A Tripartite Self

A Tripartite Self

Body, Mind, and Spirit in Early China

LISA RAPHALS

OXFORD
UNIVERSITY PRESS

Oxford University Press is a department of the University of Oxford. It furthers
the University's objective of excellence in research, scholarship, and education
by publishing worldwide. Oxford is a registered trade mark of Oxford University
Press in the UK and certain other countries.

Published in the United States of America by Oxford University Press
198 Madison Avenue, New York, NY 10016, United States of America.

© Oxford University Press 2023

All rights reserved. No part of this publication may be reproduced, stored in
a retrieval system, or transmitted, in any form or by any means, without the
prior permission in writing of Oxford University Press, or as expressly permitted
by law, by license, or under terms agreed with the appropriate reproduction
rights organization. Inquiries concerning reproduction outside the scope of the
above should be sent to the Rights Department, Oxford University Press, at the
address above.

You must not circulate this work in any other form
and you must impose this same condition on any acquirer.

Library of Congress Cataloging-in-Publication Data
Names: Raphals, Lisa Ann, 1951– author.
Title: A tripartite self : body, mind, and spirit in early China / Lisa Raphals.
Description: New York, NY, United States of America : Oxford University Press, [2023] |
Includes bibliographical references and index.
Identifiers: LCCN 2022027400 (print) | LCCN 2022027401 (ebook) |
ISBN 9780197630877 (hardback) | ISBN 9780197630891 (epub)
Subjects: LCSH: Philosophy, Chinese. | Self (Philosophy) | Mind and body. | Dualism. | Spirit.
Classification: LCC B126 .R37 2023 (print) | LCC B126 (ebook) |
DDC 181/.11—dc23/eng/20220907
LC record available at https://lccn.loc.gov/2022027400
LC ebook record available at https://lccn.loc.gov/2022027401

DOI: 10.1093/oso/9780197630877.001.0001

Printed by Integrated Books International, United States of America

This book is for John Baez.

Contents

Acknowledgments   ix
Notes on Conventions, Editions, and Transcriptions   xi

Introduction   1
    Intersecting Perspectives   2
    Mind–Body and Spirit–Body Dualism   17
    A Tripartite Self   22
    Plan of the Book   25

1. Semantic Fields of Body, Mind, and Spirit   29
    Bodies   30
    Minds   40
    Spirit(s)   46

2. Virtue, Body, and Mind in the *Shijing*   57
    Bodies in the *Shijing*   58
    Xin   65
    Spirits   72
    More on Embodied Virtue   73
    Conclusion   75

3. Mind and Spirit Govern the Body   76
    Body, Mind, and Spirits in the *Analects*   79
    The *Mozi*   83
    The Emergence of Internal Spirit in the *Guanzi*   87
    Heart–Mind as Ruler in the *Mencius*   92
    Xunzi and the Hegemony of the Heart–Mind   98
    Rulers and Ruled in the Guodian Texts   110
    The Heart–Mind Is What Is at the Center (*Xin shi wei zhong*)   112
    Heart–Mind and Spirit in the *Huainanzi* and *Wenzi*   115
    Conclusion   119

4. Body, Mind, and Spirit: A Tripartite View   121
    Yang Zhu's Discovery of the Body   122
    Mind and Spirit in the *Guanzi*   125
    The *Zhuangzi*   135
    Spirit and Body in the *Shiwen*   143
    The *Huainanzi*   149
    Conclusion   157

5. Body, Mind, and Spirit in the Guodian Manuscripts 159
   Body, Emotion, and Heart–Mind in Humans and Animals 161
   Heart–Mind and Body in the *Xingzi Mingchu* 166
   Heart–Mind and Body in the *Wuxing* 176
   Conclusion 179

6. Body, Mind, and Spirit in Early Chinese Medicine 180
   Mind–Body Dualism and Medical Texts 181
   Shén and *Xin* in the *Huangdi Neijing* 185
   Conclusion 206

   Conclusions 208
   Inner and Outer Reconsidered 211
   Personal Identity and Persistence 215
   Embodied Cognition 218

Glossary 223
Appendix 1: Time Lines 227
Appendix 2: Semantic Fields of Body, Mind, Soul, and Spirit 229
Appendix 3: The Brain in the Huangdi Neijing 231
References 239
Index 263

Acknowledgments

This book is an exploration of the boundaries between body, mind, and spirit in early China. It is also part of two ongoing interdisciplinary and intercultural explorations that have informed my scholarly work. One is the engagement between the disciplines of philosophy and history—including the history of science—from a perspective also informed by anthropology. The other is the comparative study of Chinese and Greek antiquity from a shifting viewpoint informed by all three disciplines: this book focuses on early China, but it is part of a larger comparative project. This approach is not well recognized in the contemporary academy, and for this reason I shall always be indebted to the teachers, both formal and informal, who informed and encouraged it in diverse ways: Anthony Yu, Stephen Toulmin, Gregory Nagy, A. K. Ramanujan, A. C. Graham, Sir Geoffrey Lloyd, and Michael Loewe. These debts can never be repaid; their example can only be emulated.

Several colleagues have read all or part of the manuscript at various stages: Sarah Allan, Alba Curry, Mark Csikszentmihalyi, Lothar von Falkenhausen, Martin Kern, Karyn Lai, Perry Link, Michael Puett, two anonymous readers from *T'oung-pao*, and three anonymous readers from Oxford University Press.

This project has benefited from residential fellowships and financial support from several institutions. I have received ongoing support from the University of California, Riverside. Committee on Research (COR) grants supported the initial preparation of the manuscript. A fellowship at the Harvard Center for Hellenic Studies was postponed by Covid but offered invaluable library resources and Zoom seminars.

Three chapters of this book draw on prior publications. Some of the early groundwork was done in Raphals 2015. Chapter 2 is an expanded version of Raphals 2021. Chapter 5 is based on Raphals 2019, and Chapter 6 is based on Raphals 2020.

I have benefited from discussions with graduate students Alba Curry and Ryan Harte. The heroic librarians at the Interlibrary Loan department have been a lifeline over many years.

I am also grateful to the Chinese Department of the National University of Singapore (NUS), which hosted several talks and a summer of research in 2019. I benefited from philosophical conversation partners, especially Kenneth Dean and Lo Yuet-Keung.

The ideas in this book are informed by the ideas of many scholars at all these institutions. Much of it has been presented at conference talks and invited lectures over several years. They include the Bryn Mawr Classics Colloquium, Central European University (then in Budapest), the University of California Riverside Philosophy Department, the Committee on Social Thought, University of Chicago, Hong Kong Baptist University, Shanghai East Normal University, Fudan University, Duke-Kunshan University, the conference "Comparative Global Antiquity," co-organized by Yale-NUS College and the Postclassicisms Network, Princeton University, the National University of Singapore Chinese Department, the Harvard Center for Hellenic Studies, and the Harvard Ancient Studies Visiting Lectureship.

Finally, I have benefited from discussions and correspondence with colleagues and friends: Sarah Allan, Bai Tongdong, Erica Brindley, Douglas Cairns, Cléo Carastro, Chai Jie, Alan Chan, Constance Cook, Alba Curry, Kenneth Dean, Esther Eidinow, Chris Fraser, Brooke Holmes, Elisabeth Hsu, Richard King, Karyn Lai, Liu Chun, Lo Yuet-Keung, Hui-Chieh Loy, Michael Lackner, Bill Mak, Franklin Perkins, Poo Mu-chou, Michael Puett, Michele Salzman, Eric Schwitzgebel, Mira Seo, Neil Sinhababu, Edward Slingerland, Sharon Small, Charles Stocking, Julia Strauss, Winnie Sung, Yumi Suzuki, Tan Sor Hoon, Benoit Vermander, Curie Virág, Wang Aihe, Robin Wang, and Zhou Yiqun. Responsibility for all errors and omissions is, of course, my own.

Notes on Conventions, Editions, and Transcriptions

The Pinyin transliteration system is used throughout, including in quoted text, except for the names of authors who use non-Pinyin spellings for their own names and for terms that are well known in a Latinate version (e.g., Confucius).

Chinese characters are included in the text for translated passages and where immediate reference is especially convenient. All Chinese characters are given in traditional form.

Chinese translations are my own unless otherwise indicated. Existing translations of Chinese texts are included for reference and are cited by name (i.e., Biot 1.409) rather than by name and date.

Certain key terms only lose by translation, or worse, the shortcut of translation introduces confusion by force of habit. Therefore, I have chosen to leave certain key terms as they are. These include the Chinese terms *dao* (familiar to some as *tao*), *qi*, and yin and yang. In other cases, I have retained Chinese titles, for example for the *Zuozhuan* (Zuo Transmissions).

Throughout this book, I use the following English translations for key terms for body, mind, and spirit:

BODY: Form: for *xing* 形
  Frame, occasionally limbs: for *ti* 體
  Person or embodied person: for *shēn* 身
MIND: heart–mind, occasionally mind or heart, for *xin* 心
SPIRIT: spirit for *shén* 神, in the meaning of both external spirits and internal spirit

Where possible, references are to the Chinese University of Hong Kong Institute for Chinese Studies (ICS) Concordance Series.

Chinese Standard Histories are from the Zhonghua shuju series (Beijing, 1959–) and are cited by chapter and page number (e.g., *Hanshu* 30, 1772). For the *Zuozhuan*, the modern edition of Yang Bojun (1991) is used because of its easy availability, convenience, and widespread use by other scholars.

In this and other editions that use modern pagination, references give page number, followed by section or subsection (e.g., Zuo, 849, Cheng, 10.4).

Premodern texts, excavated texts, and archaeological monographs without individual authors are cited by title. Short archaeological reports without individual authors are cited by journal (e.g., from *Wen wu*: WW 1979.19: 14–24).

The following abbreviations are used for major Chinese primary and secondary texts and journals. Full entries are found in the Bibliography.

AM	Asia Major
BEFEO	*Bulletin de l'École Française d'Extrême-Orient* (Paris)
BIHP	*Bulletin of History and Philology* (Taiwan)
BMFEA	*Bulletin of the Museum of Far Eastern Antiquities* (Stockholm)
BSOAS	*Bulletin of the School of Oriental and African Studies* (London)
CCT	*Contemporary Chinese Thought*
Dao	*Dao: An International Journal of Chinese Philosophy*
DWY	*Daojia wenhua yanjiu* (Shanghai)
EASTM	*East Asian Science, Technology and Medicine*
EC	*Early China*
EO	*Extrême-Orient, Extrême-Occident Cahiers de recherches comparatives* (Paris)
FPC	*Frontiers of Philosophy in China*
Guodian	*Guodian Chumu zhujian*
HHS	*Hou Hanshu*
HJAS	*Harvard Journal of Asiatic Studies*
HNZ	*Huainanzi*
HS	*Hanshu*
ICS	*Institute for Chinese Studies Concordance Series* (Hong Kong)
JA	*Journale Asiatique*
JAAR	*Journal of the American Academy of Religion*
JAOS	*Journal of the American Oriental Society*
JCC	*Journal of Cognition and Culture*
JCP	*Journal of Chinese Philosophy*
JCR	*Journal of Chinese Religions*
JDS	*Journal of Daoist Studies*
JRAS	*Journal of the Royal Asiatic Society*
L	Littré, E. (1839–1861) *Oeuvres completes d'Hippocrate*, 10 vols., Paris
LH	*Lunheng*
LJ	*Liji*
LS	*Huangdi neijing lingshu* (in Shibue Chūsai 澀江抽齋, 2003)
LSCQ	*Lüshi chunqiu*

MS	*Monumenta Serica*
MWD	*Mawangdui Hanmu boshu*
PEW	*Philosophy East & West*
SBBY	*Sibu beiyao*
SEP	*Stanford Encyclopedia of Philosophy*
SJ	*Shiji*
SKQS	*Siku quanshu*
SSJZS	*Shisanjing zhushu*
SW	*Huangdi neijing suwen* (Yamada Gyōkō 山田業廣, 2004)
TP	*T'oung-pao*
U	*Unschuld 2016*
UT	*Unschuld and Tessenow 2011*
WW	*Wenwu*

Introduction

Chinese philosophy has long recognized the importance of the body and emotions in extensive and diverse self-cultivation traditions. Philosophical debates about the relationship between mind and body are often described in terms of mind–body dualism and its opposite, monism or some kind of "holism."[1] Monist or holist views agree on the unity of mind and body, but with much debate about what kind, whereas mind–body dualists take body and mind to be metaphysically distinct entities.[2] The question is important for several reasons. Several humanistic and scientific disciplines recognize embodiment as an important dimension of the human condition. One version, the problem of mind–body dualism, is central to the history of both philosophy and religion. Some account of relations between body and mind, spirit, or soul is also central to any understanding of the self. Recent work in cognitive and neuroscience underscores the importance of our somatic experience for how we think and feel.[3]

Debates about mind–body dualism have become important in Chinese and comparative philosophy because of claims that Chinese thought is "holist"—including claims that there was no mind–body dualism in early China—and contrasts between supposed Chinese holism and "Western"

---

[1] Holist views include those of materialists, for whom mental states are simply physical states, and idealists, for whom physical states are really mental states. For dualists, mind and body are both real and different: neither can be assimilated into the other. For example, substance dualists, such as Descartes, believed that matter and mind were two distinct kinds of substance. The present discussion focuses on mind–body dualism only.

[2] There are multiple varieties of dualism, as well as multiple mind–body problems. For example, the term *dualism* refers to claims that, for a given domain, there are two fundamental kinds or categories of things or principles (for example, Good and Evil in theology), in contrast to monism: the theory that there is only one fundamental principle, kind, or category of thing. (It also contrasts with pluralism: the view that there are many kinds or principles or categories. In philosophy of mind, dualism refers to the theory that the mental and physical, or mind and body (including the brain), are composed of metaphysically different entities. The mind–body problem refers to problems of the relationship between mind and body or between the mental and the physical. It includes the ontological problem of distinguishing mental states from physical states and the nature of their relationship; causal questions of their mutual influence (if any); and related issues involving the nature of consciousness, intentionality, the self, and so on. See Robinson 2017.

[3] For example, Damasio 1994, 2010; Gallagher 2005; and Johnson 1993.

2   A TRIPARTITE SELF

dualism. Holist views make virtually no distinction between body and mind and spirit, and they tend to reduce all three to material or quasi-material substances, often identified with *qi* 氣.[4] Dualist views set up a distinction between a material body and a nonmaterial mind, soul, or spirit. Overall, dualist views have historically been Eurocentric, but recent claims for concepts of mind–body dualism in early China argue against the holist position in a Chinese context. Claims for Chinese concepts of mind–body dualism are part of a broader critique of a "neo-Orientalist" tendency to portray Chinese and Western thought as radically different.[5] This debate has renewed interest in the role of mind–body interactions in early Chinese thought. Much of the discourse of mind–body dualism uses a problematic binary, without acknowledgment of the very separate roles of "mind" and "spirit." Although this issue has received some attention in experimental psychology, it is often ignored in philosophical studies.[6] It also matters in a broader context, both for debates about cultural particularism and human universals, and for understanding of personal autonomy and agency.

I begin by outlining five overlapping intellectual and disciplinary perspectives that address—or somehow fail to address—problems of mind and body. In the next two sections, I focus on problems with mind–body dualism and propose an alternative view of a tripartite self. I conclude with the plan of this book and how it attempts to address these questions.

Intersecting Perspectives

A significant problem is that the entire topic is distributed among (or between) a host of problématiques and even disciplines, which often talk past each other. These include (1) studies of concepts of the body (Chinese *shēnti guan* 身體觀) or embodiment; (2) studies of the emotions, including their relations to cognition and to embodiment, across a range of disciplines; (3) studies of the mind in the context of self-cultivation, often within the discipline of ethics or philosophy, (4) studies of broader issues of selfhood,

---

[4] The term *qi*—matter energy stuff—is transliterated rather than translated throughout. Please refer to the Glossary for this and other transliterated terms.

[5] In particular, a series of studies by Edward Slingerland (2013, 2016, 2019) argue against claims that early China had no concept of mind–body dualism. This view is part of a broader critique of what Slingerland calls a "neo-Orientalist" tendency to portray Chinese thought as radically different from Western thought.

[6] For example, Richert and Harris 2008.

personhood, and, in some cases, autonomy, often within the discipline of philosophy; and (5) studies of mind–body dualism. Some of these include discussion of conceptual or root metaphors.

In addition, most studies of mind–body dualism in early China are either not comparative or anachronistically compare early Chinese texts with modern European philosophers such as Kant, Leibniz, and Spinoza. These examples illustrate the wide range of texts and methods scholars have used to explore problems of body and mind in early China and some of the very different conclusions reached.

Embodiment

In recent years, a range of studies have explored early Chinese understanding of the body. These studies vary in their themes, textual sources, and methods, but a few themes and approaches are especially prominent. One group of studies focuses on specifically Confucian texts (including some that purport to present an "early Chinese view" of the body). Roger Ames focuses on specifically Confucian understandings of the body in an important early study of Chinese views of the body. Other studies follow a particular term across one or several texts.[7]

An important study by Mark Edward Lewis on the construction of space in early China identifies an important debate about how the body arose as a means of constructing and organizing space in fourth-century (BCE) China and points to very different accounts of the body in writings associated with Yang Zhu, parts of the *Guanzi*, Mencius, and the authors of the *Zuozhuan*. Lewis's study also explores some of the consequences of depicting the body as a temporary compound of diverse elements and examines how the body was an element in a larger whole, in analogies between the body and the cosmos and between the body and the state.[8] Extensive scholarship has explored analogies between the body and the state or body politic, and analogies between the microcosm of the body and the macrocosm of the cosmos.[9]

---

[7] Y. Lo 2003, 2008; Sommer 2008, 2010, 2012. These will be discussed in more detail in Chapter 1.
[8] Lewis 2006, ch. 1: 13–76.
[9] For analogies between the body and the state, see Sivin 1995. For additional discussions of macrocosm–microcosm analogies, see Sivin 1995.

A group of Sinophone scholars have explored the study of concepts of the body from a range of disciplinary and textual perspectives.[10] Yang Rubin's study of Confucian views of the body focuses on Mencius and explores the body foundation of Confucian theories of mind and metaphysics. Yang understands the body as a complex structure of form (*xing* 形), *qi*, and spirit (*shén* 神), closely linked with the heart–mind (*xin* 心).[11] He emphasizes the importance Confucians attach to social aspects of the body, and he argues that in Confucian views, mind and body are one, Heaven and humanity are one, and inside and outside are continuous.[12] From a very different point of view, Hidemi Ishida focuses on the understanding of the body in medical texts.[13]

Roles of the Emotions

Recent studies of the emotions in Chinese philosophy also engage the boundary between body and mind and soul and spirit. Some of this investigation has centered on debates about the word *qing* 情 and on whether, how, and at what specific historical point it came to refer to emotions, but this issue is not relevant to the present inquiry.[14] Of greater relevance are investigations of the nature of the relations between the emotions, the body, and the heart–mind. These investigations fall into two very different groups.

One is the claim that emotion motivates virtuous action and, more specifically, that the correct emotions are a prerequisite for virtuous action.[15] A weak version of this view is the claim that intuitions, moral judgments, and emotions naturally work in tandem.[16] A stronger version of this view is the claim—expressed in the *Analects*, *Mencius*, *Xunzi*, and elsewhere—that emotions are central to virtuous action. But why? And how do the emotions

---

[10] See Cai Biming 1997, He Jianjun 2007, Wu Kuang-ming 1997, Yang Rubin 1993, 1996, and Zhang Zailin 2008, among others.

[11] In transliteration, I use tonal marks to distinguish *shén* 神 ("spirit") from *shēn* 身 ("[embodied] person").

[12] See Ames 1993, 1994, Yang Rubin 1993.

[13] Especially the *Huangdi neijing* (*Yellow Emperor's Classic of Internal Medicine*). See Ishida 1989, 1993.

[14] See Graham 1967, Hansen 1985, and Puett 2004, among others.

[15] For emotions and the heart–mind, see Perkins 2002. For emotions and virtuous action, see Perkins 2002, Virág 2017.

[16] See Nylan 2001: 89.

promote virtue? Do they work by influencing the body or the mind, or is there even a clear distinction?

Texts that link emotion with virtuous action give very different explanations. Warring States texts differ considerably in their accounts of the relations between emotions, primary energy, virtuous conduct, and correct ritual. A few examples suggest the range and complexity of these disagreements.

An oft-cited passage in the *Lunyu* suggests a central role of the mind, when Confucius states that at seventy he could "follow the desires of his heart–mind" (*cong xin suo yu* 從心所欲) without overstepping propriety.[17] He considered profound and spontaneous emotions to be one of the defining attributes of a perfected person, hence his repeated insistence on emotional transparency and authenticity.[18] Curie Virág argues that Confucius's emphasis on the vital role of emotions in moral life reflects a new awareness that, properly understood and integrated, the emotions could be an important source for unity and could contribute to the stable identity and continuity of the self.

A possible explanation for this view of the emotions comes from a passage in the *Zuozhuan* on ritual, which describes the ability of (correct) emotions to structure natural and primary bodily energies:

則天之明，因地之性，生其六氣，用其五行，氣為五味，發為五色，章為五聲⋯民有好惡喜怒哀樂，生于六氣，是故審則宜類，以制六志，哀有哭泣，樂有歌舞，喜有施舍，怒有戰鬥，喜生於好，怒生於惡

They pattern themselves on the brightness of Heaven, follow the inherent nature of earth, produce the six *qi* and make use of the Five Phases.[19] The *qi* form the five flavors, emerge as the five colors, and find patterns as the five sounds.... The people have likes and dislikes, pleasure and anger, sorrow and joy. These are born from the six *qi*. Thus one examines patterns and accords with categories in order to control the "six intents." For sorrow there is formalized weeping, for joy there is music and dance, for pleasure there is bestowing gifts and rewards, for anger there is warfare and fighting. Pleasure is born from likes and anger from dislikes.[20]

[17] *Lunyu* 2.4/3/1–2.4/3/2. Citations from the *Lunyu* are from the ICS series Concordance and are listed by section, page, and line number. Henceforward, citations are given in the text.
[18] Virág 2017: 27–31.
[19] Yin, yang, wind, rain, dark and light. See *Zuozhuan*, Zhao 1: 1222.
[20] *Zuozhuan*, Zhao 25: 1458–59, translation indebted to Lewis 2006: 30.

This passage describes primary and natural energies that manifest in the body as emotions and explains how they can be guided and channeled by appropriate ritual, for example, ritual mourning for sorrow and ritual music and dance for joy. The *Zuozhuan* repeatedly asserts the primacy of ritual in constituting human life by guiding emotions and bodily energies. Mencius goes one step further and argues that, to be virtuous, virtuous action must be accompanied by the right feelings.[21] For Mencius wisdom—as a "sprout" of virtue—is directly linked to the ability to feel sympathy for actual or potential suffering.[22]

For these and other Chinese thinkers who linked the emotions to virtuous action, ritual (*li* 禮) was an important component. But were correct emotions and correct ritual action the cause of virtue or the result? Confucius seems to have understood ritual as an enactment of virtue, especially the key virtue of benevolence or humaneness (*ren* 仁).[23]

Another account of the relation between emotion and ritual occurs in a text excavated from a late fourth-century tomb at Guodian 郭店 titled ""Human Nature Comes from the Mandate" (*Xingzi mingchu* 性自命出). Here, humans exist in a world of "things" (*wu* 物, including humans) and things have natures. These things, with their natures, naturally interact. But our (human) natures include particular modes of energy: emotional dispositions. As a result, these natural interactions cause us to react emotionally:

喜怒哀悲之氣，性也。及其見於外，則物取之也。

The *qi* of joy, anger, sorrow, and sadness are inherent nature. When they are manifested externally, things get a hold on them.[24]

---

[21] See *Mencius* 5A1 (on feelings toward family), 7B33 (on funeral rites). For discussion, see Perkins 2002: 209–10.

[22] See *Mencius* 2A6 and 6A6, especially. For other treatments of emotions in Mencius, see Im 1999, 2002, Nivison 1979,1996, and Wong 1991, 2002.

[23] See Pines 2002, ch. 6; Shun 2002: 67; and Virág 2017: 33–34. As Virág (2017: 42) points out, although *Analects* 9.1 claims that Confucius seldom spoke about *ren*, the term is used over a hundred times in the *Analects*, often in the context of explanations to his disciples.

[24] *Guodian Chumu, Xingzi mingchu*, strips 2–3. The Guodian Chu bamboo strip texts (*Guodian jianbo* 郭店楚簡) were unearthed in 1993 in Tomb no. 1, Guodian, Jingmen, Hubei, and probably date to the late fourth century. Quotations of the Guodian texts are from *Guodian Chumu zhujian* (henceforward *Guodian Chumu*) and Liu Zhao 2003. Texts are cited by strip numbers for the text in which they appear. For example, a passage in slip 45 of the Guodian text *Yucong* 1 is cited as *Guodian Chumu*, Yucong 1, strip 45. For simplicity of transcription, I have incorporated the Guodian editors' emendations. For example, the phrase 凡又(有)血氣者 is simply transcribed as 凡有血氣者. Translations of the Guodian manuscripts are my own but are indebted to Cook's (2012) readings of the text and survey of key scholarship. For an introduction to the Guodian texts, see S. Chan 2019. The Guodian texts are discussed in detail in Chapter 5 of this text.

The text acknowledges that these energies/emotions are inherent in human nature, so it is impracticable to try to get rid of them. Instead, as Michael Puett usefully describes it, we should isolate instances of "good" interactions and responses and:

> take that moment and make it into a ritual—which means having people re-do it, developing that same dispositional sense that occurred at that moment when (surprisingly) people acted well toward each other, thus inculcating in themselves the proper energies associated with that good response. Over time, a tradition of ritual repertoires accumulates from which humans slowly learn different ways of guiding their emotions, and thus slowly learn to have better dispositional responses toward those around them. These repertoires of ritual also train the next generation to have better dispositional responses toward those around them.[25]

Or as the Guodian text says: ritual arises from the dispositions.[26] Similarly, we can use ritual to change dangerous and malevolent ghosts into beneficent ancestors. For example, in the "Meaning of Sacrifices" chapter of the *Book of Rites*, when Zai Wo 宰我 asks Confucius about the names "ghost" and "spirit," he responds:

> 氣也者，神之盛也；魄也者，鬼之盛也；合鬼與神，教之至也。眾生必死，死必歸土：此之謂鬼。骨肉斃於下，陰為野土；其氣發揚于上，為昭明，

> The *qi* is the flourishing of spirit; the *po* is the flourishing of the ghost. Combining the ghost and the spirit is the highest teaching. All the living must die, and when they die, they must return to the earth; this is what is called ghosts. The bones and flesh die below; concealed, they become the earth of the wild fields. But the *qi* issues forth and rises up in glorious brilliance.[27]

As a result, "spirits"—the *qi* that float to Heaven after death—are worshiped as ancestors, which includes ranking ancestors into lineages and offering cult

---

[25] Puett 2010: 102–3.
[26] 體其義而節文之，理其情而出入之. *Guodian Chumu, Xingzi mingchu*, strips 17–18.
[27] *Liji* 25.24/126/5–10 (*Ji yi* 祭義).

according to lineage rank in an ancestral hall. One ritual responded to *qi* energies; another responded to *po*.[28]

A very different view is the claim that emotions interfere with self-cultivation. The *Neiye* 內業 (Inner Workings) chapter of the *Guanzi* introduces the view that the emotions—closely associated with the body and senses—threaten the mind's energies. Other scholars address the very different roles ascribed to the emotions in self-cultivation in the *Zhuangzi*.[29] In one version of the claim, they create imbalance. In a stronger version of this claim—found in medical texts especially—emotions imbalance the body to the point of causing disease.[30]

Mind, Body, and Self-cultivation

A third group of approaches discusses something analogous to what Foucault has called "the care of the self," better understood in a Chinese context as "self-cultivation" (*xiushēn* 修身) or "nurturing life" (*yangsheng* 養生). Traditions of self-cultivation fundamentally involve the care and preservation of body, mind, and spirit, but often disagree about relations between them. Some of these inquiries link the study of embodiment to the study of Chinese self-cultivation traditions. Several recent studies have emphasized the importance of embodied self-cultivation traditions, from very different points of view.

Michael Puett (2002) argues that the fourth century BCE was a turning point in Chinese understanding of the relation between humans and gods. Instead of trying to propitiate divine powers, fourth-century critics of court sacrificial practices argued that it was possible for humans to use self-cultivation practices to become a spirit and to appropriate these powers, though these thinkers disagreed on how to do so. In light of these developments, Puett emphasizes that *shén*—spirit(s)—includes both extrahuman spirits with powers over natural phenomena and also refined forms of *qi* within humans. Equally important is why Warring States thinkers began to claim that they could become spirits.[31]

---

[28] See *Liji* 25.29/17–18 (*Ji yi*). For discussion, see Puett 2010: 105.
[29] See Fraser 2011, Morgan 2018.
[30] These issues will be discussed in detail in Chapters 4 and 6.
[31] Puett 2002: 21–23 and chs. 2–5 (80–224).

Puett argues that Bronze Age sacrificial ritual was fundamentally agonistic because of the capricious nature of spirits; it was used to transform ancestors into gods and create a divine hierarchy that humans could understand and manipulate.[32] Warring States thinkers sought to reshape dominant attitudes and to reduce the distance between humans and gods through self-cultivation practices that allowed a person to become a spirit. "Self-divinization" increased individual human control and made it possible to bypass divination and sacrifice. This approach offers a very different view of Confucius's famous advice to keep a respectful distance from gods and spirits and to concentrate on human concerns.[33] It also offers new understandings of the very different self-cultivation practices described in texts as different as the *Neiye* and "Arts of the Mind" chapters of the *Guanzi*, the *Mencius*, the *Zhuangzi*, and the *Chuci*, among others.[34] These texts differ in the self-cultivation methods they recommend, but all actively engage the body, mind, and spirit through the concentration of vital essence (*jing* 精) and *qi*.

It is worth emphasizing that, from an anthropological point of view, the scenario Puett describes is widespread. In a recent posthumous collection, the anthropologist Marshall Sahlins notes that, in contrast to Western modernity, the majority of cultures throughout human history have recognized a variety of gods, ancestors, plant and animal souls, and other entities often called "spirits" not as "supernatural" beings of some mysterious kind, but as real persons—or metapersons—as immanent in human existence. These "spirits" have "the essential attributes of persons, a core of the same mental, temperamental, and volitional capacities."[35] Sahlins's point is to point to a new practice of anthropology that is consistent with this historical reality. The point for purposes of the present discussion is that interactions between humans and spirits, including the internalization of spirit and attempts to use self-cultivation to obtain spirit powers, are part of that history.

A study of *wuwei* 無為, or "acting without acting" by Edward Slingerland, argues for the centrality of *wuwei* as a spiritual ideal for thinkers as diverse as Confucius, Mencius, the authors of the *Daodejing*, *Zhuangzi*, and *Xunzi*.

---

[32] Puett 2002, ch. 1: 31–79; cf. Keightley 1978, 1998, Poo Mu-chou 1998.
[33] *Lunyu* 6.22; cf. Puett 2002: 97–101.
[34] See Puett 2002: 109–17 (*Neiye*), 122–133 (Zhuangzi), 134–40 (*Mencius*), 170–72 (the Arts of the Mind" chapters of the *Guanzi*), and 202–24 (the *Chuci*). Puett also offers a new approach to the "spirit journeys" described in late Warring States and Han sources; and argues that these claims went hand-in-hand with claims for correlative cosmology: that the cosmos was a spontaneous system,
[35] Sahlins 2022: 2. In such an "enchanted universe," the distinction between natural and supernatural becomes meaningless (2022: 36).

Slingerland describes *wuwei* as "a state of personal harmony in which actions freely and instantly from one's spontaneous inclinations," yet both manifest supreme efficacy and harmonize with the demands of conventional morality. He describes it as both a mental state, characterized by effortless unselfconsciousness, and a mode of action that accords with the normative order of the cosmos.[36] He argues that *wuwei* was central to a worldview characterized by the belief that the cosmos has a normative order in which humans have fallen away from their proper roles and modes of behavior. According to this shared view, a person who has regained this original state through *wuwei* acquires power or charismatic virtue (*de* 德). But, paradoxically, this ideal of "effortless action" can only be regained through a process of self-cultivation characterized by the need to "try not to try."

For some Warring States thinkers—Mencius, the authors of the *Daodejing*, and *Zhuangzi*, especially—*wuwei* is already inherent in our nature that conforms to natural patterns, and it can be accessed by allowing it to manifest. For others, especially Xunzi, we can attain this state only by extensive training and effort. Either viewpoint admits a tension between effortless action and the effort needed to achieve it. For both, the methods for attaining *wuwei*, as with Puett's "self-divinization," are corporeal, mental, and spiritual.

Mark Csikszentmihalyi describes a fourth-century "material virtue" tradition, exemplified in the *Mencius* and two versions of the *Wuxing* 五行 ("Five Kinds of Action") recovered from Guodian and Mawangdui 馬王堆 (Changsha, Hunan, c. 168 BCE). Csikszentmihalyi argues that these texts provide "a detailed moral psychology describing the process of the cultivation of the virtues."[37] They address the question of what a virtue is and describe virtues in terms similar to bodily humors. The book argues that material virtue is an important part of the description of a "sage" and examines a series of fourth- through second-century (BCE) texts as elements in a continuum that includes medicine, religion, and philosophy.

Csikszentmihalyi argues that a "material virtue" tradition developed as a *Ru* response to criticisms (initially in the *Mozi* and *Zhuangzi*) of their claims that "archaic" rituals were effective for either self-cultivation or the creation of social order. He considers the core texts of this tradition to be the *Mencius* and the *Wuxing*.

---

[36] Slingerland 2003b: 5, 7, 29–33.
[37] Csikszentmihalyi 2005: 7.

These texts include accounts of *jing* and *qi*, and Csikszentmihalyi applies these accounts to early Confucian ethics. He argues that for Mencius and a group of thinkers associated with Zi Si and found in excavated texts, virtue manifested physically in the body and was inseparable from it. Central to this view is an account of a material virtue grounded in the transformation of *qi*. According to both *Mencius* and the *Wuxing*, cultivation of the virtues transforms the body and appearance and is visible in a jadelike countenance and the appearance of the eyes. This view of *qi* is significantly grounded in late Warring States physiognomy and medicine. Other excavated texts on physiognomy show its importance in practical contexts, for example, a text from Yinqueshan on the physiognomizing of dogs, a Han sword physiognomy text from Juyan, and a text on the physiognomy of horses from Mawangdui. All share the view that internal *qi* is reflected in appearance and makes it possible to judge character or potential. In economic and military contexts, this meant judging the "character" of an animal or weapon. For Mencius, this theory of *qi* linked together the development of virtue and the transformed appearance of a sage. Xunzi, by contrast, rejected physiognomy as based on endowments received at birth, and thus it was not an indicator of self-cultivation.

All these ethically oriented or "normative" self-cultivation traditions involve body, mind, and spirit, often not clearly distinguished or explicitly blended. First, it could be argued that they provided the most concentrated expression of "individualism" in early China, insofar as only an individual can perform self-cultivation (*xiushēn*) or "nurture life" (*yangsheng*). Only an individual can "*xiu*" his or her "*shēn*" or "*yang*" his or her "*sheng*." In addition, as Mark Csikszentmihalyi especially has demonstrated, they are not the property of any "school" (*jia* 家). Finally, they all involve knowledge that is embodied in the immediate sense that it is gained through physical practices. These approaches place the study of the body squarely within the purview of ethics.

Selfhood, Personhood, and Autonomy

A fourth approach in several Sinological and comparative studies is to examine the role of body and mind in emerging notions of selfhood or personhood. In many cases, studies of concepts of selfhood in early Chinese texts adopt Western/modern categories of body and mind that inform, and cast, their analyses. One group is informed by a perceived antinomy between contemporary "autonomous" individuals and usually "premodern" collective notions of selfhood. Studies of "relational selfhood" focus on problems in relationships between individuals and groups, the latter including the family, family lineage (including dead ancestors), the country or state, and the world as a whole. In particular, several influential studies of "relational selves" posit a radical dichotomy between Western Kantian autonomous individuals and Chinese "relational selves."

In an early study of Yang Zhu 楊朱, John Emerson argued that Yang Zhu was responsible for "the discovery of the body" as an important philosophical innovation. In contrast to Warring States senses of self that arose out of a new political order, Yang's "physical definition of human nature" provided a new kind of freedom from notions of self previously defined by the roles imposed by state ritual (including clan identifications and ancestral obligations). By relegating these practices and relations to the realm of the "external," Yang made possible a new kind of private and nonritual mode of individual self-awareness and self-cultivation that diverges significantly from the patterns imposed by Confucian and traditional practices and relationships. As Emerson put it:

> The "discovery of the body," wherever it occurs, is part of a reconfiguration of the self/other, individual/group, and private/public relationships, leading to a new sense of self: unified and not plural, detachable from context, freed from attachments and identification, autonomous and capable of rational choice, and unambiguously located in space and time. The ancestral spirits lose most of their reality, and clan relationships become less dominant.[38]

Three types of discourse in early China address problems of the self, but most do not focus on distinctions between body, mind, and spirit. One group of studies of "relational selfhood" focuses on problems in relations between individuals and groups, the latter including the family, family lineage (including dead ancestors), the country or state, and the world as a whole. A second group addresses what in modern terms might be called questions of autonomy and agency. Studies of this kind often posit a radical dichotomy between Western Kantian autonomous individuals and Chinese

---

[38] Emerson 1996: 538; see also 533.

"relational selves," especially Ames and Rosemont's positive accounts of a "Confucian" self.[39] These studies are part of an emerging discourse on autonomy within Chinese philosophy that has questioned the applicability of Western—and especially Kantian—theories of autonomy to China, drawing almost exclusively on a small canon of broadly Confucian texts. Claims about autonomy—specifically, a dichotomy between Western autonomous Kantian and Chinese relational selves—have also been constitutive elements in debates about the nature of selfhood or personhood in premodern and contemporary China. Henry Rosemont draws a stark line between Western autonomous individuals and Confucian relational persons: "the Confucian self is not a free autonomous individual, but is to be seen relationally": as a son, father, friend, and so on.[40] He goes on to argue that there are significant differences between the two. Autonomous individuals' moral obligations respond to universal rational principles, but with no specific obligations beyond those they freely choose. Confucian relational selves have prima facie obligations to the partners of those relations—parents, children, friends, and the like—and these particularistic obligations take the place of universal moral principles.[41]

Two important and influential volumes, *The Moral Circle and the Self* and *Confucian Ethics: A Comparative Study of Self, Autonomy, and Community*, develop specifically Confucian approaches to autonomy and problems of the self, but again in a specifically Confucian context. Many other important studies of self and personhood in early China echo this approach.[42] Studies of both types do not typically dwell on relationships between the constituents of a self or person.

A third group of studies of the self address the presence or absence of traditions of individualism in China. In a recent study, Erica Fox Brindley has argued that, despite stereotypes to the contrary, multiple "individualistic" traditions are discernible in Chinese history.[43] She describes the self in early Chinese history as a "holistic" individual, but this description may

---

[39] Ames 1991, 1998; Ames et al. 1994; Rosemont 1991a, 1991b, 2006.
[40] Rosemont 2006: 10.
[41] For similar formulations, see Rosemont 1991a, 1991b.
[42] See Chong, Tan, and Ten 2003 (especially papers by Chong Kim-chong, Harold Fingarette, Karyn Lai, and Lo Yuet-Keung) and Shun and Wong 2004 (especially papers by Craig Ihara, David Wong, Henry Rosemont, and Kwong-loi Shun). For other studies see Frisina 2000, Kline and Ivanhoe 2000, Munro 2005, Nivison 1996, Nylan 1996, Tang Yijie 2003, van Norden 2000, Wong 1991, Yu Jiyuan 2001. Exceptions are Hansen 1985, Y. Lo 1992, and Yü Ying-shih 1985.
[43] Brindley 2010. For caveats on the use of the term *individualism*, see 2010: x. I have benefited from reviews of this book by Hui-chieh Loy (2011) and Hagop Sarkissian (2012).

refer less to mind–body holism than to a person always situated within the broader contexts of family, society, and the cosmos.[44] She identifies the Warring States period shift from a kinship-based political system to one based on merit as the source of opportunities to preconceive the individual as a source of agency, power, and authority. Some of these shifts involve changing views of the body. Brindley identifies two broad positions, which she calls "conformism"—conformity to an external standard—and "nonconformism" or "individualism": conformity to an internal and individual standard of judgment and action.[45] She identifies conformism with the early Mohist doctrine of "conforming upwards" (*Shang tong* 上同) and identifies "bodily conformism" with the *Daode jing*, the "Arts of the Mind" (*Xinshu* 心術) and "Inner Workings" (*Neiye* 內業) chapters of the *Guanzi*, and the text "Black Robes" (*Ziyi* 緇衣) excavated from Guodian. Brindley portrays these texts as directed to a ruler, but the *Guanzi* techniques might be pursued by anyone capable of physical and mental cultivation. She argues that a crucial shift occurred in fourth-century debates about *xing* 性 (essential nature), which opened the possibility that an individual could engage in bodily conformity with *dao*, based on the potential within individual *xing*. She attributes to the *Zhuangzi*, and even more to the *Mencius*, the view that the body is not merely a medium of authority but the "individualized source of it."[46] She thus describes a new orientation that posited universal access to divine or cosmic authority from within an individual's body.[47]

Brindley gives a strong account of relational selves (her "conformism"), self-cultivation (her "individualism"), and agency, as well as a strong historical explanation for the rise of individualism. But her account of a historically dominant conforming individualism leaves the door open to the very kind of "relational self" that she initially rejects. Further, as John Major has pointed out, Brindley's analysis does not account for political, social, and religious factors that would have enforced literal conformity and been inimical to individuality.[48] But what is significant for the present discussion is a new view

---

[44] Brindley 2010: ix–xii. Her target is a view of China as a culture dominated by Confucian values that privilege obligations to family and society in ways that overshadow the importance of the self. She argues that Chinese culture stresses achievement through relationships *with* others, rather than through separation from others, and in ways that are at odds with contemporary Western notions of individuals as free, autonomous, and independent.
[45] Brindley 2010: 21. She thus describes agency through a dual lens of conformity to external authority ("passive agency") and focuses on internal authority ("active agency").
[46] Brindley 2010: 64–70.
[47] Brindley 2010: 126.
[48] Major 2010: 334. One example is the effect of filiality (*xiao* 孝) and the limits it placed on individual agency.

of the body as part of the foundation for autonomy, especially in the texts she identifies as individualist.

In summary, in contrast to studies of the body and emotions, which in different ways foreground the role of the body in the constitution of a person, the above studies of selfhood and autonomy do not explicitly focus on relations between the embodied and cognitive aspects of a person.

Mind–Body Dualism

A fifth approach—the approach with which this introduction briefly began—is the problem of mind–body dualism. As already argued, this question addresses an important dimension of the human condition, and a view of the relations between body and mind, spirit or soul, is central to any understanding of the self.

Some studies approach mind and body by applying the study of "root" or conceptual metaphors to Chinese textual sources. Some Chinese accounts of mind and body take the form of similes and metaphors, including conceptual metaphors of the kind identified by George Lakoff, Mark Johnson, and others.[49] Lakoff and Johnson claim that most of our normal conceptual scheme is "metaphorically structured."[50] They argue that ordinary language is so immersed in conceptual metaphor that it would be very hard to do without it: "If we consciously make the enormous effort to separate out metaphorical from non-metaphorical thought, we probably can do some very minimal and unsophisticated nonmetaphorical reasoning. But almost no one ever does this."[51] They go further and make at least some claim that (metaphorical) language influences thought: a variant of the so-called Sapir-Whorf hypothesis that speakers' languages influence how they think. One explanation is a claim about the structure of the mind (and presumably, brain): that some structures of consciousness, including some level of grammar, are "hard wired" in the human mind and thus are universal and not subject to cultural variation.[52] Lakoff and Johnson make the very

---

[49] Of particular importance are Lakoff and Johnson 1980, 1999, Johnson 1987, Fauconnier and Turner 2002. For an excellent discussion of metaphor in Chinese, see Link 2013, to which the following discussion is indebted.

[50] Lakoff and Johnson 1980: 115.

[51] Lakoff and Johnson 1999: 59.

[52] Adherents of this view include Noam Chomsky (1975), Jerry Fodor (1975), and Steven Pinker (1994).

different claim that conceptual metaphors are universal because they are shaped by the shared physical experience upon which they all draw, for example, of "up" and "down," hot and cold, spatial metaphors for time, and so on. They describe this shared basis in the physical experiences as "embodiment" in the claim that "the mind is inherently embodied," and to that extent, derives conceptual commonality from shared experience.[53] In addition to the core claim that root metaphors are drawn on bodily experience, many of these structures either describe the body, mind, spirit, or person in other metaphors, or they use elements of these in other metaphorical structures.

Chinese root metaphors for mind, spirit, and body are part of a growing literature on conceptual metaphors, including their application to the study of early China. Elsewhere I have identified three very different types of metaphors of body and mind/spirit: (1) as amalgam or composite, (2) as container and contents, and (3) as ruler and ruled, where the heart–mind is a ruler governing officials, subjects, slaves, or animals.[54] Composite metaphors describe body and mind as some kind of composite or amalgam. They do not specify the structure of the composition, and they disagree on the nature of the composite and on what holds the amalgam together. Container metaphors describe the heart, mind, soul, or spirit as either contained in the body or as a container of the spirit or another heart–mind. They all can be described as weak dualism in that body and mind are described as distinct—and one cannot be reduced to the other—but they are made either of the same substances or of different substances in indissoluble relation.

I also argued that these metaphors present a spectrum of both holist and dualist positions in early Chinese (and also Greek) texts, which cannot be dismissed by a progressivist model or reduced to a simple antinomy between strongly dualist and holist views. Broadly holist metaphors include composites and containers in which the body (or mind) contains the mind or spirit (or an inner mind), or parts of the body are containers for specific psychological faculties. Broadly dualist metaphors characterize the mind or soul as ruler of the body, described as a physically distinct entity. What is of interest for the present discussion is the use of strongly dualist ruler metaphors to describe the mind in both received and excavated texts.

[53] Lakoff and Johnson 1999: 5.
[54] Raphals 2015.

Mind–Body and Spirit–Body Dualism

Another approach focuses on differences between Chinese and Western understandings of heart and mind. For example, the cognitive linguist Ning Yu has argued that Chinese cultural conceptualizations of the heart or mind differ fundamentally from Western dualism in that they understand the heart as the central faculty of both affective and cognitive activity and the source of thought, feelings, emotions, and guiding behavior. Yu argues that this cultural conceptualization differs fundamentally from the dualism of modern Western philosophy, which asserts a dichotomy between reason and emotion, in which thoughts and ideas are linked to a largely disembodied "mind" and desires and emotions with an embodied "heart."[55]

The nature of the distinction between "heart" and "mind" in Chinese philosophy is much debated. In some views, the Western distinction does not exist at all, and early Chinese philosophy understood "heart" and "mind" as one *xin* 心: "the core of affective and cognitive structure, conceived of as having the capacity for logical reasoning, rational understanding, moral will, intuitive imagination, and aesthetic feeling, unifying human will, desire, emotion, intuition, reason, and thought."[56]

A series of recent studies have argued for the importance of dualist views in early China, typically in reaction to claims that Chinese thought was predominantly or entirely holist.[57] Paul R. Goldin argues for the presence of mind–body dualism in several early Chinese texts. He notes passages in the *Zhuangzi* and *Xunzi* that seem to point to some notion of an immaterial mind or spirit, for example, someone whose material substance (his yin and yang *qi*) is disordered, but whose mind is at ease: "it seems as though the author presupposes a disembodied mental power within Ziyu that can continue to function despite massive corporeal decay. This is a significant point because it appears that we have encountered a mind-body problem."[58] A similar problem appears in the *Xunzi* in a discussion of abdication in the case of a king whose body (literally, his blood, *qi*, sinews, and energy) has declined, but whose mind (wisdom, deliberations, choices, and rejections) has not.[59] Elsewhere, Goldin notes that Chinese beliefs about ghosts and postmortem

---

[55] N. Yu 2007: 27–28; cf. Damasio 1994, Lakoff and Johnson 1999.
[56] N. Yu 2007: 28.
[57] For an influential example, see Graham 1989b: 25. For discussion, see Goldin 2003: 232. For other examples, see Goldin 2003: 243n22.
[58] Goldin 2003: 228.
[59] Goldin 2003: 231.

consciousness also suggest some form of mind–body dualism, as do the evidence of lavish grave goods (material, human, and animal) and written records in and about them.[60]

Edward Slingerland argues forcefully for the presence and importance of dualism in early China in a recent monograph and a substantial series of prior shorter studies.[61] The book is nuanced and complex, beginning with arguments against strong mind–body (or spirit–body) holism and several other claims closely associated with it.[62]

Slingerland discusses mind–body dualism as one of several reductionist "Chinese-Western" dichotomies, namely, Western dualism versus Chinese holism.[63] He argues against what he considers the strongly holist positions of Roger Ames, François Jullien, and Herbert Fingarette, among others.[64] Slingerland uses both evidence from archaeology and qualitative textual evidence to argue for "weak" mind–body dualism as a psychological universal. He argues that early Chinese thought is characterized by at least a "weak mind–body dualism," in which mind and body are experienced as functionally and qualitatively distinct, though potentially overlapping at points.[65]

Dualism and Postmortem Souls

A key point in this argument is the status of the soul after death. Chinese belief in some form of consciousness of the dead dates to the Shang oracle bone inscriptions, which include queries and petitions, both to the high god Di 帝 and to royal ancestors, who descended to earth from the abode of Di.[66] One aspect of important shifts in understandings of the afterlife between the Warring States (ca. 480–221 BCE), Qin (221–207 BCE) and Western Han

---

[60] Goldin 2015. In particular, the *Zuozhuan* account of the death of Prince Shensheng 申生 makes clear that Shensheng was believed to be able to live on in some other form after his death.

[61] Slingerland 2016, 2019. They also cite many of his earlier studies.

[62] Slingerland 2019: 33–61. These include (1) the lack of psychological interiority—associated with Herbert Fingarette's claims about the *Analects*—especially in the lack of an inner-outer dichotomy, (2) lack of a positive conception of the individual, in favor of an amalgam of social roles, and (3) lack of a conception of a soul, afterlife, or notions of personal immortality linked to them.

[63] Slingerland and Chudek 2011; critique by Klein and Klein 2012; Slingerland 2013.

[64] Slingerland 2013: 9–15; cf. Ames 1993: 149; 1994: 168; Jullien 2007: 8, 69; Lewis 2006: 20; Fingarette 1972, 2008; Santangelo 2007: 292.

[65] Methodologically (Slingerland 2013: 28), he also argues for a "Humanities-Science interface" in the use of large text databases, arguing that they provide a more "objective" alternative and serve as a corrective to cherry-picking key passages.

[66] See Poo 1998, Lai Guolong 2005, 2015, and Thote 2009. For additional discussion see Slingerland 2013.

(206 BCE–9 CE) was a changing view of the abode of the dead, with new evidence of a belief in some kind of journey after death.

Lai Guolong has surveyed material and textual evidence for accounts of postmortem journeys. Late Warring States and early Han understandings of the afterlife generally agree that a soul retains consciousness after death, with some notion of an abode of the dead. Despite their elaborate furnishings, the tomb increasingly became understood as a starting point or way station for an after-death journey. Furnishings such as travel suits, chariots, and other travel paraphernalia aided the soul in that journey. Tomb texts provided travel documents to orient the deceased in a new social, political, and cosmic order, including daybooks and other mantic texts with information on the dangers of the road. Such journeys could include passage from a family tomb to the "Yellow Springs" (*Huang quan* 黄泉) or to an unspecified underground location, movements of an ancestor between Heaven and Earth, and journeys to remote locations in the west (Mount Kunlun 崑崙山) or east (Penglai 蓬萊), and other locations such as Mount Tai (*Taishan* 泰山). There is also a shift in the identity of the protagonist of the journey from a spirit medium or other specialist to the tomb occupant. In addition, there is evidence that the war dead resided in particular locations.[67] Evidence from Baoshan, including a category of "travel paraphernalia" in the tomb inventory, provides additional evidence for belief in some kind of spirit journey and a presumably conscious deceased to undertake it.[68] These various beliefs about the status, or journey, of the deceased from tombs to a distant location all point to a "folk dualistic" view that some kind of consciousness survives death.

Slingerland argues that, although the archaeological record presents strong evidence of Shang and Eastern Zhou beliefs in continuity between the world of the living and the "spirit" world of the dead, by the late Warring States, mortuary practices show a view of the afterlife in which the dead are categorically different from the living.[69] He argues that pre-Qin writers described

---

[67] Texts from Jiudian and Baoshan suggest that the war dead resided in a place "at the edge of Mount Fu and in the wilds of Buzhou" in the remote northwest. Mt. Buzhou was considered the axis that connected the human and spirit worlds. See Lai Guolong 2005: 5–10.

[68] 相從之器所以行. For the phrase "travel paraphernalia" see *Baoshan Chumu* 2: 200–210. For discussion see Lai Guolong 2005: 31–32, using the reading of Lin Yun 1992. For further speculation about this journey see C. Cook 2006: 17.

[69] Including the ideas of souls retaining consciousness after death and some kind of land of the dead, to which the soul could travel from the tomb. Textual accounts of the afterlife that support soul–body dualism are even more explicit, including accounts of ritual practices involving "impersonator of the dead," other accounts of spirit possession, and accounts of an "incorporeal 'essential' element to the self"—a locus of personal agency and identity that leaves the body after death. See Slingerland 2019: 66–75; Lai Guolong 2005: 42; and Guo Jue 2011: 85–87.

xin as qualitatively distinct from other parts of the self and as the locus of personal identity, thought, free will, and moral responsibility.[70] Finally, he argues that, by the third century BCE, soul–body dualism becomes even more developed, with detailed accounts of ritual and religious techniques for freeing the mind/spirit from the body. Textual accounts of the afterlife that support soul–body dualism are even more explicit, including accounts of ritual practices involving a ritual "impersonator of the dead," other accounts of spirit possession, and accounts of an "incorporeal 'essential' element to the self"—a locus of personal agency and identity, that leaves the body after death. Finally, he argues that, by the Western Han, soul–body dualism becomes even more developed, with detailed accounts of ritual and religious techniques for freeing the mind/spirit from the body.[71]

Is Dualism Fundamental?

Slingerland also argues that tri- and multipartite accounts of the constituents of a person are "parasitic" on mind–body dualism because, like their dualist counterpart, they all require the separability of personal essence from the physical body. This argument for dualism requires a close association between *shén* and the cognitive functions of *xin*. He concludes:

> If there is a unifying feature behind this diversity of terminology and divisions, it is that the soul— whether designated by *shén*, *po*, *hun*, or some combination of these terms— is intimately bound up with consciousness or mind.[72]

Slingerland argues that a unifying thread behind a complex range of accounts of the physical body and its relationship to a soul or souls is

> a bipartite division between the dumb, concrete vessel that is the physical body and then a thing or collection of things that fill or inhabit this vessel.

---

[70] Slingerland 2019: 101. Rhetorically, this takes the form of two patterns: contrasting *xin* with the three words for the body and contrasting it with other organs of the body, including by conspicuous omission. He argues that *xin* is associated with the soul and personal consciousness.

[71] Slingerland 2019: 87. He notes that the model of self behind *shén* is complex and sometimes requires a tripartite model such as that of Despeux.

[72] Slingerland 2019: 90.

The latter serve as the locus/loci of consciousness, intention, and personal identity. In other words, soul–body dualism (or tripartite-ism, decipartite-ism, etc.) is fundamentally parasitic on mind- body dualism.[73]

Finally, Slingerland associates *xin* with interiority, the inner life that provides the context for choice and independent deliberation. Here he notes that this inner-outer distinction also occurs in medical texts, where the outwardly visible body is contrasted with "invisible" aspects of a person: will, spirit, and *qi*.[74]

There are several problems with the dualist view that are not limited to Eurocentrism. Chinese dualist arguments set up a problematic "body–mind" binary that conflates "mind–body" dualism and "spirit–body" dualism into one material-non-material binary that is historically Eurocentric. An additional problem is that most studies of mind–body dualism in early China are either not comparative or anachronistically compare early Chinese texts with modern European philosophers such as Kant, Leibniz, and Spinoza. Most broadly, Confucian texts in early China tend to identify mind and spirit, sometimes explicitly, and are thus friendly to this framework of analysis. But other—and in some cases under-studied—early Chinese texts and traditions present very separate roles of "mind" and "spirit."

The dualist position and the whole comparative "mind–body dualism" debate make important contributions, but still rely on Western conceptual categories based on a problematic "mind–body" binary. In an early Chinese context, there is no acknowledgment of the very separate roles of "mind" and "spirit." Most studies of "mind–body dualism" in early China collapse the categories of mind and spirit into one, which can be dualistically contrasted to the body, for example, in metaphors of the mind (or soul) as ruler of the body. Others focus on mind–body dualism during life and body–spirit dualism after death. The result is alternating treatments of "mind–body" dualism and "body–spirit" dualism. Both frameworks miss the mark for accounts of persons that assume significant and complex interactions between mind and spirit.

---

[73] Slingerland 2019: 92.
[74] Slingerland 2019: 127–33.

A Tripartite Self

Preserving the dualist framework of analysis, important dimensions of the relations between mind (and its associated faculties) and spirit or soul (and its associated faculties), can be lost, including how both relate to the body. I argue instead that there is a broad divergence between two views of a tripartite relation between body, mind, and spirit in Warring States texts. One view closely aligns mind and spirit, often in a hierarchically superior relation to the body. The other view problematizes the relation between mind and spirit, and in some cases even aligns body and spirit in opposition to mind. This group of texts includes both medical texts and texts excavated from tombs.

One contribution to Yang Rubin's influential edited volume on early Chinese views of the body presents a tripartite analysis of the person. Hu Fuchen argued that Daoist concepts of the human body are based on the relationship between the three elements of form (*xing*), *qi* and spirit. He starts from a view he traces to the *Zhuangzi*, that the life of the human body is based on *qi*.[75] He argues that, because of the tripartite structure of the human body of corporeal form, *qi* and spirit, both philosophical and religious Daoists advocated the idea of taking *qi* as the basis for self-cultivation. Spirit and body are mutually complementary, but the focus should be on refining *qi*.[76] Hu emphasizes fundamental differences between this Daoist view of the body and the views of Western culture:

> In ancient Greek mythology, the artisan Wu Yukan [Vulcan] created the body of the beautiful woman Pandora (equivalent to form), and then Zeus gave her life (equivalent to *qi*), so there is a life in the world. Pandora, they thought that the task of God's creation was completed.... The goddess of wisdom, Athena, should have added a layer of wisdom (equivalent to spirit) to her, and she would become a perfect person.[77]

The French Sinologist Catherine Despeux provides a very different approach to the dualism question. In an article titled "Souls and the Animation of the Body: The Notion of *shén* in Early Chinese Medicine," she argues against dominant contemporary Western representations of persons as a dichotomy between body (corps) and mind (esprit). She notes that questions of

---

[75] Hu Fuchen 1993: 171.
[76] Hu Fuchen 1993: 173.
[77] Hu Fuchen 1993: 174.

body and mind are typically the purview of philosophy, whereas the study of religion and even psychology are more concerned with the psyche (psyché) than the mind (esprit). Instead, she translates, and understands, the term *shén*, not as "spirit," "God," or "divinity," but as soul (l'âme), and proposes a tripartite representation of a person consisting of body, mind, and soul (l'âme):

> It seems desirable to get out of this dichotomy to analyze the vision in ancient China, especially since Western ancient thought most often referred to the trilogy body/soul/mind [corps/âme/esprit] which accords well enough with the analysis of subject and its components in Chinese culture. The Chinese equivalents of *xing* for the body, *shén* for the soul and *xin* for the heart/mind are easily found in body/soul/spirit.[78]

Despeux attributes this view to Greek thought, and especially to Aristotle's *De Anima*.

> Here we refer to a notion of the soul that is far removed from the usual modern conception and to a use of the term close to that of the ancient Greeks, for whom this notion has been the subject of heated debate. Aristotle gives a partial account of this in his treatise On the Soul.[79]
>
> The soul was seen in Greek thought as a constituent of the person with the body, the mind [esprit], and often the breath [le souffle]; it played the role of intermediary between body and mind. In Roman culture, the term spiritus "spirit" comes from spirare that evokes breath, wind and spiritus is also a translation of the Greek pneuma "breath."[80]

Despeux understands soul as an intermediary between body and mind to better understand *shén* in Chinese medicine from the second to first centuries BCE, emphasizing that soul and breath are the animating force that are essential to life.[81] This invaluable study raises several questions. One concerns the role of spirit in her trilogy of "body/soul/mind" (corps/âme/esprit). Her study focuses on the term *shén* in early Chinese medical texts, and she makes strong arguments for understanding this term as "soul" rather

---

[78] Despeux 2007: 72.
[79] Despeux 2007: 71.
[80] Despeux 2007: 72.
[81] Despeux 2007: 73–75.

than as "spirit." But in the broader context of the constituents of a person, a problem arises because the semantic field of French "esprit" includes both "mind" and "spirit," which allows at least some attributes of "spirit" to be combined with "mind."

In this book I argue for the significant presence of a tripartite model of the self in early Chinese texts, at least up to the Han dynasty. In this tripartite model, the self or person is composed of body in several aspects (including the form (*xing* 形)), frame (*ti* 體) and embodied person (*shēn* 身, all of which are discussed in detail in Chapter 1), the mind or heart–mind (*xin*), and the spirit (*shén*). I argue that there is a broad divergence between two views of a relation between body, mind, and spirit in Warring States and Han texts. The mind-centered view aligns mind and spirit in a hierarchically superior relation to the body; the spirit-centered view clearly distinguishes mind from spirit, sometimes even aligning body and spirit in opposition to mind.

The mind-centered view focuses on the heart–mind and often portrays it as the ruler of the body in metaphors that analogize the body and state. This view closely aligns the heart–mind and spirit in a hierarchically superior relation to the body; together they rule the body as a ruler rules the people or a state. The result is effectively a binary view of a person—consistent with mind–body dualisms in which there is a polarity between the body on the one hand and mind and spirit on the other. This view of the heart–mind as ruler of the body, senses, and emotions changes and develops over time. It is most prominent in the *Analects*, *Mengzi*, and *Xunzi*, but it also appears briefly in body–state microcosm–macrocosm analogies, including passages in the *Guanzi*, *Huainanzi*, and *Huangdi neijing*.

The spirit-centered view contests the mind's hegemony and gives pride of place to spirit (*shén*), often in alliance with the body and as the animating force that makes life possible. In strong versions of the spirit-centered view, spirit is distinct from, superior to, and even at odds with, the heart–mind, often operating through the body. This view is especially prominent in the *Zhuangzi*, which at times explicitly problematizes the relation between heart–mind and spirit, and in some cases even aligns body and spirit in opposition to the heart–mind. The spirit-centered view is also prominent in the "Ten Questions" (*Shiwen* 十問) text from Mawangdui, which describes spirit in close conjunction with essence (*jing* 精), *qi*, and illumination (*ming* 明), but *not* with the heart–mind.

In the context of the holism–dualism debate, the spirit-centered view is compatible with neither strong holism nor strong dualism. It clearly admits one dualist element. Since spirit was believed to leave the body at death, the spirit-centered view is compatible with the view that at death, an essential, nonmaterial aspect of the self or person separates from the material body.

But instead of reducing tripartite relations into a material-nonmaterial binary, I focus on the details of, and debates about, the nature of that tripartite relation. I also present an alternative to Despeux's tripartite view insofar as her categories of analysis are explicitly derived from Greco-Roman antiquity. Mine come from a reading of Chinese texts, with a deliberate effort to avoid importing Western categories.[82]

This approach promises to address three major gaps in the growing scholarship on mind, spirit, and body in early China. First, much of it focuses on philosophical texts, with less attention to technical literatures and excavated texts. These are the texts that align mind and spirit, and also that lend themselves to the reduction to a "mind–body" binary. Second, much of the discourse of mind–body dualism uses a problematic binary, without acknowledgment of the very separate roles of "mind" and "spirit." This can result, for example, in alternating treatments of "mind–body" dualism and "body–spirit" dualism. But by preserving the dualist framework of analysis, important dimensions of the relations between mind (and its associated faculties) and spirit or soul (and its associated faculties) can be lost, including how both relate to the body. Some studies address this issue by collapsing the categories of mind and spirit into one, which can be dualistically contrasted to the body. Others focus on mind–body dualism during life and body–spirit dualism after death. Both frameworks miss the mark for accounts of persons that assume significant and complex interactions between mind and spirit. My second group of texts, which include both medical texts and texts excavated from tombs, explore this tripartite relation in detail.

Plan of the Book

Given this plethora of approaches, the one thing that seems clear is that no one approach will be exhaustive or all-explanatory. And there is an additional danger of distorting one's textual material in the interest of accommodating it

---

[82] Nor is it clear that body, mind, and soul were the major categories of Western "Classical" analysis. The topic requires more historicization, but I would argue that the dominant categories of analysis were body/*sōma* and soul/*psychē*.

to theories and perspectives that may be quite anachronistic. Yet, sticking too closely to texts offers other problems; a text-by-text survey may be conceptually unsatisfying, and an important common thread may jump across texts, or present inconsistencies in what are in most cases, multi-authored texts.

My study of a Warring States tripartite view of a self composed of body, mind, and spirit focuses on the details of, and debates about, the relation between these elements. I argue that there is a broad divergence between two views of a tripartite relation between body, mind, and spirit in Warring States texts. One closely aligns mind and spirit, often in a hierarchically superior relation to the body. (This view is consistent with, and encourages, the reduction of a tripartite relation to the material-nonmaterial binary) The other view problematizes the relation between mind and spirit, and in some cases even aligns body and spirit in opposition to mind.

Chapter 1 surveys the classical Chinese semantic field and root metaphors for terms for body, mind, spirit, and soul, and the psychological and physical faculties associated with them. The first part of the chapter gives representative examples to show the considerable semantic stretch of these terms and illustrates how little the terms correspond, in particular, to the Anglophone semantic field that seems to underlie so many studies of this topic, especially in philosophy. Nor are body, mind, soul, and spirit neutral terms in English. They are culturally constructed and subject to historical change. For example, English "mind" has shifted from reference to emotions and moral values toward reference to reason and intellect. It has effectively replaced soul, originally a broad concept that combined religious, psychological, and moral aspects of a person.

Chapter 1 also introduces a metaphorology of Chinese root metaphors for mind, spirit, and body, as part of a growing literature on conceptual metaphors, including their application to the study of early China. It considers three very different types of metaphors of body and mind/spirit: (1) as an amalgam or composite, (2) as container and contents, and (3) as ruler and ruled, where the heart–mind is a ruler governing officials, subjects, slaves, or animals. It argues that there is a spectrum of both holist and dualist positions in early Chinese texts that cannot be dismissed by a progressivist model, or be reduced to a simple antinomy between strongly dualist and holist views. Broadly holist metaphors include composites and containers in which the body (or mind) contains the mind or spirit (or an inner mind), or parts of the body are containers for specific psychological faculties. Broadly dualist metaphors characterize the mind or soul as ruler of the body, described as a physically distinct entity. Blended metaphors include both holist and dualist elements, including the mind or soul ruling the body as part of a larger container or composite that includes both, sometimes analogized to a state or the cosmos.

Chapter 2 locates the semantic field of Chapter 1 in the *Shijing* or *Book of Odes*, one of the two earliest of the Confucian classics. In this text, spirit plays a negligible role, but both body and mind are linked to accounts of virtuous agents.

Chapters 3 and 4 present two strongly contrasting approaches to body, mind, and spirit. Chapter 3 describes a (dominant) binary view in which mind and spirit together rule the body, senses, and emotions as a ruler rules a populace or state. As Mark Lewis has argued, that rule can be harmonious or contested. The "harmonious" rule is the exception, and it primarily occurs in the *Huangdi neijing* (discussed in Chapter 6). But the "contested" view, in which the body or senses do not accept the rule of the mind, has a long history, beginning with the *Analects*. It is prominent—in very different ways—in the *Mencius* and *Xunzi*. But ruler metaphors also make brief appearances in the *Guanzi*, *Huainanzi*, in several texts excavated from Guodian, and in the recently published text *Xin shi wei zhong* 心是謂中 ("The Heart–Mind Is What Is at the Center") from the eighth volume of the Tsinghua University bamboo slip documents, published in 2018.

Chapter 4 delineates a tripartite view in which the mind's hegemony is contested, and spirit operates through the body, largely independent of the mind. These accounts privilege spirit rather than heart–mind, with spirit closely linked to essence (*jing*) and *qi*. These texts share several important common features. They all take spirit as an "internalized" faculty of persons and closely associate it with essence and *qi*. All three circulate in the body and can be stored in the heart–mind. In these texts, the correct functioning of spirit is also the source of sage-like abilities such as the ability to transform things, respond flexibly to changing circumstances, and make subtle and clear judgments. Chapter 4 begins with the "discovery of the body" in writings attributed to Yang Zhu, followed by the "Arts of the Mind" and "Inner Workings" (*Neiye*) chapters of the *Guanzi*. There follows an extensive discussion of the *Zhuangzi*'s discussion of *shén*. The last two sections of Chapter 4 discuss the treatment of spirit, essence, and *qi* in the "Ten Questions" (*Shiwen*) text from Mawangdui and the *Huainanzi*.

Chapters 5 and 6 present two historically later binary and tripartite views, respectively. Chapter 5 describes the interactions of mind, body, and emotions in texts excavated from Guodian: especially "Five Kinds of Action" (*Wuxing*) and "Human Nature Comes from the Mandate" (*Xingzi mingchu*). It focuses on accounts of the mind and spirit as rulers of the senses and emotions, and it draws on the growing scholarship on Guodian excavated texts, which are emerging as increasingly important for the study of early Chinese intellectual history. These texts focus on self-cultivation; their complex picture of body, mind, and spirit reflects the debates of earlier literature. They also consider implications of the "body–mind–spirit" problem for self-cultivation.

Chapter 6 turns to a fluid model of body, mind, and spirit, and examines the uses of *xin* and *shén* in medical texts, which are sometimes cited as examples of strong mind–body holism. Medical texts must address the role of the *xin*-heart as one of the visceral systems. In a medical context, we can identify two very different accounts of *xin*. In one, it is one of the viscera (or visceral systems); as such, it is a physical organ and is no different from any other. In another account, it is the seat of emotions and ethical and moral judgments, and it cannot be viewed primarily as a physical organ. The latter has been used in arguments for mind–body dualism. The first section of Chapter 6 surveys *xin*- and *shén*-centered views in the *Huangdi neijing* (*Yellow Emperor's Classic of Internal Medicine*). These texts describe the heart (*xin*) as an organ of the body, but they also describe the "storage" of psychological faculties such as spirit, intentions (*zhi* 志), or awareness (*yi* 意) in other organs.

1
Semantic Fields of Body, Mind, and Spirit

Body, mind, spirit, and soul are not neutral terms. They are culturally constructed and are also subject to changes of meaning over time. An example is the changing meanings of the interrelated English terms *mind*, *spirit*, *soul*, and *heart*. As Anna Wierzbicka has argued, in older strata of English, the term *mind* was closely linked to emotions and moral values and thus had important psychological and spiritual dimensions. By contrast, contemporary usage of the term focuses on reason, intellect, thinking, and knowing, with a presumed moral and emotional neutrality (emotions being more closely linked to the heart, often used in contrast to mind). Over time, Anglophone understandings of dualism between a material body and its nonmaterial counterpart have shifted from a soul–body dichotomy to a mind–body dichotomy in which mind has effectively replaced soul, a broad concept that originally combined a person's religious, psychological, and moral aspects. Wierzbicka argues that, in contemporary Anglo-Saxon usage, soul is largely restricted to religious discourse, and mind has acquired the psychological aspects of personhood. The result is, as she puts it, a new kind of dualism, "devoid of religious and moral connotations and reflecting the supreme value placed on rational thinking and knowing, rather than on other aspects of the human person."[1]

Another effect of understandings of dualism between a material body and its nonmaterial counterpart is a tendency to posit a binary "mind–body problem" based on a binary split between body and mind.

How then to escape from the categories of a broadly Cartesian modern dualism and the danger of imposing categories based on tacit claims that there is an ontological distinction between material bodies and immaterial minds, spirits, or souls?[2] Other difficulties arise by seeking to solve these problems through comparative methods, which risk assuming correspondences between the comparanda and imposing the categories of another language and

---

[1] Wierzbicka 1989: 50, cf. 48–50; N. Yu 2009: 3–4.
[2] Particularly useful is Clarke 1999, especially 3–49, to which the following discussion is indebted.

time onto historically and culturally distant texts.[3] Even native speakers of (various versions of) contemporary Chinese remain linguistically and culturally distant from Classical Chinese. The Hellenist Michael Clarke identifies three important pitfalls. The first is to assume that thought and emotion somehow imply "minds" that are separable from "bodies." The second is to assume that what survives death is a "spirit" that inhabited the "body" during life and leaves it at death. The third is to associate immaterial "minds" with immaterial "spirits" out of a shared distinction from "bodies." Clarke's method is to rely on "vigilant self-consciousness" on two points: refusing to rely on the concept of soul and refusing to assume that the essential part of a person is the same in psychological life and after death.

This section surveys the Chinese semantic fields for the key constituents of a "person." Although Classical Chinese has no near equivalents for terms such as body, mind, and soul, I divide my discussion into three sections based on terms for bodies, minds, or heart–minds, and spirits, in several senses of the term.[4] A range of philological studies have examined terms for the body, mind, and self or person, especially. These studies explore and disambiguate the semantic fields of key terms for body, mind, and person or self. Some are broad surveys of the range of terms for (usually) body and mind.[5]

Bodies

As studies by Nathan Sivin and Deborah Sommer have shown, the major Chinese terms for body differ from the English notion in important ways. They identify four main terms for the human body. *Ti* 體, the concrete physical body, was distinct from *xing* 形, the body as a structural form; *gong* 躬, the virtuous person displayed in ritual conduct; and *shēn* 身, the socialized and cultivated body person.[6]

---

[3] For example, the Swedish Sanskritist Ernst Arbman's distinction between a "body soul" and a "free soul" entails the assumption of some correspondence between early Greek and Vedic Indian beliefs. According to Arbman's (1926) taxonomy (discussed in Bremmer 1983: 8–10), a body soul endows the body with life and consciousness, is active during the conscious life of a living person, and is often divided into several parts. A free soul is usually nonmaterial and represents the individual. It is active when the body is unconscious and does not have an exact location in the body. For critique of this approach, see Clarke 1999: 43–44.

[4] Volker Scheid (2002: 27–28) argues that in English and other Indo-European languages, *body* has the implicit meaning of a vat or container. He also claims that it is categorically opposed to *mind*, a claim not supported by the Homeric evidence.

[5] For example, Y. Lo's (2003) study of the semantic field of terms for self in the *Lunyu*.

[6] Sivin 1995, Sommer 2008, to which the following discussion is indebted. The less common term *qu* 軀 also refers to the physical frame but specifically to the dysfunctional body of a petty person.

The Ti 體 Body or Frame

The *ti* body or *frame* referred to the concrete physical body, including both its major parts (the limbs) and its physical form. An example comes from the one appearance of the term in the *Analects*, where an old farmer approaches Confucius's disciple Zi Lu. Here, *ti* clearly refers to the limbs:

四體不勤，五穀不分。孰為夫子？

Your fourfold frame [four limbs] do not labor and you cannot distinguish the five grains, so who is your master? (*Lunyu* 18.7/52/25)

By contrast, Mencius (2A2) clearly refers to the entire body when he attributes to Gaozi a view of the *ti* body in which:

夫志，氣之帥也；氣，體之充也。夫志至焉，氣次焉。故曰：「持其志，無暴其氣。」

The will is the master of the *qi*; *qi* is what fills the frame. Where the will arrives, the *qi* comes after it. Therefore it is said; Take hold of your will and do not do violence to the *qi*. (*Mengzi* 3.2/15/20)[7]

It is also closely linked to ritual. This linkage is explicit in the *Liji* chapter "The Four Principles of Mourning Attire" (*Sangfu si zhi* 喪服四制):

凡禮之大體，體天地，法四時，則陰陽，順人情，故謂之禮。

The great embodiment of all rituals is that they embody Heaven and Earth, take the four seasons as models, pattern themselves on yin and yang, and accord with human emotions; as a result they are called rituals. (*Liji* 50.1/174/18–19)[8]

The first use of *ti* in the above passage refers to the "embodiment" of an abstract principle, in this case, ritual. *Ti* can also refer to the embodiment of

---

[7] Citations from the *Mengzi* are from the ICS Concordance series and are listed by section, page, and line number.

[8] Citations from the *Liji* are from the ICS Concordance series and are listed by section, page, and line number.

spiritual, cosmic, and moral states, for example, an immortal's embodiment or personification of *dao* (*tidao* 體道).

Sommer identifies the frame or *ti* body as: "a polysemous corpus of indeterminate extent that can be partitioned into subtler units, each of which is often analogous to the whole." When it is fragmented into parts, each becomes a simulacrum or retains some identification with the larger entity of which it is a constituent. This quality is particular to the *ti* body; by contrast, *xing*, *gong*, and *qu* refer to entities that occupy discrete physical frames.[9] The *ti* body is also associated with roots and plants, especially the ability of plants to multiply through cuttings rather than seeds:

> *Ti* bodies often act more like plants than like humans. When living human bodies are divided, they die: halving, quartering, or fragmenting human or animal bodies inevitably results in dismemberment or death. *Ti* bodies, however, lend themselves readily to unusual kinds of division and multiplication—processes that rarely occur with other kinds of bodies without killing them—and for *ti* bodies, division is actually tantamount to reproduction and multiplication, not death.[10]

In the Mohist canons, *ti* 體 (part) and *jian* 兼 (whole) are among the first definitions. Terms such as this are first defined briefly in the two "Canons" chapters (*Jing* 經, 40 and 41), with further details in the corresponding two "Explanations" chapters (*Jingshuo*, 經說, 42 and 43):

體，分於兼也。

A *ti* (unit/individual/part) is a portion in a *jian* (total/collection/whole). (*Mozi* 10.1.3/67/9, 40)[11]

體：若二之一，尺之端也。

For example, one of two, or the starting point of a measured length, (*Mozi* 10.3.2/78/19, 42)

---

[9] Sommer 2008: 294. For the *ji* body, see Sommer 2012. For the *Zhuangzi*, see Sommer 2010.
[10] Sommer 2008: 296.
[11] Translation after Graham 1978: 265. Citations from the *Mozi* are from the ICS Concordance series and are listed by section, page, and line number.

The Mohist canons also use the term *ti* in several definitions. One describes it as something that can be divided in the explanation for the definition of the term *gu* 故 (cause).

故，所得而後成也。

The cause of something is what it must get before it will come about. (*Mozi* 10.1.1/67/5, 40)

故：小故，有之不必然，無之必不然。體也，若有端。

Minor reason: having this, it will not necessarily be so; lacking this, necessarily it will not be so. It is a part, like having a starting point. (*Mozi* 10.3.1/78/15, 42)[12]

Like the *Liji* account of respect, this definition employs a combination of separability and continuity. The definition for *jian* (to see) also uses *ti* in its definition, to describe a limb, either part or component:

見，體、盡。

Jian (see). Part, whole. (*Mozi* 10.1/67/5, 40)

見：時者，體也；二者，盡也。

One member of a pair (?) is an individual. Two of them are "all." (*Mozi* 10.3.22/79/27, 42)[13]

Animals also have frames. For example, the Guodian text *Qiongda yishi* 窮達以時 (Poverty or Success Is a Matter of Timing) includes an argument about the unrecognized excellence (and execution) of the meritorious Wu Zixu 伍子胥 (d. 484 BCE). It concludes with a remark on the *ti* bodies of two

---

[12] Translation based on Graham 1978: 263; cf. Ames 1994: 169.
[13] Cf. Graham (1978: 329), who translates *ti, jin* as "individuals, all." Graham (1978: 265) describes *ti* and *jian* as numerical (and thus countable) "units" and "total," but any *jian* is also countable and may be a "unit" of a larger *jian*. Karyn Lai (personal communication) suggests an interesting alternative: that the frame—human, animal, or plant—is what you see when you look at the material body of a living thing.

famous horses: "That Ji was hobbled at Mount Zhang and Jin was trapped in the Qiu wilds was not because they had declined in the strength of their frames" (*ti zhuang* 體壯).¹⁴

The *Xing* Body or Form

By contrast, *xing* 形 refers to form or shape, understood as visible, solid, and three-dimensional, with clear boundaries, but it has nothing to do with a person as a whole. *Xing* literally means "form" or "shape," and it often refers to the body's outline rather than to its physical identity.¹⁵ A passage in the first chapter of the *Xunzi*, "Encouraging learning" (*Quanxue* 勸學), suggests the difference between the frame, form and embodied person (discussed below):

君子之學也，入乎耳，著乎心，布乎四體，形乎動靜。... 古之學者為己 ... 君子之學也，以美其身；

The learning of the gentleman enters the ears, fastens to the heart–mind, spreads throughout the fourfold frame [the four limbs], and embodies in action and repose.... In antiquity, learning was for oneself.... The learning of the gentleman is to improve one's person. (*Xunzi* 1/3/14–17)¹⁶

As with *ti*, *xing* can refer to the embodiment of an abstract concept, for example, in Xunzi's account of self-cultivation:

誠心守仁則形，形則神，神則能化矣。

If you cling to humaneness with a heart–mind of integrity, then you will embody it. If you embody it, then you will become spirit-like. If you are spirit-like, you can transform [things]. (*Xunzi* 3/11/4–5)

---

¹⁴ 非亡體壯也. *Guodian Chumu, Qiongda yishi*, strips 10. Textual problems surround the names and provenance of these famous horses, but the context is clearly a comparison between their inherent strength and being subdued.

¹⁵ For discussion of *xing*, see Sommer 2008: 300–2.

¹⁶ Citations from the *Xunzi* are from the ICS Concordance series and are listed by section, page, and line number. Translations of *Xunzi* are indebted to Hutton 2014 and Knoblock 1988–1994.

The noun *ji* 己 ("person," "self") is one of several terms for a person or individual that do not refer to a body. Others include the pronouns *wu* 吾 ("I," "my"), *yu* 予, and *wo* 我 ("I," "my," "me"), and *zi* 自 (a reflexive adverb for oneself).

The term *xing* (form) implies structure, and it is sometimes explicitly or implicitly contrasted with formlessness. Examples occur in excavated texts from Mawangdui and from the Shanghai Museum collection. The contrast is explicit in the description of the development of the unborn child in the "Book of the Generation of the Fetus" (*Taichan shu* 胎產書) from Mawangdui:

故人之產（也），入於冥冥，出於冥冥，乃始為人。一月名曰留（流）刑(形)

When human beings are engendered, they enter into obscure darkness, they emerge from obscure darkness, and only then do they begin to become human. The first month is called "flowing into form."[17]

The same contrast occurs in another Mawangdui text, the "Ten Questions" (*Shiwen*), in a phylogenetic (rather than ontogenetic) question about how (nonembryonic) humans acquire form, survive, and die:

黃帝問於容成曰：「民始敷淳溜（流）刑(形)，何得而生？溜（流）刑(形)成體，何失而死？

Huang Di asked of Cheng Rong: "When people first from that expanse of inchoateness flowed into form, what did they obtain that they became alive? When flowing into form completed their body frames, what did they lose that they came to die?"[18]

Here the form precedes—and constitutes—the frame. Almost identical language appears in another excavated text titled "All things flow into form" (*Fanwu liuxing* 凡物流形), which occurs in two versions in the Shanghai Museum Chu bamboo strips. It begins by asking how the things that constitute the cosmos attain a stable form:

凡物流形，奚得而成? 流形成體，奚得而不死? ⋯

---

[17] *Mawangdui Hanmu boshu* 4: 136; translated after Harper 1998: 378, cf. Sommer 2008: 302. Citations from all medical texts from Mawangdui are from *Mawangdui Hanmu boshu*, volume four, henceforward MWD4, given in the text.

[18] MWD4: 146, strip 23, trans. after Harper 1998: 393, cf. Sommer 2008: 302. Both texts use the graphs *liu* 留 instead of *liu* 流 and *xing* 刑 instead of *xing* 形.

As to things flowing into form, what do they acquire to become complete? As to [their] flowing into form and completing the frame, what do they acquire to not die?[19]

The passage goes on to pose further questions about things that have complete body frames and come to life, the meeting of yin and yang and "the harmony of fire and water" (*shuihuo zhi he* 水火之和). It then asks how human beings attain a physical form that is stable:

問之曰: 民人流形, 奚得而生? 流形成體, 奚失而死?

It is asked: as to people flowing into form, what do they acquire in order to live? As to their flowing into form and completing the frame, what do they lose that causes them to die?[20]

These questions assume a natural progression ranging from norms from heaven to the physical form of human beings and the patterning of human vital energy that derives from them.

There are important differences between body frames and body forms. Body frames involve relationships between wholes and parts; body forms involve relationships between inner and outer. Neither frames nor forms are able to multiply into parts that are analogues of a larger whole. Forms can be divided, but division typically results in death rather than reproduction. The verbal sense of *ti* means to embody within; the verbal sense of *xing* means to model from without.[21]

Important differences between frames and forms also appear in the language of excavated texts. For example, in the Guodian text "All Things Flow into Form (*Fanwu liuxing*), the pervasive unity (*yi* 一) that answers the cosmogonic questions posed by the text is identified with the "form" into which all things flow. Flowing into form is identified with "becoming complete."[22]

---

[19] See Ma Chengyuan 2008: 223, strip 1. For reconstruction and interpretation of this texts, see S. Cook 2009a and 2009b, Cao Feng 2010. For translations, see S. Chan 2015 and Perkins 2015.
[20] Ma Chengyuan 2008: 226–28, strips 2–3.
[21] Sommer 2008: 300–1.
[22] 流形成體. *Guodian Chumu, Fanwu liuxing*, strips 1–4.

The Shēn 身 Person and Gong 躬 Self

In contrast to both *ti* and *xing*, *shēn* and *gong* refer to a body, person, or "embodied person"; *shēn* can refer to the lived body or the physical person but also to the personality. As physical bodies, *shēn* have length (height) and duration (life span). The *shēn* person is the socially constructed self and displays signs of status, personal identity, moral values, character, experience, and learning. Unlike the form, that exists below the level of conscious awareness, the embodied person is self-aware and is the locus of inner reflection and self-cultivation. Embodied persons do not overlap physical boundaries with other persons. Nonetheless, they are socially permeable and can absorb nonmaterial attributes such as dishonor, disgrace, pollution, honor, and purity. For example, the *Liji* chapter "Questions of Duke Ai" (*Ai Gong wen* 哀公問) uses a plant metaphor to describe embodied persons across generations. Confucius remarks that under the reigns of the enlightened rulers of antiquity, men were respectful toward their wives and children because

君子無不敬也，敬身為大。身也者，親之枝也，敢不敬與？不能敬其身，是傷其親；傷其親，是傷其本；傷其本，枝從而亡。三者，百姓之象也。身以及身，子以及子，妃以及妃，君行此三者，則愾乎天下矣，大王之道也。

The gentleman is never without respect, and it is in respecting his [own] person that he makes it greatest. In his own person he is a branch of his parents; how can anyone dare to not have this respect to it? If he is not capable of respecting his own person, he harms his parents. In harming his parents, he harms his root; and when you harm the root, the branches follow and die. Three things are an image of the people. One's person reaches to the persons [of others], one's own children reach to the children of others, one's own wife reaches to the wives of others. If a gentleman does these three things, then he will reach the entire world; they are the way of great kings.[23]

Here, the embodied person is physically distinct from, but nonetheless continuous with, the persons of one's parents and children.

---

[23] *Liji* 28.2/135/27–29. For further discussion of *shēn* and *gong*, see Sommer 2008: 304–7.

Several passages in texts excavated from Guodian underscore the importance of embodied persons. According to *Ziyi* 緇衣 (Black Robes), in antiquity the Lord in Heaven observed King Wen's virtue and concentrated the great mandate upon his person (*qi ji da ming yu jue shēn* 其集大命于厥身, strips 36–37). According to *Taiyi sheng shui* (The Great One Gave Birth to Water), those who use *dao* are successful in their tasks and long-lived in their persons (*shi cheng er shēn chang* 事成而身長), and sages' persons avoid injury (*shēn bu shang* 身不傷, strips 11–12). According to *Tang Yu zhi dao* 唐虞之道 (The Way of Tang and Yu), the *dao* of sages is complete: "when one insists on rectifying one's person (*zheng qi shēn* 正其身) before rectifying the world (strip 2).[24]

Gong bodies are associated with the deliberate public display of virtuous conduct. They have social responsibilities but do not enjoy the fruits of labor. (*Ti* bodies, by contrast, experience sensation and pleasure; they perform labor but not in ritual contexts.) *Gong* selves have clear boundaries, which correspond to the physical frame. They do not experience self-reflection and are not measurable.

The *gong* self is the body of displayed ritual conduct, within a discrete physical form, and embodies the deliberate public display of virtuous conduct. It is used of a body that is consciously performing an action that demonstrates visually and publicly the virtuous character of the agent, typically before an audience. Such actions include ritual performance and court appearances, which are stylized and nonspontaneous, and reflect traditional values and social obligations. But *gong* bodies also act in the more spontaneous contexts of enduring hardship or performing physical labor on behalf of others or society at large. But *gong* laborers do not personally enjoy the fruits of their efforts. Even rulers and culture heroes endure such suffering and perform such labors. In the broadest sense, the *gong* body refers to the entire self or person created by *gong* actions and is often linked with the character *qin* 親, "to do in person." By contrast, *ti* bodies also perform labor but not in ritual contexts; and have indeterminate boundaries, while *gong*-body boundaries are always clearly delimited. *Gong* selves, in contrast to *shēn* persons, do not engage in self-reflection, and they are not spatially or temporally measurable. One person has one *gong* body whose identity is discrete from others' *gong*

---

[24] Used purely of a physical person, this passage could refer to straightening one's body, but that is clearly not the meaning here. Similarly, a passage from *Chengzhi* 成之 (Bringing Things to Completion) describes the governance and instruction of a noble man who first "submits his person to goodness" (身服善). See *Guodian Chumu, Chengzhi*, strip 3.

bodies; by contrast, multiple *ti* bodies may inhabit one person, and multiple human beings may participate in a common *ti* body.[25]

Finally, *shēn* and *gong* refer only to humans; by contrast, the bodies—or roots or limbs—of animals and plants are *ti* bodies.

Ritual, Solid, and Fluid Bodies

In an early study, Roger Ames makes three important points about early Chinese views of the body. First, the term *ren* 人 or "person" refers to the entire person, clearly including the *shēn*. Second, early Chinese concepts of body are fundamentally related to self-cultivation (*xiushēn*), however understood. Finally, many early Chinese projects of self-cultivation—Confucian especially—are social, and the body is closely linked with ritual enaction, which is never separate from the physical body.[26]

Medical texts offer very different views of bodies. Hidemi Ishida identifies two contrasting medical views of the body: a view of the body as occupying space or as a field (*zuo wei changyu de shēnti* 作為場域的身體) and a fluid body (*liudong de shēnti* 流動的身體). Ishida argues that, according to early Chinese views of the ontogeny of the fetus, the body was produced and contained by flowing *qi*. The visceral systems stored *qi* and were formed only after *qi* created life.[27] Ishida argues that traditional Chinese medicine uses two distinct methods to depict the body. One method, Charts of Inner Lights (*Neijing tu* 內景圖), resembles Western anatomical illustrations and depicts the solid organs of the body.[28] The other method, which he identifies with Charts of the Hall of Light (*mingtang* 明堂), depicts fluid substances flowing within the body. In his view, these are more prevalent and fundamental.[29] These "fluids" consist of *qi*, essence (*jing*), and spirit. Ishida notes that, in the medicine of the *Huangdi neijing*, the mind was understood as a liquid substance, stored in the five yin viscera, and manifested externally in five emotions that correspond to five aspects of the mind stored in the yin viscera. (The details of these passages will be discussed in Chapter 6.) He

---

[25] Sommer 2008: 294–95 and 307–9. This emphasizes that *ti* is not identical to the physical frame as normally construed in English.
[26] Ames 1993.
[27] Ishida 1993, especially 185 and 1989.
[28] For the *Neijing Tu* see Despeux 2008 and Komjathy 2008 and 2009.
[29] Ishida's example comes from a diagram of the channels in the *Leijing tuyi* (Illustrated supplement to the classic of categories), 3:14.

concludes that there are two major body concepts in early Chinese thought: a more fundamental "flowing body" and the body as residence. The mind was also considered fluid, especially linked to the five yin viscera, but flowing and pervading and regulating every part of the body. Thus, the energies of the flowing body and flowing mind are closely interrelated, and together they constitute the blood, energy, and mind circulation essential to human beings. Thus, body and mind ultimately are one, but they are clearly differentiated, with the mind pervading the whole body.[30] Yang Rubin identifies this fluid view of the body as specifically Daoist.[31]

Minds

The *Xin* 心 or Heart–Mind

Most texts attribute consciousness and thought to the *xin*, a term that refers to the mind and also clearly to the heart, located in the center of the chest.[32] It is especially difficult to translate this term in a way that avoids prejudgment, and there is no consensus on a best translation. I refer to it consistently as the "heart–mind" to avoid possibly arbitrary or equivocal translations.

The term is used pervasively in oracle bone inscriptions, the received tradition, and excavated texts. A famous passage from the *Xunzi* closely links mind and spirit:

心者，形之君也，而神明之主也，出令而無所受令 … 心不可劫而使易意，是之則受，非之則辭。

The heart–mind is the lord of the form and the master of spirit brilliance. It issues orders, but there is nothing from which it takes orders … the heart–mind cannot be compelled and made to change its thoughts. What it considers right, it accepts, what it considers wrong, it rejects. (*Xunzi* 21/104/10–12)

---

[30] Ishida 1989: 67.
[31] See Yang Rubin 1993: 21 and 1998. Notions of balanced *qi*, a body created by *qi* are pervasive in the *Daode jing* and *Zhuangzi*, but also in accounts of *qi* filling the body and generating lies in Mencius and Xunzi.
[32] For an excellent treatment of the semantics of these terms, see Y.-K. Lo 2003. This study focuses on the *Analects* of Confucius but gives a detailed account of their early history.

Several psychological attributes are associated with the heart–mind: will or intentions (*zhi* 志), knowledge or consciousness (*zhi* 知), desires (*yu* 欲), and thought or awareness (*yi* 意).

The Will (*Zhi* 志)

Central to Confucian moral psychology is the notion of intention or will. Its central role is explicit in a famous "autobiographical" remark by Confucius that, at the age of fifteen, he "set his will on learning (*zhi yu xue* 志于學).[33] Mencius also emphasizes the importance of the will (2A2), and describes its interactions with *qi*:

夫志，氣之帥也；氣，體之充也。夫志至焉，氣次焉。 故曰：『持其志，無暴其氣。』⋯志壹則動氣，氣壹則動志也。

Now as for the will, it is the commander of the *qi*; and *qi* is what fills the frame. Now the *qi* halts where the will reaches. Hence it is said: "Take hold of your will and do not abuse your qi." ... The will when blocked moves the qi. But *qi*, when blocked, also moves the will. (*Mengzi*: 3.2/15/25)

The Guodian texts are especially rich in accounts of relations between body and mind. Discussions of how the body affects the mind appear in *Zun deyi* 尊德義 (*Honoring Virtue and Propriety*) and more extensively in *Xingzi mingchu* 性自命出 (*Human Nature Comes from the Mandate*), which contains an extensive discussion of how the body and emotions affect the heart–mind. Accounts of how the heart–mind rules the body appear in *Ziyi* (*Black Robes*) and more extensively in *Wuxing* (*Five Kinds of Action*). To give one example, a passage in the Guodian text *Zun deyi* (*Honoring Virtue and Propriety*) emphasizes the mutual porosity of body and mind, and that ritual and music "nurture the heart–mind (*yangxin*) in compassion and integrity (strip 21). But it never mentions spirit. It argues that, of all the sources of virtue ritual and music are the greatest:

治樂和哀、養心於子諒，忠信日益而不自知也。

They channel happiness and harmonize sorrow, and nurture the heart/ mind in compassion and integrity, so that one's faithfulness and trust

---

[33] *Lunyu* 2.4/3/1. This passage is discussed further in Chapter 3.

increase daily without any self-awareness. (*Zun deyi*, strips 20–22, trans. Cook 2012: 2, 661–62)[34]

Here, *xin* is associated with the virtues of compassion (*zhong* 忠) and integrity (*xin* 信), and with power or virtue (*de* 德) in general but not with spirit or spirit brilliance (*shénming* 神明).[35]

Several Guodian passages discuss the will or intentions, usually of a gentleman or *junzi* 君子. One example is a saying attributed to Confucius that a gentleman "cannot be robbed of his will in life and cannot be robbed of his good name in death" (*Ziyi* strip 38). A passage in *Wuxing* explicitly links will and intentions with correct mental attitudes: "A scholar whose intentions are on the *dao* of a gentleman can be called a scholar of intentions (*zhi shi* 志士, *Wuxing*, strip 7). This passage links intentions to wisdom: "Virtue without intent will not be realized; wisdom without reflection will not get it."[36] Another passage from *Liude* 六德 (Six Virtues) suggests that intentions transcend individual will and individual persons who "hide their own will and seek to nourish the intentions of their families."[37]

The Heart–Mind as Ruler

In an important study of the body as an organization of space in early China, Mark Lewis identifies two contrasting metaphors of the body as state. In "harmonious" body-state metaphors, the mind is the uncontested ruler, and the body parts work smoothly as functions within the state In "agonistic" body-state metaphors, body parts, including the senses and, by extension, the emotions, contest the supremacy of the mind; victory of the mind creates order, but victory of other organs brings about illness or death.[38] These two contrasting uses of state-body metaphors give rise to two accounts of the heart–mind. In the "harmonious" model, the heart–mind is one of five "viscera" or "depots" (*zang* 藏), which functions are distributed

---

[34] I follow Cook's reconstruction here, which differs from that of Liu Zha (2005: 124).
[35] Other studies have explored the semantics of the "heart–mind" or "heart" in early China from a cognitive perspective. See N. Yu 2007, 2009.
[36] 德弗志不成,智弗思不得. *Guodian Chumu, Wuxing*, strips 7–8.
[37] 逸其志,求養親之志. *Guodian Chumu, Liude*, strip 33.
[38] Lewis 2006: 37–39.

harmoniously among the five. (The other four are the kidneys, liver, lungs, and spleen.) In the other account, the mind is linked to the sense organs, typically striving for independence from the rule of the mind. The "harmonious" view is most prominent in the *Huangdi neijing*. The agonistic view appears in a wide range of Warring States and Western Han texts, including the Guodian texts. These texts describe the mind as ruler of the senses, but these "ministers" consistently try to assert independence and reject hierarchical control.

An agonistic view of body and mind appears in the text *Wuxing* 五行 (*Five Kinds of Action*), excavated from tombs at Mawangdui and Guodian. Here, the heart–mind rules the body as a ruler rules a state, and the senses are its slaves. A more harmonious mind as ruler metaphor occurs in the *Ziyi*, where the people take the ruler as their heart–mind and the ruler takes the people as his *ti* body. (Both passages are discussed in detail in Chapter 5.) This metaphor analogizes the heart–mind to a ruler, but here the rulership is based on a mutual recognition between ruler and ruled.

Mind-as-ruler metaphors are prevalent in the *Guanzi*, *Mengzi*, and *Xunzi*, but these texts differ considerably in their descriptions of what rules their judgments about the heart–mind's hegemony over the body. (All are discussed in detail in Chapter 3.)

These metaphors also represent the boundaries between mind and body in a distinctive way. In the political analogy that grounds them, ruler and ruled occupy separate and distinct physical space, and are clearly separable, both as physical objects and as psychological agents. Other body–mind metaphors, such as container and contents, present a more porous interface between body and mind.

Xin as a Body Organ

A very different picture of the *xin* as heart appears in medical and recipe texts.[39] For the most part—but with some very interesting exceptions—they describe *xin* straightforwardly as the heart, an organ in the center of the chest. For example, medical texts excavated from Mawangdui, Zhangjiashan 張家山 (Jingzhou, Hubei, 196–186 BCE), and Wuwei focus on a description of ailments

---

[39] These texts had different audiences and objectives than philosophical texts. This issue is discussed in Chapter 6.

associated with the heart (*xin*) and spirit and accounts of therapies that involve them. These therapies include recipe texts from Mawangdui and cautery prohibitions from Wuwei. In these texts, spirit was considered to reside or be stored in the heart, so the heart is also involved in medical practices concerned with it. These include medical and therapeutic practices to cultivate spirit from Mawangdui and prohibitions to avoid harming it from the *Huangdi neijing* and in texts from Mawangdui.

The forty-seven references to *xin* in the Mawangdui medical manuscripts occur in only seven texts, especially in the two texts on cauterization.[40] Some are simple references to the locations and paths of vessels that enter the heart.[41] Others are lists of types of ailments associated with the vessels, such as heart pain (*xintong* 心痛) and fever of the heart (*fanxin* 煩心).[42] Some refer to the names of ailments caused by moving the vessels, where the vessel moved determines the kind of pain.[43] These are clearly physical symptoms, but some involve the emotions. For example, according to "Cauterization Canon of the Eleven Yin and Yang Vessels," moving the Yang Brilliance Vessel causes a panicky heart (*xinti* 心愓, 10, strips 43–44), and moving the Taiyin vessel causes qi to ascend and race to the heart (*shang* [] *zou xin* 上□走心, 11, strips 54–55).

The heart is also a straightforward physical organ in Mawangdui recipe texts. For example, one recipe purports to increase strength and purge foul vapors from the heart and chest.[44] All these examples clearly refer to the heart as an organ in the chest, with no particular connection to minds, emotions, or faculties of ethical judgment. An exception is a recipe to ensure the "heart-knowledge" (*liangxin zhi* 良心智) of a newborn child (126, strips 41–42).

---

[40] "Cauterization Canon of the Eleven Vessels of the Foot and Forearm" (足臂十一脈灸經) and "Cauterization Canon of the Eleven Yin and Yang Vessels" (陰陽十一脈灸經).

[41] For example, the "Cauterization Canon of the Eleven Vessels of the Foot and Forearm" describes the path of the Taiyin vessel of the forearm as going from the edge of the underarm to the heart (MWD4: 6, strips 25–26). The "Cauterization Canon of the Eleven Yin and Yang Vessels" describes the Minor Yin vessel of the forearm as going from the upper arm to the heart (MWD4: 12, strip 67).

[42] For example, the "Cauterization Canon of the Eleven Vessels of the Foot and Forearm" associates the Minor and Taiyin vessels in the foot with ailments that include heart pain and fever of the heart (MWD4: 4–5, strips 13–18). The "Cauterization Canon of the Eleven Yin and Yang Vessels" associates the Minor Yang vessel with pain in the heart and upper side (MWD4: 9, strip 39). The Taiyin vessel produces fever of the heart and heart pain (MWD4: 11, strips 54–57); and the Taiyin vessel in the forearm produces heart pain (MWD4: 12, strips 67–69).

[43] For example, moving the Minor Yang vessel causes pain in the heart and side (心與脅, MWD4: 10, strip 39). Moving the Great Yin vessel in the forearm causes heart pain and throbbing (literally like the sound "*pang pang*" 心滂滂如痛, MWD4: 12, strip 68); and moving the Minor Yin vessel in the forearm produces heart pain (MWD4: 13, strip 70).

[44] MWD4: 112, (*Yangsheng fang*), strips 144–45.

The Zhangjiashan manuscripts contain two medical texts, the *Yinshu* or *Pulling Book* and the *Maishu* or Vessel book.[45] The term *xin* appears only seven times in the *Yinshu*, typically in passages that describe techniques for addressing pain in the heart (strip 66) or "pulling heart pain" (*yinxin tong* 引心痛, strips 67–68). It also includes procedures that "manipulate" the heart by "stroking the heart (*fuxin* 撫心, strips strip 74, 84, 100) or "raising the heart" (*xingxin* 興心), apparently by lying down with the feet pressed against a wall, squeezing the chin against the abdomen, and pushing up (strip 75). Three other references discuss heart pain, heart worry, or something that harms the heart.

The *Yinshu* text does not discuss *xin*. In the *Maishu*, *xin* appears some sixteen times, often as the name of the Heart vessel, for example in the phrase *xin zhong* 心中, "in the *xin* [vessel]." The *Maishu* refers to "an ailment below the heart and side" (*zai xin qu xia* 在心胠下, 115, strip 6). It also describes "heart pain" (*xintong*), a fearful or panicky heart (*xinti* 心惕), a racing heart (*zouxin* 走心), and other similar conditions that result from manipulating or "moving" various vessels.[46]

These descriptions of the heart as a physical organ often do not mention spirit or associate spirit with the heart. Neither the *Maishu* nor the *Yinshu* mentions spirit at all; the *Maishu* does describe six constituents of the body, but spirit is not among them.[47] Recipes to treat ailments of the heart also appear in a trove of medical texts discovered near Wuwei 武威, Gansu, and they also do not associate the heart with spirit.[48]

These medical passages treat *xin* in relative isolation, in contexts that are clearly diagnostic or therapeutic. Within these contexts, the absence

---

[45] References to the Zhangjiashan texts are from Zhangjiashan 247 hao Hanmu zhujian zhengli xiaozu 2001: 113–28 (*Maishu*) and 169–86 (*Yinshu*). For translation of the *Yinshu*, see V. Lo 2014. For additional commentary, see Gao Dalun 1992 and 1995 and Peng Hao 1990.

[46] According to the *Maishu*, heart pain results from moving the Minor Yang, Yang Brilliance, and Minor Yin vessels, and moving the Minor Yang vessel produces pain in the heart and side (心與脇痛, strip 20). Heart pain also results from moving the forearm Minor Yin vessel (strip 46). Moving the Yang Ming vessel produces a panicky heart. Ailments associated with it include pain in the heart and upper side (心與胠痛, strips 24–25). Moving the Minor Yin vessel produces ailments where the heart is as if suspended (心如懸) and a panicky heart with the fear of being about to be seized by someone (心惕惕恐人將捕之, strip 40). Moving the Great Yin vessel makes *qi* ascend and race in the heart (上走心). This vessel is also associated with fatal fever of the heart alone (獨心煩死) and fatal heart pain with bloated abdomen (心痛與腹脹死, strips 33–35). A racing heart is also associated with a bitter taste in the mouth (strip 56).

[47] Bone (*gu* 骨), sinew (*jin* 筋), blood (*xue* 血), vessels (*mai* 脈), flesh (*rou* 肉), and *qi* 氣. *Maishu*, p. 125, strip 54.

[48] *Wuwei Handai yijian*, strips 44 and 63. References to strips are from Gansusheng bowuguan 1975. For a brief study and translation, see Yang and Brown 2017.

of cosmological analogies or other theoretical content is not surprising. As in the case of the multiauthored Greek Hippocratic Corpus, treatises range considerably in content and apparent audience, from the clearly medical to the rhetorical, philosophical, and cosmological. But the absence of macrocosm–microcosm and political analogies is all the more striking in contrast to the Western Han systematizing of the *Huangdi neijing*, where "harmonious" analogies also occur in clearly medical diagnostic and therapeutic contexts.

Spirit(s)

Several terms with complex semantic fields refer to spirit or "soul" (*shén* 神), which is also translated frequently as "numinous," "divine," or "spiritual." In its oldest usage, the term referred to extrahuman (or formerly human) entities, including ancestors, divine powers, and the spirit inhabitants of mountains, lakes, and forests. These extrahuman powers needed to be identified and placated. For example, several recipe texts from Mawangdui provide directions for the invocation of specified spirits through quasi-magical means, including magical recipes and incantations. In this sense, *shén* referred to the quasi-magical efficacy of spirits or objects sacred to them.

The term is also used for human beings of extraordinary sagacity who become "like" spirits. Finally, the term is used for a "spirit" quality within humans that makes them "spirit-like." Second-century theorists increasingly argued that humans, too, could attain such powers in a process Michael Puett has called self-divinization.[49]

In some medical contexts, spirit is one of the fundamental and necessary constituents of a living human being. In medical texts and self-cultivation literature, spirit is associated with the management of essence (*jing*) and *qi*, especially in the term *shénming*. This term has a range of meanings including "Spirit Illumination," "Spirit Intelligences," and/or "*Shén* and *Ming*"—*Numen* and *Lumen*, as it were.

In several of these texts, and especially in the Guodian texts, spirit is not a major element in the relationship between mind and body, but it is central to accounts of spirit brilliance and self-cultivation.

---

[49] See Puett 2002.

Extrahuman Spirits

References to external spirits are pervasive in the early literature, beginning with the oracle bone inscriptions. They appear repeatedly in the Book of Odes and the Book of Rites. In Masters texts, discussions of spirit are divided between debates about the nature of extrahuman *shén*, how humans should relate to them, and the nature and limits of their consciousness. Differences of opinion and active debates between Ru (Confucians) and Mohists are especially prominent, the former in the "core" Mohist chapters and the latter in the discourses.[50] A very different thread appears in the *Guanzi* and *Zhuangzi*, among other texts, which describe *shén* as a perceptual faculty.

Ritual texts—the *Liji* especially—address the role of sacrifice and other methods to achieve the presence of extrahuman spirits. The accounts of these texts emphasize that no single procedure guarantees success in "making the spirits descend"; rather, the ritualist approaches the spirits as if they were present, in the hope that they would be.[51] Or as the *Odes* puts it:

神之格思, 不可度思, 矧可射思

A visit from the spirits can never be foreseen, the better reason for not ignoring them.[52]

But even these procedures are linked to corporeal experience. As the *Xunzi* puts it:

卜筮視日、齋戒、脩涂、几筵、饋薦、告祝，如或饗之。物取而皆祭之，如或嘗之。毋利舉爵，主人有尊，如或觴之。

They prognosticate with turtle and milfoil to determine an auspicious day, perform fasts and purifications, sweep out the temple, lay out the tables and food offerings on the mats, and report to the invocator of the spirits as if someone were going to partake of it. They take up the

---

[50] Ding, Sixin 丁四新 (2011).
[51] Sterckx 2007: 31.
[52] *Shijing* Mao 256. Cf. Sterckx 2007: 35.

offerings and present each of them as if someone were going to taste them. They do not use a helper to raise the wine cup, but the chief sacrificer holds the cup, as if someone were going to make a toast with it. (*Xunzi* 19/98/8)

Thus, sensory memory is what ties together sacrificing descendants and ancestral spirits. Sterckx goes further and speculates that ritualists' use of their apparatus and sacred space to invite spirit energy to lodge there are equivalent to the human body of the self-cultivation adept who uses dietary regimes and meditative techniques to purify and prepare the body. As Sterckx states:

> The social power, mystery and psychological ambiguity of sacrifice in early Chinese religion lies precisely herein: in order to attract a category of powers that escape the sensory radars of ordinary mortals, the sacrificer can only find recourse to the use of a sophisticated set of visual, olfactory, sonorous and savoury tools that originate in human sensation.[53]

These included ritual robes, color, penetrating smells, foods, dances and liturgy, all part of the "functional repertoire at the disposal of the ritualist."

External spirits also appear in medical recipe texts excavated from tombs. Several Mawangdui recipes from the text "Recipes for Fifty-two Ailments" (*Wushi'er bingfang*) invoke named spirits such as the Spirit of Heaven (*Tiānshén* 天神), the Yellow Spirit (*Huángshén* 黃神), and Spirit Maidens (*Shénnǚ* 神女), associated with the sexagenary cycle.[54]

Even when understood as extrahuman entities, several texts make it clear that spirit powers are not restricted to spirits; humans can acquire them. Here a problem arises because of a scholarly tendency to discuss "human" *shén* under the rubric of philosophy and "extrahuman" *shén* under the rubric of religion. But as Roel Sterckx argues, it is important not to arbitrarily separate them and to recognize that depictions of sagehood and self-cultivation in early China should be reexamined in light of this ritual background, its imagery, and its grounding in sensation.[55]

---

[53] Sterckx 2007: 38–39.
[54] For these names and chief deities in Han popular religion, see Seidel 1982: 28–34.
[55] Sterckx 2007, especially 24 and 40.

Internal Spirit

Starting in the fourth century, the view arose that individuals could store, enhance, and refine spirits within their own person. This internal spirit was independent of ritual relations with external spirits. It was closely linked to essence (*jing*) and *qi*. Spirit as an internal capacity becomes prominent in the *Guanzi, Mencius,* and *Zhuangzi,* as well as in excavated texts from Mawangdui and Guodian. Xunzi describes it in distinctive ways, and it becomes an important component of a person in the *Huangdi neijing* and other Han medical texts. A few examples (discussed in detail in subsequent chapters) illustrate some of the range of descriptions of spirit. The *Guanzi* describes the results of the circulation of essence in the body:

靜則精，精則獨立矣。獨則明，明則神矣。神者至貴也，

[With essence] diffused throughout, they become quiescent. Being quiescent, they become of single purpose. Being of single purpose, they become detached. Being detached, they become enlightened. Being enlightened, they become spirit-like. Spirit is honored above all else. (*Guanzi* 13.1/96/24–25, *Xinshu shang* 13.36, cf. Rickett 1998: 76)[56]

有神自在身，一往一來，莫之能思。失之必亂，得之必治。

There is a spirit that of itself is present in the embodied person, at times leaving, at times entering. No one is able to contemplate it. If you lose it, there will be disorder; if you obtain it, there will be order. (*Guanzi* 16.1/116/14, *Neiye* 16.49)

It is part of the *Zhuangzi's* description of the essence of perfect *dao*:

无視无聽，抱神以靜，形將自正。　必靜必清，无勞女形，无搖女精，乃可以長生。

There is nothing to see and nothing to hear; it holds spirit in its arms with stillness, and the form will correctly align of itself. You must be still; you

---

[56] Citations from the *Guanzi* are from the ICS Concordance series and are listed by chapter, section, page, and line number.

must be pure; do not belabor your form; do not agitate your essence; then you may live long. (*Zhuangzi* 11/27/24–27)[57]

Xunzi links it to both virtue and sagacity:

誠心守仁則形，形則神，神則能化矣

If you cling to humaneness with a heart-mind of integrity, you will embody it; if you embody it, you will be spirit-like. With spirit you will be able to transform things. (*Xunzi* 3/11/4–5, *Bu gou* 不苟)

思乃精，志之榮，好而壹之神以成，精神相（反）〔及〕、一而不貳為聖人。

[Refine] your thoughts to their essence, and your intentions will flower. By attraction and singlemindedness spirit is made complete. When essence and spirit reach each other, when they are one and not dual, you become a sage. (*Xunzi* 25/121/2–3, *Cheng xiang* 成相)

These snapshot examples suggest that, while all these authors considered spirit to be of the greatest importance, they meant somewhat different things by it. It is also a matter of debate whether extrahuman spirits and internal spirit are two linked things or separate. The same term is clearly used for both extrahuman spirits who reside in heaven and hold direct powers over natural phenomena and intrahuman, highly refined forms of *qi* cultivated by some persons. But what is the relation between the two?

Roger Ames and David Hall argue for a "seamless range of meanings" between the two and a mode of thinking in which humans and divinities are continuous; that continuity reflects a fundamental view of the cosmos.[58] Michael Puett argues that these terms were importantly discontinuous. In the Bronze Age, spirit referred exclusively to extrahuman divinities, and these spirit powers were understood to be capricious and dangerous. Sacrifice and ritual were, in part, attempts to anthropomorphize the divine by means of

---

[57] Citations from the *Zhuangzi* are from the ICS Concordance series and are listed by chapter, page, and line number.
[58] Hall and Ames 1998: 236–37.

ritual that transformed spirits into ancestors and arranged them in a hierarchy that worked on behalf of the living.

According to Puett, the term *spirit* was applied only to intrahuman refined *qi* in the Warring States period, when ongoing debates about the nature of both spirits and spirit powers redefined the term in important ways.[59] Various attempts were made to use self-cultivation practices to replace divination, sacrifice, and other dominant rituals addressed to the spirit world. Advocates of these new self-cultivation practices attempted to reduce the difference between spirits and humans by redefining both. They claimed that self-cultivation practices could offer spirit-like powers to humans. Fourth-century thinkers such as Mencius and at least some of the *Zhuangzi* authors address these issues, albeit in very different ways. Puett also argues that the emergence of so-called correlative cosmology was closely related to the emergence of strong claims for the possibility of self-divinization. These third-century self-divinization advocates claimed that humans were not restricted to becoming "like spirits"; the self-divinization advocates claimed to possess techniques that actually enabled them to *become* spirits, and even to be able to leave their bodies and undertake "spirit journeys." The *Huainanzi*, in particular, builds on self-divinization and ascension literatures, and it argues for a cosmos inhabited by anthropomorphic gods and theomorphic humans.[60]

I agree with Puett in considering external, extrahuman spirit and (the various meanings of) internal, intrahuman spirit as discontinuous and different. For this reason, what I describe as the spirit-centered view could not have emerged before the fourth century (or later) and the reconsiderations of spirit that occurred at that time. That debate also involved several other terms for intrahuman faculties closely related to intrahuman spirit, as well as for the "souls" of the dead.

Shén as Life

Another meaning of *shén*, primarily in a medical context, is the animating force that maintains life in a living body. Living bodies are vivified by essence (*jing*), *qi*, and spirit, and when spirit leaves the body, it dies.

---

[59] Puett 2002: 21–23.
[60] Puett 2002, especially 26–29.

In this sense, body, mind, and spirit fit together inseparably in a living being. One account of how these parts relate comes from the "*Neiye*" (Inner Workings) chapter of the *Guanzi*:

凡人之生也，天出其精，地出其形，
合此以為人；和乃生，不和不生。

When people are born, Heaven provides essence and earth provides form. Combining, these produce a person; if they harmonize, one lives; if not, it does not live. (*Guanzi* 16.1/117/14, *Neiye* 16.49, cf. Rickett 1998: 52, 12)

Two other accounts come from the *Huainanzi*:

夫形者，生之所也；氣者，生之元也；神者，生之制也。一失位，則三者傷矣。

The form is the residence of life; *qi* is the origin of life; spirit is the governor of life. If [even] one loses its place, then [all] three are harmed. (*Huainanzi* 1/9/15–16, *Yuandao* 原道)[61]

This passage clearly links spirit to essence and *qi*. Another passage specifies their origins:

精神，天之有也；而骨骸者，地之有也。精神入其門，而骨骸反其根，

Essence and spirit are of Heaven, and bones and frame are of Earth. [At death] essence and spirit enter [Heaven's] gate, and bones and frame return to their [Earth] roots. (*Huainanzi* 7/54/27–28, *Jingshén* 精神)

These passages make clear that "mind" or "spirit" cannot be defined by one clear term or body component, taken in isolation from others. In a paper published in 1989, Hidemi Ishida argued that "mind" (which he understood broadly to include mind and spirit) was not a fixed entity dwelling in the heart or any other discrete component of the body. Rather, it was closely linked to

---

[61] Citations from the *Huainanzi* are from the ICS Concordance series and are listed by chapter, page, and line number.

qi and could move around the body with the circulation of *qi* and it could even leave the body entirely.[62] Citing many of the passages discussed above, he argued that mind was closely associated with essence and *qi* and their movement in the body, where it flowed through the channels or meridians of the visceral systems. The freedom or blockage of that flow was a determining factor in health and disease.

Shén and *Shénming*

The complexity of intrahuman spirit is also evidenced by the range of binomes in which the term *shén* occurs, including: *guishén* 鬼神 (ghosts and spirits), *shénqi* 神氣 (spirit *qi*), *shénming* 神明 (spirit illumination), *mingshén* 明神 (bright spirits), *jingshén* 精神 (essence and spirit), and *shénling* 神靈 (spirit power).[63]

Among these binomes, the compound—or binome—"Spirit [and] Illumination" (*shénming*) is especially frequent in both the received tradition and in excavated texts. This term is associated with breath cultivation practices, sexual techniques, and other macrobiotic hygiene practices. It has at least three distinct meanings in Warring States texts. The term has a range of meanings.[64]

First, it can refer to an extrahuman spirit or to a quality possessed by extrahuman spirits. Li Ling has argued that, in the *Yijing* and many other ancient texts, *shénming* is a general term whose meaning is similar to *shén*.[65]

Second, as a binome it can refer to nonspecific extrahuman "spirit intelligences." One example comes from the *Zuozhuan*, in a remark by Music Master Kuang, that the people will revere a good ruler and will "look up to him like the sun and the moon, respect him like Spirit Intelligences (*jing zhi ru shénming* 敬之如神明), and be in awe of him like thunderbolts."[66]

---

[62] Cf. Ishida 1989.
[63] For this term, see Despeux 2007, especially 73–74 and Sterckx 2007.
[64] For accounts of various aspects of the history of the term *shénming*, see Szabó 2003, Wang Zhongjiang 2016: 38–40, and Small 2018. For *shénming* as a binome referring to pairs of spirits, see Graham 1989a, especially 515; Defoort 1997: 274; Li Ling 1999: 316–31, especially 318. For accounts of it referring to the power and efficacy of extrahuman spirits, see Maspéro 1933, Harper 1998: 120, Pang Pu 2000, and Wang Bo 2001. For accounts of it as a human cognitive faculty, contrasted with the body, see Xiong Tieji 2000: 533–37, especially 533.
[65] Li Ling 2002: 37.
[66] *Zuozhuan* B9.14.6/256/23–24 ("Duke Xiang 14"). He also describes him as the "lord of spirits" 神之主.

Another example comes from a statement in the *Mozi* that "the sage kings of antiquity all believed that ghosts and spirits were spirit intelligences (*guishén wei shénming* 鬼神為神明) and could bestow calamities and blessings," but since the time of Jie and Zhou, rulers believed that ghosts and spirits lacked *shénming* and were unable to do so (12.2/108/1–2, *Gong Meng* 公孟 48). Here, *shénming* is a quality possessed by ghosts and spirits.

According to the "*Shuogua*" 說卦 commentary in the *Yijing*:

昔者聖人之作《易》也，幽贊於神明而生蓍，參天兩地而倚數，觀變於陰陽而立卦，發揮於剛柔而生爻，

The sages of antiquity made [the *Yijing*] in order to give mysterious assistance to Spirit Intelligences, and produced [procedures for using] yarrow stalks. [Assigning the number] Three to Heaven and Two to Earth, from these came the (other) numbers. They contemplated the changes in the yin and yang [lines] and established the trigrams; from the movements of the strong and weak lines, they produced the line statements.[67]

This statement might appear to support the view that *shénming* was either equivalent to *shén* or a quality of external spirits. However, the second-century commentator Xun Shuang 荀爽 (128–190 CE) describes *Shén* an *Ming* as a pair with distinct roles: "*Shén* is in Heaven, *Ming* is on Earth; *Shén* is brilliant at night; *Ming* shines in the day."[68]

A case of *shénming* as a binome that has aroused considerable discussion occurs in the opening lines of the Guodian text *Taiyi sheng shui*. It describes Heaven and Earth "completing" what appear to be two forces: *Shén* and *Ming* (*cheng shénming* 成神明), which in turn complete yin and yang and thence, the four seasons.[69]

Accounts of internal *shénming* may start from the *Neiye* and "Arts of the Mind" chapters of the *Guanzi*. They focus on the storage and concentration within the body of *qi*, essence (*jing*), and spirit.[70] It is also prominent in

---

[67] *Zhouyi* 67/85/11–12 (*Shuo gua* 說卦). Citations from the *Yijing* (*Zhouyi*) are from the ICS Concordance series and are listed by section, page, and line number.
[68] 神者在天，明者在地。神以夜光，明以晝照。Li Daoping 1994: 229. For further discussion see Li Ling 2002: 36.
[69] *Guodian Chumu*, *Taiyi sheng shui*, strips 1–6. This passage is discussed in detail in Chapter 5 of this text.
[70] Harper (1998: 120) argues that the medical texts from Mawangdui and Zhangjiashan provide examples of medical ideas that were part of the same intellectual context as the theories of the *Neiye*.

excavated texts from Mawangdui, which directly link it to the body via longevity techniques, especially "Ten Questions" (*Shiwen*).

In most of the passages discussed above, *xin* and *shén* are discussed in different contexts. In passages where *xin* refers to some kind of mental activity, accounts of mind—and its cultivation—typically focus on rites, music, and the virtues, and do not mention *shén*. Accounts of *shén* occur in the quite different context of accounts of the balance and regulation of *qi*, essence, and *yin* and *yang*, and do not focus on the heart or mind.

Hun and *Po*: the "Souls" of the Dead

Two terms refer to the "souls" of dead persons. *Hun* 魂 or "*hun*-soul" (literally "cloud soul") and *po* 魄 or *po*-soul (literally "white soul") have no English equivalent. Y.-K. Lo argues that before the sixth century BCE, the ancient Chinese believed that all humans had a "soul," which, in the south was called *hun* and in the north was called *po*. Due to cultural fusion between south and north China in about the sixth century BCE, these two sets of "single-soul" beliefs combined to create a belief in a dual *hunpo* soul. Understood as a dual soul, the *hun* (also called *hun qi* 魂氣) was considered to be *yang* and ethereal and to leave the body after death; the *po* was *yin* and material and remained with or near the corpse.[71]

One issue concerns a contrast between the postmortem fate of the body and the status of the spirit (*shén*) or "soul(s)"—*hun* and *po*, or *hunpo*—after death. Even if body, mind, soul, and spirit seem inseparable during life, a range of evidence suggests that they were believed to separate after death. A range of texts describes the departure of the spirit at death, and a range of sacrifices and rituals aimed at it. In addition, a "soul"—understood as the *hun* or the compound *hunpo*—was believed to leave the body at death. According to longstanding belief, the *hun* was believed to ascend and the *po* to remain near the corpse. Kenneth Brashier has argued that belief in separate *hun* and *po* is an elite literati tradition, but that other scholarly and popular views understood *hunpo* either as a compound or as two interchangeable terms, both linked to mental activity, consciousness, and personal identity after the death of the physical body.[72]

---

[71] For *hun* and *po* see Seidel 1982, Y. Yü 1987, Brashier 1996, and Y. Lo 2008.
[72] Brashier 1996.

In conclusion, any account of the mind and body in early China must take account of the articulation multiple "bodies" as well as multiple minds and other psychological faculties, as well as the porosities between some "bodies" and some "minds." Integrating "spirit into the picture presents other difficulties because even the boundary between external "spirits" and an internal "spirit" faculty of the individual may be less than clear. These issues are explored in detail in subsequent chapters.

The porosity between the categories of bodies and minds raises questions that will arise throughout this book and will be revisited in the Conclusions chapter at the end of this volume. The complex categories of body form, frame, and embodied person (*ti, xing,* and *shēn,* respectively), in conjunction with heart–mind and spirit, clearly present a multilayered picture of human personhood that cannot be reduced to binaries of body and mind, or even of inner and outer (*neiwai* 內外). We can also speculate that these categories are necessary to self or constitutive of it. It seems clear that any human being requires a physical form, frame, and limbs, whether or not they correspond to human norms. A more complex question is whether we can imagine a human being without a *shēn*. Can we say, for example, that a person who is brain dead or is so psychopathic as to lack the "self" of an embodied person can truly be called a human being? We can raise a similar question about nonhuman animals and other living things. Plants and animals clearly have physical frames (*ti* bodies) and forms. By contrast, only humans have embodied and ritual persons.

2
Virtue, Body, and Mind in the *Shijing*

In this chapter I survey the representations of body, mind, and spirit in the *Shijing* 詩經 or *Book of Odes* (henceforward the Odes), one of the major—and unarguably prephilosophical—texts of the Chinese tradition. This text is particularly important because of accounts of the high regard in which Confucius held it. In the *Lunyu* or *Analects*, when asked by his students what to study, Confucius places the greatest importance on the Odes which, in his view, seem to have distilled moral wisdom—or virtue—of antiquity.[1] The received Mao edition dates to the Han dynasty, but the dating of the poems in the edition is a matter of scholarly disagreement, a debate that includes the role of orality in their composition. Scholars date the initial composition to the first half of the first millennium BCE.[2] Excavated texts have suggested that multiple versions of the Odes were in circulation in Warring States China, but, for purposes of the present discussion, it is reasonable to infer that something fairly close to the received version of the Odes held this central role in Confucius's notion of virtue.[3] The Odes also presents a view of the mind that includes concepts of psychological interiority.[4]

In this chapter, I relocate these debates in the context of relations between body, mind, and spirit in the Odes. The first section examines the account of human—and animal—bodies. The second turns to uses of the term *xin* or heart-mind, including the issue of psychological interiority. The third turns to the ways in which the term *spirit* is used and how its presence or absence relates to the question of psychological interiority. I argue that, although the Odes do show psychological interiority, they do not manifest any clear expression of dualism, nor do they manifest a strong

---

[1] *Lunyu* 16.13/47/5–6 and 17.9/49/1–2; trans. Slingerland 2003: 197 and 204 (slightly modified).
[2] For discussion of some of these debates, see Shaughnessy 2015.
[3] Kern 2005.
[4] For the importance of psychological interiority in the Odes, see Slingerland's (2014 and 2018: 14, 101, and 143–46) arguments against Herbert Fingarette's (1972) claim that the *Analects* had no notion of psychological interiority, a key claim in arguments for or against mind–body dualism.

distinction between mind and spirit. The "bodies" that appear in this text are not the physical form or limbs, but rather the socially articulated and constructed body. Nor are the "spirits" that appear there interior faculties in any sense.

Bodies in the *Shijing*

In the Odes, only two of these terms refer to the bodies of humans. The term *xing* does not appear at all. *Shēn* and *gong* appear as the body and person of (usually virtuous) human beings. In contrast to later literature, the Odes never refers to human bodies as *ti*; *ti* bodies do appear, but they are the limbs or roots of plants, animals, and inanimate objects.

The uses (or absences) of embodied person (*shēn*), form (*xing*), and frame (*ti*) in the Odes are also found in the bronze inscriptions of the Zhou dynasty.[5] References to the bodies of humans are always to the (embodied) person and never to the form or frame.

Embodied Persons

The poem "Swallows" (*Yan Yan* 燕燕, Mao 28) describes the lady Zhong Ren 仲任, the Shang princess given in marriage to King Ji of Zhou and the mother of King Wen:

仲氏任只、其心塞淵。
終溫且惠、淑慎其身。

The lady Zhong Ren, her heart–mind is sincere and deep;
She is mild indeed and kind, she is good and careful of her *shēn* person.
(Mao 28.4, 6)[6]

---

[5] Citations of bronze inscriptions are by reference in *Yin Zhou jinwen jicheng* and by transcription in *Yin Zhou jinwen jicheng yinde*. Scholars differ in their transcriptions of these inscriptions. The transcriptions here follow the CHANT database. In a few cases where an archaic character was unavailable I have substituted an interpolated modern character, which is so indicated by italics. Translations are based on Cook and Goldin 2020 and Shaughnessy 1991. The contexts of these inscriptions are discussed in Cook and Goldin 2020.

[6] Citations from the Odes are from *Maoshi yinde*, Harvard concordance series. Translations are from Karlgren 1950, sometimes modified.

This brief mention underscores the extent to which virtue may be identified with the physical person. The term *shu* 淑 refers to purity and clarity and is gendered as a term for virtue in ways that *de* 德 is not.

"Yellow Birds" (*Huang niao* 黃鳥, Mao 131), one of the few poems in the Odes that can be dated, praises the three men who were buried alive with Prince Mu of Qin 穆公 at his death in 621 BCE:

誰從穆公、子車奄息。
維此奄息、百夫之特。
臨其穴、惴惴其慄。
彼蒼者天、殲我良人。
如可贖兮、人百其身。

Who follows prince Mu? Ziche Yansi
Now this Yansi, he is the champion among a hundred
Looking down on the pit [grave], terrified his trembling
That blue Heaven, it destroys our good men
If we could redeem him, a hundred men [would be worth the life of] his person. (131.1, 27)[7]

The context of the poem equates the three men's embodied persons with their lives, as they stand literally on the brink of death. But the embodied persons that are praised are not their form or even their living limbs (*ti*), but their virtuous, socially constructed persons, who accompany their lord into death. *Shēn* has a similar—if less dramatic—meaning in two other poems. "Rain without Uprightness" (*Yu wu zheng* 雨無正, Mao 194) complains that the words of rulers are unreliable, disrespectful, and do not fear heaven, admonishing them to "each be reverent in your person" (*ge jing er shēn* 各敬爾身, Mao 194.3, 46). "What Kind of Man Is That" (*He ren si* 何人斯, Mao 199) complains about an unseen visitor, "I hear his voice but do not see his person."[8]

The poem "Great Brightness" (*Da ming* 大明, Mao 236) describes the marriage of Zhong Ren to King Ji 王季 of Zhou and the birth of King Wen 文王. Here *shēn* refers to her state of pregnancy:

---

[7] Stanzas 2 and 3 repeated the same refrain for the other two: Ziche Zhonghang 子車仲行 and Ziche Zhenhu 子車鍼虎.

[8] 我聞其聲、不見其身. Mao 199.2, 47. Karlgren (149) considers the poem to be a complaint by a prince of Su against the slanders of the prince of Bao, phrased in the voice of a woman whose love no longer comes to see her.

摯仲氏任、自彼殷商、
來嫁于周、曰嬪于京。
乃及王季、維德之行。
大任有身、生此文王。

The lady Ren of the Zhong clan of Ji came from Yin-Shang
She came and married in Zhou; she became a bride in the capital
Together with [her husband] Wang Ji, she practiced virtuous conduct
Tai Ren became pregnant and gave birth to King Wen. (Mao 236.2, 59)

Lady Ren is explicitly described as virtuous (*de*) in her conduct, and this virtue is closely linked to her *shēn* person in a double sense: her ongoing practice of virtue in her embodied person, and specifically in the pregnancy that resulted in the birth of King Wen.

The poem "The Multitude" (Zheng min 烝民, Mao 260) describes the virtue (*de*) of the minister Zhong Shanfu 仲山甫:

仲山甫之德、柔嘉維則。
令儀令色、小心翼翼。

The virtue of Zhong Shanfu is mild and kind and just.
He has a good deportment, a good appearance, he is careful and reverent. (Mao 260.2, 71)

His "good appearance" refers to the coloration (*se* 色) of his face, and his mind is described as attentive (*xiao xin* 小心). He is also virtuous in obeying his ruler and in promulgating bright decrees (*ming ming* 明命). Finally, he protects the king's *gong* person (*wang gong shi bao* 王躬是保); he so much embodies the king's decrees that he serves as the king's throat and tongue (*wang zhi hou she* 王之喉舌, 260.2). He carries out the king's decrees (*wang ming* 王命) and:

邦國若否、仲山甫明之。
既明且哲、以保其身。

In the States, the princes, good or bad, Zhong Shanfu enlightened them
Intelligent and wise, he protected his person. (Mao 260.4, 71)

This poem twice refers to protecting someone, but the body of the "protected" king is a *gong*, while Zhong Shanfu, protecting himself, protects a *shēn*. Finally, Fang Luo 訪落 (Mao 287) seeks his father's counsel at the beginning of his reign and prays to him to "preserve and enlighten his person (*yi baoming qi shēn* 以保明其身, Mao 287, 77). Here, even a ruler has an embodied person.

These passages use the term *shēn* to describe the embodied person of virtuous individuals. It can feel pain and be injured, but it is primarily the socially constructed self, the bearer of status and personal identity. It embodies the accumulation of a person's moral values, character, experience, and learning.

The Bronze Inscriptions also refer to protection of the embodied person, usually of the donor or of the king. For example, in one late Western Zhou inscription, the donor, King Hu 㝬, offers sacrifices to advance the rank of his dead father so that he himself can benefit by the resulting mandate:

用令保我家、朕立㝬身。

I can use this mandate to protect our home, my position, and my person.[9]

The "announcement of merit" section of a bronze inscription sometimes includes a description of the donor's meritorious ancestors and the donor's own intention to follow their example. For example, in the *Ni zhong* 逆鐘 inscription, on the occasion of Ni's promotion, the bell donor enjoins him to take care from morning to night in his task of "protecting my person" (*ping zhen shēn* 屏朕身).[10] In an inscription on a group of bells, the donor Xing 癲 requests his deceased father and ancestors:

廣啟癲身。擢于永令(命)。...用璃(寓)光癲身。

May you broadly open my person. Promote me to eternal life ... and lodge the radiance in my person.[11]

---

[9] *Hu gui* 㝬簋, *Jinwen jicheng* 8.4317; Cook and Goldin 2020: 150.
[10] *Jinwen jicheng* 1.62; Cook and Goldin 2020: 225–26; Falkenhausen 1993b: 157–58; Kane 1982: 20.
[11] *Jinwen jicheng* 1.246; Cook and Goldin 2020: 123–25; Falkenhausen 1993a: 27. The same phrases recur at 1.252 and 255.

Other inscriptions refer to serving the ancestors or the Son of Heaven without "harm to one's person (*jue shēn* 厥身).[12] Requests for protection can also refer to protecting the person of the ruler, for example, references to guarding the king's person (*wang shēn* 王身).[13]

Gong Selves

Gong persons appear ten times in the Odes, as both men and women who have been rejected by a superior or by a husband. In several poems, a woman laments that her *gong* self (*wo gong* 我躬) is rejected by a former husband or lover. In "Valley Winds" (*Gu feng* 谷風, Mao 35), a woman addresses the husband she had thought she would spend her life with:

習習谷風、以陰以雨。
黽勉同心、不宜有怒。
采封采菲、無以下體。
德音莫違、及爾同死。

Gusts, gusts the valley winds, bring clouds and rain
I strove to be of the same [as you] in heart–mind; you should not feel anger
They gather the *feng* plant, gather the *fei*, without regard to their lower part
In my reputation for virtue, nothing is contrary [to what it should be]; I should die with you. (Mao 35.1, 7)

But he has rejected her for a new wife:

我躬不閱、遑恤我後。

My self is now not liked; how should I have leisure to be anxious for my future? (Mao 35.3, 7)[14]

---

[12] *Jinwen jicheng* 5.2824; Cook and Goldin 2020: 64.
[13] *Jinwen jicheng* 9.4467; Cook and Goldin 2020: 175–76.
[14] Some take *wo hou* 我後 to refer to descendants rather than the general future. See Karlgren 1950: 22n(f). The same lament occurs in another poem in what appears to be the voice of a dissatisfied officer who has been rejected by his superior. See Mao 197.8, *Xiao pan* 小弁, 46.

Similarly, in "Vagabond" (Meng 氓, Mao 58), a woman laments to a former husband who has rejected her: "Silently I think of it, And bemoan my *gong* self" (*gong zi* 躬自)."[15]

Elsewhere, *gong* is used of persons who labor in the face of misfortune. "The Milky Way" (Yun Han 雲漢, Mao 258) describes a drought, in which all sacrifices have been offered to the spirits, to no avail; Hou Ji 后稷 is powerless, and Shangdi 上帝 "wastes and destroys the earth below; why does he strike my *gong* self?"[16] Similarly, another poem describes a famine that has been made worse by the misbehavior of wicked officials: "will they not bring calamity on our *gong* selves?"[17] In "Crest-like Is the Southern Mountain" (Jienanshan 節南山, Mao 191), a minister is faulted because "You do not manifest a *gong* self, you do not act personally (*wu gong wu qin* 弗躬弗親); the people do not trust you."[18] This is someone who shirks *gong* labor. By contrast, the official of "Rain without Uprightness" (Mao 194, discussed above) tries to labor on behalf of his state, but his advice is not heeded:

哀哉不能言、匪舌是出、維躬是瘁。
哿矣能言、巧言如流、俾躬處休

Alas, I am unable to speak! I cannot bring out my tongue; I only exhaust myself;
How suitable to be able to speak! The artful words [of court sycophants] are like a flow; it makes themselves rest in comfort. (Mao 194.5, 45)

Finally, the *gong* embodied self, especially a ruler's, must be preserved and protected. The poem "King Wen" (Mao 235) admonishes its eponymous subject: "The mandate is not easy [easily preserved], Do not cause the extinction of your own *gong* self.[19] In "The Multitude" (Mao 260, discussed above), Zhong Shanfu protects the *gong* person of the king:

王命仲山甫、式是百辟。
纘戎祖考、王躬是保。

---

15 靜言思之、躬自悼矣. Mao 58.5, 13.
16 耗斁下土、寧丁我躬. *Yun Han* 雲漢, Mao 258.2, 69.
17 不裁我躬. "Zhou wen" 召旻, Mao 265.6, 73. In the two-stanza poem "It's No Use" (Mao 36), the speaker addresses the prince with whom he shared exile and hardship: "If it were not my lord's *gong* self, why be out here in the mire?" (微君之躬、胡為乎泥中). *Shi Wei* 式微, Mao 36.2, 8.
18 弗躬弗親、庶民弗信. Mao 191.4, 45.
19 命之不易、無遏爾躬. *Wen Wang* 文王, Mao 235.7, 58.

The king charged Zhong Shanfu: be a model to those many rulers;
Continue [the services of] your ancestors; protect the king's *gong* person. (Mao 260.3, 71)

Nonhuman *Ti* Bodies

In several *Shijing* poems, *ti* refers to the body in the sense of its limbs. According to "Valley Winds" (Mao 35, discussed above), gathered plants are not rejected because of their roots, literally their "lower limbs" (*xia ti* 下體, Mao 35.1, 7). The comparison is between the roots of the plants, which are not rejected and the wife who is. "Regard the Rat" (*Xiang shu* 相鼠, Mao 52) compares the rat, whose body always has four limbs (*you ti* 有體), with a human being, who can exist without ritual propriety (*wu li* 無禮, Mao 52.3, 11).

In "Vagabond" (Mao 58, discussed above), the narrator recalls her husband's promises of marriage. He prognosticates with both bones and stalks, and "their frames had no inauspicious word."[20] Here, *ti* could refer to their bodies as a whole or to the "limbs" of the cracks on the bone or the "branches" of the yarrow stalks. Either way, the reference is to the (now) dead bones and stalks of formerly living animals and plants. "Rushes by the Road" (Xing Wei 行葦, Mao 246) compares the complete limbs of the fast-growing plants to the unity of brothers in a family. The plants "become ample and take shape," literally; they "become ample, become limbed" (*fang bao fang ti* 方苞方體).[21]

In summary, these examples show that the "body" described in the Odes is not the form of the physical body—the frequent object of "mind–body" contrasts, nor is it the limbed body of plants and animals. In other words, it is a human and social body, the body that possesses—or lacks—virtue.

That *shēn* should be prominent in the Odes is not surprising. What is somewhat surprising is that *xing* is absent and that *ti* is applied only to nonhuman living things. In other words, even in the description of human bodies, the Odes are moving toward a normative description of specifically human behavior. This consistency is all the more noteworthy given the probable heterogeneous origins of the text. One possible explanation is a strong editorial hand, such as that ascribed by tradition to Confucius himself.

---

[20] 爾卜爾筮、體無咎言. Meng, Mao 58.2, 12–13.
[21] Xing Wei 行葦, Mao 246.1, 63.

Xin

The term *xin* appears 168 times in seventy-four of the Odes. Often it is the seat of the emotions in first-person accounts of grief and sorrow especially, but also of love, pleasure, and calm. Examples include references to "my heart" (*wo xin* 我心) or "my sorrowful heart–mind" (*youxin* 憂心) in statements such as:

憂心忡忡 / 憂心惙惙 / 我心傷悲。

My sorrowful heart is agitated /very sad /wounded with grief (Mao 14.3, *Cao chong* 草蟲)

憂心悄悄。

My anxious heart is full of trouble (Mao 26.4, 5, *Bo zhou* 柏舟)

心之憂矣。

The sorrow of my heart (Mao 27.2, 6, *Lu yi* 綠衣)

展矣君子、實勞我心。

[that princely man] afflicts my heart (Mao 33.2, 7, *Xiong zhi* 雄雉)

As Michael Carr notes in an important but little circulated study, the word "heart" is a semantic hyponym for "mind." Perhaps for this reason, Karlgren typically translates *xin* as "heart" ninety-six percent of the time and only rarely renders the term as "mind." Although other viscera are associated with emotions and consciousness, they are almost never mentioned in the Odes, and physical pain is synonymous with mental pain.[22]

So it is not surprising that in many instances, it is open to question whether *xin* primarily refers to the emotions or to cognition. For example, in "What Kind of Man Is That" (*He ren si*, Mao 199, discussed above), the (presumably female) speaker is perturbed because of a man who returns to her house but does not announce himself or come in. His heart–mind is full of dangerous

---

[22] Carr (1983: 4) is interested in instances where *xin* means "mind," rather than heart, in order to apply the Odes to the "bicameral mind" hypothesis of Julian Jaynes, which is not a concern of the present study. For statistical data on "grieved hearts," see Carr 1983: 8–15.

devices (*qi xin kong jian* 其心孔艱, 199.1); he does nothing but perturb her heart–mind (*qi jiao wo xin* 衹攪我心, 199.4), yet had he come into the house, her mind would have been relieved (*wo xin yi ye* 我心易也, 199.6). In another example, "Great Brightness" (*Da ming*, Mao 236, discussed above), King Wu is urged to have no doubts in his heart–mind (*wu er er xin* 無貳爾心, 236.7).

Psychological Interiority

One area where the boundary between feeling heart and thinking mind is difficult to draw is in the phrase *zhongxin* 中心: "the center of the heart–mind." But is this inmost faculty a feeling heart or a judging mind? In some cases, the "inmost *xin*" is linked to the "grieving heart" that is so prevalent in the *Shijing*. For example, the narrator of the short poem "Strong Winds" complains of such arrogant treatment: that "at the core of my heart I am grieved."[23] Similarly, the rejected wife of "Valley Breeze" (*Gu feng*, Mao 35, discussed above) describes her inner state as: "unwilling in the core of my heart" (*zhongxin you wei* 中心有違, Mao 35.4). Slingerland argues that her expression of reluctance (*wei*)—literally physical "opposition" or "going against"—conflicts with her "inner heart–mind" (*zhongxin*) and provides clear evidence of the conflict between one's inner psychological state and outer behavior (Slingerland 2014: 199–201). In "Glutinous Millet" (Mao 65), a sorrowful poet compares his own bowed head to a millet stalk bent by ripening grain:

行邁靡靡、中心搖搖。
知我者、謂我心憂、
不知我者、謂我何求。

I walk slowly, in my innermost heart I am shaken.
Those who know me say my heart is grieved;
Those who do not know me, ask what I am seeking.[24]

Observers of his bowed head and slow pace think he is looking for something, and they do not see that what bends him double is not a lost object but inner sorrow. The contrast is less extreme than in Mao 35, but his outer behavior does not clearly mirror his inner feelings.

---

[23] 中心是悼. *Zhong Feng* 終風, Mao 30.1, 6.
[24] *Shuli* 黍離, Mao 65.1, 14.

In both cases, the conflict between inner state and outer behavior seems to be more emotional than cognitive. The term *zhongxin* appears sixteen times in the Odes. Three things are especially interesting about them. First is the evidence they provide for psychological interiority. Second, as metaphors, they are container metaphors in that the *zhongxin* is contained within the *xin*, which is located within the body. These are among several metaphors for *xin* in early Chinese texts, and in particular, they contrast with ruler metaphors in which the *xin* rules the body as a ruler rules a state (Raphals 2015). Third, they also contrast to a very different trope in later Warring States thought in which the exterior manifests the interior.

The accounts of psychological interiority in the Odes contrast to a later *qi*-based view of a person in which a person's "inner" qualities inevitably manifest externally. Mark Csikszentmihalyi describes a fourth-century "material virtue" tradition, exemplified in the *Mencius* and two versions of the *Wuxing* 五行 ("Five Kinds of Action") recovered from Guodian and Mawangdui. Csikszentmihalyi argues that these texts provide "a detailed moral psychology describing the process of the cultivation of the virtues." He argues that material virtue is an important part of the description of a sage and that this "material virtue" tradition developed as a *Ru* response to criticisms (initially in the *Mozi* and *Zhuangzi*) of their claims that "archaic" rituals were effective for either self-cultivation or in the creation of social order.[25]

Csikszentmihalyi argues that for Mencius and a group of thinkers associated with Zi Si 子思 and found in excavated texts, virtue manifested physically in the body and was inseparable from it. Central to this view is an account of a material virtue grounded in the transformation of *qi*. According to both texts, the cultivation of the virtues transforms the body and appearance and is visible in a jade-like countenance and the appearance of the eyes. This view of *qi* is significantly grounded in late Warring States physiognomy and medicine. Other excavated texts on physiognomy show its importance in practical contexts, for example, a text from Yinqueshan on the physiognomizing of dogs, a Han sword physiognomy text from Juyan, and a text on the physiognomy of horses from Mawangdui. All share the view that internal *qi* is reflected in appearance and makes it possible to judge character or potential. In economic and military contexts this meant judging the "character" of an animal or weapon. For Mencius, this theory of *qi* linked together the development of virtue and the transformed appearance of a sage. Xunzi

---

[25] Csikszentmihalyi 2005: 7.

by contrast rejected physiognomy as being based on endowments received at birth, and thus was not an indicator of self-cultivation.

Mind and Virtue

In other cases, *xin* clearly seems to refer to the mind rather than the emotions. Carr has shown that these instances increase diachronically in the historically later sections of the Odes: the *Daya*, *Xiaoya*, and *Guofeng*.[26] But instances are not limited to the later poems. Here are a few examples:

我心匪石、不可轉也。
我心匪席、不可卷也。

My mind is not a stone; It cannot be rolled about.
My mind is not a mat; It cannot be rolled up. (Mao 26, *Bou zhou* 柏舟)

黽勉同心、不宜有怒。

[Husband and wife] should strive to be of the same mind
And not let angry feelings arise. (Mao 35, *Gu feng* 谷風)

By contrast, the poem "Jienan Mountain" (Jienanshan, Mao 191) describes a dysfunctional kingdom and criticizes the king's inability or unwillingness to "reprimand his mind" (*cheng xin* 懲心) or "change his mind" (*e xin* 訛心):

不懲其心、覆怨其正。

家父作誦、以究王訩。
式訛爾心、以畜萬邦。

he will not correct his mind, and is resentful and angry at their [attempts at] rectifying [him].

[I] Jia Fu have composed this chant, to examine the king's disorders.

---

[26] Carr 1983: 7–8 and 15–23. Carr also discusses the detailed semantic field of other mental vocabulary in the Odes, including lexical subfields for thinking and thought, for planning and pondering, for thinking broadly or worrying, and for knowing and understanding.

Ah, that you transform your mind, and nourish the myriad states! (Mao 191.9–10, 43)

"Clever Language" (*Qiao yan.* 巧言, Mao 198), another lament about injustice, contrasts appearance and reality, including the distance between others' thoughts and actions:

奕奕寢廟、君子作之。
秩秩大猷、聖人莫之。
他人有心、予忖度之。
躍躍毚兔、遇犬獲之。
荏染柔木、君子樹之。
往來行言、心焉數之。

Grand, grand the ancestral temple, a gentleman made it.
Orderly the great plans, sages made them.
Others have their minds, I can guess and measure them.
Swift run the crafty hare, but a stupid dog catches it.
Tender are the soft trees, a gentleman planted them.
The words of those who come and go, the mind can calculate their
    sense. (Mao 198.4–5, 47)

These brief references use *xin* to refer to the faculties of perception and judgment. In some cases, the term goes further and points to an "innermost" mind or heart, where the focus is on the interiority and hiddenness of one's true judgment or feelings.[27]

Several of the later poems praise rulers for their qualities of mind and explicitly link mind (*xin*) to virtue (*de*). The poem Huang yi 皇矣 (Mao 241) describes Huangdi intervening to create the Zhou dynasty, beginning with Taibo and Wang Ji. Wang Ji was friendly in his heart–mind (*yin xin ze you* 因心則友) and gained possession of the four quarters.

維此王季、帝度其心、貊其德音。
其德克明、克明克類、克長克君。

---

[27] Several other poems refer to comforting or pacifying the heart–mind. Mao 260 (Zheng min 烝民) ends with a statement that the poem is intended to comfort the heart–mind (以慰其心) of the minister Zhong Shanfu 仲山甫, who is plagued by many anxieties. Mao 262 (Jiang Han 江漢) ends with a statement when the country was settled and free from strife, the king's heart–mind was at peace (*ning*王心載寧).

> Now, this Wang Ji, Di measured his mind and established his reputation for virtue.
> In his virtue he was able to be enlightened; being capable of enlightenment he was able to be good; he was able to preside, to be ruler. (Mao 241.4, 61)

"Control" (Yi 抑, Mao 256) argues that an outwardly dignified bearing (in the sense of being repressed or restricted, *yi*) is the counterpart of inner virtue, and compares these qualities to fine wood suitable for making a *qin*:

> 荏染柔木、言緡之絲。
> 溫溫恭人、維德之基。
> 其維哲人、告之話言、順德之行。
> 其維愚人、覆謂我僭。
> 民各有心。

> Tender is the soft wood; they string it with silk.
> The mild and courteous are the foundation of virtue.
> Those who are wise—tell them lessons and they follow the path of virtue.
> Those who are stupid—they say I am untruthful:
> The people, each have their own minds. (Mao 256.9, 68)

In "Great Heaven Has a Firm Decree" (*Haotian you chengming* 昊天有成命, Mao 271), King Cheng's 成王 virtuous practices are closely linked to his heart–mind: "Continuously bright, he made his mind generous, and so he could secure tranquility."[28] Similarly, "Circling Water" (Pan shui 泮水, Mao 299) praises a ruler's officials, who "are able to enlarge their virtuous minds" (*ke guang de xin* 克廣德心).

Carr's study describes the Odes' semantic field of specifically mental activity as complex and includes thinking and thought (e.g., *si* 思 *nian* 念, *you* 悠), planning and pondering (e.g., *mou* 謀, *you* 猷, *du* 度), and knowing and understanding (e.g., *zhi* 知, *shi* 識). But it is also important to note a different aspect of the mind in the Odes: its consistent linkage with virtuous conduct in both thought and action.

---

[28] 於緝熙、單厥心。肆其靖之. *Haotian you chengming* 昊天有成命, Mao 271.1, 74.

Like the Odes, the Bronze Inscriptions associate the heart–mind with virtue. The term usually appears in the "announcement of merit" section of the inscription. It describes the virtues of the donor or his ancestor, including efforts to improve or extend virtue by broadening, brightening, or clarifying the heart–mind. For example, in the *Qin gong zhong* 秦公鐘 inscription, the Lord of Qin states that he made reverent sacrifices "in order to greatly enlighten my heart–mind" (*kuang ming you xin* 克明又心), and to stabilize and harmonize administrators and knights, and to unite his ministers.[29] Master Wang 望, the donor of the *Shi Wang ding* 師望鼎, describes his deceased father as:

> 穆穆克盟 (明) 厥心。哲(慎) 厥德。用辟于先王。
>
> Gravely, so gravely able to make his heart luminous and to carefully attend to his virtue in order to aid the Former kings.[30]

Similarly, in the *Hu gui*, Hu says that he was able to make his heart–mind broad (*huang zhi zhen xin* 簧㯱朕心).[31] Yizhe 遺者, the donor of the *Wansun Yizhe zhong* 王孫遺者鐘, proclaims that:

> 余恁(念)台心。征 (延)永余德。龢溺 民人。
>
> I remember in my heart, make far reaching and constant my virtue, and harmonize and settle the people.[32]

Other inscriptions refer to "being intelligent in my heart–mind." (*cong yu xin* 恖于心)[33]

Finally, several inscriptions combine references to protection of the person with request to open the heart–mind or to lodge light or radiance in the embodied person. For example, in the *Dong gui* 戒簋 inscription, the donor Dong 戒 prays to his deceased father and mother to:

---

[29] *Qin Wu gong zhong* 秦武公鐘. *Jinwen jicheng* 1.262–3; Cook and Goldin 2020: 250. For other instances of this phrase, see 1.247, 248, 249, 250, 266, 267, 268, and 269.

[30] *Jinwen jicheng* 5.2812; Cook and Goldin 2020: 78.

[31] *Hu gui. Jinwen jicheng* 8.4317; Cook and Goldin 2020: 150.

[32] *Wansun Yizhe zhong* 王孫遺者鐘. *Jinwen jicheng* 1.261, Cook and Goldin 2020: 272–73, Mattos 1997: 89.

[33] *Jinwen jicheng* 1.210, 211, 217, 218, 219, 220, 221, 222.

安永宕乃子戒心。安永襄戒身。

> eternally open the heart–mind of your son Dong and eternally cover his body.[34]

Another refers to Dong's mother's having:

休宕厥心。永襲厥身。

> graced his heart–mind with openness, so that she would eternally cover his body.[35]

In the *Shi Xun gui* 師訇簋, King Yi promotes and renews the command of the general Xun, and commands him to:

敬明乃心。達厶乃友干菩王身。

> be respectful, illuminate your heart–mind; and to lead your allies to guard the king's [my] person.[36]

Spirits

The term *spirit* (*shén*) as a component of a person does not arise in the Odes because accounts of spirit as a human component or capability only appear in the fourth and third centuries BCE.[37] External spirits appear as beings who make themselves known to humans in various circumstances (Mao 165.1, 166.5, 207.4–5, 212.2, 258.1, 2, 6, 264.5), including as recipients of sacrifice (209.2–6, 212.2) and the spirits of ancestors (240.2, 252.3), though not the "souls" of dead bodies. By contrast, spirit as an internal capacity of a person never appears. In marked contrast to later literature, *shén* is not a locus of human virtue in the Odes because it is not a human capability. Similarly, *shén* always refers to external spirits, in the Bronze Inscriptions.

This striking absence gives added force to arguments on self-divinization made by Michael Puett, who argues that Bronze Age sacrificial ritual was

---

[34] *Jinwen jicheng* 5.2824; Cook and Goldin 2020: 64.
[35] *Jinwen jicheng* 8.4322; Cook and Goldin 2020: 69.
[36] *Jinwen jicheng* 8.4342; Cook and Goldin 2020: 113. This phrase also occurs at 8.4469.
[37] See Puett 2002 and the discussion of *shén* in Chapter 1 of this text.

fundamentally agonistic because of the capricious nature of spirits; and it was used to transform ancestors into gods and create a divine hierarchy that humans could understand and manipulate.[38] Warring States thinkers sought to reshape dominant attitudes and to reduce the distance between humans and gods through self-cultivation practices that allowed a person to become a *shén*. "Self-divinization" increased individual human control and made it possible to bypass divination and sacrifice. This view of self-divinization offers a very different view of Confucius's famous advice to keep a respectful distance from gods and spirits and to concentrate on human concerns at *Lunyu* 6.22.[39] That attitude is entirely absent from the Odes and its account of virtue.

More on Embodied Virtue

We have already seen a suggestion that the Odes depicts virtue as a visible, external quality rather than as a quality of the inner mind. This view of virtue is also apparent in the ways in which the term *de* 德 is used in the Odes. In some poems, it simply refers to or asserts the virtue of an individual, often King Wen, or of someone "having virtue," but it says nothing about how virtue manifests or is apprehended.[40] Other poems link virtue to appearance and conduct, and conspicuously to one's *reputation* for virtuous behavior and conduct. The most frequent mention of virtue is in the phrase "reputation for virtue" (*de yin* 德音), for example, the "reputation for virtue" of the female narrator of Mao 35 (*Gu feng*), discussed above. The same phrase is used by a male admirer who praises the beautiful Meng Jiang (*mei Meng Jiang* 美孟姜) for a reputation for virtue that will never be forgotten (*de yin bu wang* 德音不忘).[41] Another man longs for a beautiful woman and "for such a reputation for virtue to come and join with me" (*de yin lai gua* 德音來括).[42] Men also have reputations for virtue. An unnamed woman praises the martiality of her

---

[38] Puett 2002: 31–79, cf. Keightley 1978 and 1998 and Poo Mu-chou 1998.
[39] See Puett 2002: 97–101.
[40] References to "the virtue of King Wen" (文之德) appear in Mao 262.6 (72), 266.1 (74), and 267.1 (74), and the eponymous poem Wen Wang 文王 (King Wen, Mao 235.6, 58) describes him as always mindful of his ancestor and cultivating his virtue (聿脩厥德). Other odes refer to the hereditary virtue of King Wu (Mao 243.2, 62), the undeflected virtue of Jiang Yuan (Mao 300.1, 80), the virtue of the rulers of antiquity (Mao 208.2, 50), the virtue of a chief of Shen (Mao 259.8, 71), and the Marquis Lu's displaying and brightening his virtue (Mao 299.4, 79).
[41] *You nü tong che* 有女同車 ("There Is a Girl in the Carriage"), Mao 83.2, 17–18. She also appears in Ode 49.
[42] *Che xia* 車舝, Mao 218.1, 53.

absent husband and ends: "so serene is my good man, so pure his reputation for virtue."[43] The Odes uses the phrase of a duke whose reputation for virtue is flawless (*Lang ba* 狼跋, Mao 160.2, 33), of a man praising his admirable guests (*Lu ming* 鹿鳴, Mao 161.2, 34), and of the reputation of a gentleman (*Xi sang* 隰桑, Mao 228.3, 57). The phrase is a refrain of praise to noble men in "There are Medlars on South Mountain": "may your virtuous fame have no end" and "may your virtuous fame be abundant."[44] Other poems praise individuals for "virtuous conduct" (*de xing* 德行).[45]

The Odes also uses the term *virtue* (*de*) for *bad* behavior. Women use the phrase *ersan qi de* 二三其德, literally "his virtue is in twos and threes," to criticize men who behave badly (*Meng* 氓, "Rogue," Mao 58.4, 13) or who are simply no good (*wu liang* 無良, *Bai hua* 白華, "White Flowers," Mao 229.7, 57). The poem "Guests" (*Bin zhi chu yan* 賓之初筵, Mao 220.4, 54) describes guests who "harm their virtue" (*fa de* 伐德) by becoming drunk and not knowing when to go home. Most striking is the poem "Grand" (*Dang* 蕩), King Wen's critique of the last Shang king. The poem excoriates him for employing violent and oppressive ministers who never should have been given power because "Heaven made them with insolent dispositions" (*tian jiang tao de* 天降慆德): literally, Heaven caused insolent or dissolute virtue to descend on them.[46] To put it differently, rather than being "good," they are "good at" and what they are good at is insolence and dissolution.

Finally, two poems associate *de* with one's appearance or demeanor. The speaker of "The People Are Burdened" (*Min lu* 民勞, Mao 253.3, 66) urges his fellow officials:

敬慎威儀、以近有德。

> Then let us be reverently careful of our demeanor, To cultivate association with the virtuous.

The poem "Demeanor" (*Yi*) begins with the assertion that outward demeanor is a sign of inner virtue (discussed above). In summary, these poems perceive virtue through the performative actions of the *shēn* and *gong* bodies of their virtuous agents. Nothing in the Odes describes virtue as internal.

---

[43] 厭厭良人、秩秩德音. *Xiao Rong* 小戎 ("War Chariot"), Mao 128.3, 26.
[44] 德音不已; 德音是茂. *Nanshan you tai* 南山有臺, Mao 172.3 and 172.4, 37.
[45] Mao 33.4, 7 (*Xiong zhi* 雄雉) and Mao 288.1, 77 (*Jing zhi* 敬之).
[46] Mao 255.2, 67 (*Dang*).

Conclusion

In summary, the Odes presents a very different body–mind–spirit landscape than do later Warring States philosophical texts three major ways. First, spirit is not part of the picture because spirits in the Odes are all external objects of prayer and sacrifice, and never internal capacities. Thus, the issue of the boundary between *xin* and *shén* does not arise.

Second, most accounts of *xin* in the Odes are the "feeling heart," and the feelings felt are primarily those of grief, anger, and powerlessness. At the same time, the *Book of Odes* clearly describes a "thinking mind," and in particular, a deeply inner or inmost mind that does not necessarily manifest externally, including its virtue. Some poems link mental character to virtue, but that virtue is manifested by action rather than by the visibly apparent *qi* that is so characteristic of later accounts.

Finally, the landscape of bodies is more diverse but also more slanted toward the social and ritual person than the formal body. The human body of the Odes is the ritual and social *shēn* or *gong* body of virtuous persons, not the form of the physical *xing* body of mind–body contrasts or the articulated frames of plants and animals. In other words, even in the description of human bodies, the Odes are moving toward a normative description of specifically human behavior.[47] That behavior includes psychological interiority but nonetheless focuses on a human "person" that is strongly defined by external appearances, manifested in the embodied (*shēn*) and ritual (*gong*) person. But the Odes does not locate virtue in the mind or soul, but instead distributes it among the *shēn* and *gong* bodies and virtuous actions of men and women who are also virtuous in their inmost minds, especially in the later poems. Given the heterogeneous origins of the poems, this consistency is all the more striking.

---

[47] For the intellectual and philosophical significance of the Odes and the importance of virtue in the person of a virtuous ruler, see Hunter 2021.

3
Mind and Spirit Govern the Body

What I have described as the mind-centered view has two separable components. The first is claims for the hegemony of the mind over the body or senses. The mind-centered view increasingly identifies virtue with the heart–mind (*xin*), often portraying it as the ruler of the body in metaphors that analogize the body and state.

The second component includes claims for correspondence or alliance between the heart–mind (*xin*) and spirit (*shén*), along with arguments for the importance of spirit. On the one hand, "mind-centered" texts argued that self-cultivation procedures could enhance internal spirit within the body; on the other hand, they identified internal spirit with virtue and with the heart–mind, in a hierarchically superior relation to the body. Together, mind and spirit rule the body just as the ruler rules the people or a state. The result is a binary view of a person as a polarity between the body and the mind/spirit.

Thus, views of the heart–mind as ruler of the body, senses, and emotions change and develop over time, including incorporating spirit into the capabilities of the mind-ruler. Although this view is most prominent in the *Analects*, *Mengzi*, and *Xunzi*, it appears in a range of texts that make body-state microcosm–macrocosm analogies, including passages in the *Guanzi* and many sections of the *Huangdi neijing*. Mind-centered descriptions of *xin* and mind as ruler metaphors provide strong arguments for mind–body—or mind/spirit–body, dualism.

In an important study of the body as an organization of space in early China, Mark Lewis identifies two contrasting metaphors of the body as state. In "harmonious" body-state metaphors, the mind is the uncontested ruler, and the body parts work smoothly as functions within the state In "agonistic" body-state metaphors, body parts, including the senses and, by extension, the emotions, contest the supremacy of the mind; victory of the mind creates order, but victory of other organs brings about illness or death.[1] These two contrasting uses of state-body metaphors give rise to two accounts of the

---

[1] Lewis 2006: 37–39.

heart–mind. In the first, "harmonious" model, the heart–mind is one of five "viscera" or "depots" (zang 藏), and psychological functions are distributed harmoniously among the five viscera. The "harmonious" view is most prominent in the *Huangdi neijing* (to be discussed in Chapter 6). In the other "agonistic" account, the mind is linked to the sense organs, typically striving for independence from the rule of the mind. The agonistic view appears in a wide range of Warring States and Western Han texts. These texts describe the mind as ruler of the senses, but these "ministers" consistently try to assert independence and reject hierarchical control.

Other Chinese texts from the fourth through first centuries BCE also describe the mind and body as a composite, but they differ in the elements of the composition, the relations of the parts of the composite, and the metaphors used to express these relations. In some texts, the body–mind is an unspecified amalgam. In others, a composite of the heart–mind and intelligence pervades and animates the living person. Yet others describe both mind and body as composites of essence (*jing*) and *qi*. Some texts describe the body as a—sometimes porous—house or container that holds the heart–mind. In others, the "containment" is distributed among a system of related organs or visceral systems that "store" a systematically related set of contents. These accounts are all broadly holist.

Accounts of spirit as part of a human being are also complex and polyvocal. Bronze Age sources consistently refer to *shén* as external spirit powers; thus, the issue of internal spirit, and thence any possible identification between *xin* and *shén*, does not arise. What does arise is a long history of disagreement about the nature of relations between humans and spirits (or humanity and Heaven) in Shang dynasty sources. On one view, they were in a state of continuity and harmony; this view is also linked to accounts of the Shang kings as shamanistic.[2] On the other view, they were in a state of tension and potential antagonism. The Shang state was fundamentally bureaucratic, and Shang kings deployed divination and sacrifice in a fundamentally agonistic *do ut des* type of give-and-take.[3]

Understandings of Shang views of the relations between humans and spirits also inform a related question: the "transformation" of recently dead ancestors into the "spirits" of the Shang pantheon of spirit powers. According

---

[2] For variants of this view and related views linking Shang kings to shamanism, see Chen Mengjia 1936, K. Chang 1983, J. Ching 1997, Eliade 1958, Hall and Ames 1998, and Wheatley 1971.

[3] For this view, see Puett 2002: 31–54, drawing on Keightley 1978, 1998, and 2014, Allan 1991, and Poo 1998.

to Michael Puett, Shang ritualists "anthropomorphized" the spirit world by turning human ancestral spirits who could guide and potentially control both Di and nature deities.[4] These rituals gave dead rulers official temple names and days on which to receive sacrifice within a sacrificial cycle. In this way, they transformed the potentially dangerous spirits of dead rulers into presumably beneficent ancestors within a rigid ancestral hierarchy.

It is a short—but transformative—step from practices that invite the spirits to enter a ritual space to practices that extend the "invitation" by inviting the spirits to enter the body (itself conceived as a ritual space). Such an imagined transformation implies a highly porous boundary between the ritual body and the ritual environment, and the internalization of spirit becomes a key issue in Warring States thought, starting from the *Mengzi* and *Zhuangzi*.

An important study by Michael Puett presents a very different alternative to the view that internal spirit is simply an extension of the ritual space. Puett argues for the emergence of "self-divinization" traditions in early China, beginning with claims in the late fourth and third centuries that humans could gain powers previously attributed to spirits through self-cultivation practices. These claims imply and give rise to a separate debate over the relation of *shén*—as a human capacity—to *xin* and to claims that the mind ruled the body and that virtue was located in this rule. The key difference is that, in this view, the relation between humans and spirits is agonistic rather than continuous or harmonious.

The first two sections of this chapter examine accounts of body, mind, and spirit in the *Analects* and *Mozi*. The remainder of this chapter examines the mind-centered view in texts that include accounts of internal spirit. The third and fourth sections address the emergence of these claims and their effects on views of body and mind in ruler metaphors in the *Guanzi* and *Mengzi*. (The other key text in which they emerge, the *Zhuangzi*, will be discussed in detail in Chapter 4.) The fifth section turns to a fully developed claim that the mind and spirit together rule the body in the *Xunzi*. The sixth section examines two very different kinds of ruler metaphor in two excavated texts from Guodian. The seventh section turns to an extensive ruler metaphor in "The Heart–Mind Is What Is at the Center" (*Xin shi wei zhong* 心是謂中), one of the excavated texts published by Tsinghua University. The last section examines the use of ruler metaphors in the second-century *Huainanzi*. (Other aspects of the *Guanzi* and *Huainanzi* will be discussed in Chapter 4.)

---

[4] See Keightley 2014 and Puett 2002, especially 52–54.

Body, Mind, and Spirits in the *Analects*

Previously, Chapter 2 argued that accounts of virtue in the Odes located it in both the body and the mind and identified it with the affective aspects of the heart. That "balance" largely continues in the *Analects*, which offers two interrelated views of the body: (1) the importance of correct alignment for both ethical and political virtue; and (2) the correct alignment of the body as a key element of ritual conduct and a central element of the efficacy of ritual. In contrast to extensive discussion of the body in the *Analects*, the heart-mind occurs only rarely, and "spirit(s)," *shén*, refers to external spirits rather than to human psychological capacities.

The *Analects:* Right Alignment and Distance from Spirits

The *Analects* describes the correct disposition of the embodied person as the basis for virtue and efficacious action. *Analects* 13.6 remarks that:

其身正，不令而行；其身不正，雖令不從。

[i]f the person is correctly aligned, then there will be obedience without orders being given. If it is not correct, there will not be obedience even though orders are given. (*Lunyu* 13.6/34/13)[5]

A similar passage (13.13/35/1) advises that government service requires no more than aligning one's embodied person correctly (*zheng qi shēn* 正其身). But those who cannot align themselves cannot correct (align) others. But what does it mean for an embodied person to be correct or to be aligned correctly?

The received view of the *Analects* understands two key normative terms— "to be straight" (*zhi* 直) and "to be upright" or "to rectify" (*zheng* 正)—as broadly synonymous. But there are important differences in their meanings. *Zheng* can also refer to the different, also normatively positive, sense of correct alignment. In this sense, *zheng* can refer to correct moral alignment ("uprightness"), but it can also involve "alignment" in broader physical, epistemological, and even cosmological senses. This understanding of *zheng* is

---

[5] Translations of the *Analects* are my own, but I have consulted and drawn on the translations of Lau 1992 and Slingerland 2003a.

linked semantically with "acting without acting" (*wuwei* 無為), explicitly so at *Analects* 15.5.[6]

In this latter sense of "pragmatically correct alignment," *zheng* refers literally to the correct orientation of one's embodied person.[7] For example, according to Confucius, a gentleman must align his stance (*zheng li* 正立), that is, assume an upright posture, before entering a carriage (10.17).

Zheng can also refer to aligning an object. For example, a gentleman maintains a dignified appearance by straightening—aligning—his robe and cap (20.2); and he does not sit if his mat is not aligned correctly (*buzheng* 不正, 10.9). Similarly, he aligns his mat before accepting a gift of meat (10.13), and he does not eat meat if it is served with the wrong sauce or is not cut correctly (*ge buzheng* 割不正, 10.8). At *Analects* 8.4, the gentleman is advised to regulate his countenance (*zheng yanse* 正顏色)—literally to rectify his facial coloring—in order to encourage sincerity and trustworthiness in others. Finally, a gentleman associates with others who follow *dao* in order to be set right by them (1.14).

The *Analects* also identifies correct alignment with good government, for example, at 12.17: "To govern (*zheng* 政) means to align (*zheng* 正). If you set an example by [your own] alignment, who will dare not to be aligned?" (*Lunyu* 12.17/32/18).[8] Finally, the *Analects* describes the sage-ruler Shun as governing, simply by aligning himself correctly to face south:

子曰：「無為而治者，其舜也與？夫何為哉，恭己正南面而已矣。」

The Master said, "As for one who ruled by means of *wuwei* was it not Shun? How did he do it? He made himself reverent and aligned himself [in the ritually correct way] facing south, and that was all. (*Lunyu* 15.5/42/9)[9]

This use of *zheng* is very different from "straight" or "upright" (*zhi*), a term the *Analects* opposes to crookedness, indirection, and craft. Confucius specifically recommends setting the straight over the crooked at *Analects* 2.19:

---

[6] This view of *zheng* is not unique to the *Analects*. *Zheng* in this sense of "correct alignment" also appears in the Odes and in a range of Warring States texts roughly contemporaneous to the probable composition of the *Analects*, especially the "Inner Workings" (*Neiye*) chapter of the *Guanzi* 管子. For details of this argument, see Raphals 2014.

[7] For discussion of the semantic range of *shēn*, see Y. Lo 2003.

[8] For other examples of *zheng* as correct government, see *Analects* 13.3 and 14.16.

[9] This passage raises the possibility that correct alignment is itself a form of indirect action. See Raphals 2014 and Slingerland 2003b.

哀公問曰：「何為則民服？」孔子對曰：「舉直錯諸枉，則民服；舉枉錯諸直，則民不服。」

Duke Ai asked: "How can we ensure that the people will be obedient?" Confucius replied: "Raise up the straight over the crooked and the people will be obedient. Raise up the crooked over the straight and the people will not be obedient." (*Lunyu* 2.19/4/6–7)

Confucius repeatedly describes ritual as a powerful technique for aligning the body correctly and for aligning body and mind. (There are also close philological links between the terms for ritual (*li* 禮) and the *ti* 體 body.) The importance of the body to ritual is further underscored in a remark attributed to Confucius in the *Liji*. Asked about "three things that don't exist" (*sanwu* 三無), he replies:

無聲之樂，無體之禮，無服之喪，此之謂三無。

Soundless music, disembodied ritual, and mourning without [mourning] clothes—these are what is called the three things that don't exist. (*Liji* 30.2/138/10–11, *Kongzi xianju* 孔子閒居)[10]

In other words, for Confucius, ritual is inherently embodied and would be incomprehensible otherwise. As such, ritual is performed by an embodied person (*shēn*) or by a ritual person (*gong*), never by a form or a frame.

The Heart–Mind in the *Analects*

The importance of the body to virtuous conduct and ritual is further underscored by the conspicuous absence of *xin* in the *Analects*. The term *xin* occurs only five times and without reference to either bodies or spirits:

子曰：「吾十有五而志于學，三十而立，四十而不惑，五十而知天命，六十而耳順，七十而從心所欲，不踰矩。」

---

[10] When asked for further clarification, Confucius refers to the Odes (Mao 1.3): "My deportment has been dignified and good, Without anything wrong that can be pointed out"—there is the ritual without embodiment ("威儀逮逮，不可選也," 無體之禮也, *Liji* 30.2/138/12, *Kongzi xianju*). For further discussion, see Lewis 2006: 14.

The Master said: "At fifteen, I set my will on learning. At thirty, I took my place. At forty, I had no doubts. At fifty, I understood the mandate of Heaven. At sixty, my ear was compliant. At seventy, I could follow the desires of my heart–mind without going beyond the rule [the carpenter's square]." (*Lunyu* 2.4/3/1–2)

Here the heart–mind is linked to desires. The metaphor of the carpenter's square further emphasizes the theme of physical alignment in this account of virtue attained in old age. By contrast, a second passage focuses on the heart–mind, describing Yan Hui as capable of spending three months with "nothing in his heart–mind but humaneness" (6.7/12/19).

A third passage refers to the ability of music to reflect the player's inner nature. It relates that Confucius was playing on the stone chimes in the state of Wei. A passerby remarked that "there is something on his mind (*you xin* 有心)! How he beats the chime stones!" (*Lunyu* 14.39/41/4–7). A fourth passage criticizes someone who eats all day and does not apply his mind to anything (*wu suo yong xin* 無所用心, 17.22/15/14). The fifth recounts Shun's sacrificial prayer when passing on his throne to Yu. Shun claims to have concealed nothing and urges Yu to use his heart–mind to examine Shun's actions (20.1/57/1–2).

The first passage refers to the affective state of a person in a mature state of self-cultivation. The third builds on the assumption that Confucius's musical performance reflects his inner state. But neither passage comments on the nature of the mind or its relation to other components of a person.

Like the Odes, the *Analects* clearly uses the term *shén* to refer to spirits—extrahuman powers—rather than to signify human psychological capacities. Confucius is famously reticent about them and "does not discuss prodigies, feats of strength, disorderly chaos or spirits" (7.21). He even defines wisdom as an attitude in which one "respects spirits but keeps them at a distance" (6.22). Finally, he admonishes his disciples not to be distracted by the service to spirits in the afterlife, but rather to concentrate on life in this world (11.12). Nonetheless, ancestors and spirits are central to his moral program, and as such, they are an important part of his thinking. At a discussion of sacrifices, he remarks that one should sacrifice to the dead and to the spirits as if the spirits are present (*ji shén ru shén zai* 祭神如神在, *Lunyu* 3.12/5/24).

These remarks are in no sense claims that spirits did not exist, but rather they signal that humans should not engage with them or try to influence them. As Puett puts it, spirits have great potency, but humans should not speak of them or worry about them. The purpose of ritual should be not to influence spirits, but to cultivate ourselves. Spirits should be revered, but the highest way to revere them is not to try to influence them.[11]

In summary, the *Analects* has much to say about the body, especially the embodied person, but relatively little about mind or spirit. It combines a strong interest in ritual—for human purposes—with respectful distance from spirits.

The *Mozi*

The treatment of body, mind, and spirits in the *Mozi* is significantly divided between the early Mohist doctrines, which discuss spirits at length, and definitions of body and mind, which occur in the epistemological chapters.[12]

Mohists on the Mind

In contrast to the *Analects*, the term *xin* occurs over fifty times in the *Mozi*. In some instances, it clearly referred to affective states, such as "not having a peaceful heart" (*wu an xin* 無安心, 1.1/1/10) or "having no remorse in his heart" (*wu yuan xin* 無怨心, 1.1/1/12). But, in other instances, *xin* seem to refer to a clearly cognitive faculty, often used to describe a gentleman or superior person. For example, "Cultivating One's Person" (*Xiushēn* 脩身) (ch. 2), argues that even purveyors of underhanded counsel will not gain support as long as a gentleman ensures that:

譖慝之言，無入之耳，批扞之聲，無出之口，殺傷人之孩，無存之心，

---

[11] Puett 2002: 98.

[12] The *Mozi* refers to texts and teachings associated with Mo Di 墨翟 (fl. c.430 BCE). The *Mozi* consists of seventy-one *pian*, of which eighteen are no longer extant, in six groups. Books 1–7 date from the mid- to late third century BCE and contain summaries of Mohist doctrines. Books 8–38 consist of ten "triads" (with seven chapters lost) that expound the ten doctrines of the early Mohist school and date from the mid- or late fifth century. Books 39 to 40 are critiques of the Ru school (Fei Ru 非儒), and do not present Mohist doctrines (39 is lost). Books 40 to 45, the "Later Mohist" texts or "Dialectics" (*Mo bian* 墨辯) include two chapters of "Canons" (*Jing* 經, chs. 40 and 41), two "Explanations" of the Canons (*Shuo* 說, chs. 42 and 43), and two lost chapters on ethics and language (chs. 44 and 45). The Later Mohist texts are fragmentary and complex, and probably date from the late fourth to mid-third centuries. Chapters 46 to 50 are "Dialogues" of sayings and conversations attributed to or involving Mozi and probably date to the mid- to late fourth century. Chapters 51 to 71 (ten have been lost) address defensive strategy and military engineering. See Fraser 2016: 12–14. For further information on the structure and dating of the Mohist texts, see Durrant 1977–78, Graham 1985 and Meader 1992.

there are no slandering words coming in his ears, no threatening sounds going out of his mouth, and no [thought of] killing or harming others' children abiding in his heart–mind. (*Mozi* 1.2/2/14, ch. 2)

The same chapter describes a gentleman as wise, and wisdom is linked to the mental faculty of discrimination:

慧者心辯而不繁說

For those who are intelligent, their minds make distinctions, but they are not complicated in their speech. (*Mozi* 1.2/3/2, ch. 2)

Even incapable rulers have minds and try to think:

不能為君者，傷形費神，愁心勞意，然國逾危，身逾辱。

Those who are not able to be gentlemen wear out their forms, exhaust their spirits, tax their heart–minds and belabor their thoughts, and yet their states are even more in danger and their persons even more humiliated. (*Mozi* 1.3/4/23–24, ch. 3)

Other passages in the *Mozi* use *xin* to refer to faculties that arguably are both affective and cognitive, but certain passages include cognitive activity, for example, the comment in "Exaltation of the Virtuous, 2" (*Shangxian xia* 尚賢下) that when rulers reward the meritless and punish the innocent: "it makes the people become distanced in mind and disjointed in frame" (*you xin jie ti* 攸心解體, *Mozi* 2.3/15/16, 9).

In summary, although the heart–mind continues to be an affective faculty that feels peace, grief, and the like, accounts of the mind as an explicitly cognitive faculty that discriminates and thinks first seem prominent in the *Mozi*.

Spirits in Early Mohism

The early Mohist doctrines include extensive discussion of external spirits and postmortem consciousness. Confucius and the early Mohists agreed on the importance of the correct performance of sacrificial rituals but for very different reasons. The early Mohists recommended constant attention to extrahuman spirits in accounts of "ghosts and spirits" (*guishén* 鬼神), and focused on three issues: (1) whether they existed; (2) whether they had consciousness (*ming* 明)—understood as whether they were aware of human right and wrongdoings and rewarded good and punished evil—and (3) critiques of Ru attitudes and practices regarding ghosts and spirits.

In the Mohist canon, respect for the spirit world was based on certainty about the existence of spirits as external extrahuman entities. "Explaining Ghosts" (*Minggui* 明鬼, chs. 29–31) presents many examples of workaday interactions between humans and spirits, including during sacrifice.[13] Accounts of spirit manifestations focused on events that demonstrated human shortcomings, moral or practical and material.[14] They believed that spirits were not only conscious (*ming*), but that spirits had foreknowledge of human actions and could reward the worthy and punish the unworthy:

偕若信鬼神之能賞賢而罰暴也，則夫天下豈亂哉！

Now, if we could persuade the people under Heaven to believe that ghosts and spirits are capable of rewarding the worthy and punishing the wicked, then how could there ever be disorder in the world? (*Mozi* 8.3/50/26–27, ch. 31, Sterckx 2007: 28)

The early Mohists also believed that the dead have consciousness.[15] The view that human consciousness survived death differs in emphasis from the later Mohist definition of "life." Like Aristotle's account of the faculties of the soul, where the living body is inextricably joined to the soul, the Mohist definition defines life as the union of the physical form and awareness (discussed below).

Early Mohist views of spirit also manifest in their critiques of Ru ritual practices. On the one hand, they opposed Ru funerary rituals because their expense and duration impoverished the living without directly addressing the (conscious) dead. Mohist belief in sacrifices to the spirits rose from their belief in both the consciousness of the dead and the moral power of the spirits. By contrast, Confucius's "respectful distance" acknowledges ghosts

---

[13] See Sterckx 2007: 26–30.
[14] Additional accounts of the perspicacity of ghosts and spirits come from the Shanghai Museum's excavated Chu manuscripts, "The Perspicuity of Ghosts and Spirits." See *Guishén zhi ming* 鬼神之明 (On the perspicacity of ghosts and spirits) in Ma Chengyuan 2005 (*Shanghai bowuguan* vol. 5): 307–21. For discussion, see Brindley 2009 and Ding Sixin 2006 and 2011.
[15] 死人有知. *Mozi* 8.3.51/68/24 (*Minggui xia* 明鬼下, 31), cf. Graham 1978: 281.

and spirits but does not rely on them. Mohist "spirit perspicacity" relies on their prescience and power as an arbiter of human conduct.

Later Mohist Definitions

Several definitions in the epistemological chapters of the Mohist canon provide important information on fourth- or third-century understandings of how bodies and minds were constituted. The dialectical chapters define *ti* as limbs or "parts" in contrast to wholes, but what then are the "parts" of a person? The dialectical chapters describe mind or sentience "holding together" (*chu* 處) the physical living body. According to "Explanations, 2":[16]

生，形與知處也。

Life: the form being located with the intelligence. (*Mozi* 10.1.43/69/25, ch. 43, cf. Graham 1978: 280)

Here, *chu* seems to refer to spatial position; a person is alive as long as the form is located with—shares the same space as—the intelligence or consciousness.[17] The Mohist text also notes two situations in which a body is alive but not sentient. It defines sleep as "the intelligence (*zhi* 知) not knowing of anything";[18] and defines dreaming as "supposing to be so while asleep."[19]

This passage describes the intelligence and the physical form (*xing*) as distinct entities (described by distinct words and graphs) that nonetheless share a location in space. Insofar as they share a location, we might be tempted to take this view as holist.

Finally, the Mohist text argues that both a living physical body and sentience are prerequisites for life in a human being.

It is also interesting that the logical implications of this coexistence in physical space are not explored. The text does not address the question of what happens to the body–intelligence composite after death, when the intelligence

---

[16] The two chapters titled "Canons" (chs. 40 and 41, *Jing shang* 經上 and *Jing xia* 經下), were probably written and compiled between the late 4th and mid-3rd centuries BCE and consist of terse statements. Two chapters of "Explanations" (chs. 42 and 43, *Shuo shang* 說上, *Shuo xia* 說下), provide commentary on them.
[17] Graham 1978: 282.
[18] 臥，知無知也, *Mozi* 10.1.45/68/29, ch. 40, trans. Graham 1978: 280.
[19] 夢，臥而以為然也, *Mozi* 10.1.47/69/33, ch. 40), trans. Graham 1978: 280.

no longer holds together the physical form. Finally, this passage identifies life itself as this coexistence; it implies that the mind cannot survive the body and that the body requires the animation of the heart–mind to be alive at all.

The Emergence of Internal Spirit in the *Guanzi*

The *Guanzi* offers several accounts of body, mind, and personhood. Accounts of living persons as composites of body, mind, and spirit appear in chapters concerned with the nature of the heart–mind: two chapters titled "Arts of the Mind," 1 and 2 (*Xinshu shang, xia* 心術上, 下, chs. 36 and 37) and "Inner Workings" (*Neiye*, ch. 49).[20] The *Guanzi* is a complex and composite text, and it presents polyvocal views of body, mind, and spirit. (Spirit-centered views in the *Guanzi* will be discussed in Chapter 4. The present discussion is limited to ruler metaphors in the *Guanzi*.)

The Heart–Mind as Ruler

Several *Guanzi* passages describe the mind as a ruler, of both subordinate officials and the people as a whole. "Ruler and Officials, 2" (*Junchen xia* 君臣下) (ch. 31), clearly analogizes the position of the heart–mind in the body (of which it is a physical part) to that of the ruler in the state (of which he is a part):

君之在國都也，若心之在身體也。道德定於上，則百姓化於下矣。
戒心形於內，則容貌動於外矣。

The ruler occupying the capital of his state is like the heart–mind occupying the person's frame. When *dao* and *de* are established above, the people will be transformed below. When a sincere heart–mind forms internally,

---

[20] All three present considerable textual complexities. For example, order in the *Guanzi* text does not reflect age. "Inner Workings" is the last of the chapters, but it is considered to be the oldest. "Arts of the Mind, 2" (*Xinshu xia*) is closely related to it and appears to develop ideas from it, while "Arts of the Mind, 1" (*Xinshu shang*) is a completely separate work, but a fourth chapter, "The Pure Mind" (*Baixin* 白心, ch. 38), expands on several concepts from both "Inner Workings" and "Arts of the Mind, 1." An additional difficulty is that "Arts of the Mind, 1" consists of "statements" and "explanations" of them, and there is considerable debate about the authorship of the latter, especially. Guo Moruo 郭沫若 argued that the *Neiye* and *Xinshu* chapters were written by the Jixia Academy scholar Song Xing 宋鈃 (385–304 BCE). In Guo's view (1944: 247), the statements were written by Song Xing, and the explanations were notes by his students. For discussion of these chapters, see Rickett 1998: 15–16 and 32–39.

it manifests in physical appearance externally. (*Guanzi* 11.1/83/12–13, *Junchen xia* 11.31).[21]

Here, the mind's influence on the body is described by the metaphor of a ruler transforming the people, with no intermediary described. The emphasis is on the unity of the state as a whole. The rulership metaphor is expressed differently in "Arts of the Mind, 1," where the mind's rule is over the body and the senses, described as subordinate officials:

心之在體，君之位也。九竅之有職，官之分也。心處其道，九竅循理。嗜欲充益，目不見色，耳不聞聲。

The heart–mind occupying the frame [is like] a ruler occupying his throne. The duties of the nine apertures are the divisions [in the responsibilities] of officials. If the heart–mind is at rest in *dao*, the nine apertures function properly. If lust and desire occupy it fully, the eyes do not see colors and the ears do not hear sounds. (*Guanzi* 13.1/95/25–26, *Xinshu shang* 13.36)

Here, the hegemony of the heart–mind is over the body, described metonymically by its nine apertures. The senses are mentioned only incidentally: when desires fill the body, they do not work correctly.

The "Explanation" to this passage further emphasizes the regulatory role of the heart–mind and places more emphasis on the role of the senses. It describes the organs of sight and hearing as officials (*guan* 官), who seem to function in a harmony with the mind-ruler. The *Guanzi* also describes the art of the mind as acting without acting (*wuwei*):

心之在體，君之位也。九竅之有職，官之分也。耳目者，視聽之官也，心而無與視聽之事，則官得守其分矣。夫心有欲者，物過而目不見，聲至而耳不聞也，故曰：「上離其道，下失其事」。故曰，心術者，無為而制竅者也。故曰：君。

The heart–mind occupying the frame [is like] a ruler occupying his throne. The functions of the nine apertures resemble the separate responsibilities

---

[21] Translations of the *Neiye* draw on Puett 2002, Rickett 1998, and Roth 1999. Here and in other *Guanzi* passages, line breaks, which in the original are in rhymed verse, are eliminated for the sake of brevity.

of officials. The ears and eyes are the officials for sight and hearing. If the heart–mind does not interfere with the activities of sight and hearing, the officials will be able to maintain their separate responsibilities. Now if someone's heart–mind is filled with desires, the eyes do not see when things pass by and the ears do not hear when there are sounds. Thence it is said: "If those on high depart from *dao*, those below will be lax in work." Hence it is said: The art of the heart–mind lies in controlling the apertures through *wuwei*. Therefore it is described as: "ruler." (*Guanzi* 13.1/96/16–18, *Xinshu shang* 13.36)

Both the passage and the explanation specify a superior–subordinate relation between the mind and senses. The second metaphor, the ruler of officials, is part of a description of the entry and cultivation of essence (*jing*) and spirit, a process that is possible only when the mind's hegemony is fully established.

Essence (Jing) and Qi

The "Arts of the Mind" chapters present a view of body and mind that closely links the mind to *jing* and *qi*. One passage describes the composite of body and mind as a house that can become the dwelling of spirit illumination (*shénmíng*):

潔其宮，開其門，去私毋言，神明若存。

Clean your mansion, open its gates! Once you have eliminated partiality and are without speech, spirit illumination will appear. (*Guanzi* 13.1/96/7, *Xinshu shang* 13.36)

According to the explanation to this passage, "mansion" refers to the mind and "gates" to the senses.[22] But it is striking that neither house nor gates take priority: the mind is a house surrounded by gates and is cleaned by a good airing out, which does not necessarily require opening the gates.

The key activity is a deliberate emptying to make possible a spontaneous replacement by spirit illumination. The replacement is effected by the

---

[22] Specifically, the eyes and ears. See *Guanzi* 13.1/96/16 (*Xinshu shang* 13.36).

circulation of *jing*. It introduces a process (discussed in detail in Chapter 4) that leads to the practitioner becoming "enlightened (*ming* 明) and "spirit-like." The passage concludes by returning to the house-cleaning metaphor:

故館不辟除，則貴人不舍焉，故曰不潔則神不處。

If the hall is not opened up and cleaned out, the honored one will not stay in it. Therefore it is said: "If you do not make a clean sweep, spirit will not remain." (*Guanzi* 13.1/96/24–26, *Xinshu shang* 13.36)

This passage never mentions the mind. Here the heart–mind is simply a dwelling that spirit will enter and inhabit if the circumstances are correct.

"Arts of the Mind, 2" also describes both body and mind as composites of *jing* and *qi*. A discussion of how to cultivate "power" (*de* 德, a quasi-magical power or virtue, in the sense of "good at") begins with the claim that power can only develop when the physical form is correctly aligned:

形不正者德不來，中不精[靜]者心不治。正形飾德，萬物畢得。

If the form is not correctly aligned, power will not come. If what is within is not quiescent, the heart–mind cannot govern. Align the form and cultivate power; then all things may be fully grasped. (*Guanzi* 13.2/98/1, *Xinshu xia* 13.37)

This passage describes body and mind wodrking together for a common goal: the acquisition of a power associated with sages and the legendary rulers of antiquity. But how do they do it? The passage next points to a potential conflict between the senses and the mind:

無以物亂官毋以官亂心此之謂內德。　是故意氣定然後反正。氣者，身之充也。行者，正之義也。充不美，則心不得。

Not to let things disorder the senses and not to let the senses disorder the heart–mind, this is called inner power. And so, once thought and *qi* become stable, it [the form] becomes correctly aligned of itself. *Qi* is what fills the embodied person; in conduct, right alignment should be the guiding principle. If what fills [the person] is not good, the heart–mind will not succeed. (*Guanzi* 13.2/98/1–3, *Xinshu xia* 13.37)

This passage views the senses and mind as a composite. It identifies inner power with an equilibrium that prevents disorder from arising in the mind through the influence of the senses. The actions of the body (including sense perception) are distinguished from the actions of the mind, but they are not described as ontologically different. Nor does this passage claim rulership of the mind over the senses, though it does point to its important normative functions, and argues that correctly ordered heart–minds affect the body:

人能正靜者，筋肕而骨強。... 昭知天下，通於四極。金心在中不可匿。外見於形容，可知於顏色。

As for people who can exercise both right alignment and quiescence, their muscles are firm and their bones sturdy ... they are brilliant and understand the entire world; they penetrate to its four extremes. A complete heart–mind within cannot be concealed. Outwardly it can be seen in the appearance of the form, and it can be observed in the complexion. (*Guanzi* 13.2/98/24–26, *Xinshu xia* 13.37)

Here the combination of correct alignment (whether of body or body and mind) and mental quiescence strengthens muscle and bone, but the physical manifestations of self-cultivation are not limited to a well-toned physique. The state of their heart–minds is manifest in bodily appearance (*xingrong* 形容), and coloration (*yanse* 顏色). The passage also points to the potential for disorder if the senses affect the mind excessively. Finally, the passage underscores the immediate way that body and mind affect each other.

What is this passage arguing against? Its strong claim is that self-cultivation depends not just on textual study, but on physical and possibly meditative practices. Similar claims are made in Mencius's description of his ability to cultivate his "flood-like *qi*" (*haoran zhi qi* 浩然之氣, 2A2), discussed below.[23]

In summary, the *Neiye* describes the creation of spirit in a three-part temporal sequence. In an initial stage (described here), a well-regulated heart–mind rules the senses. In two subsequent stages, spirit enters the body–mind via the circulation of *jing* and *qi*. (These will be discussed in Chapter 4.)

---

[23] Mark Csikszentmihalyi (2005) identifies this kind of argument with a "material virtue" tradition, exemplified in the *Mengzi* and the *Wuxing* or "Five Kinds of Action," recovered from tombs at Guodian and Mawangdui.

Heart–Mind as Ruler in the *Mencius*

The mind-centered view first becomes prominent in the *Mengzi* (frequently Latinized as *Mencius*). Here I focus on three important aspects of Mencius's view of body, mind, and spirit: his emphasis on the importance of *xin*, including its role as the ruler of the body and senses; his view of spirit as a capacity beyond even sagacity; and the relationship of these two views to his understanding of the body.

The Mind

Unlike Confucius, who had little to say about the heart–mind, Mencius refers to it repeatedly, in several contexts: (1) accounts of the "unperturbed mind" and subsequent account of the cultivation of *qi* (2A2); (2) the association of *xin* with virtue in his account of the four sprouts of virtue (2A6); and as (3) the "greatest" part of a person, in contrast to the senses (6A15).

The conversation between Mencius and King Hui of Liang 梁惠王 at 1A3 begins with King Hui claiming that he exerts his mind to the utmost (*jinx*in 盡心) on behalf of his state (1.3/1/19–20). At 1A7, Mencius remarks that only a gentleman (*shi* 士) can have a constant heart–mind (*hengxin* 恆心) even if he lacks the constant means of support; the people do not have this quality, and so there is nothing that they will not do (1.7/6/19–20). This difference is the explicit reason for Mencius's call for an enlightened rule to ensure that the people's livelihood is secure.

Mencius, like the *Guanzi* authors, is actively concerned with self-cultivation by means of the refinement of *qi*. He describes *qi* as filling the frame but commanded by the will (*zhi*). At 2A2 he claims to have attained an "unperturbed mind" (*budongxin* 不動心) at the age of forty. He adds that attaining this state is not inherently difficult and that Gaozi 告子 attained this state at an even younger age (3.2/15/1 and 5). Gongsun Chou 公孫丑 asks for an explanation, and Mencius disagrees with Gaozi's claim that if one fails to understand words, one should not worry about it in one's heart–mind. He goes on to describe the will as the ruler of the *qi* that pervades the body.[24] Mencius also notes that when the will is blocked, it moves the *qi*, but when *qi* is blocked, it moves the will (3.2/15/25). Gongsun then asks about his strong

---

[24] *Mengzi* 3.2/15/20–21, as previously discussed in Chapter 1.

points, and Mengzi describes one of them as being good at nurturing his "floodlike *qi*" (*haoran zhi qi* 浩然之氣), which is then described at length (3.1/15/29 and 3.1/16/1–6).

Unlike the *Guanzi*, the *Mengzi* does not link *qi* with either essence or spirit; the term *essence* (*jing*) does not appear in the *Mengzi* at all. Like the *Guanzi*, Mencius uses a container metaphor in describing the body as a container of the heart–mind. But in Mencius's version, the container is filled by flood-like *qi*. The container is also permeable. *Qi* can both enter the body and emanate from it without loss: "If you nurture it with straightness and there is no impediment, it will fill the space between Heaven and Earth" (3.2/16/1). Here, the body becomes a model of the interpenetration of self and cosmos.

Another aspect of that permeability is Mencius's description of the self as transparent, in the sense that the state of the heart–mind is visible in body. According to 4A15, when a person is "upright within the breast" (*xiong zhong zheng* 胸中正), the pupils of the eye are clear and bright (7.15/38/14–15). According to 7A21:

君子所性，仁義禮智根於心。其生色也，睟然見於面，盎於背，施於四體，四體不言而喻。

That which a gentleman makes his true nature—humaneness, rightness, the rites and wisdom—is rooted in his heart–mind. They manifest in his coloration, giving the face a sleek appearance, and also shows in the back and extend to the four limbs. (13.21/69/14–15)[25]

In these accounts of mind and body as composites and containers, mind and body are spatially inseparable.

The Heart–Mind in Mencian Moral Psychology

An unmoved heart–mind is important because of its role in managing the will or intentions (*zhi*) and indirectly the *qi*, and because of the connection of both to rightness and propriety (*yi* 義). The unmoved heart–mind nourishes floodlike *qi*, but only if it itself is nourished with rightness and propriety. As Kwong-loi Shun puts it, ideally, for the heart–mind to be unmoved, the will,

---

[25] For translations of the *Mengzi* I am indebted to Lau 1984 and Gassmann 2011.

which guides *qi*, must accord with rightness and propriety. But to support the will, it is necessary to cultivate one's *qi*, and this is why Mencius identifies his ability to nourish his floodlike *qi* as one of his strong points. As Shun puts it: the role of the unmoved heart–mind is to make the will conform to rightness and propriety (*yi*), and to cultivate *qi* to support these directives, thereby putting *yi* into practice.[26]

Mencius thus innovates by linking *qi* cultivation to moral excellence. As Alan Chan puts it, Mencius uses "floodlike *qi*" to signify the moral vigor of a sage. *Qi* thus shapes the heart–mind, and this is the fundamental insight that underlies Mencius's approach to the ethical life. Chan agrees with Shun in taking the will as the aim or direction of the heart–mind, which in turn clarifies the relationship between *qi* and the heart–mind because well-nourished *qi* is necessary to set the heart–mind in a firm direction. But it is not sufficient because the heart–mind can also be set in the wrong direction.[27]

The claim that *qi* fills the body was conventional by this time, but the claim that the heart–mind commands it (via the will) is more complex. It is not clear whether Mencius thinks that *qi* will always follow the directives of the heart–mind because it is the will, rather than the heart–mind, that directly controls the *qi*. As Chan puts it: "Eating hot chili pepper, being slapped in the face, being afraid of making a fool of oneself in a learned conference, and practically everything we do or that is done to us will have an impact on our *qi*, which in turn would move the heart in certain ways."[28] So if the heart–mind is to command the *qi*, it must be able to control its affective and cognitive movements, especially likes and dislikes. It is this focus on the importance of the heart–mind's control of the *qi*, and how to achieve it, that distinguishes Mencius's approach to self-cultivation from Gaozi's.

The problem is that the heart–mind does not have a fixed direction.[29] For both Gaozi and Mencius, training the will (*chi zhi* 持志) is very similar to cultivating *qi* (*yangqi* 養氣). But for Mencius, Gaozi is wrong in saying that the heart–mind can provide the proper direction when words cannot.[30] The *Zuozhuan*, Gaozi, and *Mengzi* (and also the *Zhuangzi* and the Guodian texts)

---

[26] Shun 1997: 75–76 and 84. For defense of the argument that *yi* in some sense derives from the heart–mind, see Shun 1997: 85–109. This issue is in turn fundamental to Mengzi's disagreement with Gaozi's claim that *yi* is external.
[27] A. Chan 2002: 43 and 47.
[28] A. Chan 2002: 50–51. For the following discussion, I am indebted to A. Chan 2002.
[29] This point is also clear in the Guodian text *Xingzi mingchu*, which will be discussed in detail in Chapter 5.
[30] This point is emphasized by the commentators Huang Zongxi 黃宗羲 (1610–1695) and Jiao Xun 焦循 (1763–1820). See A. Chan 2002: 52–57.

agree that it is crucial to regulate will carefully so that it does not succumb to the dictates of excessive *qi*. Chan suggests that Mencius made an important distinction. Gaozi identifies human *qi* with the "*qi* of the blood" (*xueqi* 血氣). Mencius argues that *qi* can be nourished so as to become one with rightness and propriety: floodlike *qi*. Given an accepted view that tastes affect the *qi*, floodlike *qi* can flourish only if it is nourished consistently by rightness and propriety. By contrast, Gaozi seems to think that *qi* cultivation depends on learning from external sources. Mencius disagrees and takes the source of rightness to be internal, possibly in the heart–mind. Chan argues that the heart–mind "likes" rightness and propriety by natural inclination, which is why feelings of commiseration or respect, generated by *qi*, arise naturally from the heart–mind, a point that is pursued in 2A6.

At 2A6, Mencius elaborates on the claim that all persons have a heart–mind that cannot endure the sufferings of others (*buren ren zhi xin* 不忍人之心), and this "mind" is the basis of the four sprouts of virtue (3.6/18/4). He goes on to identify four innate tendencies in human nature, and he argues in two ways that they are universal. First, anyone who does not have them is not a human being:

由是觀之，無惻隱之心，非人也；無羞惡之心，非人也；無辭讓之心，非人也；無是非之心，非人也。

From this we may observe that anyone who is without a heart–mind for empathy and compassion is not human; anyone who is without a heart–mind for shame and repulsion is not human; anyone who is without a heart–mind for politeness and respect is not human; and anyone who is without a heart–mind for right and wrong is not human. (*Mengzi* 3.6/18/7–8)

Mencius identifies these four tendencies as the origins of the four major virtues. Importantly, he identifies the subject of each tendency as a *xin*: the *xin* that is sensitive to the sufferings of others is the starting point or "sprout" (*duan* 端) of humaneness (*ren*); the *xin* that feels shame and dislike is the start of rightness and propriety (*yi*); the *xin* that feels modesty and courtesy is the start of ritual propriety (*li* 禮); and the *xin* that distinguishes right and wrong is the start of wisdom (*zhi* 智, *Mengzi* 3.6/18/8–9).

Second, these four "heart–minds" are as inherent in and essential to our makeup as is having four limbs to our bodies: "People have these four sprouts just as they have four limbs."³¹ These "tendencies" cannot be clearly classified as either affective or rational, and the result is a distinctive conception of practical reason.³² As Robert Gassmann has observed, people's desires and aversions are outward signs of corresponding "hearts": referring to the capacity to choose between alternatives and assess them according to social values and rules or norms. In other words, they refer to the power of the mind for reflective or self-reflective awareness.³³

The previous two sections have shown how Mencius expands the notion of *xin*. Unlike the early Mohists, who focus on the cognitive possibilities of discrimination and thought, Mencius redefines the heart–mind as a central part of ethical life. This is the context for his brief account of the relation of the heart–mind to the senses. At 6A15 Mencius responds to the question of why some people are great and others petty. He responds that what matters is which part of a person guides and controls: those who follow the great part of themselves are great; those who follow the petty part are petty, so some are guided one way and others another:

耳目之官不思，而蔽於物…心之官則思，思則得之，不思則不得也。

The offices of the eyes and ears cannot think, and can be confused by things . . . the office of the heart–mind can think, and is successful only if it does think; otherwise, it will not find the answer. (*Mengzi* 11.15/60/27–28)

Here he describes the relation of the heart–mind to the senses in an account of ethical failure. This account has two components. First, he explains ethical failure as people following their less important part (the senses) instead of their greater part (the heart–mind). Second, he makes the positive claim that ethical ideals can be attained as long as the heart–mind reflects or thinks (*si* 思).

This passage seems to locate ethical failure in the senses.³⁴ It stops short of asserting that the heart–mind is—or rather should be—the ruler of the senses. But the claim is implicit, since only a ruler guides and controls the

---

[31] 人之有是四端也，猶其有四體也. *Mengzi* 3.6/18/9.
[32] See D. Wong 1991 and Shun 1997.
[33] Gassmann 2011: 245–48. He also makes a very interesting link between the invisibility of the heart–mind and the *Guanzi*'s account of a "mind within the mind."
[34] See Shun 1997: 175–77.

organs or officials under it. The full version of the claim will be put forward by Xunzi and is discussed in the next section.

The Mencius–Gaozi debate—and materials in the Guodian texts that seem to support Gaozi's position—also raise broader questions about psychological motivation, what is internal and what is external. An important concern behind these debates was the question of whether moral resources are internal and inherent, as part of human nature, or external and not available in the same way.[35]

Spirit in the *Mengzi*

Shén appears only three times in the *Mengzi*, one of which is a clear reference to external spirits.[36] The two other passages describe internal *shén* but in quite different terms than does the *Guanzi*. At 7A13, Mencius contrasts the influence of a gentleman with that of a hegemon (*ba* 霸) and a true king (*wang* 王). A hegemon makes the people happy; a true king makes them deeply content; they progress toward good without awareness of his influence. But a gentleman:

夫君子所過者化，所存者神，上下與天地同流

Where a gentleman passes through, he transforms; where he abides, he manifests spirit. Above and below and Heaven and Earth flow together. (*Mengzi* 13.13/68/19–21)

Here spirit is clearly an internal capacity that manifests in the ethically, politically, and even cosmologically active influence of a gentleman, which surpasses that of even a true king.

Spirit is at the apex of a different moral hierarchy at 7B25, where someone asks about the meanings of the terms *good* (*shan* 善) and *trustworthy* (*xin* 信):

可欲之謂善，有諸己之謂信，充實之謂美，充實而有光輝之謂大，大而化之之謂聖，聖而不可知之之謂神。

---

[35] A number of these issues are discussed at length in K. Lai 2019a. The Guodian materials will be discussed in detail in Chapter 5.

[36] At 5A5 he describes Yao transmitting rulership to Shun by putting him in charge of the sacrifices: "He made him head sacrificer and the hundred spirits accepted them [the sacrifices]; which showed that Heaven accepted him" (使之主祭而百神享之，是天受之, *Mengzi* 9.5/48/27). The context is Mencius's argument that a ruler cannot "give" the empire to another: only Heaven can do so. The acceptance of the sacrifices by all the spirits was a demonstration of their consent.

Being capable of desiring it is called "good"; to have it in oneself is called "trustworthy"; to be filled with it and make it substantial is called "beautiful"; to be filled with it, make it substantial, and have glorious brilliance is called "great"; to be great and then to transform it is called "sage"; to be a sage but to be impossible to be understood is called "spirit." (*Mengzi* 14.25/76/4)

This passage delineates a hierarchy of excellences, of which spirit is at the head and is beyond even the merit of a sage.

These passages clearly portray *shén* as an internal quality and, in the case of 7B13, a state above even sagehood. Following Puett's arguments about self-divinization, they position Mencius as one of several fourth-century thinkers who claimed that, with correct self-cultivation, divine powers could reside in humans. Mencius also asserts the mind's rule over the senses, but he does not push it very far. He uses the language of *qi*, but not the broader self-cultivation language that links *qi* to essence and spirit. Nor does Mencius link his account of spirit to claims about the heart–mind and its rulership of the body. That step is taken by Xunzi.

Xunzi and the Hegemony of the Heart–Mind

Mencius gives a new importance to *xin* by taking this affective and cognitive capacity as the source point of moral development. In doing so, he positions it as more important than the senses and their associated desires and aversions. He also introduces internal *shén* as something that goes beyond even sagehood and the moral excellence attributed to *xin*.

Xunzi goes several steps further in several ways. First, he makes explicit what is implicit in Mencius. Xunzi affirms that the heart–mind is not only the "greater part" of a person; it is ruler of the body and the senses. He does this in explicit analogies between the management of a state and the governance of the body. Second, probably drawing on the Mohists, he links *xin* explicitly with thinking and cognitive processes. He makes it and them central. As Paul Goldin puts it, "In many respects, the heart–mind is the keystone of Xunzi's philosophy, the one piece that links together all the others."[37]

[37] Goldin 2018.

In particular, it is the means to discover *dao*. Some scholars link the heart–mind to a new notion of autonomy. Finally, possibly drawing on the *Guanzi*, Xunzi explicitly links the activity of the heart–mind to spirit, as Mencius does not.

Xin as Ruler of Body and Senses

For Xunzi, the heart–mind is a "ruler" in multiple senses. According to the "Discourse on Heaven" (*Tianlun* 天論, Xunzi 17), Heaven constitutes the heart–mind as ruler of the body and the senses as its ministers:

天職既立，天功既成，形具而神生，好惡喜怒哀樂臧焉，夫是之謂天情。耳目鼻口形能各有接而不相能也，夫是之謂天官。心居中虛，以治五官，夫是之謂天君。

When the work of Heaven has been established and the accomplishments of Heaven have been completed, the form is set and spirit arises. Liking, dislikes, happiness, anger, sorrow, and joy are contained therein—these are called one's Heavenly Dispositions. The eyes, ears, nose, and mouth each has its own form and its respective objects and they cannot assume each other's abilities—these are called one's Heavenly Officials. The heart–mind inhabits the central cavity so as to govern the Five Officials; for this reason it is called one's Heavenly Lord. (*Xunzi* 17/80/9–10)[38]

Here the ruler metaphor coincides with a container metaphor: the body is the container of the heart–mind, which inhabits its central cavity (*zhongxu* 中虛). That containment within the body is explicitly linked to the heart–mind's ability to govern, on the analogy of a ruler centrally positioned in his state. But this container is also semiporous. Information moves from the outside in, but the passage also makes clear that orders and instructions issue from the inside out.

---

[38] For translation see Hutton 2014: 176. Translations of Xunzi are based on Hutton 2014; I have also consulted Knoblock 1988–1994. For a similar view of the senses, see 12/60/13–14: an argument that people should perform their specifically allotted tasks, just as the eyes, ears, mouth, and nose cannot perform each other's work (人習其事而固，人之百事，如耳目鼻口之不可以相借官也).

Xin and Cognition

Xunzi also considers the heart-mind as the source of cognition and moral judgments. It is the heart-mind that has the potential to know *dao*, which in turn allows it to make correct judgments. Xunzi is explicit that the heart-mind, rather than the spirit, is the source of this capacity. According to "Undoing Fixation" (*Jiebi* 解蔽, Xunzi 21), this capacity comes from three qualities: emptiness (*xu* 虛), unity (*yi* 壹), and stillness (*jing* 靜):

> 人何以知道？曰：心。心何以知？曰：虛壹而靜。心未嘗不臧也，然而有所謂虛；心未嘗不兩也，然而有所謂壹；心未嘗不動也，然而有所謂靜。人生而有知，知而有志；志也者，臧也；然而有所謂虛；不以所已臧害所將受謂之虛。心生而有知，知而有異；異也者，同時兼知之；同時兼知之，兩也；然而有所謂一；不以夫一害此一謂之壹。心臥則夢，偷則自行，使之則謀；故心未嘗不動也；然而有所謂靜；不以夢劇亂知謂之靜。

How do people know *dao*? I say: with the heart-mind. How does the heart-mind know? I say: it is through emptiness, unity, and stillness. The heart-mind is never not storing something, but even so it has what is called emptiness. The heart-mind is never not of two [minds], yet it nonetheless has what [is] called unity. The heart-mind is never not in motion, but it still has what is called stillness. People are born and have awareness; with awareness they have intention. To have intentions is to be holding something; yet, there is something called emptiness. Not to let what one is already holding harm what one is about to receive is called emptiness. The heart-mind is born and has awareness. With understanding comes awareness of differences. These differences are known at the same time, and when they are known at the same time, this is to be of two [minds], yet, there is what is called unity. Not to let one idea harm another idea is called unity. When the heart-mind sleeps, it dreams. When it relaxes, it goes about on its own. When one puts it to use, it forms plans. Thus, the heart-mind is never not in motion, but nonetheless, there is what is called stillness. Not to let dreams and worries disorder one's understanding is called stillness. (*Xunzi* 21/103/25—104/4, Hutton 2014: 228)

Xunzi describes this stillness by the metaphor of a mirror, specifically, the mirroring quality of a pan of still water:

故人心譬如槃水，正錯而勿動，則湛濁在下而清明在上，則足以見
鬚眉而察〔膚〕理矣。微風過之，湛濁動乎下，清明亂於上，則不
可以得大形之正也。心亦如是矣。

Hence, the human heart–mind may be compared to a pan of water. If you place the pan upright and do not move it, the mud sinks to the bottom, and the water on top is clear enough to see your beard and eyebrows and to examine the lines on your face. But if a slight wind passes over it, the submerged mud is stirred up from the bottom, and the clarity of the water at the top becomes disturbed, so it is impossible to get a correct impression of the whole form. The heart–mind is just like this. (*Xunzi* 21/105/5–7, Hutton 2014: 231)

Xunzi also underscores the role of the heart–mind in making cognitive judgments based on the inputs of the senses and the body. The context is a discussion in "Rectifying Names" (*Zhengming* 正名) on how the heart–mind differentiates different kinds of things, and how these distinctions should be reflected in correct names. The passage focuses on the hegemonic activity of the heart–mind. It begins with a description of the various kinds of information that are differentiated (*yi* 異) by the senses and by the body overall:

形體、色理以目異；聲音清濁、調竽、奇聲以耳異；甘、苦、鹹、
淡、辛、酸、奇味以口異；香、臭、芬、鬱、腥、臊、漏庮、奇臭
以鼻異；疾、癢、凔、熱、滑、鈹、輕、重以形體異；說、故、
喜、怒、哀、樂、愛、惡、欲以心異。

Form and structure, color, and pattern are differentiated by means of the eyes. Notes, tones, clear highs, muddy lows, mode, measure and strange sounds are differentiated by means of the ears. Sweet, bitter, salty, bland, piquant, sour, and other strange flavors are differentiated by the mouth. Fragrant, foul, flowery, rotten, putrid, sharp, sour, and other strange smells are differentiated by the nose. Pain, itch, cold, hot, slippery, sharp, light, and heavy are differentiated by the form and frame. Persuasions, reasons, happiness, anger, sorrow, joy, love, hate, and desire are differentiated by the heart–mind. (*Xunzi* 22/108/16—109/1, Hutton 2014: 238)[39]

---

[39] The term *xingti* seems to refer to form and structure at the beginning of the passage, but to the body in the second usage. For musical technical terms, see Knoblock 1994, 3: 336.26.

Here, each corporeal faculty undertakes its own proper area of discrimination. What the heart–mind differentiates, however, is not sensory input. The heart–mind differentiates emotions, desires, and reason. So far, the activity of the heart–mind parallels that of the senses. Then things shift, and the *xin* takes on a unique role:

心有徵知。徵知，則緣耳而知聲可也，緣目而知形可也。然而徵知必將待天官之當簿其類，然後可也。五官簿之而不知，心徵知而無說，則人莫不然謂之不知。此所緣而以同異也。然後隨而命之，同則同之，異則異之。

The heart–mind has the power to judge its awareness. If it judges its awareness, then by following along with the ears it is possible to know a sound, and by following along with the eyes one can know a form. However, judging awareness must await the Heaven-given faculties to appropriately encounter their respective kinds, and only then can it work. If the five faculties encounter them but have no awareness, or if the heart–mind judges among them but has no persuasive explanations [for its judgments], then everyone will say that such a person does not know. These are what one follows and uses to distinguish the same and the different. Only after doing this does one then follow it up by naming things. One treats similar things as similar and different things as different. (*Xunzi* 22/109/1–5, Hutton 2014: 238)

Xunzi's moral psychology is distinctive because of this account of *xin* as including higher-order critical reflection. His new cognitive emphasis is grounded in two claims. The first is that the heart–mind engages in critical or reflective thinking. The second is that reflective thinking is not natural and is a product of deliberate effort. Xunzi defines the activity of the mind as "reflection" (*lu* 慮) and defines the result of such reflection as "deliberate artifice" (*wei* 偽):

性之好、惡、喜、怒、哀、樂謂之情。情然而心為之擇謂之慮。心慮而能為之動謂之偽；慮積焉，能習焉，而後成謂之偽。

The feelings of liking, disliking, happiness, anger, sadness and joy in one's nature are called "dispositions." When there is a certain disposition and the heart–mind makes a choice on its behalf, this is called "reflection." When the heart–mind reflects and one's abilities act on it, this is called "deliberate artifice." That which comes into being through accumulated reflection and training of one's abilities is also called "deliberate artifice." (*Xunzi* 22/107/23-24, Hutton 2014: 236)[40]

Finally, the *Xunzi* describes the heart–mind as a craftsman and good political order as the warp and weft of woven cloth:

心也者，道之工宰也。道也者，治之經理也。心合於道，說合於心，辭合於說。正名而期

The heart–mind is the craftsman and overseer of *dao*. *Dao* is the warp and pattern of good order. When the heart–mind fits with *dao*, when one's persuasions fit with one's heart–mind, when one's words fit one's persuasions, then one will name things correctly and procure agreement. (*Xunzi* 22/110/7-8, Hutton 2014: 241)[41]

Here the accuracy of the craftsman (*gong* 工) *xin* leads to its hegemony as an overseer or governor (*zai* 宰).

In summary, Xunzi presents the heart–mind as the faculty that rules the body, engages in cognition and reflection, and apprehends and even oversees *dao*. In this new account, *xin* has a new and unique autonomy to govern. This autonomy includes the ability to accept what it thinks right, choose among emotions, and approve and disapprove of desires: "What the heart–mind deems to be right it accepts; what it deems wrong it rejects."[42] The definition of "reflection" at the beginning of "Rectifying Names" (ch. 22) describes the heart–mind choosing on behalf of some dispositions over others.[43] Finally, the heart–mind approves and disapproves of desires:

故欲過之而動不及，心止之也，心之所可中理，則欲雖多，奚傷於治！欲不及而動過之，心使之也。心之所可失理，則欲雖寡，奚止於亂！故治亂在於心之所可，亡於情之所欲。

---

[40] On this point, see J. Lee 2005: 42.
[41] According to Wang Xianqian's 王先謙 (1842–1918) commentary to this passage: "a craftsman is able to accomplish things; an overseer is able to rule over them." See Wang Xianqian 1988: 423.
[42] 是之則受，非之則辭. *Xunzi* 21/104/12.
[43] *Xunzi* 22/107/23, discussed above.

Thus, when the desire is excessive but the action does not match it, this is because the heart–mind prevents it. If what the heart–mind approves of conforms to the proper patterns, then even if the desires are many, what harm would they be to good order? When the desire is lacking but the action surpasses it, this is because the heart–mind compels it. If what the heart–mind approves of misses the proper patterns, then even if the desires are few, how would it stop short of chaos? Thus, order and disorder reside in what the heart–mind approves of, they are not present in the desires from one's dispositions. (*Xunzi* 22/111/6–9, Hutton 2014: 244)

This description goes well beyond both the *Guanzi* and the *Mengzi*. The *Guanzi* described the heart–mind as able to govern the senses, but also as susceptible to being disturbed by emotions and desires. The *Mengzi* took it as the emotional source for morality, but Xunzi's notion of the autonomy of the heart–mind establishes it as the active agent of self-cultivation. Janghee Lee argues that Xunzi wanted to redefine *xin* in a new way, with these key philosophical features. According to Lee, Xunzi uses *xin* in two senses: in a technical philosophical sense as the faculty of self-governance, but also in nontechnical ways in common use in the late Warring States, for example, as an organ of the body (the "heart") and accounts of "*xins*" that seek profit, desire comfort, harbor resentment and ill will, and engage in deception.[44]

Understood thus as a bodily organ, *xin* is the site of all psychological phenomena, including sensation, emotion, and desires; but it depends on this faculty of self-governance, which includes the sense of appropriateness (*yi*). But for the heart–mind to engage in critical thinking, it must have a volitional power that allows it to be independent of desires and emotions, thereby addressing the problems raised in the *Guanzi*'s account of the rulership of *xin*. The heart–mind's autonomy is what allows it to supervise the senses, emotions, and desires; its faculty of appropriateness is what allows it to engage in deliberate effort.[45] On this view, human morality has only a tenuous connection with Heaven, and a very close connection with the activity of the heart–mind.[46] This view also accounts for what Antonio Cua calls the "functional distinction" between the body and mind.[47]

---

[44] On this point see J. Lee 2005: 36–38.
[45] Given Xunzi's analogy between the body and state and mind and ruler, "autonomy" potentially refers to both personal and some version of political autonomy.
[46] J. Lee 2005: 37–40.
[47] Cua 1985: 139 and 199–200nn3, 4.

Mind and Spirit

Xunzi's third innovation is his explicit linkage of the heart–mind to internal spirit and to "spirit illumination" (*shénmíng*). External spirit, internal spirit, and *shénmíng* all occur in the *Xunzi*. Xunzi understands external spirit as the fact that the cosmos operates as it does:

不見其事而見其功，夫是之謂神。

We cannot see the activity, but we can see the accomplishments. This is what we call spirit. (*Xunzi* 17/80/6)[48]

Several times Xunzi refers to a "spirit intelligence" (*shénmíng*) in ways that seem to refer less to an internal capacity than to an external agency: For example, according to "The Strong State" (*Jiangguo* 彊國, Xunzi 16), when ritual and music are cultivated:

百姓貴之如帝，高之如天，親之如父母，畏之如神明。

The common people honor their ruler like Shang Di, they look up to him like Heaven, they feel as close to him as to their own parents, and they fear him like a spirit intelligence. (*Xunzi* 16/75/13–14)

Here *shénmíng* clearly seems to be some kind of extrahuman entity. But Xunzi is also explicit that humans have internal spirit. In "Self Cultivation" (*Xiushēn*, ch. 2), he describes methods for controlling *qi* and nourishing the heart–mind. One of the desiderata is to become "spirit-like":

凡治氣養心之術，莫徑由禮，莫要得師，莫神一好。夫是之謂治氣養心之術也。

In the arts of controlling *qi* and nourishing the heart–mind, nothing is more direct than following ritual, nothing is more important than getting a good teacher, and nothing is [more] spirit-like than single-minded liking [of these practices]. These are called the arts for controlling *qi* and nourishing the heart–mind. (*Xunzi* 2/6/9–10)

---

[48] Cf. Puett 2002: 185–88, to which the following discussion is indebted.

The discussion of how to nourish the heart–mind continues in "Nothing in Excess" (*Bugou* 不苟, ch. 3), which recommends integrity (*cheng* 誠) as the best way to cultivate the heart–mind (*yangxin* 養心). With integrity, it only remains to cling to humaneness (*ren*) and conduct oneself with appropriateness (*yi*):

誠心守仁則形，形則神，神則能化矣；誠心行義則理，理則明，明則能變矣。變化代興，謂之天德。

If, with a heart–mind of integrity, you cling to *ren*, you will embody it; if you embody it, you will be a spirit; if you are a spirit, you will be able to transform things. If, with a heart–mind of integrity, you conduct yourself with *yi*, you will become well-patterned; if you are well-patterned, you will become enlightened; if you are enlightened, you will be able to bring about change. To bring about change and transform in succession is called Heavenly virtue. (*Xunzi* 3/11/4–5)

But spirit is not inherently moral; it can be used for vicious purposes. According to "Against the Twelve Masters" (*Fei shier zi* 非十二子), some people are:

知而險，賊而神，為詐而巧，（言）無用而辯，（辯）不（給）（惠）〔急〕而察，治之大殃也。

Knowing but dangerous, harmful but spirit-like, skilled at deceit but clever, [their words] are without use, but engaged in argumentation. [Their arguments] do not benefit the people, but they pursue these investigations; they are a great calamity for good government. (*Xunzi* 6/23/7–9)

Unlike Mencius, who considers spirit a capacity that surpasses even sagehood, Xunzi clearly locates spirit within the bounds of sagehood. As Roel Sterckx puts it: "He conceives of *shen* as a spirit-like power that transforms the world into a harmonious order through the efficiency of its ruler who is able to govern without apparent effort. A notion of order and hierarchy, both social and cosmic, underlies Xunzi's use of *shen*."[49] According to "The Rules of a King" (*Wangzhi* 王制, Xunzi 9), the order that results from the sage's activity is *shén*:

---

[49] Sterckx 2007: 27.

上以飾賢良，下以養百姓而安樂之。夫是之謂大神。

Above it is used to adorn the worthy and good; below it is used to nourish the hundred families and give them pleasure. This is called the Great Divinity. (*Xunzi* 9/38/18–19)

But in "Achievements of the Ru" (*Ruxiao* 儒效, ch. 8), Xunzi goes further and claims that the sage who does this is also spirit-like:

曷謂一？曰：執神而固。曷謂神？曰：盡善挾（洽）〔治〕之謂神。〔曷謂固〕？〔曰〕：萬物莫足以傾之之謂固。神固之謂聖人。

What is meant by being one? I say: it is to hold fast to spirit and to be firm. What is meant by being spirit[-like]? I say: to achieve the utmost goodness and to uphold proper order is called being spirit[-like]. To be so that none of the ten thousand things can overturn you is called being firm. One who is spirit[-like] and firm is called a sage. (*Xunzi* 8/31/3–5)

The passage continues that the sage is the manager of *dao* (*dao zhi guan* 道之管), who manages the way of all under Heaven, unifies the way of the hundred kings.[50]

Xunzi is especially interested in the ability of an enlightened ruler to use spirit to transform the people. An enlightened lord uses power, *dao*, commands, judgments, and punishments to control the people: "Thus his people's transformation by *dao* is spirit-like" (*ruo shén* 如神, 8/31/5).

Finally, the importance of spirit is recapitulated in two late chapters. "Working Songs" (*Cheng xiang* 成相, ch. 25) contains a song about spirit. The previous verse praised the intention to achieve order and the importance of integrity. The text now turns to the gentleman who has these qualities:

處之敦固、有深藏之能遠思。
　思乃精，志之榮，好而壹之神以成，精神相（反）〔及〕、一而不貳為聖人。

[50] 聖人也者，道之管也：天下之道管是矣，百王之道一是矣. *Xunzi*.

Dwell in it amply and firmly, store it deeply within, and thus you will be able to reach far in thoughts.

[Refine] your thoughts to their essence, and your will will flower. By attraction and unity is spirit made complete. When essence and spirit reach each other, when they are one and not dual, you become a sage. (*Xunzi* 25/121/2–3)

Finally, the last chapter in the *Xunzi*, "Yao Asked" (*Yao wen* 堯問, ch. 32), discusses Xunzi's influence:

今之學者得孫卿之遺言餘教，足以為天下法式表儀，所存者神，所（遇）〔過〕者化。

When scholars of today obtain Xunzi's remaining words and the teachings he left behind, they are sufficient to be models and standards for all under Heaven. Wherever they reside, that place enjoys a spirit-like state. Wherever they pass by, that place becomes transformed. (*Xunzi* 32/150/8–9, Hutton 2014: 342–43)

In other words, the text claims not only that Xunzi himself achieved a "spirit-like" state, but that other scholars who follow his teachings will achieve such a state and confer its benefits wherever they reside.

In summary, Xunzi's account of *xin* departs from those of his predecessors in several important ways. For Mencius, what differentiates the gentleman from ordinary people is "holding on to one's heart–mind," but this "heart–mind" is preserved by means of benevolence and the rites.[51] In other words, as Goldin puts it, Mencius's "thinking" is moral thinking.[52] By contrast for Xunzi, the way to self-cultivate is to follow the rituals of the sage kings; but the only autonomous agent who can choose to use that method is the heart–mind. Xunzi needs the heart–mind as the conscious agent that desires goodness and completion. (Given Xunzi's negative view of human nature, goodness—or even its starting points—is not something humans have inherently.) For Mencius, the basis of morality is inherent; for Xunzi, morality must come from external sources. For Mencius the heart–mind is the seat of morality; for Xunzi it is the agent that incites us to

---

[51] 君子所以異於人者，以其存心也。君子以仁存心，以禮存心。*Mengzi* 8.28/43/32.
[52] Goldin 1999: 2.

attain morality.[53] Xunzi also differs in important ways from the authors of the *Neiye*. The concern of the *Neiye* is how to transform the heart–mind; Xunzi's concern is how to transform one's inherent nature (*xing*) by means of the heart–mind. The *Neiye* attempts to return to the heart–mind's original state; Xunzi wants to evolve from originally brutish nature.[54]

Finally, Xunzi links his account of the active heart–mind with *shénming*, a term with a complex range of meanings (as previously discussed in Chapter 1). Xunzi seems to almost reinvent the term. He uses it consistently to mean "spirit illumination" or "spirit enlightenment," a quality linked to an exalted state of the cognitive activity of the mind.[55]

Three points are distinctive about Xunzi's view of *shénming*. First, he argues that *shénming* comes spontaneously as a result of correct self-cultivation practices:

積土成山，風雨興焉；積水成淵，蛟龍生焉；積善成德，而神明自得，聖心備焉。

If you accumulate enough earth to complete a mountain, wind and rain arise from it; if you accumulate enough water to complete a deep pool, water dragons will live in it. If you accumulate enough goodness to complete virtue, you will attain *shénming* of yourself, and the heart–mind of a sage is complete therein. (*Xunzi* 1/2/9–10, Hutton 2014: 3)

Second, it is in principle available to everyone, and it is not the unique potential of a gentleman or a ruler. As "Human Nature Is Bad" (*Xing'e* 性惡, ch. 23) puts it:

今使塗之人伏術為學，專心一志，思索孰察，加日縣久，積善而不息，則通於神明、參於天地矣。故聖人者，人之所積而致矣。

Now if you were to make people on the street submit themselves to study and practice learning, if they concentrated their heart–minds and unified their wills, if they pondered, queried, and thoroughly investigated, if they

---

[53] Goldin 1999: 36.
[54] Goldin 1999: 31.
[55] Jia Jinhua 2014, Knoblock 1988: 252–55, Machle 1992. *Shénming* is discussed in Chapter 1 of this text.

added up days upon days and connected to this long period of time, if they accumulated goodness without stopping, then they would connect to spirit illumination, and would form a triad with Heaven and Earth. Therefore, becoming a sage is something that people achieve through accumulation. (*Xunzi* 23/116/13–14, Hutton 2014: 254)

Third, and especially important for the present discussion, *shénmíng* is a property of the heart–mind. Xunzi begins (ch. 21) by asserting that the heart–mind is both the ruler of the body and the master of *shénmíng*:

心者，形之君也，而神明之主也，出令而無所受令 . . . 故口可劫而使墨云，形可劫而使詘申，心不可劫而使易意，是之則受，非之則辭。

The heart–mind is the lord of the form and the master of *shénmíng*. It issues orders, but there is nothing from which it takes orders . . . thus, the mouth can be compelled either to be silent or to speak, and the body can be compelled, either to contract or to extend itself, but the heart–mind cannot be compelled to change its thoughts. What it considers right, one accepts, what it considers wrong, one rejects. (*Xunzi* 21/104/10–12, Hutton 2014: 229)[56]

In summary, Xunzi not only asserts the rulership of the heart–mind over the body; he also links that rulership to a mastery of the "spirit illumination" of *shénmíng*, thereby closely associating spirit-like powers with the activity of the mind and assimilating them to the normative activity of the mind.

Rulers and Ruled in the Guodian Texts

Paul Goldin argues that several previously unknown Confucian texts from Guodian should be understood as doctrinal material deriving from a single tradition of Confucianism dateable to around 300 BCE. He argues that these texts are especially close to the *Xunzi* and anticipate several of his important ideas. These texts contain a number of key ideas that distinguish them from

---

[56] For further discussion of the heart–mind's hegemony, see Robins 2014.

Mencian Confucianism, including the conception of the ruler as the "mind" (*xin*) of the state.[57]

The Guodian Chu Slips 郭店楚簡 were unearthed in 1993 in Tomb no. 1, Guodian, Jingmen, Hubei, in the latter half of the Warring States period. The Guodian texts are especially rich in accounts of relations between body and mind, and they will be discussed in detail in Chapter 5. They are mentioned briefly here because they contain several prominent ruler metaphors. Two Guodian texts present a strongly political analogy in which the heart–mind rules the body as a ruler rules a state. They compare the heart–mind to the ruler of a state and the body or the senses to its ministers or officials, or to slaves.

Perhaps the strongest account comes from the text *Wuxing* 五行 (*Five Kinds of Action*), excavated from tombs at Mawangdui and Guodian, which describes the senses and body as "slaves of the heart–mind."[58] This passage is the one instance of which I am aware of a Chinese ruler metaphor in which the heart–mind is a ruler of slaves, rather than the people, or ministers. In a very different metaphor in the text *Ziyi* ("Black Robes"), the people take the ruler as their heart–mind, and the ruler takes the people as his body frame.[59] This metaphor analogizes the heart–mind to a ruler whose authority arises from mutual recognition and assent between ruler and ruled. These two passages, from two different Guodian texts, present two very different metaphors of the mind as ruler. One is an agonistic relationship in which the heart–mind governs the body as an iron-handed master; the other is a harmonious relationship in which the ruler's authority arises from mutual recognition between himself and the people.

Goldin locates these metaphors in the context of Xunzi's broad analogy between polity and personhood. He argues that kingdoms are affected by both their underlying resources and the policies of their rulers. Xunzi considers a ruler's policies to be fundamental for a kingdom's ultimate success or failure, regardless of their resources. There is a close analogy to mind and body. People consist of their inherent natures (*xing*) and their deliberate effort (*wei*). For Xunzi, it is human effort (*wei*) that determines ultimate success or failure as human beings: "all that matters are the mind and its decision

---

[57] Goldin 2005: 36–37.
[58] 耳目鼻口手足六者，心之役也. *Guodian Chumu, Wuxing*, strip 45, discussed in further detail in Chapter 5.
[59] 子曰: 民以君為心，君以民為體. *Guodian Chumu, Ziyi*, strips 8–9, discussed in further detail in Chapter 5.

112 A TRIPARTITE SELF

to follow (or not to follow) the Way." Goldin notes a similar argument in the *Ziyi* passage discussed above. The body taking peace in what the mind is fond of and the people desiring what the lord is fond of refer, not to the natural resources of the state or the inherent nature of the person, but to the initiatives and choices of the ruler. The Guodian editors have even suggested that Xunzi's language is based on Guodian section 94.[60] Nonetheless, there are important differences between the *Xunzi* and the Guodian texts, including Xunzi's more systematic approach to a range of philosophical problems. Either way, it seems reasonable to link the ruler metaphors in the Guodian manuscripts with Xunzi's account of the heart–mind as ruler of the body.

The Heart–Mind Is What Is at the Center (*Xin shi wei zhong*)

A metaphor resembling Xunzi's heart–mind ruler comes from a recently published excavated text that focuses on the heart–mind's centrality. Volume Eight of excavated texts acquired by Tsinghua University includes a text titled "*Xin shi wei zhong*" 心是謂中: "The Heart–Mind Is What Is at the Center."

The Tsinghua Bamboo Slips (*Qinghua jian* 清華簡) were acquired by Qinghua (Tsinghua) University in 2008 as an alumni donation. Because they were illegally excavated and obtained on the black market, they have no provenance, but they probably come from Hubei or Hunan and probably date to the Warring States period.[61] The collection is extensive, and volumes continue to be published. "The Heart–Mind is What Is at the Center" is less than one page in length. It consists of 236 characters written on seven bamboo slips and is divided into three paragraphs. Here is a provisional translation of it in its entirety.

心是謂中

The Heart–Mind Is What Is at the Center[62]

---

[60] Goldin 2005: 45 and 45–50, especially 50n94. See *Guodian Chumu*, 164n16.
[61] For an introduction to these manuscripts see Liu Guozhang 2016.
[62] *Qinghua daxue cang Zhanguo zhujian* 2018: 148–52. This transcription follows the emendations of the editors, and only includes nonstandard characters when necessary. I have benefited from discussions of this text on the website "Bamboo and Silk Manuscripts" (www.bsm.org.cn).

MIND AND SPIRIT GOVERN THE BODY   113

心，中。處身之中以君之，目，耳，口，肢⁶³ 四者為相⁶⁴，心是謂中。心所為美惡，復訶⁶⁵ 若影⁶⁶，心所出小大，因名若響。【一】心欲見之，目故視之；心欲聞之，耳故聽之；心欲道之，口故言之；心欲用之，肢故舉之。心，情⁶⁷ 毋有所至，百體【二】四相莫不恬湛⁶⁸。為君者其監於此，以君民人。

The heart-mind is the center. It occupies the center of the body in order to be a lord over it. The eyes, ears, mouth and limbs, these four are helpers, the heart-mind is what is at the center. What the heart-mind likes and dislikes, returning from it is like shadows; (1) the great and small things that emerge from the heart-mind cause names to be like echoes. When the heart-mind desires to see something, the eyes see it; when the heart-mind desires to hear something, the ears hear it; when the heart-mind desires to say something, the mouth says it; when the heart-mind desires to make use of something, the limbs take it up. When the heart-mind and inner dispositions do not seek to attain anything, the body and (2) four helpers will never not be calm and docile. One who acts as a ruler must pay attention to this [the relationship between heart-mind and body] in order to [understand how to] be a lord over the people.

人之有為，而不知其卒，不惟謀而不度乎？ 如謀而不度，則無以【三】知短長，短長弗知，妄作衡觸，而有成功，名之曰幸。幸，天；知事之卒，心。必心與天兩事焉，果成，盍心謀之，稽之，度【四】之，鑒之。聞訊視聽，在善之據，心焉為之。

When people act, they do not know the end results; do they not only plan but not [know how to] measure accurately? If you plan without accurate measurement, then you do not (3) know the long and short of things. If you do not know the long and short of things and are lost and chaotic but still gain success and merit, this is called fortuitous luck. Fortuitous luck is from Heaven; knowing the end results is from the

---

63 Reading 纏 as zhi 肢, "limbs." By contrast Cao Feng (2019: 6) reads it as zhong 踵, "heels."
64 Reading 叟 as xiang 相. For the reading zhi 助, see Li Xueqin 2018: 149n2.
65 For reading he 何 as he 訶, see Cao Feng 2019: 6n1 and Chen Minzhen 2018.
66 For reading 傿 as 影, see Chen Wei 2018 and Cao Feng 2019.
67 I follow the editors' reading of 情. For reading as 靜, see Cao Feng 2019: 6.
68 Reading 畾 as tian 恬 and 淺 as zhan 湛, after Cao Feng 2019: 6n2.

heart–mind. It must be the case that both the mind and Heaven work and things eventually succeed. The calm and quiet heart–mind makes plans, investigates, measures, (4) and inspects. That it inquires, smells, observes and listens and depends on being good at collecting [that information, and thus makes correct decisions] is because the heart–mind works in it [the body].

斷命在天，苛疾在鬼，取命在人。人有天命，其亦有身命，心厭為【五】死，心厭為生。死生在天，其亦失在心。君公、侯王、庶人、平民，其毋獨祈保家沒身於鬼與天，其亦祈諸口【六】與身。【七】

Exhausting one's life span is determined by Heaven; physical illness is determined by ghosts; but taking hold of one's destiny is determined by people. People have life spans determined by Heaven; they also have life spans determined by their persons [shēn]. The heart–mind is responsible for (5) death; the heart–mind is also responsible for life. Death and life are matters of Heaven, but losing them is a matter of the heart–mind. Rulers, dukes, lords, kings, the common people, and the masses should not only pray for their families and persons [shēn] to ghosts and to Heaven; they should also pray to their own [mind] (6) and person [shēn] (7).[69]

Several points are important and striking about this manuscript. First, it clearly identifies *xin* as both the center of the body and the ruler of the senses. Second, the second and third sections emphasize the specifically cognitive functions of the heart–mind. Its activity of cognition, moral judgment, and appraisal is precisely what other organs of the body do not have. Further, the perception and evaluation performed by the heart–mind is both descriptive (measurement) and normative (judgments of right and wrong). Because of its cognitive role, the heart–mind can interpret and use what the body hears, sees, smells, examines, etc., to make good decisions. This cognitive function is so powerful that it compares with Heaven and can even determine life and death. The claims made for *xin* here resemble claims made for spirit in the *Huainanzi*.

[69] *Qinghua daxue cang Zhanguo zhujian* 2018: 149.

Heart–Mind and Spirit in the *Huainanzi* and *Wenzi*

Both claims that the heart–mind is the ruler of the body and statements that link it with internal spirit appear conspicuously in the *Huainanzi* and *Wenzi*.[70] Of these texts, the *Wenzi* presents particular complexities because the discovery of a *Wenzi* text in a tomb dated to 55 BCE whose contents are significantly different from the received *Wenzi*.[71] All the *Wenzi* passages that discuss *xin* and *shén* also appear in the *Huainanzi*, and none of them appear in the *Dingxian Wenzi*. For this reason, I provisionally take them as later interpolations and discuss them under the rubric of the *Huainanzi*.

Perhaps the simplest version of the metaphor occurs at the beginning of *Huainanzi* 10, "Profound Precepts" (*Moucheng* 繆稱). Here the ruler metaphor is turned on its head: instead of asserting that the heart–mind is like a ruler, it asserts that the ruler of a state is like the heart–mind:

主者，國之心(也)。心治則百節皆安，心擾即百節皆亂。

The king is the heart–mind of his country. When the heart–mind governs [peacefully], the hundred joints [of the body] all are at peace; when the heart–mind is agitated, the hundred joints are all in disorder. (*Huainanzi* 10/82/19)[72]

Here, the crux of the argument is that stable government creates harmonious order and agitation creates disorder, in both body and state. But the treatment or mind ruler metaphor in the *Huainanzi* is more complex because of the relation between three terms: the heart–mind, "Essence and Spirit" (*jingshén*), and spirit (*shén*).

"Essence and Spirit" (*Jingshén* 精神, *Huainanzi* 7) is an account of human ontogeny and cosmology and is probably closely linked to the

---

[70] The *Huainanzi* 淮南子, a collection of scientific and philosophical essays from the court of Huainan, is attributed to Liu An 劉安 (c. 179–122 BCE), King of Huainan.

[71] References to the *Wenzi* 文子 first appear in the Han dynasty. A bamboo strip copy of the text was discovered in the tomb of King Huai 懷王 of Zhongshan (Dingzhou 定州, Hebei), dated to 55 BCE. For accounts of this text and the "proto-Wenzi" it suggests, see Le Blanc 2000 and Van Els 2015.

[72] Cf. *Wenzi* 6/29/16–17, *Shangde* 上德. For translations from the *Huainanzi* I am indebted to Major et al. 2010.

Daodejing. It begins by describing the sources of the human body and person:

夫精神者，所受於天也；而形體者，所稟於地也。

Essence and Spirit are what we receive from Heaven; the form is what we are given by Earth. (*Huainanzi* 7/55/7)[73]

There follows an account of the development of the human embryo in the womb, which ends by describing a system of regulation between the five yin organs and the five senses:

形體以成，五藏乃形，是故肺主目，腎主鼻，膽主口，肝主耳，脾主舌。

In this way the form and frame are completed and the five *zang* organs are formed. Therefore, the lungs regulate the eyes; the kidneys regulate the nose; the gall bladder regulates the mouth; the liver regulates the ears; and the spleen regulates the tongue. (*Huainanzi* 7/55/10).[74]

On this understanding, the senses probably should not be understood as distinct from the body, since each is controlled by one of the five yin organs (to be discussed in detail in Chapter 6). The *Huainanzi* goes on to describe a series of correlations of between the body and the cosmos, leading to the rulership of the heart–mind:

故頭之圓也象天，足之方也象地。〔天〕有四時、五行、九解、三百六十（六）日，人亦有四支、五藏、九竅、三百六十（六）節。天有風雨寒暑，人亦有取與喜怒。故膽為雲，肺為氣，（肝）〔脾〕為風，腎為雨，（脾）〔肝〕為雷，以與天地相參也，而心為之主。

Therefore, the roundness of the head is in the image of Heaven; the squareness of people's feet is in the image of Earth. Heaven has four seasons, five phases, nine regions, and 366 days. People have four limbs, five *zang* organs, nine apertures, and 366 joints. Heaven has wind, rain, cold, and heat; people

---

[73] Cf. *Wenzi* 3/12/11–12, *Jiushou* 九守.
[74] Cf. *Wenzi* 3/12/19–20, *Jiushou*. The five *zang* organs: see Chapter 6 and the Glossary.

have taking, giving, joy, and anger. Therefore, the gall bladder parallels the clouds, the lungs parallel air, the liver parallels wind, the kidneys parallel rain, and the spleen parallels thunder. In this people form a triad with Heaven and Earth, and the heart–mind is the ruler of this. (*Huainanzi* 7/55/11–14)[75]

It is not obvious why this series of parallels leads to a claim for the rulership of the heart–mind, which is not analogized to Heaven or any particular governing property of Heaven. An identical version of the passage occurs in the *Wenzi*. "The Nine Protections" (*Jiushou* 九守, *Wenzi* 3) contains a series of statements attributed to Laozi, and these passages are among them.

Huainanzi 7 goes on to describe the healthy movement of Essence and Spirit (*jingshén*) in the body, and the visible and tangible health of body and senses that result when all flows well. It returns to the governing role of the heart–mind:

耳目清、聽視達，謂之明。五藏能屬於心而無乖，則教志勝而行不僻矣。教志勝而行（之）不僻，則精神盛而氣不散矣。

When the ears and eyes are clear, and hearing and vision are acute, we call it clarity. When the five yin organs can be subordinated to the heart–mind and [function] without error, then the vigor of the will is victorious and the circulation [of *qi*] is not awry. When fluctuations of the will are vanquished and the circulation is not awry, essence and spirit are abundant and *qi* is not dispersed. (*Huainanzi* 7/55/21–22)[76]

In this state, a person functions in accordance with the underlying patterning of the cosmos (*li* 理) and is able to attain equanimity (*jun* 均) and penetrating awareness (*tong* 通). At this point, it becomes clear that essence and spirit (*jingshén*) are not the same as spirit:

通則神，神則以視無不見〔也〕，以聽無不聞也，以為無不成也。

When you are penetrating, you become [like] spirit; once you are [like] spirit, your vision has nothing unseen, your hearing has nothing unheard, and your actions have nothing incomplete. (*Huainanzi* 7/55/23–24)

---

[75] Cf. *Wenzi* 3/12/19–23, *Jiushou*.
[76] Cf. *Wenzi* 3/13/3–5, *Jiushou*.

Here the *Wenzi* version diverges and omits the "spirit" stage:

五藏能屬於心而無離，則氣意勝而行不僻，精神盛而氣不散，以聽無不聞，以視無不見，以為無不成。

When the five *zang* organs can be subordinated to the heart–mind and their function misses nothing, *qi* and thought are victorious and the circulation [of *qi*] is not awry; essence and spirit are abundant and *qi* is not dispersed; thereby your hearing has nothing unheard, your vision has nothing unseen, and your actions have nothing incomplete. (*Wenzi* 3/13/19–23)

The *Wenzi* passage goes on to explain that the senses and the desires of the body dissipate essential spirit, which can be preserved by cultivating serenity and avoiding the distractions of the senses.

As the argument continues, it returns to the ruling activity of the heart–mind:

精神澹然無極，不與物（散）〔殽〕，而天下自服。故心者，形之主也；而神者，心之寶也。形勞而不休則蹶，精用而不已則竭，是故聖人貴而尊之，不敢越也。

Essence and spirit are calm and without limit, they are not dissipated amid external things, and the world naturally submits to them. Therefore, the heart–mind is the ruler of the form; spirit is the treasure of the heart–mind. When the form labors and does not rest, it becomes exhausted; when essence is used unceasingly, it runs out. Therefore sages honor and venerate it and do not dare let it dissipate. (*Huainanzi* 7/57/2–3)[77]

Here, as in the *Xunzi*, the heart–mind is closely linked to spirit. But this passage has a different emphasis from Xunzi's claims for *xin* and *shén*. Here the context is an injunction that sages preserve their essence and, by implication, their spirit. The danger seems to be that spirit, the "treasure" stored and preserved in the heart–mind, can be diminished through the heart–mind's role as master of the body. In other words, these two functions of the heart–mind—ruling the body and preserving essence and spirit—are in potential opposition. Other passages in late Warring States and Han texts also contrast

---

[77] Cf. *Wenzi* 3.1/13/23–24, *Jiushou*.

attractions and desires associated with the senses and the body to the normative judgments of the heart–mind.[78]

In summary, although these *Huainanzi* passages begin to link *xin* and *shén*, their goal is not to promote the dominance of *xin*, but rather the ultimate importance of spirit, the subject of Chapter 4.

Conclusion

This chapter has surveyed claims for the hegemony of the heart–mind across a range of Warring States and Han texts. These texts make several different arguments. The first, a point that might seem obvious or trivial, is to assert the importance of the heart–mind and to hold that the heart–mind has the capacity to make normative or cognitive distinctions. Such arguments first appear in the *Analects* and continue to appear in the *Mozi, Guanzi, Mencius,* and *Xunzi*. These texts pursue and amplify this basic claim in very different ways. The *Analects* and *Mencius* clearly focus on the affective capacities of the "heart" in the heart–mind in guiding desires. The *Mozi, Guanzi,* and *Xunzi*, by contrast, call attention to the cognitive capacities of the heart–mind. In describing this difference, I do not imply that the two are in any way mutually exclusive, but I do note the difference in their respective emphases. Indeed, for Xunzi it is crucial, since his moral psychology is closely linked to his highly cognitive account of the mind. His views may well be indebted to the Mohists and the *Guanzi*, and they are closely paralleled by the accounts of the centrality of the mind in the Guodian texts and the "The Heart-Mind Is What Is at the Center."

A second claim is that the heart–mind in some sense is more important than, or has some command over, the body or senses. Versions of this assertion first appear in the *Guanzi* and *Mencius*, and also appear in the *Xunzi* as well as in texts excavated from Guodian and in the Tsinghua University bamboo slip texts. This point is closely linked to a third view: the specific assertion that the heart–mind *rules* the body or senses. This view is usually expressed as a metaphor that compares the mind's hegemony over the body to a ruler's hegemony over a state. Ruler metaphors—the extreme for assertions of the hegemony of the heart–mind—appear in the *Guanzi, Xunzi, Huainanzi, Wenzi* in excavated texts from Guodian, and in the Tsinghua University bamboo texts.

---

[78] For additional citations and discussion, see N. Yu 2007, 2009; Slingerland 2013: 16–17.

But the "rulers" in these metaphors do different things and serve very different rhetorical purposes. In the *Xunzi*, the Guodian texts, and the Tsinghua University bamboo texts, the central claim is the rulership of the heart–mind. Some assert that claim through the agonistic metaphor of command over (presumably unwilling) slaves rather than presumably cooperative officials. In the *Guanzi*, *Wenzi*, and *Huainanzi*, the claim is not the rulership of the mind, but rather the ultimate importance of spirit. These texts mention the rulership of the mind only in passing; the real importance of the mind is its links to spirit, to which it is assimilated. The same might be said of the *Xunzi*, but I would argue that Xunzi assimilates spirit to the mind, rather than mind to spirit.

The role of spirit leads to a fourth point: claims for correspondence or alliance between mind and spirit. Hand-in-hand with arguments that self-cultivation procedures could enhance spirit in the body, a second set of claims in some texts identified internal spirit with virtue, as well as the heart–mind. These identifications closely align the heart–mind with spirit in a hierarchically superior relation to the body. Together, heart–mind and spirit rule the body as a ruler rules the people or a state. The result is effectively a binary view of a person—consistent with mind–body dualism—in which there is a polarity between the body and the mind or spirit.

4
Body, Mind, and Spirit
A Tripartite View

Chapter 3 explored a series of texts that progressively emphasized the importance of the heart–mind as the locus of feeling, moral judgment, and cognition, leading to claims that the heart–mind ruled the body and senses. In some cases, that rulership was linked to internal spirit. I now turn to a group of texts that emphasize the importance of spirit and explicitly privilege the body as a site of self-cultivation. In some cases they marginalize, or even disparage, the heart–mind. As discussed in Chapter 3, while both the *Analects* and ritual texts emphasize the importance of the body in the performance of correct ritual, the *Mengzi* and *Xunzi*, for different reasons, subordinate it to the heart–mind.

The texts described in this chapter all take spirit (*shén*) as an internalized faculty of persons, and understand it as central and crucial to self-cultivation.[1] They describe a system of interactions that closely link spirit with essence (*jing* 精) and *qi*. *Jing*, the product of refined *qi*, circulates in the body. If it is sufficiently still (*jing* 靜) and unified (*yi* 一), it can be transformed into spirit and stored in the heart–mind. Spirit thus depends on an adequate supply of *jing* and *qi*. Finally, the correct functioning of spirit is the source of sagelike abilities; the ability to transform (*hua* 化) things, to respond flexibly to changing circumstances, and to make subtle and clear judgments.

I begin with a new understanding of the importance of the body in textual fragments attributed to the fourth-century figure Yang Zhu 楊朱 (fl. ca. 370–350 BCE). The remaining four sections of the chapter address views of body, mind, spirit in the *Guanzi*, *Zhuangzi*, the *Shiwen* ("Ten Questions") text from Mawangdui, and the *Huainanzi*.

---

[1] Chiu 2016; cf. Graham 1989b: 95–105, Roth 1990: 13–18, and Chen Guying 2006: 41–54.

Yang Zhu's Discovery of the Body

Chapter 3 described what might be called a "discovery of the mind" in the late third century by Xunzi in his new understanding of the cognitive "mind" in the heart–mind. I now turn to a very different and earlier discovery of the body. Accounts of how Confucius or others used their bodies in the performance of rituals—descriptions of the proper way to stand, bow, walk, and so on—show how concern with ritual developed into a concern for training the body.[2] But the body became a central issue in Chinese thought in the fourth century BCE when the school of Yang Zhu and the *Neiye* chapter of the *Guanzi* theorized it as the site of self-cultivation.[3]

No text is attributed to Yang Zhu, so Yangist ideas are known only from others' accounts, often by philosophical enemies. Accounts of him appear in the *Mengzi*, *Lüshi Chunqiu*, and *Huainanzi*; and four chapters of the *Zhuangzi* contain what is now considered Yangist material.[4] As Mark Lewis notes, concern over the body figures in all presentations of Yangist doctrines, and the core of Yangist teachings was the supreme value of life and the body: "Preserving one's nature" entailed nourishing bodily energies and developing bodily powers.[5]

Mencius describes Yang Zhu in clearly hostile terms at 3B9 and 7A26:

楊氏為我，是無君也。

Yang is "each for oneself"; this is to be without a lord. (*Mengzi* 6.9/35/1)

楊子取為我，拔一毛而利天下，不為也。

Master Yang held to "each for oneself"; if plucking a single hair would benefit the entire world, he would not do it. (*Mengzi* 13.26/70/4)

A less hostile version in the *Huainanzi* describes a doctrine of:

全性保真，不以物累形。

Keep one's nature intact, guard one's true self, and not tie down one's form with external objects. (*Huainanzi* 13/123/21–22, "*Fan lun*" 氾論)

---

[2] For examples, see Lewis 2006: 14–16.
[3] See Emerson 1996 and Lewis 2006, to which the following discussion is indebted.
[4] Chapters 28 ("Yielding the Throne"), 29 ("Robber Zhi"), 30 ("Discourse on Swords"), and 31 ("The Old Fisherman"). See Graham 1989b: 54–59.
[5] Lewis 2006: 17.

Doctrines ascribed to Yang Zhu also appear as titles of sections of the *Lüshi chunqiu*: "Life as Basic" (*Bensheng* 本生, ch 1.2), "Giving Weight to Self" (*Zhong ji* 重己, ch. 1.3), "Fundamental Desires" (*Qing yu* 情欲, ch. 2.3), and "Awareness of the Purpose of Action" (*Shen wei* 審為, ch. 21.4).[6] Other passages identify *xing* 性, "nature" with *sheng* 生, "life." In other words, keeping one's nature intact meant preserving one's true self or what is "genuine" (*zhen* 真), but also preserving one's health, safety from danger, and living out one's natural lifespan. As the old fisherman of *Zhuangzi* 31 observes of Confucius:

恐不免其身，苦心勞形以危其真。嗚乎，遠哉其分於道也。

> I fear he will not be able to extricate his person from disaster. By causing suffering in his heart–mind and exhausting his form, he is endangering his genuineness. Oh my, he is indeed far removed from *dao*. (*Zhuangzi* 31/92/27)

Other Yangist stories in the *Zhuangzi* describe individuals rejecting rulership and power in order to preserve their health and physical well-being. In some cases, these ideas are taken to the point of caricature in assertions about the absurdity of exchanging bodily parts for external objects, such as a hair for the world in the Mencius passages quoted above. Several passages in the *Liezi* also take up this theme.[7]

What is so important about these fragmentary and possibly contrarian passages? John Emerson argues that Yang Zhu's major innovation was the "discovery of the body."[8] He argues that Warring States thinkers redefined the relationship between the individual and the state, resulting in both a new political order and a new sense of self. Yang's new emphasis on preserving one's inner nature offered freedom from public ritual roles and the clan identifications and obligations to the spirits that went with them and had previously defined them. By defining ritual, honors, and clan relations as external conditions, Yang Zhu made possible new forms of self and self-awareness. In the earlier clan ritual world, people did not identify with individual bodies because, in ancient China (as in contemporary Melanesia), persons were "dividuals": plural selves defined by multiple

---

[6] See Graham 1989b: 55.
[7] See Lewis 2006: 18–20.
[8] Emerson 1996: 533.

relationships.[9] These socially and ritually defined selves did not either identify with or depend on the physical body.

Emerson argues that Yang's doctrines introduced and enabled the identification of persons with their physical bodies. This "discovery of the body" involved a reconfiguration of self/other, individual/group, and private/public relationships. The result was a new sense of self that was unified (rather than plural), context-independent (rather than context-grounded), autonomous, and clearly located in space and time. As a result, both ancestral spirits and clan relationships lost force and reality.

Many classical texts asserted that status and honor did not necessarily reflect real merit. Yang Zhu made the stronger claim that real worth is completely independent of official status or honor. He rejected all public identities as unreal and recognized only the private world of "nature" and the body.

As Lewis notes, by the mid-Warring States period, the trope of the body and life as markers of supreme value had become conventional. This "body" was defined in spatial terms as a central self set against external objects, rather than a Western dualistic opposition between body/matter and mind or soul/spirit. The mind was part of the body; it was essentialized and refined, but of the same substance. Properly cultivated and protected, it could generate spirit-like powers (*shén*). As Lewis puts it, early Chinese thinkers portrayed the body as a center within a field of rival forces. Properly developed, it could manifest and radiate its own force. This model of the body first appeared in the Yangist doctrines, and it was successively adopted by rivals to articulate their own positions.[10]

In summary, awareness of the body as a site of development and power first emerged in Chinese thought in the fourth century BCE. It became a topic of discourse that was used by different traditions to articulate their own values and priorities. It was originally identified as central in Yangist doctrines on the importance of protecting one's own life and self, and avoiding external attractions that could compromise the integrity of the body. These ideas are further developed in the *Neiye* and "Arts of the Mind" chapters of the *Guanzi*, *Zhuangzi*, the *Shiwen* text from Mawangdui, and the *Huainanzi*.

---

[9] A "dividual" is a person who is composed of parts shared with others, and who can only be given a separate identity by artificially separating these bonds. Examples in Western societies include parent–child pairs and married couples. For dividuality, see Strathern 1988, especially 12–15 and 275–88.

[10] Lewis 2006: 20. As he puts it, the body became problematic as one spatial unit defined in opposition to others, rather than in binary oppositions between body and mind.

Mind and Spirit in the *Guanzi*

Perhaps the strongest initial statement of the view that *shén* is an intrahuman capacity comes from the "Inner Workings" (*Neiye*) chapter of the *Guanzi*, which significantly breaks down barriers between humans and external spirits. Puett has shown that the *Neiye* makes new claims that humans have the potential to gain powers like those of external spirits. By correctly cultivating essence (*jing*) and *shén* in a settled heart–mind, humans can gain the "divine" powers necessary to control things in the world and to understand good and ill auspices without the aid of external spirits via ritual and mantic practices.[11]

I largely agree with this view, but I prefer some difference of emphasis. Closely following the order of argument of the text, I read the *Neiye* as making three claims about the development of spirit. First are a set of claims about *jing*: that *jing* is the basis of both physical life and sagacity, that human *shén* and external spirits are composed of the same stuff (*jing*), and that *jing* is identified with the sage, with wisdom (*zhi*), and with virtue or inner power (*de*).

The text then turns to three related claims about the mind: that a settled heart–mind can align the senses and form the lodging of *jing*; that *jing* can lodge only in a heart–mind that is settled (*dingxin*); and that cultivating the heart–mind (*xiuxin* 脩心) and making its thoughts tranquil makes it possible to attain *dao*. Finally, the text turns to a set of claims about spirit: that it is an internal faculty that can unify and transform and that it is linked to the One and to *dao*. It also describes methods for the cultivation of spirit by aligning the body and settling the heart–mind so that inner power (*de*) enters on its own, with the result that one is "like a spirit" (*ruo shén*).

The *Guanzi* ruler metaphors discussed in Chapter 3 addressed the first part of this process: the need for a "settled heart–mind" before *jing* and *qi* could be circulated and cultivated in the body. But the rulership of the heart–mind is not the goal of self-cultivation; it is a preliminary stage in the development of spirit. As self-cultivation proceeds, attention shifts from the mind to the body, the circulation of *jing*, and the entry of spirit. Correspondingly, the metaphoric language shifts from mind as ruler metaphors to a new metaphor of mind as the container of the all-important spirit, just as body is the container of the mind. I begin with the account of body, mind, and spirit in the *Neiye*, and then I turn to important differences between it and the "Arts of the Mind" chapters.

---

[11] See Puett 2002: 109–17, to which the following discussion is indebted. For a broader account of the structure of the *Neiye*, see Roth 1999: 99–123.

The *Neiye*

The *Neiye* begins by identifying essence or *jing* as highly refined *qi* that is identified with life and that is also linked to the development of spirit:

凡物之精，（此）〔比〕則為生。下生五穀，上為列星。流於天地之閒，謂之鬼神；藏於胸中，謂之聖人。

It is always the case that the essence of things is what makes them be alive. Below it generates the five grains; above it creates the ordered stars. When it flows between Heaven and Earth, we call it ghosts and spirits; when it is stored within a person's chest, we call that person a sage. (*Guanzi* 16.1/115/17–18, *Neiye* 16.49)

In other words, sages contain the same *jing* as external spirits, and the only difference is that spirits are pure *jing*, while humans are a mixture of *jing* and form. Here, the chest is a container in which *jing* can be stored (*zang* 藏), literally put away in a treasury. *Jing* is identified with both spirit and sageliness.

The *Neiye* describes the heart–mind as naturally complete and developed but vulnerable to harm from emotional attachments:

凡心之刑，自充自盈，自生自成。其所以失之，必以憂樂喜怒欲利。

It is always the case that the form of the heart–mind is full and replete of itself, and develops and becomes complete of itself. What causes it to lose them is sorrow, happiness, joy, anger, desire and [seeking] profit. (*Guanzi* 16.1/115/22–24, *Neiye* 16.49)[12]

The text argues that heart–mind must be settled if it is to become a lodging place for essence (*jing*) and eventually for spirit. According to the *Neiye*, sages conform to the values of Heaven and Earth, and as a result, are not transformed by their seasonal changes and alternations. The result is a settled heart–mind:

---

[12] Reading *xing* 刑 as *xing* 形. Roth (1999: 50) translates this phrase as "all the forms of the mind are naturally infused and filled with it [*jing*]." I take these verbs as intransitive and read it as "In all cases, the form of the mind is full and replete of itself" (cf. Rickett 1998: 40). Unlike Roth, I thus do not read this passage as saying that *jing* inherently resides in the mind. The commentaries differ on the meaning of *xin zhi xing* 心之刑. Ma Yuancai (1990: 8) states that it refers to various exemplary mental states mentioned throughout. Zhao Shouzheng (1989, 2:122) interprets it as referring to the physical structure of the heart–mind. This difference does not affect the issue of the relationship of *jing* to the mind.

BODY, MIND, AND SPIRIT   127

能正能靜，然后能定。定心在中，耳目聰明，四枝堅固，可以為精舍。精也者，氣之精者也。氣，道乃生，

Only one who is capable of correct alignment and capable of stillness is, as a result, capable of being settled. When a settled heart-mind is present within, the ears and eyes are keen and bright, and the four limbs [lit. branches] are durable and strong, is it possible to create a lodging place for essence. As for essence, it is the essence of *qi*. When *qi* is guided, it [essence] is generated. (*Guanzi* 16.1/116/2–3, *Neiye* 16.49)

The passage thus specifies three separate preconditions for *jing* finding a lodging place (*she* 舍). The heart-mind must be settled, but the senses must be keen and the body (the four limbs) must be strong and enduring. In other words, body and mind must cooperate to refine *qi* into *jing*. This cooperation is not described as rulership.

The *Neiye* next describes the entry of spirit and spirit illumination into the body:

一物能化謂之神，一事能變謂之智。化不易氣，變不易智，惟執一之君子能為此乎！執一不失，能君萬物。君子使物，不為物使，得一之理。

To unify things and be able to transform them is called spirit. To unify affairs and be able to alter them is called wisdom. To transform but not alter *qi*, to alter but not change wisdom: only the gentleman who holds fast to the One is able to do this! By holding fast to the One and not losing it, you can rule over the myriad things. The gentleman controls things, and is not controlled by them. He obtains the pattern of the One. (*Guanzi* 16.1/116/6–7, *Neiye* 16.49)

The text returns to the correct alignment of the body and the spontaneous entry of spirit illumination (*shénming*):

形不正，德不來；中不靜，心不治。正形攝德，(天仁地義，)[13]　則淫然而自至神明之極，照乎知萬物。中（義）守不忒，不以物亂官，不以官亂心，是謂中得。

---

[13] I follow Roth (1999: 222n59) and Haloun 1951 in taking 天仁地義 as the gloss of an unknown commentator rather than the original text. I have modified the ICS text accordingly and do not include it in the translation.

128 A TRIPARTITE SELF

If the form is not aligned, inner power will not come; if the center is not tranquil, the heart-mind will not be well ordered. Align the form, hold fast to inner power, and the extremity of spirit illumination will gradually arrive of itself, so brilliant it knows the myriad things. Hold it fast within and do not be excessive. Do not allow things to disorder the senses, and do not allow the senses to disorder the heart-mind. This is called obtaining it within. (*Guanzi* 16.1/116/11–12, *Neiye* 16.49)

The text then elaborates on spirit, which also naturally resides in the body:

有神自在身，一往一來，莫之能思。失之必亂，得之必治。敬除其舍，精將自來。精想思之，寧念治之，嚴容畏敬，精將至定。得之而勿捨，耳目不淫。

There is a spirit that of itself is present in the person, sometimes going, sometimes coming, no one is able to contemplate it. If you lose it, disorder must occur; if you obtain it, there must be order. Clean its lodging place carefully, and essence will come in of itself. Refine your thoughts and contemplate it; make your memories tranquil and put it in order. Be reverent, generous, dignified, and respectful, and essence will arrive and settle. Obtain it and do not disperse it, and the ears and eyes will never go astray. (*Guanzi* 16.1/116/14–15, *Neiye* 16.49)

The text then describes how regulation of the mind leads to regulation of the senses:

我心治，官乃治；我心安，官乃安。治之者心也，安之者心也。

If my heart-mind is regulated, the senses [lit. officials] are thereby regulated. If my heart-mind is at peace, the senses are at pace as a result. What regulates them is the heart-mind; what makes them at peace is the heart-mind. (*Guanzi* 16.1/116/18–19, *Neiye* 16.49)

It is noteworthy that here, the mind is not described as "ruling" the senses. Instead, regulation of the senses occurs naturally once the mind is regulated.

Taken together, these four passages offer a picture of complex interactions between body, mind, and spirit. The first passage begins with unifying attention and consciousness. That unity is described as "spirit" but is closely identified with both wisdom and the transformation of *qi* in the body. The second passage emphasizes that correct alignment of the body is the prerequisite for both an ordered heart–mind and the entry of spirit illumination. The series of imperatives here—"do not allow"—refer to the management of both the senses and the heart–mind.

The third passage returns to spirit, which it describes as naturally present within a person (*shēn*) and moving freely in and out of the body. This passage makes it clear that spirit, rather than the heart–mind, is the key to internal order: "if you lose it, disorder must occur." The *Guanzi* never speaks of "losing" one's mind but repeatedly warns against losing one's spirit, which, unlike the heart–mind, can move in and out of the body. The passage also emphasizes that spirit (and spirit illumination) naturally align the senses: "obtain it and retain it, and the eyes and ears never go astray." The fourth passage shifts back to the role of the heart–mind: it regulates the body and puts it at peace.

There are important differences between the treatment of the mind in the *Neiye* and its description in other chapters of the *Guanzi*. The ruler metaphor introduced in Chapter 3 appears in two chapters of the *Guanzi*: "Ruler and Officials" (*Junchen xia*, ch. 31) and "Arts of the Mind" (*Xin shu shang*, ch. 36), both of which describe the heart–mind as a ruler of officials using the term *prince* or *ruler* (*jun* 君). In the *Neiye*, the heart–mind clearly regulates or "orders" (*shi* 治) the body but does not "rule" (*jun*) it. The underlying metaphor of the *Neiye* is not a ruler regulating subordinates; it is the concentration of essence within a porous inner container whose "treasure" illuminates from within.

The *Neiye* next turns to a metaphor of double enclosure:

心以藏心，心之中又有心（馬）〔焉〕。彼心之心，（音）〔意〕以先言。（音）〔意〕然后形，形然后言。言然后使，使然后治。不治必亂，亂乃死。

The mind therefore stores the mind; within the mind there is also another mind in it. In that mind within the mind, awareness comes before words. Only after there is awareness is there form; only after there is form are there words; only after words is there control; only after there is control is there regulation. If there is no regulation, there will inevitably be disorder. If there is disorder, there will be death. (*Guanzi* 16.1/116/21–22, *Neiye* 16.49)[14]

The awareness of this "mind within the mind" (*xin zhi xin* 心之心) seems to operate before sensory input; in contemporary terminology it is precognitive. It is also at risk from the activity of the mind: if knowledge overwhelms the mind, it loses its vitality. Importantly, it is not identified with *shén*.

There are physical markers of the inner mind in the settled mind. Another passage describes it as the wellspring of *qi*, which strengthens the body and produces sagacity:

精存自生，其外安榮，內藏以為泉原，浩然和平，以為氣淵。淵之不涸，四體乃固；泉之不竭，九竅遂通。乃能窮天地，被四海。中無惑意，外無邪菑。心全於中，形全於外，不逢天菑，不遇人害，謂之聖人。

When essence is present, it produces life of itself; externally, it is settled and flourishing; internally, one can store it in order to make it into a fountainhead. Floodlike, harmonious and tranquil, it acts as the depths of the *qi*. As long as the depths do not go dry, the four limbs are firm. As long as the fountainhead is not exhausted, the nine apertures thereupon open. Thus they can exhaust the limits of Heaven and Earth and cover the four seas. If there are no delusions within, there will be no disasters without. If the heart–mind is complete within, the form will be complete without; one will not meet with disasters from Heaven or injuries from other people, and [this person] we call a sage. (*Guanzi* 16.1/116/24–26, *Neiye* 16.49)

Here the body is a container that stores *jing*, which is literally "treasured within" (*nei zang* 內藏). As a result, it becomes a source of *qi*, which strengthens the body and even produces sagacity.

The last part of the *Neiye* returns to three key points with which it began. The first is the need to concentrate *qi* and align the body correctly:

（搏）〔摶〕氣如神，萬物備存。能（搏）〔摶〕乎？能一乎？能無卜筮而知吉凶乎？能止乎？能已乎？能勿求諸人而之己乎？思

---

[14] I translate *xin* as "mind" here for fluidity; cf. Rickett 1998: 46–47, 8.2–8.3.

之，思之，又重思之。思之而不通，鬼神將通之。非鬼神之力也，
精氣之極也。

Concentrate your *qi* like a spirit and the myriad things will all reside within. Can you concentrate? Can you unify? Can you not engage in crack-making and stalk casting [divination] and yet understand good and ill auspice? Can you stop? Can you reach an end? Can you not seek from others and obtain it in yourself? Think about it, think about it, and think about it again. If you think about it but do not penetrate, the ghosts and spirits will penetrate it. This is not due to the power of the ghosts and spirits; it is due to the ultimate point of essential *qi*. (*Guanzi* 16.1/117/6–8, *Neiye* 16.49)

Second, the *Neiye* returns to the importance of the body:

四體既正，血氣既靜，一意（搏）〔摶〕心，耳目不淫，雖遠若近。

When the four limbs are aligned, and the blood and *qi* are stilled, unify your awareness, concentrate your heart–mind, and your ears and eyes will never go astray, and even what is distant will be like what is near. (*Guanzi* 16.1/117/10, *Neiye* 16.49)

Finally, it returns to the claim that people are composites of form (*xing*) and essence (*jing*):

凡人之生也，天出其精，地出其形，合此以為人。和乃生，不和不生。察和之道，其（精）〔情〕不見，其徵不醜。平正擅匈，論治在心，此以長壽。忿怒之失度，乃為之圖。節其五欲，去其二凶，不喜不怒，平正擅匈。

As for the birth of humans, Heaven brings forth their essence; Earth brings forth their form; they combine like this to constitute a human being. When they [*jing* and form] harmonize, there is life: when they do not, there is not life. If we examine the way of harmony, its essence cannot be seen, its signs cannot be classified. When there is arrangement and regulation in the heart–mind, this thereby gives long life. Joy and anger cause one to lose the measure; therefore, design for [how to deal with them]. Moderate the five desires; expel the two evils; do not be joyous and do not be angry;

and balance and right alignment fill the chest. (*Guanzi* 16.1/117/14–16, *Neiye* 16.49)

To reiterate several points in Puett's study, the argument of the *Neiye* turns on three interrelated terms: *qi*, essence, and spirit. *Qi* is refined into essence, and essence is refined into spirit. By aligning their bodies and settling their heart–minds, sages create a stable container for essence. From it, spirit, gives access to the rest of the (monistic) cosmos. By bringing their *qi* into accord with the patterns of the cosmos, sages gain mastery over things, so an important goal of self-cultivation is to retain spirit within the double container of body and mind. The result is, literally, the powers of spirits, gained without recourse to the mantic techniques of religious specialists. As Puett puts it, the *Neiye* authors are thus teaching humans how to usurp powers that otherwise belong to spirits and also to appropriate abilities that ritual specialists claim as their own.[15]

In conclusion, the *Neiye* clarifies three important points about body, mind, and spirit. First, the self-cultivation techniques described in the *Neiye* clearly require the participation of body, mind, and spirit but in different ways. The process begins with aligning the body, which in turn aligns the mind; once regulated, the mind recursively regulates the senses but without having to "rule" them. At this point, spirit lodges in the body of itself. The result is a human who holds powers normally ascribed to external spirits. Second, this process clearly requires three elements that do not reduce to two and thus is not well described in dualist terms. The initially separate but eventually circular engagement of both body and mind are necessary to create the conditions that produce internal spirit. A dualist account of this process would end with the dyad of body/mind and spirit. Third, both external and internal spirit are "constructed" by human activity. External spirits are "created" by ritual activity. Internal spirit is created by the psychophysical techniques described here.

The "Arts of the Mind"

The themes of the cultivation of *qi*, essence, and spirit also are central to the two "Arts of the Mind" chapters of the *Guanzi*. Some two-thirds of "Arts of

---

[15] Puett 2002: 115–16 and 109–16.

the Mind, 2" parallels the central section of the *Neiye*, but in different order and with different emphases. Scholarly accounts of these chapters focus on whether they were written by Huang-Lao Daoists connected to the Jixia Academy.[16] What is most important about this debate for purposes of the present discussion is evidence that the *Neiye* is the older text, written in the fourth century, and that the *Xinshu* chapters derive from it.

Key ideas from the *Neiye* also appear in the *Xinshu 2*. One passage describes the inner mind and its system of double containment in the same terms as in the *Neiye*:

心之中又有心。意以先言，意然後刑，刑然后思，思然后知。凡心之刑，過知失王。

Within the mind there is also another mind. Awareness comes before words; only after there is awareness is there form; only after there is form is there thought; only after there is thought is there understanding. It is always the case that if the form of the mind is overwhelmed by too much knowledge it loses vitality. (*Guanzi* 13.2/99/3–4, *Xinshu xia* 13.37)[17]

The fifth "Explanation" in *Xinshu* 1 reiterates the *Neiye* claim that an adept can become "spirit-like" by concentrating essence:

世人之所職者精也。去欲則宣，宣則靜矣，靜則精。精則獨立矣，獨則明，明則神矣。神者至貴也，故館不辟除，則貴人不舍焉。故曰「不潔則神不處」。

That which manages all people is essence. If you eliminate desires [it] will circulate; when it circulates you will become still; when you are still you will become essential [of essence]. When you are essential you will be establish yourself alone. When you establish yourself alone, you become enlightened; when you are enlightened you become a spirit. Spirit is what is most honored. Therefore, if the hall is not opened up and cleaned out, an honored person will not reside in it. Therefore it is said: "If you do

---

[16] It has been claimed that key sections of the *Guanzi* were written by Song Xing 宋鈃 (371–289 BCE) and Yin Wen 尹文 (350–285 BCE), whom the *Hanshu* identifies as key Huang-Lao thinkers at the Jixia Academy. See Rickett 1985: 56–58 and 65–70, Chen and Sung 1998, Roth 1999: 23–30, and Chen Guying 2007: 31–41.

[17] Cf. *Guanzi* 16.1/116/21–22, *Neiye* 16.49, discussed above. I follow Rickett (1998: 63) and Guo Moruo in taking *xing* 刑 as *xing* 形 and *wang* 王 as *sheng* 生.

not make a clean sweep spirit will not remain." (*Guanzi* 13.1/96/24–26, *Xinshu shang* 13.36)[18]

This passage never mentions the mind, which, in the context of this passage, seems to be little more than a passive container that, under correct circumstances, spirit can enter and inhabit.

Puett notes that the claims of the *Xinshu 2* go beyond those of the *Neiye*. Both share a monistic cosmology, but in *Xinshu 2*:

執一而不失，能君萬物，日月之與同光，天地之與同理。

聖人裁物，不為物使。心安是國安也，心治是國治也。　治也者心也，安也者心也。

One who grasps the One and does not lose it can be ruler of the myriad things; share the brilliance of the sun and moon; and share ordering patterns with Heaven and Earth.

The sage regulates things, and is not controlled by things. When the [sage's] heart–mind is at peace, the state is at peace; when the [sage's] heart–mind is ordered, the state is ordered. (*Guanzi* 13.2/98/13–16, *Xinshu xia* 13.37)

This passage differs from the *Neiye* in important ways. Here, grasping the One confers not only access to the cosmos, but the powers of Heaven.[19] The passage compares the heart–mind of the sage to the ruler of a state, but what the sage rules here is not the body but the world: the sage "can be the ruler of the myriad things" (*neng jun wanwu* 能君萬物).

The *Guanzi* has long been recognized as an important source for ideas associated with Huang-Lao Daoism.[20] The relevance of this question for the present discussion is the emphasis on the cultivation of *jing* and *shén*, which ancient sources recognize as a central concern of Huang-Lao. For example, in the last chapter of the *Shiji*, Sima Qian describes the Daojia as: "making people's essence and spirit (*jingshén*) concentrated and unified."[21]

---

[18] Cf. Rickett 1998: 76, also discussed previously in Chapter 3.
[19] As Puett points out (2002: 171–72), this account defines the sage in the same terms as spirit.
[20] A second group of texts closely identified with Huang-Lao are four texts from Mawangdui: the *Jingfa* 經法 (Canon: Law), *Shida jing* 十大經 (Ten Great Classics), *Cheng* 誠 (Aphorisms), and *Daoyuan* 道源 (Dao the Origin). Some scholars consider them to be the lost "Four Books of the Yellow Emperor" (*Huangdi sijing*). For translation see Yates 1997.
[21] 道家使人精神專一. *Shiji* 130: 3289.

The *Zhuangzi*

The *Zhuangzi* is distinctive for both a negative view of the heart–mind and a highly positive view of cultivating spirit, but with very different goals than those of the *Guanzi*. In considering views of the body, mind, and spirit in the *Zhuangzi*, I begin in each case with the roughly fourth-century views of the Inner Chapters and then turn to views from later periods in the Outer Chapters.

The *Zhuangzi* on the Heart–Mind

The second chapter of the *Zhuangzi* mentions the rulership of the heart–mind only to ridicule its apparent arbitrariness. It suggests that there is no inherent reason that the *xin* should be the lord and the body its "vassals and concubines" (*chenqie* 臣妾). The *Zhuangzi* explicitly rejects taking the heart–mind as a ruling authority and any claim that it has a superior ability to respond and judge:

> 若有真宰，而特不得其眹。可行己信，而不見其形，有情而无形。百骸，九竅，六藏，賅而存焉，吾誰與為親？汝皆說之乎？其有私焉？如是皆有為臣妾乎？其臣妾不足以相治乎？其遞相為君臣乎？其有真君存焉？如求得其情與不得，無益損乎其真。

> There seems to be a genuine governor, but it is peculiar that we cannot get any indication of it. That it can go and stop is believable, but we do not see its form; it has a genuine nature but is without form. The hundred joints, nine openings, six viscera are all complete and present in it [the body], but which should I deem closest to me? Are you pleased with them all, or are you partial to one? And if it is like this, do you take all of them to be its servants and concubines? And are not the servants and concubines sufficient to rule each other? Or do they take turns being each other's lords and servants? Or is there a genuine lord present among them? That we seek to grasp its genuine nature and do not succeed does not either add or detract from its genuineness. (*Zhuangzi* 2/4/1–4)[22]

---

[22] Translations of the *Zhuangzi* are indebted to Graham 1981, Mair 1994, and Ziporyn 2020.

As the passage continues, the *Zhuangzi* rejects the authority of any "complete heart–mind" (*chengxin* 成心):

夫隨其成心而師之，誰獨且無師乎？奚必知代而心自取者有之？愚者與有焉。未成乎心而有是非，是今日適越而昔至也。

If you follow the completed heart–mind and make it your master, who could be alone and without a master? Why should it be only those who understand the alternation [of things] and whose heart–minds approve their own selections who have one? The foolish also have one. For there to be judgments of so and not-so/right and wrong that are not yet formed in the heart–mind would be "to go to Yue today and arrive yesterday." (*Zhuangzi* 2/4/9–10)

Clearly, Zhuang Zhou or the Zhuangist authors of the Inner Chapters do not consider even a complete heart–mind to be a reliable guide. This passage has occasioned a great deal of scholarly debate because of the tendency to want to find a real ruler somewhere.[23] An alternative is to view spirit as a state in which people act spontaneously. As such, spirit is latent when it is not actively being concentrated. It operates in a subtle state of active passivity.[24]

The *Zhuangzi* also makes positive recommendations about the management of the heart–mind. Chapter 4 of the *Zhuangzi* describes a process of "forgetting" and "fasting the heart–mind":

若一〔汝〕志，无聽之以耳而聽之以心，无聽之以心而聽之以氣！聽止於耳，心止於符。氣也者，虛而待物者也。唯道集虛。虛者，心齋也。

Unify your intentions; don't listen with the ear, but rather listen with the heart–mind; don't listen with the heart–mind; but rather listen with *qi*! Listening stops at the ear, the heart–mind at the tally. As for *qi*, it is something that is empty and awaits things. Only *dao* gathers emptiness. Emptiness is the fasting of the heart–mind. (*Zhuangzi* 4/10/1–2)

---

[23] Some consider the "real ruler" to be the "real self" (Chen Guying 2001: 35, 47, Tang Junyi 2005: 187), others take it to be the heart–mind (Wang Bo 2004: 161–63), the spirit (Slingerland 2003b: 198–99), or even *dao* (Graham 1981: 51). See Chiu 2016: 42.

[24] For these views, see Billeter (2009: 17, 50–51, 55) and Chiu (2016: 44).

Is there a connection between the *Zhuangzi*'s account of the completed heart-mind and the importance of "forgetting" and fasting the heart-mind? One possibility is that the completed heart-mind becomes inflexibly firm and no longer responsive to the world. The processes of forgetting and fasting free the heart-mind from these constraints. This possibility could explain the *Zhuangzi*'s strong criticism of the completed heart-mind, without corresponding disapproval of the heart-mind itself.[25]

The *Zhuangzi* also emphasizes that emotions harm the heart-mind; importantly, they include the normative dispositions of humaneness and propriety (*ren yi*). They also harm the body:

人大喜邪？毗於陽；大怒邪？毗於陰。陰陽並毗，田時不至；寒暑之和不成，其反傷人之形乎！

Are people too happy? They are excessive in yang; are they too angry? They are excessive in yin. When yin and yang are excessive, the four seasons do not arrive on time; the harmony of cold and heat is not complete; does this not in turn harm the form? (*Zhuangzi* 11/26/14–15)

The passage continues that keen sight and hearing seduce the emotions by color and sound. A similar tendency applies to normative dispositions. Humaneness and propriety (*ren yi*) cause disorder and confusion; rites and music cause ingenuity and dissolution; sagacity and wisdom cause artifice and fussiness (11/26/19–21). The passage adds that the *junzi* should:

苟能无解其五藏，无擢其聰明；尸居而龍見，淵默而雷聲，神動而天隨，從容无為。

Avoid dissipating your five *zang* viscera; avoid overextending your hearing and sight. Stay still as a corpse, but with a dragon countenance; stay silent as the abyss, but with the sound of thunder; the spirit moves and Heaven follows; possessed in calm, it acts by not acting. (*Zhuangzi* 11/26/26–27)

---

[25] Karyn Lai has proposed this explanation (personal communication).

Lao Dan goes on to give a similar assessment of the nature of the heart-mind: "Constrained, it sinks; encouraged, it rises; sinking or rising can imprison or kill it."[26]

Finally, the *Zhuangzi* describes the clarity of the fasted heart-mind as clear like a mirror:

水靜則明燭鬚眉，平中準，大匠取法焉。水靜猶明，而況精神！聖人之心靜乎！天地之鑑也，萬物之鏡也。

When water is still, its clarity mirrors the whiskers and eyebrows; it is fitting and accurate, so the great craftsman takes it as his standard. When water is still, it is clear like this; how much more so is a pure spirit! The heart-mind of the sage is still thus! Heaven and Earth mirror it and it is a looking glass for the ten thousand things. (*Zhuangzi* 13/34/15–16)[27]

Understood this way, still water is not truly still; it continues to flow in almost invisible motion. In the same way, the spirit can be both still and in motion.[28] But as Chiu points out, it is the wrong move to take the spirit-infused heart-mind as an authority (instead of the completed heart-mind). The fasted heart-mind is transformed in ways that avoid the problems of the completed heart-mind. The fasted and transformed heart-mind instead responds like a clear mirror, but it is not an authority.

Concentrating Spirit

The *Zhuangzi* describes cultivating spirit in two ways, one negative and one positive. Negatively, it describes the fasting of the heart-mind, discussed above. Positively, it repeatedly refers to "concentrating *shén*." In the first chapter, a daemonic person makes grain ripen and protects animals from plagues by "concentrating *shén*" (*shénning* 神凝, 1/2/16). The second chapter describes realized persons as "spirit-like" (*zhìren shén yǐ* 至人神矣, 2/6/17). For the *Zhuangzi*, the heart-mind's judgments and responses differ from (and are inferior to) those of a spirit person.

---

[26] 女慎無攖人心。人心排下而進上，上下囚殺. *Zhuangzi* 11/26/30–31.
[27] The *Zhuangzi* also describes the heart-mind of a realized person as being like a mirror: 至人之用心若鏡 (7/21/21).
[28] For this point, see Chiu 2016: 47.

The third chapter, "The Lord of Nurturing Life" (*Yangsheng zh*u 養生主), conspicuously links spirit to the exercise of skill in its depictions of hyperaware individuals who excel at the performance of a craft or skill. Stories of this type begin with the butcher Pao Ding and continue in the Outer Chapters (discussed below). It describes the method of the skilled butcher Pao Ding 庖丁. He is explicit that spirit, rather than technical expertise or rarefied perceptions, is behind his skill, as he sees with his spirit rather than his eyes:

臣以神遇而不以目視，官知止而神欲行。

I use spirit and do not see with the eyes. The senses [lit. officials] know to stop, and the spirit moves as it desires. (*Zhuangzi* 3/8/5)

Importantly, his speech begins with the claim that what he values is *dao*, which goes beyond skill; at the end of his speech, Lord Wenhui exclaims that Pao Ding's words have taught him how to nurture life (*yangsheng*, 3/8/11). It is worth noting in passing that this chapter also ascribes spirits to animals. It mentions a marsh pheasant that seeks food and drink but avoids a cage because "even if treated as a king, its spirit would not be happy" (3/8/15).

Several passages in the *Zhuangzi* refers to spirit "dwelling within" (*she*) in terms reminiscent of the *Neiye*. These begin in the fourth chapter, in a passage linked to the fasting of the heart–mind, described above:

是之謂坐馳。夫徇耳目內通而外於心知，鬼神將來舍，而況人乎！是萬物之〔所〕化也，禹舜之所紐也，伏戲、几蘧之所行終，而況散焉者乎！

This is what is called riding at a gallop while sitting. Permit your ears and eyes to penetrate internally and push the knowledge of the heart–mind to the outside, then ghosts and spirits will come and inhabit, and how much more so the human! This is the transformation of the myriad things. (*Zhuangzi* 4/10/7–9)

Here the goal is not to control things but to be in accord with the ongoing transformation of things.

Another account, in the eleventh chapter, describes the cooperation of the body and an indwelling spirit in an account of Huang Di's search for longevity. He seeks out the recluse Kong Tongzi and asks him how to regulate his body to achieve longevity.[29] Kong describes an "essence of perfect *dao*" (*zhidao zhi jing* 至道之精):

> 无視无聽，抱神以靜，形將自正。必靜必清，无勞女形，无搖女精，乃可以長生。目无所見，耳无所聞，心无所知，女神將守形，形乃長生。... 慎守女身，物將自壯。

> There is nothing to see and nothing to hear; it holds spirit in its arms with stillness, and the form correctly aligns of itself. You must be still; you must be pure; do not belabor your body; do not agitate your essence; then you may live for long. When the eyes have nothing that they see and the ears have nothing that they hear and the heart–mind has nothing that it knows, your spirit will guard your form and it will live long.... Watch over and preserve your person, and all things will of themselves give it vigor. (*Zhuangzi* 11/27/24–27)

A passage in the Outer Chapters links nourishing the heart–mind with cultivating or releasing the spirit. In a discourse between Yun Jiang 雲將 (Cloud General) and Hong Mang 鴻蒙 (Vast Obscurity), the latter gives advice on self-cultivation:

> 心養。汝徒處无為，而物自化。墮爾形體，吐爾聰明...解心釋神，莫然无魂。

> The nourishment of the heart–mind. Simply abide in *wuwei*, and things transform of themselves. Let the form and frame fall away; cast out hearing and vision ... release the heart–mind; free the spirit; be as still as if without a [cloud] soul. (*Zhuangzi* 11/28/16–18)

Several passages seem to privilege spirit over the heart–mind, but what about the relation of the spirit to the body? Other passages describe the body protecting the spirit or the spirit leaving the body.[30] One passage in *Zhuangzi* 12 refers to the body protecting the spirit. It describes the emergence of fate (*ming* 命), things (*wu*), form or principle (*li*), and physical form (*xing*) from

---

[29] 治身奈何而可以長久？*Zhuangzi* 11/27/22–23.
[30] Cf. *Zhuangzi* 12/32/10, discussed above.

original nonbeing: Bodily form protects the spirit; form and spirit each have their own models."³¹ Another refers to the spirit leaving the body. A gardener tells Zigong that:

汝方將忘汝神氣，墮汝形體，而庶幾乎！而身之不能治

If you would just forget your spirit *qi* and let your form and frame fall away, you'd almost be there.. But you can't even govern your own person. (*Zhuangzi* 12/32/10)

Later in the same chapter, the response to a question about spirit people is that: "the spirit rises, mounted on the light, while the form vanishes."³² The chapter extols the spirit of realized persons and describes nourishing it. Persons of kingly virtue (*wangde* 王德) can see where there is no light and hear where there is no sound. Therefore, in the depths of the deep they can perceive things; in the spiritness of spirit they can perceive *jing*.³³

Another passage describes the *dao* of nourishing spirit, which requires purity, stillness, and the complex acting by not acting (*wuwei* 無為):

純粹而不雜，靜一而不變，惔而無為，動而以天行，此養神之道也。

Plain and pure, to be unblended, still and unified, to be unchanging, tranquil, [to act by] *wuwei*, in motion to walk with Heaven, this is the *dao* of nourishing spirit. (*Zhuangzi* 15/42/7–8)

Spirit and Skill

The idea that the concentrated *shén* of a spirit-like person is linked to the exercise of skill appears once in the Inner Chapters in the story of the butcher Pao Ding (discussed above). The topic receives more sustained attention in chapter 19, which describes several individuals of paramount skill, whose

---

31 形體保神，各有儀則. *Zhuangzi* 12/31/11.
32 上神乘光，與形滅亡. *Zhuangzi* 12/33/8.
33 故深之又深而能物焉，神之又神而能精焉. *Zhuangzi* 12/30/5–6.

expertise requires concentrating and unifying intentions and attention. One example is the hunchback cicada catcher:

> 吾處身也，若厥株拘；吾執臂也，若槁木之枝；雖天地之大，萬物之多，而唯蜩翼之知。吾不反不側，不以萬物易蜩之翼。

> I empty my person like a rooted tree stump; I hold my arms like the branch of a withered tree; for all heaven and earth's vastness and the myriad things' greatness, I am only aware of the wings of the cicada. I don't wander or waver, and would not change all the myriad things for the wings of a cicada. (*Zhuangzi* 19/50/14–15)

This passage is not a description of fasting the heart–mind, but it uses the same technique for a different purpose. Similarly, when asked about his skill, the bell stand maker Woodworker Qing (Zi Qing 梓慶) describes his preparations for making a bell stand as "fasting to still the heart–mind" (*zhai yi jing xin* 齊以靜心):

> 輒然忘吾有四枝形體也。當是時也，無公朝，其巧專而外骨消；然後入山林，觀天性；形軀至矣，然後成見鐻，然後加手焉。

> I forget that I have four limbs and a form and frame. During this time there is no "my lord's court"; the skill of it concentrates and outside distractions melt away; only then do I go to the mountain forest to observe Heaven's inherent nature of the wood. The form's aptitude reaches its peak; and only then do I completely see the bell stand; and only then do I put my hand to it. (*Zhuangzi* 19/52/6–8)

Similarly, in the story of the skilled ferryman in chapter 19, Yan Hui describes the ferryman to Confucius as rowing "like a spirit" (*ruo shén*, 19/50/18).

Whether or not they use the term *shén*, these accounts all describe cultivating the spirit by fasting or minimizing the influence of both the body and the heart–mind.

Spirit is also associated with clear understanding of a kind sometimes attributed to the heart–mind. For example, when someone asks Confucius why he understood something yesterday but not today, Confucius replies that he understood it yesterday because his "spirit" side (*shénzhe* 神者) had anticipated the answer, but today he is muddled because he is using his "nonspirit" aspects (*bushénzhe* 不神者, 22/63/12).

In summary, concentrating and stabilizing spirit seem to be prerequisites for the clear and perceptive understanding of a "spirit person" (*shénren*). This account of realized spirit goes well beyond any kind of purely intellectual prowess. The Zhuangzian Confucius praises the spirit of "utmost persons" (*zhiren* 至人) as psychologically and even physically impervious. They cannot be tricked or seduced (intellectually or physically). Life and death cannot transform them, and they range from the highest mountain to the deepest wellspring.[34] Finally, the *Zhuangzi* describes a pure and unified spirit as being able to influence things outside the body. The final chapter describes the realized individuals of antiquity as complementing spirit illumination, nurturing the myriad things, harmonizing with all under heaven, and benefiting the hundred clans.[35]

For all their similarities, the *Zhuangzi* and *Guanzi* take very different attitudes toward the heart–mind. Both agree on the need to stabilize (*ding* 定) both heart–mind and spirit. For example, the *Zhuangzi* describes a sage's heart–mind as a clear mirror like still water, but the context is the power of a pure spirit (13/34/16). It describes the *dao* of nourishing spirit as still, unified, and unchanging (15/42/8). Woodworker Qing fasts to calm his heart–mind (19/52/6–8, all discussed above). In these accounts, excellence of both heart–mind and spirit consists in stillness, obtained through fasting and forgetting. By contrast, the *Neiye* locates *dao* only in the heart–mind, a "homunculus-like" "mind within the mind." And in the *Guanzi*, a spirit housed within the heart–mind could easily take on the role of the "true ruler" the *Zhuangzi* rejects wholesale.

Spirit and Body in the *Shiwen*

The "Ten Questions" (*Shiwen*) text from Mawangdui contains an extended account of breath cultivation that link both spirit and spirit illumination to the body via longevity techniques. The text is organized as ten questions by a range of individuals. In the first four, the Yellow Emperor asks a series of questions on how to extend the life of the body and of spirit. Question 1 concerns how living things move and grow:

天師曰：爾察天之情？陰陽為正，萬物失之而不繼，得之而贏。食陰擬陽，稽於神明。

---

[34] 死生亦大矣，而无變乎己，況爵祿乎！若然者，其神經乎大山而無介，入乎淵泉而不濡. *Zhuangzi* 21/59/22–23.
[35] 配神明，醇天地，育萬物，和天下，澤及百姓. *Zhuangzi* 33/97/21.

144 A TRIPARTITE SELF

> The Heavenly Teacher said: When you examine heaven's nature, yin and yang are the rulers. Having lost them, the myriad creatures are discontinued; having obtained them, they thrive. Eat yin and secure yang; attain spirit illumination. (MWD4, 145 [*Shiwen*], strips 1–2, Harper 1998: 385)[36]

Here, as in several other responses, spirit illumination is the result of what appear to be breath or sexual techniques. Question 1 continues with a "recipe to penetrate spirit illumination":

> 靜而神風，拒而兩持，參築而毋遂，神風乃生，五聲乃對。翕毋過五，致之口，枚之心…此謂復奇之方，通於神明。天師之食神氣之道。

> Still your spirit wind, make fast your two racks, triply pound, and let nothing escape. The spirit wind then is born; the five tones then are matched. Suck it in not more than five times, bring it to the mouth, and still it with the heart–mind…. This is called the doubly marvelous recipe to penetrate spirit illumination. The way of the Heavenly Teacher to eat spirit vapor. (MWD4, 145 (*Shiwen*), strips 3–7, Harper 1998: 386–88)

In Question 3, he asks Cao Ao 曹熬 what causes (premature?) death and longevity. Here, spirit illumination is portrayed as the result of a procedure to extend longevity:

> 長生之稽，偵用玉閉。玉閉時避，神明來積。積必見章

> The procedure for living long is to carefully employ the jade closure. When at the right times the jade closure enfolds, spirit illumination arrives and accumulates. Accumulating, it invariably manifests radiance. (MWD4, 146 (*Shiwen*), strips 17–18, Harper 1998: 390–91)

Cao Ao describes nine sexual techniques, of which the eighth produces longevity and the ninth makes it possible to "penetrate spirit illumination" (*tong yu shénming* 通於神明).[37]

---

[36] Transcription of the *Shiwen* follows the emendations of the editors, and only includes nonstandard characters when necessary. Translations are from Harper 1998, sometimes modified.

[37] "Cao Ao's way for coitus with Yin and cultivating spirit *qi* 曹熬之接陰治神氣之道. See MWD4, 146 (*Shiwen*), strips 22–23, Harper 1998: 391. For other accounts of "engendering spirit illumination" (*chan shénming* 產神明) see MWD4, 163 (*Tianxia zhi dao tan*), strips 17–24, Harper 1998: 427.

Question 4 begins with the Yellow Emperor asking Rong Cheng 容成 a question about human longevity:

民始蒲淳溜形，何得而生？溜形成體，何失而死？

When people first spread out purity and flowed into form, what did they obtain [to cause them] to live? When, having flowed into form and completed their frames, what did they lose [to cause them] to die? (MWD4, 146 (*Shiwen*), strip 23; cf. Harper 1998: 393)[38]

What is being asked here? According to Harper, the term *flowing into form* refers to the early gestation of the embryo during pregnancy.[39] But this question closely resembles a question at the beginning of a text titled "All Things Flow into Form" (*Fanwu liuxing* 凡物流形), which occurs in two versions in the Shanghai Museum Chu bamboo strips. It begins by asking how the things that constitute the cosmos attain a stable form:

凡物流形, 奚得而成? 流形成體, 奚得而不死? ... [1]

As to things flowing into form, what do they acquire to become complete? As to [their] flowing into form and completing their frames, what do they acquire to not die?[40]

The passage goes on to pose further questions about things that have complete bodies and come to life, the meeting of yin and yang and "the harmony of fire and water" (*shui huo zhi he* 水火之和). It then asks how humans attain stable physical form:

民人流形, 奚得而生? [2] 流形成體, 奚失而死? ... [3]

As to people flowing into form, what do they acquire in order to live? As to their flowing into form and completing their frames, what do they lose in order that they die?[41]

---

[38] The editors read *pu* 蒲 as *fu* 敷 or *bu* 布 and xing 刑 as xing 形.
[39] Harper 1998: 393n2.
[40] See Ma Chengyuan 2008: 223, strip 1. For reconstruction and interpretation of this text, see Cao Feng 2010 and Cook 2012. For translations, see S. Chan 2015: 285–99 and Perkins 2015: 195–232. Transcription follows the emendations of the editors.
[41] Ma Chengyuan 2008: 226, 228, strips 2–3.

146 A TRIPARTITE SELF

In that text, embryology recapitulates cosmogony. I will argue that it also does so in the *Shiwen*.

Rong Cheng's answer to Huangdi's question on how to preserve life and extend longevity focuses on the need to observe and be in accord with the cycles of Heaven and Earth. The *Shiwen* describes a number of techniques to do this, including techniques to attain *shénming*:

故善治氣摶精者，以無徵為積，精神泉溢，翕甘露以為積，飲瑤泉靈尊以為經，去惡好俗，神乃溜刑。

Those who are skilled at cultivating *qi* and concentrating essence accumulate the signless. As a result, essence and spirit overflow like a fountain. Inhale the sweet dew to amass it; drink from the jade fountain and numinous wine vessel to circulate it. Drive out the bad, be fond of the customary, and spirit will flow into form. (MWD4, 146–47 (*Shiwen*), strips 28–29, Harper 1998: 394)

The passage seems to say that spirit will fill the body as it did at birth, but is the context ontogenic or cosmogonic? I would argue that it is both. The result is health and longevity. There follows a description of dietary constraints and breathing exercises, with the result that the form possesses a cloud-like radiance; filled with essence, it is able be long-lasting.[42] The passage ends with the injunction to:

以長為極。將欲壽神，必以腠理息。

Make long duration your ideal. If you wish to make spirit long-lived, you must breathe with the skin's webbed pattern. (MWD4, 147 (*Shiwen*), strips 36–37, Harper 1998: 396.)

It continues that "the essence of cultivating *qi* (*zhiqi zhi jing* 治氣之精) is to exit from death and enter into life"; "to fill the form (*cong xing* 充形) with this [*qi*] is called concentrating essence" (*bo jing* 摶精).[43] The problem is that essence inevitably leaks out of the body and thus must be supplemented.[44] By

---

[42] 則形有雲光。以精為充，故能久長. MWD4, 147, (*Shiwen*), strips 33–35, Harper 1998: 396.
[43] *MWD4*, 147 (*Shiwen*), strips 38–39, Harper 1998: 396.
[44] 精出必補. *MWD4*, 147 (*Shiwen*), strip 39, Harper 1998: 396.

solidifying what is below and storing up essence, the *qi* does not leak out.[45] As a result, the practitioner becomes a spirit and is liberated from form.

This "spirit flowing into form" (*shén ji liu xing* 神乃溜刑) and this procedure for filling the form with *qi* echo the cosmogonic processes described in *Fanwu liuxing*. The goal is clearly to prolong the longevity of both the spirit and the physical form through what appears to be a breath procedure. There is no suggestion that this procedure enhances the heart or the mental faculties. Here *shén* is clearly linked with the body, but not particularly with the mind.

The Mawangdui editors' text of Question 4 ends at strip 41.[46] Qiu Xigui argues from context to move strip 40 elsewhere and append a section from Question 6 (strips 52–59).[47] The appended passage introduces the heart–mind by describing a gentleman who uses it to regulate his activities:

心製死生，孰為之敗？　慎守勿失，長生累世。累世安樂長壽，長壽生於蓄積。被生之多，上察於天，下播於地，能者必神，故能形解。

When the heart–mind controls death and life, who is defeated by them? Carefully hold it and do not lose it, and long life continues across ages. For continuous ages you are peaceful and joyous, and possess longevity. Longevity is born of growth and accumulation. As for the fullness of that life: above it scans Heaven and below it spreads over Earth. One who is capable inevitably becomes a spirit, and as a result, is capable of release from form. (MWD4, 148 (*Shiwen*), strips 55–56, Harper 1998: 397–98)

The basis for this emendation is overall context, but it may have the unintended consequence of introducing a *xin* as ruler metaphor into an account of cultivating *jing* and *qi*, a context where it is otherwise absent.

Another possible link between heart–mind and spirit occurs in Question 10, where King Zhao of Qin asks Wang Qi about a technique to "suck in *qi* to achieve essence illumination" (*xi qi yi wei jingming* 吸氣以為精明). Wang Qi urges him to "make the heart–mind even like water" (*ping xin ru shui* 平

---

[45] 實下閉精，氣不漏泄. MWD4, 148 (*Shiwen*), strips 54–55, Harper 1998: 396.
[46] *MWD4*, 147 (*Shiwen*). See also Zhou Yimou and Xiao Zuotao 1988: 374–75.
[47] See Qiu Xigui 1992: 525–27. Harper's translation follows this emendation. See Harper 1998: 396–97n7.

心如水) and to "not let the heart–mind be nervous and flurried" (*xin wu chu dang* 心毋怵蕩).[48] The end result is that:

精氣淩健久長。神和內得，魂魄皇〔皇〕
Essence and *qi* are congealed, hardy and long-lasting. Spirit harmony is obtained inside; *hun* and *po* are gleaming. (MWD4, 152 (*Shiwen*), strip 100, Harper 1998: 411)

At this point we may ask whether we should read the *Shiwen* as a continuous sequence—with the implication that they ultimately connect *xin* and *shén*—or as discrete questions, where they do not. Insofar as the first four questions are all attributed to Huangdi and the remaining six to others, there seems no reason to take them as a continuous sequence.

The *Shiwen* clearly shares both vocabulary and concerns with the *Guanzi*, but does it share the monistic cosmology of the *Guanzi*? Puett argues that the *Shiwen* authors are not necessarily committed to an explicitly monistic cosmology, and seems to suggest a divide between *qi*, essence, and spirit on the one hand and "form" on the other. His argument is that, while the text is not conclusive, the argument is couched in a dualistic framework because the *Shiwen* does not clearly describe forms as unrefined *qi*, and thus as being of the same basic stuff as *qi*, essence and spirit. Question 4's account of the separation of spirit from form seems to posit an ontological distinction between spirit and material form, but that distinction is not made explicit.[49]

Other Mawangdui passages refer to *shén* or *shénming*, without reference to the heart–mind. "Conjoining Yin and Yang" (*He yinyang*) echoes the language of Question 4 of *Shiwen* with a description of a sexual technique to achieve *shénming*: "enter the dark gate, ride the coital muscle, suck the essence and spirit upward."[50] Another passage describes a sequence of movements to "penetrate spirit illumination" (*tong shénming* 通神明).[51] A third passage describes a technique whose result is that "essence and spirit enter and are deposited, then engendering spirit illumination."[52] These passages all link spirit with *qi* and yin and yang, without reference to the heart–mind.

---

[48] *MWD4*, 152 (*Shiwen*), strips 97–98, Harper 1998: 411.
[49] Puett 2002: 209–14.
[50] 入玄門，御交筋，上飲合精神. *Mawangdui Hanmu boshu 4*, 155 (*He yinyang*) strip 104, Harper 1998: 414–15.
[51] MWD4, 155 (*He yinyang*), strips 112–14, Harper 1998: 418.
[52] 精神入藏，乃生神明. MWD4, 156 (*He yinyang*), strip 133, Harper 1998: 422.

In conclusion, in most of the passages discussed above, the heart–mind and spirit are described in different contexts. In passages where *xin* refers to some kind of mental activity, accounts of mind—and its cultivation— typically focus on rites, music, and the virtues, and do not mention spirit. Accounts of spirit occur in the quite different context of accounts of the balance and regulation of *qi*, essence, and yin and yang, and do not focus on the heart–mind.

By contrast, links between the heart–mind and spirit become prevalent in medical literature from approximately the first century BCE and later, starting with the *Huangdi neijing*, which repeatedly links them. Several passages describe the heart as storing spirit (*xin zang shén* 心臟神).[53] According to another passage, the heart is the residence of *shén* and essence. When it is damaged, spirit leaves and the person dies.[54] Finally, one passage describes the heart as the source of *shénming*: "the heart is the official that acts as ruler; *shénming* originates in it."[55]

The *Huainanzi*

Several chapters of the *Huainanzi* seem to repeat arguments that are familiar from the texts considered so far: that humans and spirits have the same composition, that anthropomorphic spirits and theomorphic humans both inhabit a monistic and patterned cosmos, and that by practicing self-cultivation a person can effectively become a spirit. The *Huainanzi* reworks these themes in complex ways that bear on its accounts of mind and spirit.[56]

Yuandao

"Originating in the Way" (*Yuandao* 道原) opens with a cosmology of *dao* and *de*, not unlike the *Daodejing* and "The source of *dao*" (*Daoyuan* 道原),

---

[53] *Suwen* 23: 153 (*Xuanming wu qi* 宣明五氣) and 62: 334–35 (*Zhou jing lun* 調經論); *Lingshu* 8.2, 291(*Benshén*) and 78.5.2, 472–73; (*Jiuzhen lun* 九鍼論). For translations, see Unschuld and Tessenow, 1:409 and 2:102, respectively, and Unschuld, *Lingshu*, 152–53 and 735.

[54] LS 71.2, 447 (*Xieke* 邪客); Unschuld, *Lingshu*, 639–40.

[55] 心者，君主之官也，神明出焉. SW 8: 76–77 (*Linglan midian lun* 靈蘭秘典論); Unschuld and Tessenow, *Suwen*, 1: 155–56.

[56] For the background and nature of the *Huainanzi*, see Le Blanc 1985, Roth 1991, Major 2003, Vankeerbergen 2001, and Puett 2002. Translations of the *Huainanzi* are my own but are indebted to Major et al. 2010 and Puett 2002.

150　A TRIPARTITE SELF

one of the "*Huangdi sijing*" texts from Mawangdui. The *Huainanzi* version describes two spirits who put the cosmos to right:

泰古二皇，得道之柄，立於中央。神與化遊，以撫四方。

The two august lords of high antiquity grasped the handles of *dao* and established themselves in the center. Their spirits wandered with transformation and thereby pacified the four quarters. (*Huainanzi* 1/1/10)

In the cosmos it describes, self-cultivated adepts could control the spirits that controlled the natural forces of wind and rain, and could gain tremendous powers:

神托于秋豪之末，而大與宇宙之總。其德優天地而和陰陽，節四時而調五行。

Their spirits could concentrate [on things as minute as] the tip of an autumn hair or as great as the entirety of space and time. Their power made Heaven and Earth bountiful and harmonized yin and yang; it set the boundaries of the four seasons and regulated the Five Phases. (*Huainanzi* 1/1/13–15)

It is noteworthy that these adepts do not transcend their material bodies. They roam the universe but remain in an embodied state:

是故疾而不搖，遠而不勞，四支不動，聰明不損，而知八紘九野之形埒者，何也？執道之柄，而游於無窮之地也。

This is why they are fast but not agitated, go far but do not tire, their four limbs do not move, their keen hearing and clear sight do not diminish, and even so they understand the forms and boundaries of the eight outlying regions and the nine fields of the heavens. How can this be? By grasping hold of the handles of the Way and roaming in the lands that are without limits. (*Huainanzi* 1/2/10–11)

As Puett points out, this is a political reading of the Inner Chapters of the *Zhuangzi*, and describes a nonagonistic mode of rulership. Nonagonistic rule of this kind is ascribed to the sage-emperor Shun, who "grasped mysterious power in his heart–mind (*zhi xuan de yu xin* 執玄德於心), and his transformations so fast it was like a spirit (*ruo shén* 若神, 1/4/18–20).[57]

Here, the *Yuandao* chapter seems to accept a tradition common to the *Neiye* and *Huangdi neijing* that takes *qi* as the fundamental source, viewing the physical body, *qi*, and spirit as the formative elements of a human being. It stresses the need to keep all of them properly aligned:

夫形者，生之所也；氣者，生之元也；神者，生之制其也。一失位，則三者傷矣。

The form is the residence of life; *qi* is the origin of life; spirit is the governor of life. If [even] one loses its place, then [all] three are harmed. (*Huainanzi* 1/9/15–16)

Therefore, sages thus ensure that each keeps to its appropriate position, maintains its own function, and does not interfere with the others. The passage continues:

故夫形者非其所安也而處之則廢，氣不當其所充〔也〕而用之則泄，神非其所宜〔也〕而行之則昧。此三者，不可不慎守也。

If the form dwells where it is not safe it will be destroyed, if [the use of] *qi* does not match what replenishes it, it will drain away. If spirit acts in a manner it ought not, it will become benighted. These three must be guarded attentively. (*Huainanzi* 1/9/16–18)

It is only possible for people to see and hear clearly, maintain the weight of their physical bodies, and make perceptual and moral judgments because *qi* fills their bodies and spirit directs them.[58]

These passages emphasize that spirit must control the form, and the form must provide a lodging place for spirit:

故以神為主者，形從而利；以形為制者，神從而害。

Thus, if one takes spirit as the master, the form will follow and will benefit. If one takes the form as controlling, spirit will follow and be harmed. (*Huainanzi* 1/10/3)

---

[57] See Major et al. 2010: 59, Puett 264–65.
[58] 氣為之充而神為之使也. *Huainanzi* 1/9/22–23.

As a result, over time, essence and spirit are depleted. Eventually, "the form closes its openings and spirit has nowhere to enter."[59]

Here, spirit-like theomorphic humans have control over the natural phenomena of the cosmos, but—unlike the *Neiye*—that control is spontaneous, effortless, and nonagonistic: "Therefore sages nourish their spirits, harmonize and soften their *qi*, and pacify their forms, and so submerge, float, and turn downwards and upwards along with *dao*.[60] They are as comfortable in it as if taking off clothes, but when they use it, it is like shooting a crossbow. In this way they welcome all transformations and respond to all matters.[61]

Several chapters of the *Huainanzi* seem to repeat arguments that are familiar from the texts we have considered so far: that humans and spirits have the same composition, that both anthropomorphic spirits and theomorphic humans inhabit a monistic and patterned cosmos, and that by practicing self-cultivation a person can effectively become a spirit. The *Huainanzi* reworks these themes in complex ways that bear on its accounts of mind and spirit.

Jingshén

Chapter 7, "Essence and Spirit" (*Jingshén* 精神), is a detailed account of the compound of essence and spirit.[62] Like *Taiyi sheng shui*, it begins with a cosmogony in which the cosmos emerges spontaneously, but two spirits—who also emerge spontaneously—align, plan, and orient it. It then moves to an account of the origin and nature of the bodies, minds, and spirits of human beings, which are composed of refined *qi*. All three are described in a typology of *qi* (in various forms and densities), but also in terms of their complex interrelationships.

精神〔者〕，天之有也；而骨體者，地之有也。精神入其門，而骨體反其根，我尚何存？

Essence and spirit are of Heaven, and the bones and frame are of Earth. When essence and spirit enter [Heaven's] gate, and bones and frame return to their [Earth] roots, how can I still survive? (*Huainanzi* 7/54/27–28, *Jingshén*)

---

[59] 形閉中距，則神無由入矣. *Huainanzi* 1/10/4–5.
[60] 是故聖人將養其神，和弱其氣，平夷其形，而與道沈浮俯仰. *Huainanzi* 1/10/8–9.
[61] 如是，則萬物之化無不遇，而百事之變無不應. *Huainanzi* 1/10/10.
[62] There is a difference of opinion on how to understand this term. For Essence and Spirit, see Puett 2002. For Quintessential Spirit, see Major et al. 2010.

Here, the goal of self-cultivation seems to be to keep them together as long as possible because the combination of essence and spirit (*jingshén*) is the basis of both the body and consciousness, as well as the basis of sagehood. The passage goes on to identify both tranquility and *dao* with spirit illumination: "stillness and vastness are the dwelling of *shénmíng*; emptiness and lack of differentiation are where *dao* resides."[63] Taken together, these passages link *shénmíng* with both stillness and Heaven.

The chapter then turns to the origins of both spirit and the body in the context of the development of the human embryo:

夫精神者，所受於天也；而形體者，所稟於地也。故曰：「一生二，二生三，三生萬物。萬物背陰而抱陽，沖氣以為和。」故曰一月而膏

Essence and Spirit is what we receive from Heaven; the form and frame is what we are given by Earth. Therefore it is said: "The one generates the two; the two generate the three; the three generate the myriad things. The myriad things carry yin on their backs, embrace yang and, through the blending of *qi* become harmonious." (*Huainanzi* 7/55/7–8)

In this passage, when the one generates the two and generates the myriad things, the monistic cosmos divides and generates yin and yang, which in turn constitute the human embryo. As Puett points out, this is a very different ontogeny from that of the *Shiwen* or *Fanwu liuxing*. Here, spirit does not flow into form; rather, the process of birth and development is a process of *qi* gradually acquiring differentiated physical form. As a result, the person that emerges from ontogeny is fundamental composed of both physical form and spirit. Ontogeny culminates in the formation of the *zang* viscera:

十月而生。形體以成，五藏乃形，是故肺主目，腎主鼻，膽主口，肝主耳。

In the tenth month, birth occurs. In this way, the form and frame are thus complete, and the five *zang* viscera take form. Therefore, the lungs govern the eyes; the kidneys govern the nose; the gall bladder governs

---

[63] 夫靜漠者，神明之宅也；虛無者，道之所居也. *Huainanzi* 7/55/4.

the mouth; the liver governs the ears; and the spleen governs the tongue. (*Huainanzi* 7/55/9–10).[64]

This account derives significant portions of the body from Heaven and is explicit about the analogies between the human microcosm and a cosmic macrocosm:

故頭之圓也象天，足之方也象地。天有四時、五行、九解、三百六十六日，人亦有四支、五藏、九竅、三百六十六節。天有風雨寒暑，人亦有取與喜怒。故膽為雲，肺為氣，肝為風，腎為雨，脾為雷，以與天地相參也，而心為之主。

Therefore, the head is round like Heaven, the feet are square like Earth. Heaven has four seasons, five phases, nine points, and 366 days. Humans also have four limbs, five repositories, nine orifices, and 366 joints. Heaven has wind, rain, cold, and heat; humans also have taking, giving, happiness, and anger. Therefore, the gall bladder is clouds, the lungs are *qi*, the liver is wind, the kidneys are rain, and the spleen is thunder. They thereby form a triad with Heaven and Earth. but the heart–mind is the master. (*Huainanzi* 7/55/11–14).

This microcosm–macrocosm analogy emphasizes the concern of the chapter: how to maintain the alignment of both the human body and the cosmos: "Therefore blood and *qi* are the flowering of humanity, and the five *zang* viscera are the essence of humanity."[65] As a result, the ability to concentrate blood and *qi* in the five *zang* viscera is of the greatest importance.[66] It results in the reduction of desires and clarity of perception:

五藏能屬於心而無乖，則淫志勝而行不僻矣。淫志勝而行不僻，則精神盛而氣不散矣。精神盛而氣不散則理，理則均，均則通，通則神，神則以視無不見〔也〕，以聽無不聞也，以為無不成也。

If the five *zang* viscera can be subordinated to the heart–mind, and their functioning is without error, distracted attention will be overcome and

---

[64] See Puett 2002: 272–84, to which the following discussion is indebted.
[65] 是故血氣者，人之華也；而五藏者，人之精也。*Huainanzi* 7/55/19–20.
[66] 血氣能專於五藏。*Huainanzi* 7/55/20.

the movement [of *qi*] will not be awry. When distracted attention is overcome and the movement [of *qi*] is not awry, then Essence and Spirit will be abundant and *qi* will not dissipate. When Essence and Spirit are abundant and *qi* does not dissipate, you will be patterned. When you are patterned, you become well balanced. When you are well balanced, you become penetrating. When you are penetrating, you become a spirit. A spirit, your vision has nothing unseen, your hearing has nothing unheard, and your actions have nothing incomplete. (*Huainanzi* 7/55/21–24)

In other words, according with the underlying patterns of the cosmos literally makes one a spirit, which implies neither transcendence nor control over nature per se. What this does require is to prevent essence from dissipating and spirit from leaving the body.

夫孔竅者，精神之戶牖也；而(氣志) [血氣]者，五藏之使候也。耳目淫于聲色之樂，則五藏搖動而不定矣。五藏搖動而不定，則血氣滔蕩而不休矣。血氣滔蕩而不休，則精神馳騁於外而不守矣。

Now, the orifices [of the body] are the doors and windows of Essence and Spirit, and *qi* and will are the followers of the five *zang* viscera. If the ears and eyes are enticed by the pleasures of sound and color, the five *zang* viscera will sway and will not be settled. If the Five *zang* viscera sway and are not settled, blood and *qi* overflow and do not stop. If blood and *qi* overflow and do not stop, Essence and Spirit rush to the outside and are not preserved. (*Huainanzi* 7/55/27—7/56/2)

By contrast, the passage continues, one who can settle the five *zang* viscera and preserve essence and *qi* within the body can witness both past and future. As Puett points out, ironically, a generally Zhuangzian cosmology is being appropriated to argue that the sage does possess control over aspects of the cosmos. But it is a form of control very different from that advocated by other texts such as the *Neiye*.

The "Essence and Spirit" chapter then presents a strongly contrasting picture, not of the sage, but of the Perfected Person (*zhenren* 真人). Such persons "embody the foundation and embrace their spirits in order to wander in the confines of Heaven and Earth" (7/57/11). They forget their five *zang* viscera and lose their bodies (7/57/15–16). Like the *Zhuangzi*'s spirit person, they are oblivious, and allow their spirits to roam free:

同精於太清之本，而游於忽區之旁 。有精而不使者，有神而不(行)[用]，... 居而無容，處而無所，其動無形，其靜無體，存而若亡，生而若死，出入無間，役使鬼神

They share essence with the root of great clarity, and so they wander beyond the boundless. They possess essence but do not give it orders; they possess spirit but do not move it. . . . At rest they have no likeness, in place they have no location, in movement they have no form, in stillness they have no frame. They are present but absent; they are alive but seem to be dead; they emerge from and enter what has no dimension, and use ghosts and spirits as their servants. (*Huainanzi* 7/57/21–22 and 7/57/24–7/58/1)

So for Perfected Persons, spirit is not so much liberated from the body as unaffected by it:

故形有摩而神未嘗化者，以不化應化，千變萬抮而未始有極。

Thus, although the form disappears, the spirit is never transformed, and if you use what does not transform to respond to transformation, even a thousand transformations and ten thousand alternations will not begin to reach a limit. (*Huainanzi* 7/58/6–7)

Perfected Persons thus coexist with Heaven and Earth in the same correct alignment that was originally created by the spirits. As Puett observes, the understanding of the sage in "Essence and Spirit" is probably indebted to texts like the *Neiye*, interpreted in a broadly Zhuangzian framework.

Here, the cosmos is set up by the primordial spirits, so it needs spirits to be properly aligned. But they do this spontaneously and out of their natures, not in order to impose their will on the cosmos. As microcosms of the cosmos, humans have spirit, and when they practice self-cultivation and become like spirits; they also engage in a spontaneous connection with the patterns of the cosmos. In other words, "Essence and Spirit" claims that its self-cultivation methods can link a realized person with the patterns of the universe; and this connection is made through the correct cultivation and alignment of both body and spirit. For both sages and the Perfected, it is important to be patterned in this way because the patterns were originally established by the spirits, following their own inherent natures. So the more spirit-like one becomes, the more spontaneously one follows these patterns.

Conclusion

We can trace a different awareness of the relation of the body and spirit through several stages. First, awareness of the body as an important site of "self-care" first appears in the fourth-century doctrines ascribed to Yang Zhu. Yangist doctrines emphasized the need to protect one's physical person by avoiding dangerous attractions such as the allure of wealth and status.

The *Neiye* and "Arts of the Mind" chapters of the *Guanzi* focus on a different aspect of self-cultivation: the development of internal spirit, including the role of the body in that development. Crucial to that development is essence (*jing*), which the *Neiye* positions as the basis of physical human life, the root of sagacity, and common to both human spirit and external spirits. In the process of lodging and refining essence in order to create spirit, the heart–mind serves as an intermediary by aligning the senses and providing a lodging place for essence. The *Neiye* describes spirit as naturally present in the embodied person (*shēn*), but by nature something that comes and goes. It is only stabilized by a combination of correct alignment of the embodied person and the stabilizing activity of a settled heart–mind. Once settled, spirit and spirit illumination naturally align the senses. As a result, the adept becomes "like a spirit."

The *Neiye* makes the heart–mind an essential part of the self-cultivation—or self-divinization—process. In the *Zhuangzi*, by contrast, it is an obstacle to self-cultivation. Various *Zhuangzi* chapters underline the need to both "concentrate spirit" (*shénning*) and "fast the heart–mind" (*xinzhai*). Other passages praise "spirit people" (*shénren*) and reiterate the importance of spirit—but never the heart–mind—to the exercise of the high-order skills that characterize the "skill stories" of the Outer Chapters, especially.

The *Shiwen* prominently uses the language of essence, *qi* and spirit, but in the context of self-cultivation and longevity practices rather than the treatment of illness. Its focus is longevity techniques and cultivating spirit illumination, but it also describes procedures for cultivating *qi* to concentrate essence. But unlike similar passages in the *Guanzi*, the heart–mind has

158　A TRIPARTITE SELF

no involvement in these procedures, most of which are breathing or sexual techniques.

The *Huainanzi* reworks these arguments in different ways, especially in the first (*Yuandao*) and seventh (*Jingshén*) chapters. Both present a cosmos populated by anthropomorphic spirits and theomorphic humans who have mastered self-cultivation techniques. The first chapter, like the *Neiye*, understands the physical body, *qi*, and spirit as formative elements of a person, all of which must be properly aligned. Here the lodging place for spirit is the body, not the heart–mind. The seventh chapter frames the human body as a microcosm of the cosmos and focuses on the nature of essence and spirit as the Heaven-derived components of a person. In particular, it focuses on the necessity to and means of using self-cultivation practices to keep essence and spirit together in a process that only incidentally involves the heart–mind.

5
Body, Mind, and Spirit in the Guodian Manuscripts

This chapter considers the relationship between body, mind, and spirit as described in the Guodian corpus. A significant body of research has already been done on moral psychology in the Guodian, and considerable scholarship on these texts investigates their specifically Confucian history.[1] Here I address the treatment in several Guodian texts of interrelations between body and mind, especially how they affect each other and the place of the Guodian material in the broader context of debates about mind–body dualism.

Three important themes concerning body and mind recur in the Guodian manuscripts overall. First are accounts of the constituents of both humans and animals, specifically discussions of the nature of the body or physical person, basic emotions (*qing* 情), and the mind.[2] Second is a discussion of the nature of specifically human mental qualities, especially the heart–mind, spirit, and intentions or will. Spirit is discussed in "The Great One Gives Birth to Water" (*Taiyi sheng shui* 太一生水). A related and third important theme—accounts of mutual relations between mind and body—deals with both how the body, and with it the emotions, affect the mind and how the heart–mind directs or rules the body. Discussions of how the body affects the mind appear in "Honoring Virtue and Propriety" (*Zundeyi* 尊德義) and more extensively in "Human Nature Comes from the Mandate" (*Xingzi mingchu* 性自命出), which contains an extensive discussion of how the body and emotions affect the heart–mind. Accounts of how the heart–mind rules the body appear in "Black Robes" (*Ziyi* 緇衣) and more extensively in "Five Kinds of Action" (*Wuxing* 五行). Additional relevant passages are found in "Poverty or Success Is a Matter of Timing" (*Qiongda yishi* 窮達以時),

---

[1] Chan 2009b, 2011, 2012, 2019; Csikszentmihalyi 2005; Pang Pu 2000–2001.
[2] Due to an extensive debate about the meaning of the term *qing* 情 (Puett 2004, Middendorf 2008 among others), I transliterate rather than translate this term throughout.

"The Way of Tang and Yu" (*Tang Yu zhi dao* 唐虞之道), "Bringing Things to Completion" (*Chengzhi* 成之), "Six Virtues" (*Liude* 六德), and four texts titled "Thicket of Sayings" 1–4 (*Yucong* 語叢). The *Xingzi mingchu*, *Wuxing* (discussed in this chapter) and other Guodian texts have equivalents in texts excavated from other Warring States and Han tombs, but these are beyond the scope of the present discussion.[3]

We find a scale of views on the relation between mind and body in the Guodian texts. The *Xingzi mingchu* in particular presents weak mind–body dualism, in apparent differences between the body's passive response to sensation and emotion, and the capacity of the mind to use active agency to control those responses, especially through thinking or reflection (*si* 思).

At one end of the scale is a strong mind–body dualism in several passages in *Wuxing* ("Five Kinds of Action") and *Ziyi* ("Black Robes"). These texts present metaphors that compare the heart–mind to the ruler of a state and the body or the senses to its ministers or officials or to slaves. At the other end of the spectrum is a robustly holist view of *qi* as unifying body and mind. Here, similarities between the "flow" of *qi*, sound, and music are the conduit that makes possible moral transformation through music.

The first section takes up several passages from the Guodian manuscripts that describe relations between body, mind and emotions as constituents of both humans and animals. These passages make it clear that animals, as well as human beings have *qi*, *qing*, and intentions. However, the potential ability of the heart–mind to interact with *qing* and intentions seems to be unique to humans. For humans, our essential nature (*xing* 性) affects fundamental emotions (*qing*), which in turn move the heart–mind.

The next section discusses Guodian accounts of the constitution of a (human) person, including the body or physical person and its relationship to heart–mind, virtue, and self-cultivation. The third section takes up an extensive discussion of the relation between body and mind in the *Xingzi mingchu* and *Wuxing*. The fourth section turns to the strong dualism of ruler–ruled metaphors in the *Wuxing* and *Ziyi*; and a strongly holist view of sound and music in the *Xingzi mingchu* and elsewhere.

---

[3] The Shanghai Museum texts include a version of the *Xingzi mingchu* titled "Discussion of Qing and Xing" (*Xingqing lun* 性情論, Ma Chengyuan 2001, Ji Xusheng 2004). Another version of the *Wuxing* was excavated from Mawangdui (*Mawangdui Hanmu boshu* 1980: 17–27, Csikszentmihalyi 2004: 312–71).

Body, Emotion, and Heart–Mind in Humans and Animals

Several passages from the Guodian manuscripts describe the relations between the bodies, minds, and emotions of humans and other animals. A passage from the *Yucong* ("Thicket of Sayings") describes the constitution of humans and animals as follows:

凡有血氣者，皆有喜有怒，有慎有莊，其體有容有色，有聲有嗅有味，有氣有志。物有本有卯[4]，有終有始。

In general, all things that have blood and *qi* have happiness and anger, caution and gravity. Their frames have appearance and color, they have sounds, smells and flavors, they have *qi* and intentions. In all cases living things have roots and branches; they have ends and beginnings. (*Guodian Chumu, Yucong* 1, strips 45–49)

The important reference to "all things that have blood and *qi*" (*you xueqi zhe* 有血氣者) makes it clear that the passage does not limit itself to human beings, since "blood and *qi*" is common to humans and other animals.[5] The passage also shows that, in addition to shared physical constitution, humans share three things with other animals: (1) fundamental emotions and desires—the basic emotions of joy and anger and the basic responses to desire of satisfaction (when desires are satisfied) and suffering (when they are not); (2) the four sensory modalities of sight, hearing, smell, and taste; and (3) *qi* and intentions.

Although the above passages affirm that emotions and desires are common to "all things that have blood and *qi*," a passage in the *Xingzi mingchu* suggests that a complex relation to the heart–mind seems unique to humans:

道四術，唯人道為可道也。其三術者，道之而已。詩、書、禮、樂，其始出皆生於人。

Dao has four arts, but only the human *dao* is worthy to take; as for the [other] three arts, if you take them, that is all. The beginning and emergence of the

---

[4] After Li Tianhong (2003) and Cook's (2012, 2:814–15) reading of the character 峜 as *ben* 本 (root) and 卯 as *biao* 標 (branches). For simplicity of transcription, I have incorporated the Guodian editors' emendations, primarily based on Liu Zhao 2003.

[5] Raphals 2018, Sterckx 2007.

Odes, Documents, Ritual, and *Music* all were from the human. (*Guodian Chumu, Xingzi mingchu,* strips 14–16)

This point is explicit in a second *Yucong* I passage that identifies the intentions with the heart–mind:

容色，目司也。聲，耳司也。嗅，鼻司也。味，口司也。氣，容司也。志，心司。

Appearance and color are a matter of the eyes, sound is a matter of the ears, smell is a matter of the nose, flavor is a matter of the mouth. *Qi* is a matter of appearance, intentions are a matter of the heart–mind. (*Guodian Chumu, Yucong 1,* strips 50–52)

It is important to note that this passage does not specifically refer to humans, insofar as animals also have intentions. However, the reference to appearance or demeanor (*rong* 容) probably does indicate that the passage is intended to describe humans, though the notion that animals can have demeanor will be instantly familiar to anyone who has ever lived with a cat.

A third passage from *Yucong* 3 emphasizes the specific importance of the heart–mind:

縱志，益。存心，益。

To raise oneself by intentions is advantageous. To care for one's heart–mind is advantageous. (*Guodian Chumu, Yucong 3,* strip 15)

Taken together, these passages suggest that it is the heart–mind that can take charge of the perceptions, emotions, and desires common to all animals, and to cultivate it is beneficial.

The Human Constitution

Passages in several Guodian texts underscore the importance of the body and give passing accounts of the *shēn* person and its relationship to the heart–mind, virtue, and self-cultivation. "Black Robes" (*Ziyi*) makes it clear that a "person" is in some fundamental sense material and physical, when it states that: in antiquity, the Lord in Heaven observed King Wen's virtue and concentrated the great mandate upon his person (*shēn*, strips 36–37). According to *Taiyi sheng shui*, those who use *dao* to carry things are successful in their tasks and are long-lived in their persons (*shēn chang* 身長); in the case of sages, their achievements are successful and their persons are not injured (*shēn bu shang* 身不傷, strips 11–12). Another passage in "Honoring Virtue and Propriety" (*Zundeyi*) describes how the body affects the mind and emphasizes the porosity of the two. According to this text, ritual and music: "nurture the heart-mind (*yangxin*) in compassion and integrity, so that faithfulness and trust increase daily without any self-awareness (*zizhi* 自知, strip 21).

That a "person" is both physical and psychological is made clear in a discussion of the virtue of benevolence (*ren* 仁). "The Way of Tang and Yu" (*Tang Yu zhi dao*) concludes with the observation that: "when one insists on rectifying one's person (*zheng qi shēn* 正其身) before rectifying the world, the *dao* of sages is complete" (strips 2–3). This passage, used purely of a physical person, could refer to straightening one's body, but that is clearly not the meaning here. Similarly, another passage from "Bringing Things to Completion" (*Chengzhi*) describes the governance and instruction of a gentleman who before undertaking oversight of the people first "submits his person to goodness" (*shēn bao shan* 身服善, strip 3). The passage continues: if he "lacks it in his person" (*wang hu qi shēn* 亡乎其身) and merely preserves it in words, the people will not follow him, no matter how much he piles up commands (strips 4–5). This discussion opposes the use of punishments and penalties to government by virtue and specifically by those who *embody* virtue in their persons.

The term *ti* is also applied to the bodies—and powers—of animals. For example, "Poverty or Success is a Matter of Timing" (*Qiongda yishi*) includes an argument that excellence—moral or physical—does not necessarily result in recognition. Thus, the meritorious Wu Zixu (d. 484 BCE) was executed but not because his wisdom had declined. The passage concludes with the bodies of two famous horses: "That Ji was hobbled at Mount Zhang and Jin was trapped in the Qiu wilds was not because they had declined in the strength of their frames."[6]

Several passages discuss the will or intentions, usually of a gentleman or *junzi*. For example, "Black Robes" (*Ziyi*) attributes a saying to Confucius that a gentleman "cannot be robbed of his intentions in life and cannot be robbed

---

[6] 驥駒張山騹窒於卲筌, 非亡體壯也. *Guodian Chumu, Qiongda yishi*, strips 9–10. Textual problems surround the names and provenance of these famous horses, but the context is clearly a comparison between their inherent strength and being subdued.

of his good name in death" (strip 38). *Wuxing* explicitly links intentions with correct mental attitudes: "A scholar whose intentions are on the *dao* of a gentleman can be called a scholar of intentions.[7] The passage continues by linking intentions to wisdom: "Virtue without intention will not be realized; wisdom without reflection will not get it."[8] Another passage from "Six Virtues" (*Liude*) suggests that intentions transcend individual will and the individual person who "hides his own will and seeks to nourish the intentions of his family."[9]

Spirit in the Guodian Manuscripts

Spirit is not a significant term in the Guodian texts overall.

An exception is "The Great One Gives Birth to Water" (*Taiyi sheng shui*), where spirit illumination (*shénmíng*) is a central term. Spirit illumination is formed from the consecutive joinings of The Great One (Taiyi), Heaven and Earth. Spirit illumination in turn forms yin and yang, which in turn form the four seasons:

太一生水，水反輔太一，是以成天。天反輔太一，是以成地。天地復相輔也，是以成神明。神明復相輔也，是以成陰陽。陰陽復相輔也，是以成四時。

The Great One gave birth to water. Water returns to join with the Great One, and they thereby complete Heaven. Heaven returns to join with the Great One, and they thereby complete Earth. Heaven and Earth return and join with each other and thereby complete *Shén* and *Ming*. *Shén* and *Ming* return and join with each other and thereby complete yin and yang. Yin and yang return and join with each other and thereby complete the four seasons. (*Guodian Chumu, Taiyi sheng shui*, strips 1–2)

Thus:

四時者，陰陽者之所生也。 陰陽者，神明之所生也。 神明者，天地之所生也。 天地者，太一之所生也。

---

[7] 士有志於君子道謂之志士. *Guodian Chumu, Wuxing*, strip 7.
[8] 德弗之志不成，智弗思不得. *Guodian Chumu, Wuxing*, strips 7–8.
[9] 逸其志，求養新之志. *Guodian Chumu, Liude*, strip 33.

The four seasons are what is born from yin and yang. Yin and yang are what is born from *shén* and *míng*; *shén* and *míng* are what is born from Heaven and Earth; Heaven and Earth are what is born from the Great One. (*Guodian Chumu, Taiyi sheng shui*, strips 4–6)

Several other points are noteworthy about this cosmogony. It all arises from Taiyi, and Heaven is part of the process rather than its apex. The complementary entities, *shén* and *míng*, are born from The Great One via Heaven and Earth, and they precede even the creation of yin and yang.[10] Finally, this occurrence of *shén* and *míng* is distinctive in the Guodian texts.

The only other time the terms *shén* and *míng* appear together in the Guodian manuscripts is in "The *Dao* of Tang and Yu" (*Tang Yu zhi dao* 唐虞之道):

古者堯生於天子而有天下，聖以遇命，仁以逢時，未嘗遇〔不明〕並於大時，神明均從，天地佑之。縱仁，聖可與，時弗可及矣。

In antiquity, when Yao arose [was born] to be the Son of Heaven and possessed the world, he received his mandate with sagacity and met his time with humanity. Before he ever received [his mandate and] stood together with the great times, the spirit intelligences were [set] to favor him, and Heaven and Earth assisted him. (*Guodian Chumu, Tang Yu zhi dao*, strips 14–15, cf. Cook 2012, 2: 559–60)

Here, *shénming* seems to refer to a high degree of wisdom or cognition associated with internal spirit, or with the powers of external spirits.[11] It appears to be interchangeable with *shén*, in possible contrast to the above passage from *Taiyi sheng shui*.[12]

---

[10] There is considerable disagreement about whether and how to associate *shén* with Heaven and *míng* with Earth in this passage. Wang Bo (2004: 273–76) suggests that they refer to the sun and the moon, respectively. Li Ling (2002: 36–38) is in partial agreement but notes the variability of the term (discussed above). Pang Pu (2000: 194–95) takes *míng*, not as the sun or moon, but as the essence of light: in its function of cultivating all things, it is also known as *shénming*. For discussion, see Allan 2000: 524–32; Li Ling 1999: 317–18; Robinet 1999; and Wang Bo 2001: 220.

[11] An example of the former is a statement in the *Guoyu* 國語 (Tales of the States) that the spirit illumination (*shénming*) of King Wuding was such that, despite his sageliness and wisdom, he still considered his rule incomplete and pondered the Way for three years 昔殷武丁能聳其德，至于神明，以入于河，自河徂亳，於是乎三年默以思道. *Guoyu* 17 (Chu 1.8), 554. The Shang dynasty King Wu Ding 武丁 reigned from 1324–1266 BCE.

[12] Additional cases are discussed in Chapter 1.

Heart–Mind and Body in the *Xingzi Mingchu*

I now turn to how the body motivates the heart–mind and how the heart–mind rules the body. The *Xingzi mingchu* is significant for any discussion of mind and body because it provides a detailed discussion of the relationship between human nature and self-cultivation. In this context, it discusses and links several key concepts, including *xing* 性 (essential nature), *qing* (genuine emotions), *xin* (heart–mind), *zhi* (will, intentions), *qi*, and the use of artifice (*qiao* 巧, *wei* 偽).

The *Xingzi mingchu* includes both accounts of human motivation as a passive response to external forces and the active role of the heart–mind in shaping responses to the world by forming stable intention that override the influence of external forces and emotional responses to them (Perkins 2009).

A "Body Moves Mind" Model of Human Motivation

The *Xingzi mingchu* begins with a statement about clearly human (and not animal) nature and the importance of both environment and habit:

> 凡人雖有性，心無定志，待物而後作，待悅而後行，待習而後定。喜怒哀悲之氣，性也。及其見於外，則物取之也。性自命出，命自天降。

> In general, although people have a nature, their heart–minds do not have fixed intentions. They await things and only then act; they await pleasure and only then go; they await habit and only then stabilize. The *qi* of happiness, anger, grief, and sorrow is by nature. When it arises and is visible externally, things take hold of it. Nature emerges from the mandate; the mandate descends from Heaven. (*Guodian Chumu, Xingzi mingchu*, strips 1–3)

Here, fixed intentions emerge only when they are taken in hand because it is the nature of the intentions of the heart–mind (*xin zhi zhi* 心之志) to act only when induced. In other words, on this account, the heart–mind is passive. But the passage continues:

> 道始於情，情生於性。始者近情，終者近義。知【情者能】出之，知義者能入之。好惡，性也。所好所惡，物也。善不【善，性也】所善所不善，勢也。

Dao begins in *qing*; *qing* is born from nature. Its beginning is close to *qing*, but its ends are close to propriety. Those who understand [*qing*, are able] to make it emerge; those who understand propriety are able to incorporate it. Liking and disliking are matters of nature; what is liked or disliked are matters of things. Approval and disapproval are matters of nature; what is approved and not approved are matters of situational power. (*Guodian Chumu, Xingzi mingchu*, strips 3–5)

This passage indicates two ways in which mental dispositions potentially influence the body. First, *dao* is closely linked to basic emotions, which may be subject to intervention or control. Second, although what we like and dislike may be a matter of external objects (things), perceived through sensation, what we choose to approve and disapprove are matters of choice through situational power and advantage (*shi* 勢). The passage continues:

凡性為主，物取之也。金石之有聲，【也，弗扣 不鳴】。雖有性，心弗取不出。凡心有志也，無與不【可。心之不可】獨行，猶口之不可獨言也。

In general, nature acts as lord, and things take hold of it. The sounds of bronze [bells] and stone [chimes] [emerge only when they are struck.] Although [humans] have natures and heart–minds, if nothing takes hold [of them] they do not emerge. In general, heart–minds have intentions, but they forget them and do not act. [That the heart–mind cannot] act alone is like the mouth alone being unable to speak. (*Guodian Chumu, Xingzi mingchu*, strips 5–7)

This fragmentary passage clearly describes a heart–mind that requires external stimulation through the body. The passage continues that people have a common nature (*qi xing yi* 其性一) but differ in how they use their heart–minds:

四海之內其性一也。其用心各異，教使然也。凡性或動之，或逆[13]之，或交之，或礪之，或出之，或養之，或長之。凡動性者，物也；逢/逆性者，悅也；交性者，故也；礪性者，義也；出性者，勢也；養性者，習也；長性者，道也。

---

[13] Reading 逨 as *ni* 逆 (oppose), after Huang and Xu 1999, Li Ling 2002, and others. *Guodian Chumu* glosses it as 逢(?). For further discussion, see Cook 2012, 2: 705n61.

168 A TRIPARTITE SELF

> Within the four seas their nature is one. But in their use of the heart–mind each is different, and this is due to the direction of their education. As for inner nature in general, some things move it, some go against it, some restrain it, some sharpen it, some make it emerge, some nourish it, some grow it. In general, what causes inner nature to move is things; what goes against it is pleasure; what restrains it causes/precedents; what sharpens it is rightness; what makes it emerge is circumstance; what nourishes it is practice; what grows it is *dao*. (*Guodian Chumu, Xingzi mingchu*, strips 9–12)

In this scale, sages (*sheng ren* 聖人) have a key role because of their ability to literally embody correct values:

聖人比其類而論會之，觀其先後而逆順之，體其義而節文之，

> The sages compared their categories and arranged and assembled them; observed their precedence and deference and put them in conformity, embodied propriety in their frames, and gave it regularity and pattern. (*Guodian Chumu, Xingzi mingchu*, strips 16–17)

Franklin Perkins (2009: 119) describes this as a simple stimulus-response model of human psychology and motivation, but a somewhat different approach is to examine relations between body and mind, especially the *Xingzi mingchu*'s emphasis on sensation as the "stimulus" by which the body influences the heart–mind.

The Heart–Mind Takes Charge

The passages discussed above suggest an outer-inner porosity in which, without fixed nature or intentions, the complex of the body, sensations, and emotions all move the heart mind, with no account of any agency in choosing how to respond to sensory and emotional stimuli. But other passages in the *Xingzi mingchu* suggest the existence of a more authentic heart–mind that is not at the mercy of these patterns.

One passage recommends use of the heart–mind in thinking (*si zhi yong xin* 思之用心) as an alternative to the heart–mind being buffeted constantly by the inputs of the body and emotions, but even here, its relation to thought is complex:

凡憂思而後悲，凡樂思而後忻。凡思之用心為甚。難[14]，思之方也。其聲變則【心從之矣。】其心變則其聲亦然。

In general, it is only after thinking that worry becomes sorrow; in general, it is only after thinking that happiness becomes delight. In general, use of the heart–mind in thinking is deep. The difficulty is in the directions of thinking. When the sound changes, [then the heart–mind changes], when the heart–mind changes, then the sound also changes. (*Guodian Chumu, Xingzi mingchu*, strips 31–33)

Here, dwelling on emotions intensifies them. The passage also presents something of a "chicken and egg" problem in that emotions (described in terms of sound, either music or the human voice) affect the heart–mind, which affects them in return.

Other passages underscore the importance of the activity of the heart–mind: "As for *dao* in general, the techniques of the heart–mind rule."[15]

凡學者求[16]其心為難，從其所為，近得之矣，不如以樂之速也。

As for learning in general, seeking the [genuine] heart–mind is difficult. It is by following that which is done that one comes close to getting it, it is not like using the speed [immediacy] of music. (*Guodian Chumu, Xingzi mingchu*, strip 36)

This passage clearly recommends a heart–mind that, although difficult to access and less directly available than the influence of music, is more genuine and thus preferable. It draws on earlier accounts of the potential of music to elevate or degenerate the moral faculties, but it does not pursue the issue at length. The passage continues:

---

[14] I follow the *Guodian Chumu* editors' reading of *nan* 難. See Cook 2012, 2: 723n211 for other readings.
[15] 凡道，心術為主. *Guodian Chumu, Xingzi mingchu*, strip 14.
[16] For 甾 for 求 see Qiu Xigui 1998: 183n35.

雖能其事，不能其心，不貴。求其心有偽[17] 也，弗得之矣。人之不能以偽也，可知也。

Although you may be able to [accomplish] an undertaking, if you cannot [attain] the heart-mind, it is not valuable. If in searching for the heart-mind there is artifice, you will not attain it. [Thus] that people cannot [attain it] by using artifice is [something] we can know. (*Guodian Chumu, Xingzi mingchu*, strips 37–38)

How then, according to the *Xingzi mingchu*, is this difficult state to be attained? One passage gives a clear negative recommendation: that artifice (*wei*) is incompatible with the genuine heart-mind.[18]

The passage continues by contrasting different components of a person on which one might rely in a descending scale that gives preference to the heart-mind:

凡用心之躁者，思為甚。用智之疾者，患為甚。用情之至者，哀樂為甚。用身之弁者，悅為甚。用力之盡者，利為甚。目之好色，耳之樂聲，鬱陶之氣也，人不難為之死。

In general, for those who use the agitation of the heart-mind, their thinking is deep. For those who use the speed of knowledge, their anxiety is deep. For those who use the extremity of their *qing*, their grief and happiness are deep. Of those who use the agitation of their persons, their satisfaction is deep. Of those who use the limit of their force, their benefit is deep. The eyes' love of color and the ears' love of sound create unassuaged joy or anxiety. It is not difficult for people to die of this. (*Guodian Chumu, Xingzi mingchu*, strips 42–44)[19]

The passage contrasts those who rely on thinking and knowledge with those who rely on emotion and the sensations and physical force of the

---

[17] Clear consensus reads 為 as *wei* 偽, artifice. Slip 38 is broken after 可知也, and scholars disagree about what to interpolate. I follow Liu Zhao (2003: 90, 100) and Cook (2012, 2: 727–28nn241–44) in reading *bu*. Qiu Xigui (1998: 183n39) interpolates 其 ("if one commits the transgression ten times").

[18] The remainder of slip 360 contains several textual problems but seems to indicate that with no more than ten tries, the heart-mind must lie therein (其心必在焉), and its manifestations can be examined.

[19] Qiu Xigui (1998: 183n42) reads *bian* 弁 as *bian* 變 (erratic); Chen Wei (2002: 204) reads *ji* 急 (agitated). For discussion of other readings of *yutao* 鬱陶, see Cook 2012, 2: 732n287.

body. The latter may bring short-term satisfaction, but the consequences can be fatal.

So far, the argument seems to be that careful use of the heart–mind and thinking can circumvent the dangers posed by the body and emotions. But self-regulation by means of the heart–mind is not sufficient because even correct conduct—faced with distracting sensations and emotions—can still degenerate into ostentation or dissolute or degenerate behavior if the heart–mind does not have the right dispositions (strips 44–47). But how is it to get them?

The *Xingzi mingchu* ends with a description of how a *junzi* can take charge of intentions (*zhi zhi* 執志). It starts by stressing the need for genuineness and the destructiveness of cunning and artifice:

進欲遜而毋巧，退欲易而毋輕，欲皆文而毋偽。君子執志必有夫皇皇之心，出言必有夫簡簡之信.

In advancing one should be modest and not cunning; in withdrawing one should be somber and not frivolous. In all cases one should be finely patterned but not artificial. The gentleman in taking charge of his intentions must have a broad-minded heart–mind; in speaking words, he [must] have a straightforward trustworthiness. (*Guodian Chumu, Xingzi mingchu*, strips 64–66)[20]

The passage continues that he must display an appropriate appearance in guest ritual, a respectful appearance in sacrificial ritual, and a grief-stricken appearance in mourning ritual (strips 66–67).

The passage ends with a perplexing sentence, which does not occur in the Shanghai Museum version and which scholars construe in two entirely different ways. It reads:

君子身以為主心。

(1) Gentlemen use their persons to master their heart–minds.

(2) Gentlemen know their persons are ruled by the heart–mind. (*Guodian Chumu, Xingzi mingchu*, strip 67)

---

[20] I follow Li Ling (2002: 108) and Cook (2012, 2: 748) in reading *su* 肅 (solemn, somber). *Guodian Chumu* and Liu Zhao (2003: 106) do not transcribe the graph 騫. For readings of *wang* 往 and *jian* 柬[簡], see Cook 2012, 2: 748nn402, 403.

At issue is whether the heart–mind rules, guides, or expresses itself through the body, or whether the body shapes, forms or rules the heart–mind. As written, the obvious construction of the sentence is reading (1) above, in which the phrase is read straightforwardly to mean: "Gentlemen use their [embodied] persons to master their heart–minds" and the body is clearly doing the ruling. Liu Xinlan and Pang Pu opt for the body as ruler: According to Liu Xinlan, the phrase refers to gentlemen's attention to their own conduct to correct the heart–mind. According to Pang Pu, "The gentleman uses his self to master his heart–mind." Li Tianhong agrees with their readings and suggests that *zhu* 主 has the sense of "to preserve" or "to maintain." Shirley Chan takes it as "it is the body that he uses to master the heart–mind." Perkins suggests the following reading: "use their bodies to master their heart–minds."[21]

Other scholars take the meaning to be reading (2) above, that the heart–mind rules the body. This meaning requires some kind of emendation, and several have been proposed. Liu Zhao thinks the phrase should read *junzi shēn yi xin wei zhu* 君子身以心為主: "for gentlemen the embodied person takes the heart–mind as master." In a later publication he translates it as: "The body of a gentleman realizes/embodies the heart–mind." Chen Wei takes *wei* to mean "for the sake of" and *zhu* as "to maintain" and gets "the embodied person is used to master the heart–mind." Guo Yi interpolates *yu* 於 between "ruler" (*zhu*) and "heart–mind" (*xin*) to get: "*junzi shēn yi wei zhu yu xin* 君子身以為主於心; here too the gentleman takes the embodied person to be under the control of the heart–mind. Liao Mingchun takes the phrase to mean "using the embodied person to express/reflect the heart–mind" (*yi shēn wei zhu xin* 以身為主心), with *zhu* understood as "to express" or "to reflect," with the meaning: "the gentleman takes the embodied person as an expression of the heart–mind."[22]

---

[21] See Liu Xinlan 2000: 354–55, Pang Pu 2000–2001: 53, Li Tianhong 2003: 197, S. Chan 2009a: 379n44, and Perkins 2009: 118–19, 128. For a summary of these views, see Li Tianhong 2003: 196–97). Other advocates of (1) include Liu Xinlan (2000: 5), who reads the passage in the sense that the solemnity of one's external deportment (*shēn*) serves to mold the heart–mind. Other advocates of (2) include Ding Yuanzhi (2000: 119) and Zhao Jianwei 趙建偉 (1999). For further discussion of this passage, see Perkins 2009 and Cook 2012, 2:749–50n408.

[22] See Liu Zhao 2000: 89 and 2003: 106; Chen Wei 2002: 201; Guo Yi 2001: 264; and Liao Mingchun 2001: 168–69.

A Holist View of Mind and Body

The *Xingzi mingchu* also supports a strongly holist view of mind and body. As Lee-moi Pham has argued, the *Xingzi mingchu* asserts that *qi*, sound, and music all share a quality of "flowing and fulfilling."[23] This shared quality is what makes it possible for music to guide *qi* in passing through both body and mind in ways that ultimately further moral self-cultivation. According to Pham, the *Yucong* 1 account of the common emotional endowment of humans and animals constructs a "body–mind–*qi* mode of discourse," which is common to the shared outlook of the Guodian texts.[24] In this view, it is the very permeability between mind and body, expressed in the flow of *qi*, that makes it possible for music to be so fundamental to self-cultivation.

The logic of this argument is as follows: (1) claims for the importance of stimulation via sensations and basic emotions, as a basic feature of human nature; (2) the special suitability of music to stimulate the emotions via sensation; (3) the ability of thought or reflection and other activities of the heart–mind to produce emotions and other affective states; and (4) the common grounding of body, *qing* and heart–mind in *qi*.[25]

The argument begins with a set of claims for the importance of stimulation due to the setup of human nature. Humans' heart–minds develop intentions only when stimulated in a positive way (*jue* 悅). Such stimulation leads to goal-directed action. These motivating stimuli include basic emotions (*qing*), which are described as constellations of *qi*.[26] The *Xingzi mingchu* compares human nature (*xing*) to "a vibrating system" in which resonance can occur as in musical instruments, which only emit sound when struck. So in order to stimulate *qi* to provoke emotional response, things in the external world must "grab" attention and thereby stimulate response and action (strips 5–6). Unlike other animals, humans need to learn (*xue*) in order for their heart–minds to acquire a specific direction (strips 5–8). This is done by "using the heart–mind" (strip 9).

An important effect of sensation is the ability of sound—specifically music—to stimulate the basic emotions, which in turn move the heart–mind. But is the original stimulus from sound or from the emotions behind

---

[23] 充盈流動的特質. Pham Lee-moi 2013: 54.
[24] 身心氣的論述模式. Pham Lee-moi 2013: 62; cf. *Yucong* 1, strips 45–49, discussed earlier in this chapter.
[25] The first three steps of this analysis are indebted to Middendorf 2008, especially 146.
[26] *Xingzi mingchu*, strips 1–2, quoted above.

it? This passage seems to ground the original stimulus in the emotions that produce music:

凡聲，其出於情也信，然後其入拔人之心也厚。

As for sounds in general, when it is credible that they [truly] emerge from the *qing*, and then enter and capture the human heart–mind, it is profound. (*Guodian Chumu, Xingzi mingchu*, strip 23)

The *Xingzi mingchu* stresses the importance of music in educating the heart–mind because music (both ancient and contemporary) affects the heart–mind quickly and directly:

凡古樂龍心，益樂龍指，皆教其人者也。

ancient music makes a dragon of [stirs] the heart–mind; extravagant music makes a dragon of [stirs] the desires; both are things that can instruct the people. (*Guodian Chumu, Xingzi mingchu*, strip 28)

The passage continues that both extreme music (*yue* 樂) or happiness (*le* 樂, the same graph has both meanings) and extreme mourning or grief (*bei* 悲) bring out the utmost of their affections:

其性相近也，是故其心不遠。

Their natures are similar; therefore, their heart–minds are not far apart. (*Guodian Chumu, Xingzi mingchu*, strips 29–30)

Ulrike Middendorf makes four points about the influence of sound and music on *qing*. First, the *Xingzi mingchu* considers sound to be "trustworthy" (*xin* 信), whether in the form of laughter, the singing voice, the sound of musical instruments, or its symbiosis with vision in dance.[27] This trustworthiness is what makes sound able to influence its listeners so profoundly (strips 23–26). Second, music has a specific ability to change people's affective states and to teach moral (or immoral) values (strips 26–28). Third, strong emotions—especially grief and joy—tend to be followed by their opposites

[27] Middendorf 2008: 147–48.

(strip 29). Fourth, thinking or reflection (*si*) also influences the quality of emotions; anxious thoughts lead to sadness, joyous thoughts to delight (strips 32–33). Musical education is especially facilitated by a "seeking of the heart–mind" (*qiu qi xin* 求其心, strip 36), aided by the "trustworthiness" of sound and the correct "orientation of *qing*" (*qing zhi fang* 情之方, strip 40).

To this point, the analysis gives no explanation for interactions between body and mind beyond the specific case of the trustworthiness of sound. I now turn to a more systematically holist account of body and heart–mind in the *Xingzi mingchu* based on the nature of *qi* in constituting both. As Pham Lee-moi puts it: "the body's coloration and appearance is the container of the activity of the heart *qi* (*xin qi zuoyong de rongqi* 心氣作用的容器), and through the body, heart–mind, intentions, and *qi* affect each other reciprocally. Blood and *qi* guide the *qi* of virtuous intentions, and complete the process of self-cultivation."[28]

Once we see body and mind as a continuum of *qi*, other passages admit of new interpretations. An example is *Xingzi mingchu*, strips 43–44 (discussed earlier), which compares the effects of relying on the heart–mind, knowledge, *qing*, and the body. It concludes that the senses' love of color and sound create a "*qi* of unassuaged joy or anxiety" (*yutao zhi qi* 鬱陶之氣) that can be fatal. The passage continues:

有其為人之節節如也，不有夫謇謇之心則采。有其為人之謇謇如也，不有夫恆怡之志則縵[慢]。

For those who conduct themselves step by step [steadily], if they do not have a straightforward heart–mind, they become ostentatious [overadorned]. For those who conduct themselves in a straightforward manner, if they do not have intentions of permanent joy, they become indolent. (*Guodian Chumu, Xingzi mingchu*, strips 44–45)[29]

Pham links this *qi* of unassuaged joy or anxiety to the account of body, mind, and *qi* in the *Xingzi mingchu*. This *qi* of joy or anxiety is present in the sensory organs, in the eyes' love of color, or in the ears' love of sound.

---

[28] 道德志氣. Pham Lee-moi 2013: 62.
[29] There are several readings for the binome *jian jian*, including 謇謇 (Li Ling 1999), 柬柬 (Cook 2012, 2: 732–34) and 謇謇 (Pham 2013: 67). Another textual problem concerns 采, which Pham reads as *nie* 餒, "dispirited." A third is 慢, which I follow Guo Yi (2001) in reading as 縵. Pham reads 亟治之志則慢, "if they do not have intentions of urgent government, they become indolent."

The heart-mind moves and initiates the faculties of creatures composed of blood and *qi*, but if there is an excess of *yutao zhi qi* pent up within the body, it cannot flow and circulate smoothly. As a result, people can easily die of it.[30]

Similarly, an undisciplined (*fang zong* 放縱) heart-mind, wisdom, *qing*, body, and force lead to excess in reflection (*si*), anxiety (*huan* 患), grief and joy (*ai le* 哀樂), and the like. This accumulation results in agitation (*zao* 躁), illness (*ji* 疾), and other problems (strips 42–44, quoted above). These five so-called mental, emotional, and physical forces, Pham argues, can be reduced to two: the heart-mind and the body. It is the activity of the heart-mind and body together that produce restlessness, illness, extreme anxiety, and other extreme reactions, which in turn stimulate excesses of blood and *qi* (in the medical senses of these terms) that lead to extreme physical reactions. It is in this sense that the eyes' love of color and the ears' love of sound cause a *qi* of unassuaged joy or anxiety. Pham's point is that all these conditions are caused by overabundant *qi* (*qi sheng* 氣盛). Left alone in that state, it can be fatal. She concludes, "body, heart, and *qi* are equal to each other."

The interest of this argument for the present discussion is its relatively holist account of body and heart-mind. It is also noteworthy that this argument does not focus on any special trustworthiness of sound, but rather on the embodied nature of all sensation and the close interactions between body and mind.

Heart-Mind and Body in the *Wuxing*

"Five Kinds of Action" (*Wuxing*) presents a different set of claims for porosity between body and mind, where the heart-mind affects the body. A full account of that text is beyond the scope of the present discussion, but a few passages warrant mention.[31] The context in the *Wuxing* is a discussion of whether "Five Kinds of Action" take shape from within (*nei* 內) or without (*wai* 外). The five kinds of action are the five virtues of humaneness (*ren*), propriety (*yi*), ritual propriety (*li*), wisdom (*zhi*), and sagacity (*sheng* 聖) Those that take place from within are described as "virtuous action" (*de zhi xing* 德之行); those that arise from without are simply "action" (*xing* 行, strips 1–3).

---

[30] *Guodian Chumu, Xingzi mingchu*, strips 43–44 (quoted above), Pham Lee-moi 2013: 74.
[31] For the *Wuxing*, see especially Csikszentmihalyi 2004, to which the following WX translations are also indebted (see Appendix 2: 277–310).

The Inner Heart–Mind

It is in this context that the *Wuxing* discusses several states of the "inner heart–mind" (*zhong xin* 中心):

君子無中心之憂則無中心之智，無中心之智則無中心【之悅】，無中心【之悅則】不安，不安則不樂，不樂則無德。

If the gentleman lacks the anxiety of the inner heart–mind, he will also lack the wisdom of the inner heart–mind. If he lacks the wisdom of the inner heart–mind, he will lack the [joy of the] inner heart–mind. If he lacks [the joy of] the inner heart–mind [then he will] not be at peace; if he is not at peace then he will not be happy; if he is not happy then he will lack virtue. (*Guodian Chumu, Wuxing*, strips 5–6)

The five conducts are also closely linked to reflection or contemplation (*si*). To be essential, contemplation requires the virtue of humaneness; to be extensive, it requires wisdom; to be effortless, it requires sagacity.[32] The *Wuxing* also links different dispositions of the inner heart–mind (*neixin*) with different outward dispositions. To use one's inner heart–mind in relating to others (*yi qi zhong xin yu ren jiao* 以其中心與人交) is joy. Transferring the joy of the inner heart–mind to brothers results in closeness, which in turn extends to produce the feeling of kinship or familiality (*qin* 親). Kinship in turn extends to love (*ai* 愛), and love for fathers and then for others produces humaneness (*ren*). The passage concludes:

中心辯然而正行之，直也。

To make discriminations in the inner heart–mind and then to orient it correctly in conduct is to be upright. (*Guodian Chumu, Wuxing*, strips 33–34)

In summary, both the *Xingzi mingchu* and the *Wuxing* present accounts of how the heart–mind is motivated by sensation and emotion, but they also give an account of how the heart–mind can use reflection to form stable intentions. Several scholars have stressed the importance and agency of the heart–mind. Jiang Guanghui describes this agency as free will. Ding Sixin argues that it

---

[32] 不仁，思不能清。不智，思不能長。⋯【不】仁，思不能清。不聖，思不能輕. *Guodian Chumu, Wuxing*, strips 9 and 11.

transcends the embodied person (*chaoyue shēnti* 超越身体). Perkins usefully characterizes them as concerned with avoiding what the Greeks called *akrasia*: weakness of the will.[33] For purposes of the present discussion, the important point is that there is a strong degree of interaction between the body and heart–mind that resists classification as strongly dualist or strongly holist.

The Mind as Ruler

The *Wuxing*, like the Xunzi, presents a mind-centered view of the relations between body and mind, in an analogy in which the heart–mind rules the body as a ruler rules a state:

耳目鼻口手足六者，心之役也。心曰唯，莫敢不唯；諾，莫敢不諾；進，莫敢不進；後，莫敢不後；

The ears, eyes, nose, mouth, hands, and feet—these six are the slaves of the heart–mind. When the heart–mind says "acquiesce," none dares not acquiesce; [when it says] "promise," none dares not promise; [when it says] "advance," none dares not advance; [when it says] "go back," none dares not go back. (*Guodian Chumu, Wuxing*, strips 45–46)[34]

The force of this analogy is to emphasize the power of the heart–mind as ruler, which none can disobey. It is a contrast to a different mind-ruler analogy in "Black Robes" (*Ziyi*), which foregrounds consensus between ruler and ruled:

子曰：民以君為心，君以民為體，心好則體安之，君好則民欲之。故心以體廢，君以民亡。

The Master said: The people take the ruler as their heart–mind; the ruler takes the people as his frame. When the heart–mind is fond of something, the frame is at peace with it; when the ruler is fond of something, the people desire it. Therefore, the heart–mind [may] be maimed by the frame, and the ruler [may] be destroyed by the people. (*Guodian Chumu, Ziyi*, strips 8–9.)

---

[33] See Jiang Guanghui 2000–2001: 34, Ding Sixin 2000: 303–4, and Perkins 2009: 130. For other accounts, see Andreini 2006: 162 and Perkins 2009: 127–128.
[34] For the reading of "slaves" 役, literally, "corvée labor," see Liu Zhao (2003). For further discussion of this metaphor, see S. Chan 2009b.

Conclusion

In this analysis, I have attempted to read the Guodian corpus as a more-or-less unified text (rather than as a collection of separate "Confucian" and "Daoist" writings), with a coherent account of problems of self-cultivation.[35] Indeed, as Middendorf points out, although none of its ideas are new or unique, the *Xingzi mingchu* in particular presents a compact "review" of the key Warring States positions on human nature and basic emotions (*xing* and *qing*), self-cultivation, and virtue, and all these topics inherently involve the relation between body and mind.[36]

Therefore, it is perhaps surprising to see that the Guodian corpus does not present a unified position on the relationship between body and mind, but rather offers a range of views on relations between them. Positions range from a strong dualism in some passages in the *Wuxing* and *Ziyi* to a strong holism in some readings of the *Xingzi mingchu*. Other passages seem to present an intermediate position (which could be described as either weak mind–body dualism or weak mind–body holism).

Two passages in *Wuxing* and *Ziyi* compare the heart–mind to the ruler of a state and the body to his subordinates. In the *Ziyi* passage, the subordinates are the people. In the more striking *Wuxing* passage, the subordinates are slaves. This latter passage is especially striking—and indeed anomalous—in light of a range of Warring States' heart–mind–ruler comparisons that take the body as the ruler's ministers or officials.[37]

At the other end of the spectrum is a robustly holist view of *qi* unifying—and equalizing—body and mind. Here, similarities between the "flow" of *qi*, sound, and music are the conduit that makes possible moral transformation through music. A more conventional reading of the *Xingzi mingchu* is also more dualist, by virtue of privileging the ability of the heart–mind to create fixed intentions as part of the process of self-cultivation.

In conclusion, this range of positions shows the volatility of the question of the interrelations between body and mind, and their importance in the virtue-based strategies that are central to Guodian accounts of both self-cultivation and state organization.

---

[35] On this point, see Csikszentmihalyi 2005 and Slingerland 2008, among others.
[36] Middendorf 2008: 145.
[37] For fuller discussion, see Raphals 2015.

6
Body, Mind, and Spirit in Early Chinese Medicine

This chapter proposes that some medical texts present a more decentralized and corporeal view of body–mind integration than do most early Chinese philosophical writings.[1] In particular, the notions of mind (*xin*) and spirit (*shén*), as well as other psychophysical attributes of a person, can be found to be more closely integrated with various aspects of the body (*xing, shēn, ti*). Especially in the *Huangdi neijing* 黃帝內經, much of the importance of *xin*—when it does not clearly refer to the heart alone—is as the container or lodging place of spirit rather than as the seat of consciousness and moral judgment. In what follows, I translate *xin* as "heart" insofar as it refers to the physical organ in the body, for example, as the dwelling place of spirit, or in comparison to the lungs and liver. However, it is important to remember that it is a "psychophysical" heart that also refers to the "mind," as it does in other Warring States and Han texts.[2]

There is no denial of notions of dualism in many early Chinese philosophical texts where mind, often as the "ruler" of the body or the senses, is aligned with spirit, in distinction to the body; and in some philosophical texts *shén* is closely associated with sagehood.[3] But another view—this one of texts in Daoist and *Huangdi neijing* traditions—problematizes the connection between mind and spirit, and in some cases even aligns body and spirit in opposition to mind. Dualism tends to reduce spirit to mind, insofar as all

---

[1] This chapter has benefited from discussion following presentations at the University of Chicago, Central European University, Hong Kong Baptist University, and National University of Singapore, and from comments by anonymous reviewers at *T'oung-pao*.

[2] I thus differ from the strongly holist view that there is nothing qualitatively distinctive about *xin* as a physical organ in the *Huangdi neijing*. But limiting the meaning of *xin* to "physical heart only" ignores the many associations of *xin* and *shén* with emotions, judgment, and other psychological capabilities. In addition, the account of *xin* and *shén* in the *Huangdi neijing* also has similarities to passages of self-cultivation literature such as the *Guanzi* 管子 (see note 70 below), where *xin* clearly refers to the mind as well as the physical heart.

[3] The details of the latter argument are beyond the scope of the present discussion. For an account of the philosophical importance of spirit, see Puett 2002.

A Tripartite Self. Lisa Raphals, Oxford University Press. © Oxford University Press 2023.
DOI: 10.1093/oso/9780197630877.003.0007

"nonbody" aspects of a person are identified with consciousness, intention, and cognition; but according to the *Huangdi neijing*, *shén* as the animating force that literally keeps the body alive cannot be collapsed into mind.

The first section of this chapter surveys several dualist and tripartite views of body, mind, and spirit or soul in early Chinese medical texts. The second section examines the uses of *shén* in the *Huangdi neijing* and argues that much of the importance of *xin*—when it does not clearly refer to the heart alone—is as the container of lodging place of *shén* rather than as the seat of consciousness and moral judgment.

Mind–Body Dualism and Medical Texts

Slingerland's account of mind–body dualism in early China extends to pre-Han medical texts which, in his view, distinguish between an immaterial—and largely invisible—spirit and a tangible, visible, material body. He holds that the soul—however designated—is intimately bound up with consciousness or mind, intention, and personal identity, and that there is a bipartite division between the physical body and what fills or inhabits it.[4] In a specifically medical context, he states that the *Huangdi neijing*, though primarily concerned with the material body, presupposes "a backdrop that assumes spirit–body dualism" through contrasts between spirit and the body, or between "inner" moods, feeling, and emotions and the external, visible realm of the physical body.[5]

Tripartite Views

By contrast, Catherine Despeux proposes a tripartite representation of a person consisting of body (*corps*), mind (*esprit*), and soul (*âme*), to better understand *shén* in Chinese medicine in the second and first centuries BCE, emphasizing that soul and breath are the animating forces essential to life.[6] Slingerland acknowledges the tripartite medical view of the person advanced by Despeux but considers the tripartite view to be "parasitic on mind–body

---

[4] Slingerland 2019: 90 and 92.
[5] Slingerland 2019: 82–83, citing Messner 2006: 41–63.
[6] Despeux 2007: 73–75. For a different tripartite view of persons as consisting of form, *qi*, and spirit, see Hu Fuchen 1993: 171–92.

182　A TRIPARTITE SELF

dualism" because it ultimately requires the separability of personal essence from the physical body.[7]

Despeux understands soul as being intermediary between body and mind to better understand spirit in Chinese medicine from the second to first centuries BCE, emphasizing that soul and breath are the animating force essential to life.[8] She considers spirit from five specifically medical perspectives: the heart as the seat of the soul, the relation of *shén* to five of the viscera, the possibility that *shén* are plural, with a multitude of spirits in the body, the movements of *shén* within the body, and finally, the role of spirit in the animation of the body. The latter sections include substantial discussion of excavated materials from Wuwei and Dunhuang that illustrate this movement, which appears to be absent in the *Huangdi neijing*.

Despeux argues that the possibility of multiple spirits moving in the body is complicated by a tendency of the *Huangdi neijing* and other medical texts to not make explicit distinctions between singular and plural. This ambiguity is especially problematic for discussions of *shén*, since the term could refer to either (one) spirit or to spirits. She also notes that technical texts do not always offer explicit arguments regarding key ideas. Without explicit knowledge of their evolution and range of meaning, we must glean information from occurrences of the conceptual vocabulary in diverse contexts, through study of networks of related terms and their contexts.[9]

Several preliminary points are worth making before turning to my own discussion. First, Hu Fuchen and Despeux take very different points of view on which constituent of the person is fundamental: Hu focuses on *qi* and Despeux on *shén*. This difference may be explained by differences of context. Hu's interest in cultivating *qi* is Daoist self-cultivation practices. In the medical texts of interest to Despeux, the body dies when spirit leaves it.

Despeux's preference for understanding *shén* as "soul"/âme reflects this important point. (It is also worth noting that French "esprit" means both "mind" and "spirit," possibly conflating the two—or preserving resonances of "spirit"—in a way that is not possible in English.) The choice of "soul" rather than "spirit" for *shén* also draws on Aristotle's *De Anima*, particularly on his

---

[7] Slingerland 2019: 92. He also notes (87) that the model of self behind *shén* is complex, and sometimes requires a tripartite model such as that of Despeux.
[8] Despeux 2007: 73–75.
[9] See Despeux 2007: 73.

argument that the faculties of the soul are multiple. This point is helpful for Despeux's account of multiple spirits within the body, but her account of soul/*shén* differs from Aristotle's in two important ways. His "souls" are not distinct souls but rather five distinct faculties (*dunameis*), and these faculties form a hierarchy.[10]

In medical texts, as in other contexts, dualist frameworks of analysis lose important dimensions of the relations between mind (and its associated faculties) and spirit or soul (and its associated faculties), including how both relate to the body.[11] An important example is the enormous importance of spirit as the animating force that vivifies the body; this cannot be collapsed into "mind." Despeux's invaluable study significantly avoids the dualistic scheme but raises several questions. One concerns the role of spirit in her trilogy of "body/soul/mind" (corps/âme/esprit). In her study of *shén* in early Chinese medical texts, she makes strong arguments for understanding *shén* as "soul" rather than "spirit." In the broader context of the constituents of a person, a problem arises because the semantic field of French "esprit" includes both "mind" and "spirit," which allows at least some attributes of "spirit" to be combined with "mind."

This chapter continues the argument for a tripartite view of a person consisting of body, heart–mind, and spirit. In particular, in early medical literature, especially excavated texts from Mawangdui and Zhangjiashan, *xin* is not necessarily identified with *shén*, nor is it necessarily presented as metaphysically distinct from every other bodily organ. Hence, these sources do not confirm the dualistic paradigms that have been inferred from texts such as the *Xunzi*, and even from the very mixed picture of the *Huangdi neijing*. This point is important because of two tendencies in contemporary scholarship. One is to treat *xin* and *shén* as essentially equivalent references to a mind–spirit amalgam within a dualistic scheme. The other is to understate the importance of *shén* as soul or breath, in the sense of the animating force that life requires. In addition, discussions of both *shén* and *shénming* (spirit illumination) support a tripartite model of the person in early Chinese texts,

---

[10] *De Anima* describes six faculties of the soul that are, to varying degrees, common to all living things: nutrition (and reproduction, *threptikon*), desire (*orektikon*), sensation (*aisthētikon*), locomotion (*kinētikon kata topon*), imagination (*phantasia*), and reason (*nous*). Plants have only the faculty of nutrition. Animals with sensation also have desire, but imagination [*phantasia*] is more obscure. Only humans have the faculty of reason (*to dianoētikon te kai nous*). See Aristotle, *de Anima* 414a29–414b1 and 414b15–19.

[11] A different problematic approach is to focus on mind–body dualism during life and body–spirit dualism after death. Both frameworks miss the mark for accounts of persons that assume significant and complex interactions between mind and spirit.

184 A TRIPARTITE SELF

at least up to the Han dynasty, in which persons are composed of body (*xing, ti, shēn*), heart–mind (*xin*), and spirit (*shén*), along with *hunpo, ling,* and so on.[12]

Issues of Genre and Audience

Medical texts presumably had different purposes and audiences than philosophical texts. The status of *xin* as the center of cognition and moral judgment is a central issue in philosophical texts but not in medical texts. By contrast, the central role of spirit as a prerequisite for life is clearly key to medical contexts. Meanwhile, medical writers sought to use cosmologies that had elsewhere been applied to government to explain medicine. They also drew on other technical traditions, including those of recipe masters (*fangshi* 方士) and diviners. The medical arrangement of these ideas also became significant for a new ideology that associated the structure of the cosmos to that of both the human body and the state.[13]

Despite important differences of genre and audience, medical texts are important for an understanding of early Chinese debates about the constituents of a person and the understanding of body, mind, and spirit. For example, the anonymous physicians/compilers of the *Huangdi neijing* corpus are interested in promulgating and validating an acupuncture-based model of the body, especially in the *Lingshu* 靈樞 (Numinous Pivot). As one might expect from a multiauthored compilation, the *Huangdi neijing* includes multiple accounts of *xin* and *shén* and may also speak to an ongoing tension or competition between philosophical lineages and technical expertise traditions in early China.

Medical texts are particularly relevant to "holism–dualism" debates because medical texts are often cited as examples of strong mind–body holism, especially in claims that in medical texts, the *xin*/heart is a physical organ, no different from any other.[14] By contrast, in many philosophical texts, the heart–mind is the seat of emotions and ethical and moral judgments, and cannot be viewed primarily as a physical organ. It is this view that in part

---

[12] The semantic field of terms for the body is discussed in Chapter 1.

[13] See Despeux 2007: 72, and Sivin 1995. For the broader context of medical writing, see Harper 1999: 91–110, and 2001: 99–120. For linkages between the formation of professional groups and books that codified their professional knowledge, see Li Ling 1993.

[14] For discussion of this issue, see Slingerland 2019: 42–45 and 302.

informs claims for mind–body dualism. Medical texts add to the range of perspectives on these issues.

Shén and Xin in the *Huangdi Neijing*

There are three known texts of the *Huangdi neijing*. The *Suwen* 素問 (Basic Questions) was compiled by Wang Bing 王冰 in 762, and the *Lingshu* was compiled in the twelfth century.[15] A third text, the *Taisu* 太素 (Great Basis), compiled by Yang Shangshan 楊上善 in the seventh century, was preserved in Japanese editions of the *Huangdi neijing*.[16] Much of the content of all three is believed to date from the Han dynasty.[17] Following the work of Nathan Sivin, David Keegan, and Paul Unschuld, I take the *Huangdi neijing* as a multiauthored compilation of smaller units whose dates are uncertain.

Before turning to mind and spirit, something should be said about the "body" in the *Huangdi neijing*. Five terms for the body occur extensively in the *Huangdi neijing* and appear to be used fairly interchangeably.[18] In the *Huangdi neijing*, there are no obvious differences in meaning between these terms, and in some cases several are used in a single paragraph, without apparent differences in meaning.[19]

I identify three major rubrics or thematic accounts of *xin* and *shén* occur in short passages in the *Huangdi neijing*. Only one corresponds to the *xin*-centered view that is so prevalent in late Warring States and Han philosophical texts. In the interests of brevity, I exclude from the discussion passages where *xin* is described purely as a bodily organ, and focus on contexts where

---

[15] Citations from the *Suwen* are from Yamada Gyōkō 山田業廣, *Suwen cizhu jishu* 素問次注集疏, ed. Cui Zhongping 崔仲平 et al. (Beijing: Xueyuan chubanshe, 2004, hereafter SW). Translations are from Unschuld and Tessenow 2011, sometimes modified. Citations from the *Lingshu* are from Shibue Chūsai 澀江抽齋, *Lingshu jiangyi* 靈樞講義, ed. Cui Zhongping et al. (Beijing: Xueyuan chubanshe, 2003, hereafter LS). Translations are based on Unschuld 2016, sometimes modified.

[16] Kosoto Hiroshi 1981. For discussion, see Sivin 1998: 29–36.

[17] Sivin dates the contents of the *Suwen* to the first century BCE; Keegan and Unschuld date its language and ideas to between 400 BCE and 260 CE. Some content may be considerably later. See Yamada Keiji 1979: 67–89; Sivin 1993: 196–215; Keegan 1988; Unschuld 2003: 1–7, 26–43, 59–65, and 77–80; and Ma Jixing 1990.

[18] Most frequent are the terms *xing* (the physical form, 305 times) and *shēn* (the embodied person, 252 times). The term *ti* (the limbed body) occurs seventy times. The compounds *shēnti* 身體 (twenty-one times) and *xingti* 形體 (six times) are less frequent. The term *gong* 躬 does not occur. For the semantic field of terms for the body see Sivin 1995: 5–37 and Sommer 2008: 293–324.

[19] For example, see Tessenow and Unschuld 200. A full examination of this issue is beyond the scope of the present study.

186   A TRIPARTITE SELF

it has significant interactions with possibly nonmaterial aspects of a living person.[20]

I begin with *Lingshu* 8, "Taking Spirit as the Foundation" (*Benshén* 本神). It provides an extensive and important discussion of the role of *xin* and *shén* in the body and offers three interrelated claims, which also appear in other chapters: (1) that *shén* is the foundation of all life; (2) that the five *zang* 藏 viscera store five psychological faculties, including *shén*;[21] and (3) that emotional excess harms the five *zang* viscera, especially the heart (*xin*), which stores *shén*. The text also makes a series of pentic correspondences between the five *zang* viscera, five psychological capacities, and five emotions. All this is described from a therapeutic viewpoint. These provide a context for: accounts of *xin* as ruler of the body or the viscera.

"Taking Spirit as the Foundation"

Lingshu 8 begins by asserting the foundational importance of *shén*: "For all methods of needling, it is first necessary to consider *shén* as the foundation."[22] An explanation follows that the five *zang* viscera store six constituents of the body, but excess or indulgence causes them to leave the viscera: "when essence is lost, *hun* and *po* fly and scatter; thought and will are disordered. Wisdom and forethought leave the body."[23] The text identifies spirit with the emergence of life, and the heart–mind as merely something that "manages things":

---

[20] The term *xin* occurs with great frequency in the *Huangdi neijing* (563 instances). Using concordance searches, I focused on co-occurrences of *xin* and *shén*. In particular, I excluded contexts that describe *xin* as a bodily organ that include (but are not limited to) references to "harming the heart" (*shang xin* 傷心), "heart *qi*" (*xinqi* 心氣), references to the heart as a location in the body, for example "a disease in the heart" (*bing zai xin* 病在心), references to the heart vessel and other mentions of the heart in connection with other vessels, and accounts of the five *zang* viscera that do not involve spirit or psychological attributes.

[21] The *Huangdi neijing* distinguishes two kinds of viscera. Five *zang* 臟 (modern form 藏) "depots" or "treasuries" (the heart, lungs, liver, spleen, and kidneys) are concerned with transformation and storage. Five *fu* 腑 (modern form 府) viscera (the gall bladder, stomach, large and small intestine, urinary bladder) provide reception and passage. See SW 4.99, Unschuld and Tessenow 2011: 1: 89.

[22] 凡刺之法，先必本于神. LS 8.190, Unschuld 2016: 147, *Jiayi jing* 1.1.

[23] 精失、魂魄飛揚、志意恍亂、智慮去身者. LS 8.190, Unschuld 2016: 147. The six components are: blood (*xue* 血), the vessels (*mai* 脈), camp *qi* (*yingqi* 營氣), guard *qi* (*weiqi* 衛氣), essence (*jing*), and spirit (*shén*). The terms "camp *qi*" (*yingqi*) and "guard *qi*" (*weiqi*) refer to "constructive" and "protective" *qi*, respectively. Both are military terms, and they refer to two types of *qi* in the body that were believed to protect it and ward off intruders. See Unschuld and Tessenow 2011: 1: 18. For reading *yingqi* 營氣 as *yingweiqi* 營衛氣 see Unschuld 2016: 147.

故生之來謂之精，兩精相搏謂之神，隨神往來者謂之魂，並精而出入者謂之魄，所以任物者謂之心，心有所憶謂之意，意之所存謂之志，因志而存變謂之思，因思而遠慕謂之慮，因慮而處物謂之智。

Therefore, the origin of life is called essence; the clash of two [kinds of] essence is called *shén*. What comes and goes following spirit is called *hun*; what enters and leaves along with essence is called *po*. What is responsible for things is called the *xin*; what *xin* reflects upon is called thought/intention. What preserves thought/intention is called will; to preserve and change something because of will is called reflection. To reach a vision long afterwards because of reflection is called concern. To understand how to regulate things because of concern is called intelligence. (LS 8.191–95, cf. Unschuld 2016: 148–49; *Jiayi jing* 1.1–2)

Zhang Jiebin's 張介賓 (1563–1640) commentary on this passage glosses the "two *jing*" as the essence of yin and yang. Understood thus, the interactions of yin and yang essence—the origin of life—produce *shén*, which is thus associated with the origin of life and precedes *xin*.

Lingshu 8 has an identical parallel in the first chapter of the *Huangdi zhenjiu jiayi jing* 黃帝針灸甲乙經 (Huangdi's A-B Classic of Needling and Moxibustion), the "Treatise on Essence, Spirits, and the Five *Zang* Viscera" (*Jingshén wuzang lun* 精神五藏論). The treatise begins with a statement that all needling methods take their basis in spirit; and that blood, vessels, camp and guard *qi*, essence, and spirit are all stored in the five *zang* viscera. It then asks about the meaning of *jing*, *shén*, *hun*, *po*, *xin*, and other associated terms.[24] The clear dating of the *Jiayi jing* means that these ideas in *Lingshu* 8 can be dated to no later than 260 CE.[25]

Lingshu 8 next explains how emotional excesses affect the viscera and injure the body, *shén* in particular. The context is an account of balance by those who understand how to nurture life (*zhi zhe zhi yangsheng* 智者之養生). Among other measures, "they harmonize their emotions and inhabit their homes in calm":[26]

是故怵惕思慮者則傷神，神傷則恐懼，流淫而不止。因悲哀動中者，竭絕而失生。喜樂者，神憚散而不藏。愁憂者，氣閉塞而不行。盛怒者，迷惑而不治。恐懼者，神蕩憚而不收。

---

[24] See *Jiayi jing*, 1.1 (=LS 8.190).
[25] Huangfu Mi 皇甫謐, *Huangdi sanbu zhenjiu jiayi jing xinjiao* 黃帝三部針灸甲乙經新校, 1–5.
[26] 和喜怒而安居處. LS 8.194, Unschuld 2016: 149.

Therefore, when there is fear in pondering and consideration, it harms spirit. When spirit is harmed, fears flow in excess and without end. When grief and sorrow excite, the center [*qi*] is exhausted, [their flow] is interrupted, and one loses one's life. Those who are happy and joyous make their *shén* disperse and scatter, so it cannot be stored. Those who are worried and sad make their *qi* closed and blocked, so it cannot move. Those who are full of rage are confused and cannot be cured. Those who are in fear make their *shén* disseminate, so it cannot be brought under control. (LS 8.195–96, Unschuld 2016: 149; cf. *Jiayi jing* 1.2)

Emotional excess is particularly destructive to the heart because of its effect on spirit. When fear causes injury to spirit, it causes people to lose their sense of self.[27] The passage goes on to make a series of pentic correlations between the five emotional states, injury to the five *zang* viscera, and death during the five seasonal periods. Worry and sadness (*chouyou* 愁憂) injure the spleen and thought; sorrow and sadness (*bei'ai* 悲哀) harm the liver and *hun*; joy and pleasure (*xile* 喜樂) injure the lungs and *po*; abounding rage (*shengnu* 怒) injures the kidneys and will.[28] The text also emphasizes the need to take into account consultors' emotional or affective states. In order to practice needling effectively, the practitioner must determine whether *jing*, *shén*, *hun*, and *po* are still present or have been lost.[29]

Lingshu 8 then describes a system of storage of psychophysical aspects of a person in the five *zang* viscera, including storage of spirit in the heart:

肝藏血，血舍魂，肝氣虛則恐，實則怒。 脾藏營，營舍意，脾氣虛則四肢不用，五藏不安，實則腹脹，經溲不利。 心藏脈，脈舍神，心氣虛則悲，實則笑不休。肺藏氣，氣舍魄，肺氣虛則鼻塞不利，少氣，實則喘喝，胸盈仰息。5腎藏精，精舍志，腎氣虛則厥，實則脹。

The liver stores blood; blood hosts *hun*. When liver *qi* is depleted, there is fear; when it is replete, there is rage. The spleen stores camp *qi*; camp *qi* hosts thought. When spleen *qi* is depleted, the limbs are useless and the five *zang* viscera are not at peace. When it is full, the abdomen is distended, and

---

[27] 恐懼自失. LS 8.196–198, Unschuld 2016: 150.
[28] LS 8.199, Unschuld 2016: 150–51.
[29] 是故用鍼者，察觀病人之態，以知精神魂魄之存亡. LS 8.199, Unschuld 2016: 151; cf. *Jiayi jing* 1.5.

menses and urine do not flow freely. The heart stores the vessels; the vessels host *shén*. When heart *qi* is depleted, there is grief; when it is full, there is unceasing laughter. The lungs stores *qi*; *qi* hosts *po*. If lung *qi* is depleted, the nose will be blocked. [The *qi*] does not flow freely and there is shortness of breath. The kidneys store essence; essence hosts will. When kidney *qi* is depleted, there is receding [*qi*]; when it is full, there is distension. (LS 8.199–201, Unschuld 2016: 152–53; *Jiayi jing* 1.3)

The purpose is clearly diagnostic; excess or deficiency of the *qi* associated with each of the viscera can manifest as an emotion whose presence can be used to diagnose the imbalance. These three ideas are widely represented in the *Huangdi neijing*.

Several of these accounts of spirit indicate that it is stored in and associated with the heart. Descriptions of the heart storing spirit occur in pentic correspondences between the five *zang* viscera, five psychological faculties they store, and five diagnostic manifestations, sometimes involving the emotions. For example, *Suwen* 23 and *Lingshu* 78 present straightforward correlations in which the *zang* viscera are containers that store (rather than rule). The *xin/shén* complex has no special privilege:

心藏神，肺藏魄，肝藏魂，脾藏意，腎藏志，是謂五藏所藏。

The heart stores spirit; the lungs store *po*; the liver stores *hun*; the spleen stores thought; the kidneys store will. These are the so-called "what the five *zang* viscera store" (SW 23.569–70, Unschuld and Tessenow 2011: 1: 409)

五藏：心藏神，肺藏魄，肝藏魂，脾藏意，腎藏精志也。

The five *zang* viscera: the heart stores spirit; the lungs store *po*; the liver stores *hun*; the spleen stores thought; the kidneys store essence and will. (LS 78.1070; Unschuld 2016: 735)[30]

A different pentic account occurs in *Suwen* 62, which includes five fundamental constituents that create the physical form of the person (*shēnxing* 身形):

---

[30] *Lingshu* 78 presents a longer series of correlations between the human body and the nine regions of the cosmos (LS 78.1056; Unschuld 2016: 727).

夫心藏神，肺藏氣，肝藏血，脾藏肉，腎藏志，而此成形。志意通，內連骨髓，而成身形五藏。

Now, the heart stores spirit, the lungs store *qi*, the liver stores blood, the spleen stores flesh, the kidneys store will, and this completes the form. Will and thought penetrate [everything], in the interior they link up with bones and marrow, thereby completing the form of the person and the five *zang* viscera. (SW 62.1211, Unschuld and Tessenow 2011: 2: 102)[31]

This passage offers interesting counterevidence to texts that support claims for a radical distinction between the physical body and some kind of mind, consciousness, or will that inhabits it. Here, there is no clear distinction between "containers" (*xin* and the other *zang* viscera) and their contents: *shén* and the other psychological attributes are aspects of the person.[32]

In contrast to the pentic correspondences in *Huangdi neijing*, the *Nanjing* (*Classic of Difficult Issues*)—another possibly early text related to the *Huangdi neijing* tradition—organizes its account of the problem of spirit(s) and the five viscera in the framework of "Five Agents" (*wuxing* 五行) cosmology. Difficult Issue 34 is a discussion of the five *zang* viscera, their correlations with the sets of five sounds, colors, smells, and tastes, the fluids they control, and seven *shén*:

五藏有七神，各何所藏耶？ 然：藏者，人之神氣所舍藏也。 故肝藏魂，肺藏魄，心藏神，脾藏意與智，腎藏精與志也。

The five *zang* viscera have seven spirits; which lodges in each of them respectively? It is like this: The *zang* viscera are storage depots containing people's spirit *qi*. Thus, the liver stores *hun*; the lungs store *po*; the heart stores spirit; the spleen stores thought and wisdom; the kidneys store essence and will. (*Nanjing benyi* 34.170, trans. after Unschuld 1986: 367)

This *Nanjing* passage repeats and amplifies the accounts in the *Lingshu*, but some of the commentaries make the interesting addition that spirits or psychological capacities move in the body, either entering and leaving,

---

[31] According to the Wang Bing commentary, *zhiyi* 志意 (which Unschuld and Tessenow translate as "mind") is an encompassing reference to the five spirits (SW 62.1211, Unschuld and Tessenow 2011: 2: 103n7).

[32] Other chapters describe the heart as storing *qi*. For example, SW 18 describes the *qi* from the viscera penetrating the heart and how the heart stores the *qi* of the blood and the vessels in summer (藏真通於心，心藏血脈之氣也; SW 18.407, Unschuld and Tessenow 2011: 1:305).

or circulating within it. According to Hua Shou's 滑壽 (1304–1386) commentary:

魂者，神明之輔弼也，隨神往來謂之魂。魄者，精氣之匡佐也，並精而出入者謂之魄。神者，精氣之化成也，兩精相薄謂之神。

Hun is an assistant to spirit illumination; what follows *shén* in its comings and goings is called *hun*. *Po* is an aid to essence *qi*; what leaves and enters together with essence is called *po*. Spirit is a transformation product of essence *qi*; when the two essences [of yin and yang] interact, [the result] is called spirit. (*Nanjing benyi*, 34.170, Unschuld 1986: 371)

The commentary's suggestion that spirit moves within, into, or out of the body, Despeux also finds in the *Jiayi jing*. Moreover, Six Dynasties texts clearly develop the idea of multiple *shén* in the body, but the question is whether such accounts can be attributed to the (presumably earlier) *Huangdi neijing*, where they are not explicit. Despeux suggests that the names of acumoxa points in the *Jiayi jing* at least suggest a similar view of multiple spirits in multiple parts of the body.[33] Both the *Nanjing* and the *Jiayi jing* clearly refer to the "comings and goings" (*wanglai* 往來) of *shén*, but the problem with the "multiple spirits" claim is that what follows the movements of *shén* is called *hun*, and *hun* is singular insofar as it is contrasted with *po*, thought, and so on. It is doubtful that these questions can be resolved for the *Huangdi neijing*, but they do add to a view of *shén* as decentralized and corporeal.

Spirit as the Foundation of Life

The central role of spirit in maintaining life also appears in accounts of the natural life span. *Suwen* 1 begins with an account of the long-lived sages of highest antiquity who "were able to keep form and spirit together and to exhaust their years allotted by heaven."[34] The chapter ends with a description of sages who externally did not belabor their form and internally did not suffer

---

[33] See Despeux 2007: 80–82; note her translation of *shén* as "soul." Daoist texts describe spirits from the Daoist pantheon entering and inhabiting specific parts of the body, but also "indigenous" spirits that normally reside there, as well as meditation and visualization techniques to preserve both. See Despeux 1987: 54.
[34] 能形與神俱，而盡終其天年. SW 1.20; Unschuld and Tessenow 2011: 1: 31–32.

from reflection and worry. As a result, "their form and frame did not deteriorate and their essence and spirit did not dissipate."[35]

Lingshu 54, "The Years Allotted by Heaven" (*Tiannian* 天年) explicitly associates *shén* with allotted life span, elsewhere described as "mandate" or destiny (*ming* 命). It describes the storage of *shén* in the heart as part of the normal ontogeny of a human being, beginning with its origins in the developing embryo: "The [*qi* of one's] mother constitutes the basis; that of the father serves as shield. Loss of spirit results in death; those who keep spirit survive."[36] Huang Di 黃帝 asks what kind of *qi* constitutes spirit (*he zhe wei shén* 何者為神), and is told:

血氣已和，營衛已通，五藏已成，神氣舍心，魂魄畢具，乃成為人。

When blood and *qi* are in harmony, when the camp and guard [*qi*] penetrate [the body], when the five *zang* viscera are complete, when spirit *qi* has settled in the heart, and when *hun* and *po* are mature, then a person is completed too. (LS 54.778, Unschuld 2016: 514)

This passage indicates a close connection between *xin* with *shén* because spirit is stored in the heart as spirit *qi*, and the completion of that process is essential for the formation of a person.[37] The account of life span continues with an explanation of how the *qi* associated with the yin and yang viscera becomes depleted over the course of a normal life cycle. At the age of ten, blood and *qi* penetrate the five *zang*, but by the age of sixty, they slow down and heart *qi* begins to weaken, as if affected by grief. At eighty, lung *qi* weakens and the *po* departs. By one hundred, "all five *zang* are depleted and spirit *qi* has all left [the body]. Only the physical appearance and the skeleton remain, and that is the end."[38] This passage describes the "completion" of a person as spirit *qi* settling in the heart and

---

[35] 形體不敝，精神不散. SW 1.38; Unschuld and Tessenow 2011: 1:44. For *jing shén* as "essence and spirit," see Tessenow and Unschuld 2008: 210–11, and Zhongguo zhongyi yanjiuyuan and Guangzhou zhongyi xueyuan 1995: 1672. Unschuld notes the use of *jing* in several compounds, including "essence light" (*jingguang* 精光), "essence qi" (*jingqi* 精氣), "essence brilliance" (*jingming* 精明), and "essence fluid" (*jingye* 精液), but consistently understands *jing shén* as "essence and spirit."
[36] 以母為基，以父為楯，失神者死，得神者生也. LS 54.778, Unschuld 2016: 514.
[37] For the compound *shénqi* ("spirit *qi*"), see Tessenow and Unschuld 2008: 367–68.
[38] 五藏皆虛，神氣皆去。形骸獨居而終矣. LS 54.783, Unschuld 2016: 516–18.

the maturation of *hun* and *po*; it also associates the departure of *shénqi* with impending death.[39]

Several *Suwen* passages discuss the importance of preserving spirit *qi* (*shénqi*). *Suwen* 2 describes appropriate activities and regulation for each season, including "collecting spirit *qi* puts autumn *qi* in balance."[40] *Suwen* 3 notes that if one does not follow the sequence of the seasons correctly, guard *qi* dissipates and *qi* is diminished.[41] Finally, several *Suwen* passages give technical instructions for needling to preserve and balance spirit *qi*.[42]

Xin as Ruler of the Visceral Systems

Accounts of spirit being stored in the heart (and mind) also occur in passages which state that the *xin* is the ruler of the other viscera. *Suwen* 8 identifies specific functions in the body with specific government functions. *Xin* is the ruler, but its subjects are the other four *zang* viscera, which act as its officials:

心者，君主之官也。神明出焉。肺者，相傅之官，治節出焉。肝者，將軍之官，謀慮出焉。

The heart is the official that acts as ruler; spirit illumination originates in it. The lungs are the official that acts as minister and mentor. Order and moderation originate in it. The liver is the official that acts as general. Planning and deliberation originate in it. (SW 8.237, Unschuld and Tessenow 2011: 1:155–56)[43]

These "officials"— *guan* 官 is probably analogous to "office" or *zang*, "storehouse"— maintain the life of the body, which dies if they do not perform correctly. This passage seems to be a medical expression of a view of polity that

---

[39] LS 54.778 and 54.783. *Shénqi* is also associated with the heart, the eyes, the *hun* and *po*, the blood, and the joints. For the eyes and heart, see SW 81.1402 and 1405 (Unschuld and Tessenow 2011: 2:724 and 727) and LS 80.1091 (Unschuld 2016: 755). For *hun* and *po*, see LS 12.351, for blood LS 18.441, and for the joints LS 1.52.

[40] 收斂神氣，使秋氣平. SW 2.45, Unschuld and Tessenow 2011: 1: 48–49. The Wang Bing commentary explains that agitation of spirit can inflame desires, which harm harmonious *qi* and unbalance autumn *qi*.

[41] SW 3.62, Unschuld and Tessenow 2011: 1:62. SW 3.82 (Unschuld and Tessenow 2011: 1: 78) also states that "when *yin* and *yang* are balanced and sealed, essence and spirit are in order" 陰平陽秘，精神乃治. In particular, cold can cause *yang qi* to be unstable and spirit *qi* (*shénqi*) to drift.

[42] SW 27.625 and 62.1214, Unschuld and Tessenow 2011: 1:452, and 2: 105–6.

[43] The phrase 君主之官也，神明出焉 also occurs in the two apocryphal chapters of the Suwen (chs. 72 and 73).

194 A TRIPARTITE SELF

prioritizes equilibrium between emperor and ministers, but also the harmonious flow of different kinds of constituents within the body.⁴⁴

Both Paul Unschuld and Mark Edward Lewis point out that, in contrast to the early second-century BCE medical texts preserved at Mawangdui 馬王堆 and Zhangjiashan 張家山, the *Huangdi neijing* indicates the increasing importance of a new model of corporeal/political relations, both as a model for structuring space and as a new understanding of the need for harmony or equilibrium between the emperor and his officials.⁴⁵ Accounts of *xin* as ruler of the body are part of a dominant narrative in Warring States and Han philosophical texts such as *Guanzi*, *Mencius* 孟子, *Liji* 禮記, *Xunzi* 荀子, *Lüshi chunqiu* 呂氏春秋, *Wenzi* 文子, and *Huainanzi* 淮南子.⁴⁶

Other passages describe *xin* as the ruler of the viscera, but as we will see, that label is in the service of something else. For example, *Lingshu* 36 describes the *xin* as ruler over both the *zang* and *fu* viscera and assigns offices somewhat differently:

五藏六府，心為之主，耳為之聽，目為之候，肺為之相，肝為之將，脾為之衛，腎為之主外。

As for the five *zang* and six *fu* viscera, the heart is the ruler: the ears are the listeners, the eyes are the observers, the lungs are the prime minister, the liver is the general; the spleen is the guardian; the kidneys are the governors of the outer regions. (LS 36.632; Unschuld 2016: 384–85)

This passage is part of the answer to a question about the movement of fluids in the body. The next passage explains that the liquids from the five *zang* and six *fu* viscera all normally pour into the eyes. When the heart feels grief, all the liquids come together and flow as tears. It may be that the heart's role as "ruler" is what makes the fluids coalesce to flow as tears; the text does not say so directly. Even so, the point of the passage is to explain tears, not to assert the rulership of *xin*.⁴⁷ By contrast, *Suwen* 8 focuses on the role of the

---

⁴⁴ The *Huainanzi* also refers to the heart as the "ruler of the five *zang* viscera" (夫心者，五藏之主也). See *Huainanzi* 1/8/9–10.
⁴⁵ See Unschuld 1985: 79–83, and Lewis 2006: 37.
⁴⁶ For accounts of rulership of the mind see Geaney 2002: 17–18; Raphals 2015: 132–82; Sabattini 2015: 58–74; and Unschuld 1985: 100.
⁴⁷ A similar passage occurs at *Lingshu* 28: grief excites the heart, which causes the *zang* and *fu* viscera to sway or shake, opening the stem vessels and resulting in tears. It describes the heart as

heart as ruler. Other passages also describe *xin* as the ruler of the viscera but in the service of some other point.

Lingshu 71 describes the heart as the ruler of the other viscera, but also asserts that it is the residence of spirit, and that spirit is the *sine qua non* for life itself:

心者，五藏六府之大主也。精神之所舍也。其藏堅固，邪弗能容也。容之則心傷，心傷則神去，神去則死矣。

The heart is the great ruler of the five *zang* viscera and six *fu* viscera; it is where essence and spirit reside. As long as this *zang* viscera is firm and stable, evil [*qi*] cannot be permitted [entry]. If it is permitted, the heart is damaged; if the heart is damaged, spirit leaves; if spirit leaves, [the person] dies. (LS 71.934, Unschuld 2016: 639–40)

Here, the importance of *xin* — and its rulership of the other viscera — is a function of the presence of spirit, which is essential for survival. It presents a strong contrast to claims—for example in *Suwen* 8—that the importance of *xin* arises from its role as ruler of the other viscera, and not merely as the container of spirit.[48] This range of sometimes incompatible statements on *xin* within the *Huangdi neijing* compilation may reflect diverse textual origins.

Protecting Spirit

The role of spirit in maintaining life implies the need for therapeutic practices to protect it. Two subthemes derive from the therapeutic orientation of the *Huangdi neijing*: (1) accounts of the effects of emotions, especially the effects of grief on *xin* and *shén*; and (2) therapeutic techniques for protecting and

---

"the ruler among the five *zang* and six *fu* viscera. 心者，五藏六府之主也. LS 28.566; Unschuld 2016: 333. However, the point of the passage is to explain the causes of tears and weeping, not to assert the rulership of the *xin*.

[48] LS 80 makes a similar claim for the primacy of *shén*. It describes the eyes as the source of spirit *qi* (*shénqi* 神氣): "Camp and guard [*qi*] and *hun* and *po* pass through there [the eyes] continuously; they are where spirit *qi* is generated. Therefore, when *shén* is exhausted, *hun* and *po* dissipate, and will and thought are disturbed" 營衛魂魄之所常營也，神氣之所生也。故神勞則魂魄散，志意亂. As a result, "the eyes are the emissaries of the heart. The heart is the residence of *shén*" 目者，心使也。心者，神之舍也. LS 80.1091, Unschuld 2016: 755–56.

enhancing spirit. Several passages focus on the emotions as a source of potential harm to spirit.

As noted in the previous section, grief excites the heart and harms the viscera, resulting in tears. Similarly, *Lingshu* 66 notes that grief and worry harm the heart; double cold harms the lungs; and rage and anger harm the liver.[49] While these passages do not mention *shén* explicitly, harming the heart is dangerous to *shén* because it dwells in the heart.

Other passages are explicit that harming the heart injures spirit. *Lingshu* 35 describes how either draining a depletion or supplementing a repletion causes spirit to leave its residence, with multiple adverse consequences.[50] *Lingshu* 67 describes some cases in which spirit is excited, and its *qi* moves even before a needle is applied.[51] These passages describe spirit in quasi-material terms, as a substance that can be moved, depleted, or forced out of the body.

A very different approach to avoiding harm to spirit is to prohibit needling specific parts of the body at specific times of the calendar. *Lingshu* 61, "Five Prohibitions" (*Wujin* 五禁), describes a system of such prohibitions, based on the ten heavenly stems of the sexagenary cycle. On days when a given stem is active, the corresponding parts of the body should not be needled:

甲乙日自乘，無刺實，無發蒙於耳內。
丙丁日自乘，無振埃於肩喉，廉泉。
戊己日自乘四季，無刺腹去爪寫水。
庚辛日自乘，無刺關節於股膝。
壬癸日自乘，無刺足脛，是謂五禁。

On the days occupied by *jia* and *yi*, one must not pierce a repletion, and one must not conduct an enlightening [piercing] at the ear.
On the days occupied by *bing* and *ding*, one must not conduct a "shaking off dust" [piercing] at the shoulder, at the throat, and at the *lianquan* [opening].
On the days occupied by *wu* and *ji* and during the four time periods [representing the earth branches associated with the phase of wood], one must not pierce the abdomen and one must not conduct the "[finger/toe] nail clipping" [piercing] to drain water.

---

[49] 憂思傷心，重寒傷肺，忿怒傷肝. LS 66.899, Unschuld 2016: 611.
[50] 寫虛補實，神去其室. LS 35.623, Unschuld 2016: 379.
[51] LS 67.902; Unschuld 2016: 614. The context is individual differences in temperament and treatment.

On the days occupied by *geng* and *xin*, one must not pierce the joints at the upper thigh and knees.
On the days occupied by *ren* and *gui*, one must not pierce the feet and the lower legs; these are the so-called Five Prohibitions. (LS 61.830–31; Unschuld 2016: 561–62)

The second prohibition governs the shoulder and throat. The "shaking off dust" technique was used to treat *yang qi* moving into the chest when it should not, thus potentially affecting the heart and harming *shén*. The *Lingshu* passage does not explicitly refer to the heart or spirit, but calendric prohibitions in excavated texts do. For example, according to cautery prohibitions in medical manuscript texts from the first-century CE site of Hantanpo 旱灘坡, Wuwei 武威, cautery in the wrong place at the wrong time in a person's life was presumably fatal. One text, titled *Huangdi zhibing shénhun ji* 黃帝治病神魂忌 (Taboos of the Yellow Emperor for Treating Ills and [Protecting] *shénhun*), cautions against cauterizing the Heart vessel: "When a person is one year old, do not cauterize the heart, or there will be death within ten days."[52] The explicit reason for the prohibition is to protect *shénhun* 神魂 (either *shén* and *hun* or a compound *shénhun*). However, fine-grained timing of cautery prohibitions is necessary only if *shén* and *hun* change locations in the body over the course of a life span: in other words, if they move within the body in a regular fashion.

Detailed accounts of mobile spirits in the body occur in medieval medical sources, including Dunhuang manuscripts from the ninth/tenth centuries, which describe prohibitions on acupuncture and cautery based on the location and movement of a "human spirit" (*renshén* 人神) that was believed to change location in the body on a calendrical cycle.[53] *Renshén* prohibitions appear in the *Huangdi zhenjiu hama ji* 黃帝鍼灸鍼蟆忌 (*The Yellow Emperor's Toad Prohibitions for Acupuncture and Cautery*), a lost text dateable to between the Han and Sui dynasties. Much of its content is preserved by extensive quotation of the *Huangdi hama jing* 黃帝鍼蟆經 (The Yellow Emperor's Toad canon) in the oldest extant Japanese medical text, the *Ishinpō* 醫心方

---

[52] 人生一歲毋灸心，十日而死. *Wuwei Handai yijian* 1975: 4, slip 21. See also Yang and Brown 2017: 241–301. Their translation is based on Akahori Akira 1978: 75–107. Despeux (2007: 82) points to this text as the oldest known Chinese evidence of a concept of a mobile spirit.
[53] See Harper 2003: 471–512; and 2005: 134–64; Arrault 2010: 285–332.

(Recipes at the Heart of Medicine) completed in 984 by Tamba Yasuyori 丹波康賴.[54] The *Ishinpō* identifies specific times in life to avoid when the *renshén* is migrating from one location to another.

The *Ishinpō* identifies locations for *renshén* based on age, day of the month, and days to avoid when the *renshén* is migrating from one location to another. It also gives locations at various times of the day for the five "spirits": *hun*, *po*, *shén*, will (*zhi*), and intentions (*yi*):

凡平旦至食時魂在中府，魄在目眥，神在膀胱，志在天窗，意在人中。
禺中魂在人中交，魄在口左右，神在中庭，志在天窗，意在人中。
日中魂在氣陰迎，魄在厥陰，神在目眥曲澤，志在陰谷，意在太陰。
日昳至晡時魂在期門，魄在尺澤，神在目，志在臍，意在晴明。

From the time of dawn to the [first] meal *hun* is in *Zhongfu*, *po* is in the eyelids, *shén* is in the bladder, will is in *Tianchuang*, intentions are in *Renzhong*.
Approaching midday *hun* is in *Renzhong jiao*, *po* is in the left and right sides of the mouth, *shén* is in *Zhongting*, will is in *Tianchuang*, intentions are in *Renzhong*.
At midday *hun* is in *Qiyin ying*, *po* is in *Jueyin*, *shén* is in the eyelids and Q*uze*, will is in *Yingu*, intentions are in *Taiyin*.
From the time of dusk to the time *bushi*, *hun* is in *Qimen*, *po* is in *Chize*, *shén* is in the eyes, will is in the navel, and intentions are in *Qingming*. (*Ishinpō* 2.71, cf. Hsia et al. 1986, 1:286–94)

Calendric prohibitions on acupuncture and cautery based on the movements of *renshén* are also described by the seventh-century physician Sun Simiao 孫思邈 in his *Qianjin yaofang* 千金要方 (Essential Recipes Worth a Thousand in Gold). According to Sun, in order to practice acupuncture or cautery, one must know the patient's yearly motion (*xingnian* 行年) and suitable and prohibited times, as well as the location of the *renshén*, to

---

[54] The *Huangdi zhenjiu hama ji* is listed in the *Suishu* 隨書 bibliographic treatise. The *Huangdi hama jing* 黄帝鍼蟆經 is preserved in an 1823 Japanese woodblock edition (rpt. Beijing: Renmin weisheng chubanshe, 1984) and is quoted extensively in the *Ishinpō*. See V. Lo 2001: 61–99.

ensure that its location does not correspond to the prohibited periods.[55] Sun also describes harm to *renshén* in extensive monthly food prohibitions of specific types of meat or fish, to avoid harming the *renshén* or the *renshén* and *qi*. For example: "in the first month do not eat tiger, panther or fox meat; they harm *renshén*."[56]

Ninth- to tenth-century (CE) calendars excavated from Dunhuang also indicate the location of *renshén* in the body at different times in cycles of nine or twelve years.[57] The manuscript P2675V° gives another version of calendric *renshén* prohibitions:

甲乙日頭丙丁日在眉戊己日腹[][]日在心壬癸日在足

On *jia* and *yi* days it is at the head. On *bing* and *ding* days it is at the eyebrows [shoulders]. On *wu* and *ji* days it is at the abdomen. On [*geng* and *xin*] days it is at the heart. On *ren* and *gui* days it is at the feet.[58]

Some scholars consider *renshén* systems to be a later elaboration of *Lingshu*-type prohibitions. In this view, the *Lingshu* system had no shifting *shén*, and this element was added later. However, Donald Harper argues for a shared iatromantic background between the Wuwei cautery prohibitions and *Lingshu* 61, "Five Prohibitions." Both use the ten heavenly stems of the sexagenary cycle, arranged in pairs. The *Lingshu* system has no mobile *shén*, but with one exception, its prohibited locations correspond to the *renshén* system for the ten heavenly stems in the Dunhuang manuscript P2675V°. In this view, the first-century CE Wuwei cautery prohibitions provide a relatively early account of mobile *shén* understood

---

[55] 先知行年宜忌，及人神所在不與禁忌相應即可. *Qianjin yaofang* 89.8a. Subsequent sections describe its location in different parts of the body at different ages (89.11a–b) and describes prohibited locations for specific days of the month (89.12a–b). Similar prohibitions appear in his *Qianjin yifang* 千金翼方 (Supplementary Prescriptions Worth a Thousand Gold). For comparable passages from the *Qianjin yifang*, see Harper 2004: 154 and 163nn53, 58.

[56] 正月勿食虎豹狸肉傷人神. *Qianjin yaofang* 80.14a. Chapter 80 lists *renshén* food prohibitions for nine months of the year: rabbit 兔肉 (month two), horse 馬肉, deer 鹿肉 and roebuck meat 麋肉 (month five), wild goose 鷺肉 and duck 鴈肉 (month six), chicken 雞肉 (month eight), dog meat 犬肉 (month nine), carp intestine and fish roe 鯉魚腸魚子 (no month specified), pork 豬肉 (month ten), the meat of rats and swallows 鼠肉鷰肉 (month eleven), and beef 牛肉 and crab meat 蟹鼈 (month twelve). See *Qianjin yaofang* 80.9b–20b.

[57] See Arrault 2010. For further discussion see Despeux 2007: 83–86.

[58] Cong Chunyu 1994: 209. See Cong's annotations for "shoulders" and for the interpolation of *geng xin* and cross-references to the *Qianjin yaofang*. For discussion of this passage see Harper 1999: 103 and 108n41.

in terms of prohibitions on acupuncture and cautery.[59] In any case, what matters for the purposes of the present discussion is, first, that the Wuwei cautery prohibitions (like the *Huangdi neijing*) identify harming spirit with damage to the heart, and, second, that their focus of interest is not on the heart, but on *shén*.

In the *Huangdi neijing*, accounts of avoiding harm to spirit focused on its lodging place, the heart, and specifically on the role of some emotions as sources of damage to the heart, and thence, to spirit. In the few cases where discussions of emotions as sources of harm occur in excavated medical texts, the topic is handled rather differently. The *Yinshu* 引書 text from Zhangjiashan describes emotional disharmony as a cause of illness, but its context is an explanation of why individuals of different social classes fall ill for different reasons. It explains that the common people become ill frequently and die easily because they cannot regulate their *qi*. As a result, their yin declines early and they are unable to counteract it, but the nobility fall ill for different reasons:

貴人之所以得病者，以其喜怒之不和也。喜則陽氣多，怒則陰氣多，是以道者喜則急呴，怒則劇吹，以和之。吸天地之精氣，實其陰，故能無病。

The reason that nobility become ill is that they do not harmonize their joy and anger. If they are joyful, their yang *qi* is excessive; if they are angry their *yin qi* is excessive. Therefore, following *dao*, when they are joyful they should exhale (warm breath) quickly, and when they are angry they should increasingly puff out (moist breath) in order to harmonize it. If they breathe in the essence *qi* of heaven and earth and solidify their yin, they will be able to be without illness.[60]

Here, preservation of health is specifically linked to harmonizing emotions and moderating yin and yang *qi* rather than the *Huangdi neijing* explanation of unregulated joy and anger harming the heart and liver or the need to preserve *shén* in the heart or elsewhere. Excess emotion is linked to illness

---

[59] Harper 2005: 152 and 162n48.
[60] *Zhangjiashan Hanmu zhujian (247 hao mu)* 185, slips 106–10. For translation, see V. Lo 2014: 116–18. The passage continues that lowborn people become ill due to exhaustion from labor, hunger, and thirst, and ignorance of how to keep warm and breathe correctly. For additional commentary, see Gao Dalun 1995 and Peng Hao 1990.

specifically among the nobility. For all social classes the causes of declining *yin qi* are material rather than moral; and regulating *qi* is linked to breathing techniques that preserve *yin qi* and health.[61]

Finally, *Lingshu* 1 addresses how the actions of a practitioner can harm spirit, emphasizing that skilled practitioners care about treating spirit: unrefined practitioners treat the body while outstanding ones treat spirit.[62] It cautions on how to avoid damage to spirit by inserting the needle straight, with a firm grip. The passage continues:

神在秋毫…方刺之時，必在懸陽及與兩衛。神屬勿去，知病存亡。

Spirit is concentrated in [the space of] an autumn hair.... At the moment of piercing [the focus of attention] must be on the suspended yang and on the two guards. Spirit [must] remain attached and must not leave. [In this way] one knows whether the patient will survive or perish.[63]

Other chapters describe the care physicians must take of their own spirit in order to treat others effectively.[64]

In summary, several points are noteworthy about the foregoing accounts of *xin* and *shén* in medical texts of the *Huangdi neijing* tradition and beyond. First, *xin* is closely associated with *shén*, but in what way? Although some passages assert the role of *xin* as the ruler of the other viscera and the body, they do so in the context of asserting the importance of *shén* as the *sine qua non* of the life of the body. Second, accounts of *shén* describe it as a fundamental constituent of the body, sometimes in contrasts between spirit and physical form but pervasively in accounts of *shén* as fundamental to life, especially in *Lingshu* 8 and 54. Other chapters discuss how to enhance and protect *shén* (including by therapeutic techniques and by self-cultivation) and address sources of potential harm to it (including excess emotion, heterodox *qi*, and incompetent medical practice).

---

[61] SW 77.1334 (Unschuld and Tessenow 2011 2:666–67); LS 66.886 (Unschuld 2016: 603).
[62] 麤守形，上守神. LS 1.32, Unschuld 2016: 36. This point is made even more strongly in LS 3, which glosses and amplifies this passage (LS 3.90, Unschuld 2016: 75–76).
[63] LS 1.40–42, Unschuld 2016: 41.
[64] LS 9 emphasizes the need for practitioners to concentrate their own *shén* in order to treat that of a patient (9.235, Unschuld 2016: 170–71). LS 75 describes the "spirit illumination" (*shénming*) of an expert practitioner necessary to practice effective needling on the five *zang* viscera (LS 75.994, Unschuld 2016: 681).

Third, the *Huangdi neijing* identifies five distinct psychological capacities associated with *xin*, including *shén*, *hun*, and *po*. But there is no clear separation between mind and body: it is not possible to separate a material organ such as the liver from the non- or quasi-material *hun* stored within it. These texts are striking for their "corporealization" of consciousness. Despite passing claims for the rulership of *xin*, they effectively decentralize consciousness, removing control from the mind and distributing it among the five *zang* viscera.[65]

Dualism Reconsidered

At this point, one might object that in medical texts, with their specific concerns, we can identify a spirit–body dualism in which medical *shén* substitutes for philosophical *xin*. Indeed, two *Suwen* passages suggest some kind of spirit–body dualism in a contrast between a clearly material body and a possibly immaterial spirit. They mention four corporeal ("form") viscera (*xingzang* 形藏) and five "spirit viscera" (*shénzang* 神藏), identified with the five *yin* viscera: heart, lungs, spleen, liver, and kidneys:

故形藏四，神藏五，合為九藏，以應之也。

Thus, the corporeal *zang* viscera are four, the spirit *zang* viscera are five. Together this makes nine *zang* viscera to correspond to them. (SW 9.251, Unschuld and Tessenow 2011: 1: 168)

故神藏五，形藏四，合為九藏。

Thus, the spirit *zang* viscera are five, the corporeal *zang* viscera are four. Together this makes nine *zang* viscera. (SW 20.483, Unschuld and Tessenow 2011: 1: 356)

The problem is that neither the *Suwen* nor the *Lingshu* specify or discuss "corporeal" or "spirit" viscera. These terms occur only twice in the

---

[65] I am grateful to an anonymous reviewer from *T'oung-pao* for emphasizing the importance of this point.

Huangdi neijing, and not at all in the *Nanjing* or *Jiayi jing*, although they appear repeatedly in Tang sources.[66] In other words, there may well be an argument for spirit–body dualism in later medical sources, but not in the *Huangdi neijing*.

Are there other passages that address the possibility of spirit–body dualism in the *Huangdi neijing*? The *Huangdi neijing* repeatedly links spirit to essence (*jing*) and *qi* in the constitution of a person, and several passages combine *shén* with clearly material aspects of the body in their accounts of yin and yang, *shén*, and *jingqi*.[67] Lingshu 5 describes proper storage of spirit in the body as the union of corporeal form and *qi*:

調陰與陽，精氣乃光，合形與氣，使神內藏。

Balancing yin and yang [*qi*] causes essence *qi* to become luminous. Uniting form and *qi* causes spirit to be stored internally. (LS 5.158; Unschuld 2016: 123)

Here, the union of the clearly corporeal *xing* and at least partially corporeal *qi* causes the storage of *shén*. In other words, there is no contrast between a corporeal body and some kind of noncorporeal spirit. *Shén* is also described as a component of the body in *Lingshu* 18:

營衛者，精氣也。血者，神氣也。故血之與氣，異名同類焉。

Camp and guard [*qi*] are essence *qi*. Blood is spirit *qi*. Hence blood and *qi* may have different names, but they are the same in kind. (LS 18.441; Unschuld 2016: 265)[68]

---

[66] See, for example, Dunhuang manuscript P3477, "Xuan Gan's Pulse Canon" (*Xuan Gan mai jing* 玄感脈經), for the four corporeal and five spirit viscera; Ma Jixing et al. 1998: 153. Here, the corporeal viscera are the temples (*toujiao* 頭角), ears and eyes (*ermu* 耳目), mouth and teeth (*kouchi* 口齒), and the center of the chest (*xiongzhong* 胸中). The five spirit viscera are the *zang* of the *Huangdi neijing*: the heart, lungs, liver, spleen, and kidneys. See Wang Shumin 2005a and 2005b, especially 54 and 395, respectively; and E. Hsu 2010: 107–84, especially 156–59. For discussion of Dunhuang manuscripts and the *Huangdi neijing*, see Harper 2010.

[67] Accounts of *jing* and *qi* are prominent in earlier philosophical literature, especially in the "Arts of the Mind" and "Inner Workings" chapters of the Guanzi, as was previously discussed in Chapters 3 and 4.

[68] Here *shénqi* seems clearly to refer to the spirit *qi* that must settle in the heart as part of the completion of the body, but *shén* and *qi* can also occur as separate terms. A similar problem occurs with *jingqi* (essence *qi*) and *jing* and *qi*.

This passage answers a request for an explanation about why blood and *qi* have different names but are "the same in kind" (*tong lei* 同類). It defines camp and guard *qi* as essence *qi* and blood as spirit *qi*, and it identifies both with the physical body. *Lingshu* 12 also describes the storage of *shén* and *qi* (as distinct from "spirit" alone in *Lingshu* 5):

五藏者，合神氣魂魄而藏之。六府者，受穀而行之，受氣而揚之。經脈者，受血而營之。

The five *zang* viscera unite spirit, *qi*, *hun*, and *po* and store them. The six *fu* viscera receive grain and transmit it; they receive the *qi* and disperse it. The conduit/stream vessels receive the blood and circulate it. (LS 12.351; cf. Unschuld 2016: 216)

Lingshu 52, "Guard *Qi*" (*Weiqi*), makes a similar point:

五藏者，所以藏精神魂魄者也。六府者，所以受水穀而行化物者也。其氣內干五藏，而外絡肢節。

The five *zang* viscera are what stores essence, spirit, *hun*, and *po*. The six *fu* viscera are what receives water and grain, and what processes and transforms things [ingested substances]. Their *qi* internally seeks to reach the five *zang* viscera; externally they link the limbs and the joints. (LS 52.765; Unschuld 2016: 501)

Here the storage is accomplished by the *zang* viscera rather than by the union of the body and *qi*. The context, however, is different since these passages are contrasting the collective functions of the five *zang* and six *fu* viscera. Nonetheless, like *Lingshu* 5, these passages describe the material storage of *shén*, *hun*, and *po* in the body.

Lingshu 47, "Taking the *Zang* Viscera as the Foundation" (Benzang 本藏), also describes the *zang* viscera as storing spirit, *hun*, *po*, essence, blood, and *qi*:

志意者，所以御精神，收魂魄，適寒溫，和喜怒者也。...志意和，則精神專直，魂魄不散，悔怒不起，五藏不受邪矣。...五藏者，所以藏精神血氣魂魄者也。

Will and thought are what serve to rein in essence and spirit, control *hun* and *po*, take charge of cold and heat, and harmonize joy and rage.... When will and thought are harmonized, essence and spirit are focused, *hun* and *po* do not dissipate, regret and rage do not emerge, and the five *zang* viscera do not receive evil [*qi*].... The five *zang* viscera are what stores essence, spirit, blood, *qi*, *hun*, and *po*. (LS 47.706–707; Unschuld 2016: 447–48)[69]

The focus here is on the regulatory role of will and thought (*zhi yi* 志意)—linked to the kidneys and spleen—in storing and regulating the components of a person necessary to survival and in preventing their dissipation through harmful emotions or pernicious external *qi*. *Xin* is strikingly absent from this discussion.

Several other passages discuss the importance of "essence and spirit" (*jing shén*). For example, *Suwen* 1 describes the presence of essence and spirit as the basis of health and longevity.[70] *Suwen* 3 links *jing* and *shén* to the *qi* of Heaven—the basis of the life span—and to *shénming*: "Hence when the sages concentrated essence and spirit, and when they ingested the *qi* of Heaven, they corresponded to spirit illumination" 故聖人傳精神, 服天氣, 而通神明.[71] Yet other passages associate *shén* with locations other than the *xin* in the body. One is the joints: "The so-called joints, they are the locations where spirit *qi* passes, where it exits and enters; they are neither skin, flesh, sinews, nor bones."[72]

In summary, the *Huangdi neijing* tradition reflects what may be fundamental differences of genre in treatments of the relation between *shén* and *xin* in philosophical versus at least some medical texts. *Shén* is of central importance in both genres but for different reasons. From the therapeutic perspective of medical texts, it is the basis of life and health rather than—associated with *xin*—the locus of cognition and moral judgment, as in many philosophical texts. In the *Huangdi neijing*, much of the importance of *xin*—when not simply the heart—is its role as the storehouse or dwelling of *shén*. Similarly,

---

[69] Here and in most instances, Unschuld translates *jing shén* as "essence spirit" rather than as "essence and spirit" and *zhi yi* as "mind" rather than "will and thought"; see, for example, SW 78 (SW 78.1349, Unschuld and Tessenow 2011: 2: 680), and SW 14 (SW 14.324, Unschuld and Tessenow 2011: 1: 236–37).

[70] SW 1.23 and 38, Unschuld and Tessenow 2011: 1: 34 and 44. See also SW 14.324, Unschuld and Tessenow 2011: 1: 236–37, and SW 78.1349, Unschuld and Tessenow 2011: 2: 680.

[71] SW 3.62, Unschuld and Tessenow 2011: 1: 60–61. The Wang Bing commentary adds that only sages who have attained *dao* are able to transmit essence and spirit.

[72] 所言節者, 神氣之所遊行出入也, 非皮肉筋骨也. LS 1.52; Unschuld 2016: 47.

accounts of the injurious effects of emotions on *xin* and *shén* are focused on preserving the essential role of *shén* in maintaining life, health, and longevity.

Not all medical texts reflect consistent differences from philosophical texts, in part because of terminological and conceptual tensions within the *Huangdi neijing* corpus and tradition, but also because of the rich diversity of medical thought itself. To give two brief examples, early Han medical texts from Zhangjiashan are not concerned with the relationship between *shén*, *xin*, and the body; and some passages in *Huangdi neijing*, such as the passages from *Lingshu* 5 and 18 discussed earlier, even seem to advance a weak monism.

Accounts of *xin* as ruler of the body or the senses also occur in the context of *xin* as the locus of *shén*, including in pentic correlations featuring both. I would suggest that these medical materials remain relevant to philosophical discussions of *shén* and *xin* because they intersect with the latter in treatments of self-cultivation where *shén* is linked to *jing* and *qi* as well as to *shénming*.[73]

Conclusion

In the medical texts surveyed here, cognitive and moral aspects of *xin* receive little attention. By contrast, *shén* is an important topic: as an essential element that must be protected from harm in needling prohibitions, and as a key goal of self-cultivation practices for health and longevity. Self-cultivation involves the balance and regulation of *qi*, *jing*, *yin* and *yang*, and *shén* as both spirit *qi* (*shénqi*) and spirit and essence (*jing shén*). This intellectual landscape contrasts strongly with excavated philosophical texts that describe *xin*—and its cultivation—in terms of rites, music, and the virtues, and do not mention *shén*.

Nonetheless, *shén* is closely associated with *xin* in the *Huangdi neijing*. As the above discussion has shown, different passages describe that connection in different ways. Some use container metaphors in which *xin* is the dwelling place of *shén*, including in pentic correlations in which the five *zang* viscera correspond to five "spirits." Others, less commonly,

---

[73] Examples include the "Arts of the Mind" chapters of the *Guanzi* and the "Ten Questions" (*Shiwen*) text from Mawangdui, which were previously discussed in Chapters 3 and 4.

present ruler metaphors in which *xin* and *shén* rule the body as a ruler rules a state.[74] Many hermeneutic and textual issues complicate our understanding of the *Huangdi neijing* and excavated medical texts. Nonetheless, in most cases, *shén* is the important element. This is not surprising, given the repeated claim in the *Huangdi neijing* that *shén* is the basis of life. In early medical literature, *xin* is not necessarily identified with *shén* and is not represented as being metaphysically distinct from the other viscera. These points are important because they contrast so strongly with the dualistic paradigms that have been inferred from the early Chinese philosophical mainstream.

In conclusion, if we were to derive views of body, mind, and spirit purely from the philosophical mainstream, we could easily adopt a dualist mind–body view, represented especially by ruler metaphors in which the heart-mind and spirit are contrasted to, and rule, the body. The *Huangdi neijing* presents a different picture in which the relation of *xin* to the body and to *shén* is more complex. In contrast to the dualistic view of the person wherein a compound "mind–spirit" rules and regulates the body as a ruler does a state, it presents a corporeal view of persons as bodies, minds, and spirits. In this view, spirit is closely linked to essence and *qi*. It is significantly corporeal, fluid and mobile, and body and spirit are not easily distinguished. This nuanced and polyvocal picture shows the limitations of a simple antinomy between holism and dualism as ways of looking at early Chinese conceptions of the self.

---

[74] For additional accounts of the heart-storing spirit (*xin zang shén* 心藏神), see SW 23.569 and 62.1211 (Unschuld and Tessenow 2011: 1: 409, and 2: 102); LS 8.199–201 and 78.1070 (Unschuld 2016: 152–53 and 735). For spirit leaving when the heart is damaged, see LS 71.934; Unschuld 2016: 639–40. For "the heart as the ruler of the body and the source of *shénming*" 心者，君主之官也，神明出焉, see SW 8.237; Unschuld and Tessenow 2011: 1: 155–56.

Conclusions

This book surveys the complex interrelations between bodies, minds, spirits, and souls in early China. I end by summarizing these results, suggesting their implications, and sketching several areas for possible future research. Chapter 1 introduced the complex semantic field of bodies, minds, spirits, and souls. Chapter 2 argued that the *Book of Odes* (and Bronze Inscriptions) present a different body–mind–spirit landscape than do later Warring States: philosophical texts. Spirits are all external, and the "heart–mind" is primarily a "feeling heart." But the Odes also clearly describes a thinking, inmost mind, and a strong sense of psychological interiority. Its landscape of human bodies focuses on the interiority and behavior of embodied and ritual persons, in contrast to the many descriptions of the forms and frames of plants and nonhuman animals. The Odes offers a normative description of specifically human behavior that includes both psychological interiority and the external appearances presented by embodied (*shēn*) and ritual (*gong*) persons of men and women who are virtuous (or not) in their inmost minds.

Chapter 3 surveyed claims for the hegemony of the heart–mind across a range of Warring States and Han texts. These texts assert the primacy of the heart–mind and its capacity to make cognitive and normative judgments. The *Analects* and *Mencius* focus on its role in guiding desires, while the *Mozi*, *Guanzi*, and *Xunzi* focus on its cognitive capacities, especially the *Xunzi*. The same emphasis appears in excavated texts from Guodian and "The Heart-Mind Is What Is at the Center." These texts also describe the heart–mind as ruling, and more important than, the body or senses, typically in metaphors that compare the mind to the ruler of a state. Texts vary in what the ruler rules, ranging from subordinate officials to slaves. In some cases, the hegemony of the heart–mind is based on its role as the dwelling of spirit, where the heart–mind and spirit function as an amalgam rather than as two interacting faculties. The result is a binary view of a person in two senses. One is the polarity between the body and the mind or spirit. The other is the agency of the heart–mind–spirit amalgam as the ruling and active part of the polarity, with the body as both ruled and passive. Both are consistent with mind–body dualism.

Chapter 4 turned to a very different arrangement of body, heart–mind, and spirit in the *Neiye* chapter of the *Guanzi*, the *Zhuangzi*, the *Shiwen* text from Mawangdui, and the *Huainanzi*, beginning with awareness of the body as an important site of self-care in doctrines attributed to Yang Zhu. These texts focus on the concentration of essence (*jing*) as part of the development of internal spirit. These processes crucially involve the body and cause the adept to become "like a spirit." In these texts, the role of the heart–mind varies. In the *Neiye*, it is an essential part of the self-cultivation process. In the *Zhuangzi*, by contrast, it is at times an obstacle to that process, hence the latter's recommendations to "concentrate spirit" and "fast the heart–mind."[1] In the *Shiwen* the cultivation of essence, *qi*, and spirit leads to health and longevity, without involvement of the heart–mind. The "Essence and Spirit" chapter of the *Huainanzi* frames the body as a microcosm of a cosmos in which essence and spirit are Heaven-derived components that must be kept together and retained.

Insofar as the Guodian texts appear to be, and have been read as, a kind of summary of late Warring States thought, their accounts of body and heart–mind are especially important. They present no unified view, ranging from the strong dualism of the *Wuxing* and *Ziyi* to the possible holism of the *Xingzi mingchu*. The *Wuxing* and *Ziyi* compare the heart–mind to the ruler of a state and the body to his subordinates, to the people, or to slaves. Some readings of the *Xingzi mingchu* are robustly holist views of *qi* unifying and equalizing body and mind, in which similarities between the "flow" of *qi*, sound, and music make possible moral transformation through music. Dualist readings of the *Xingzi mingchu* privilege the heart–mind's capacity to generate fixed intentions. Other texts suggest intermediate positions that could be described as weak mind–body dualism or weak mind–body holism. Taken together, the range of opinion in the Guodian texts demonstrates the importance of interrelations between body and mind, as central to their virtue-based accounts of both self-cultivation and state organization.

By contrast, the medical texts surveyed in Chapter 6 have little concern for cognitive and moral aspects of the heart–mind. But they are extremely concerned with spirit, both as a vital element that must be protected from

---

[1] The Zhuangist authors seem to be quite critical of the completed heart–mind, but other passages refer more positively to a *xin* that is not fixed, and some of the skill masters (for example, the wheelwright Lun Bian) use their heart–minds in ways the Zhuangist authors endorse.

harm and as a key goal of self-cultivation practices for health and longevity. These texts also describe self-cultivation procedures based on the balance and regulation of essence, *qi*, and spirit. The *Huangdi neijing* also associates spirit with the heart, both as the container in which it dwells and as the co-ruler of the other *zang* viscera. But the underlying medical reason for the importance of spirit is that *shén* is the basis of life, which cannot exist without it. The *Huangdi neijing* presents a very different picture than the philosophical mainstream. In contrast to dualist "mind-rulers" it presents a corporeal view of persons as bodies, minds, and spirits, in which spirit is closely linked to essence and *qi*, and body and spirit are not easily distinguished.

These chapters link treatments of the body and embodiment to accounts of the heart–mind and self-cultivation. They also offer new perspectives on the problem of mind–body dualism by suggesting a tripartite structure in which the heart–mind and spirit are distinct capacities that do not align in a dualist manner. The texts surveyed here clearly present many instances of what I will call "x-body dualism," where "x" may be the heart–mind, spirit, or some amalgam of the two. But other texts treated here present compelling evidence that the heart–mind and spirit cannot be reduced to an "x" in dualist relation to the body, which itself is complex and multivocal.

An alternative is a more nuanced position. It recognizes that some degree of dualism is fundamental or even "hard-wired" in the human brain, but that does not mean that we should reduce our understanding of personhood, cognition, and so on, to x-body dualism. In addition, we must give due weight to the legacy of mind–body dualism within Western philosophical traditions in order to consider alternatives.

But the defining feature of mind–body dualism in Western philosophy is not simply "dualism" in the sense of perceiving mind and body as fundamentally different. Rather, it is the view that agency resides in the mind and that the body has no part in it, beyond following the mind's orders.[2] When cognition is understood as the sole prerogative of the mind, agency becomes an aspect of mental states rather than embodied action. Real alternatives to this appear in spirit-centered accounts such as the Zhuangist alignment between body and spirit and the *Guanzi*'s alignment of body, heart–mind, and spirit. Even mind-centered accounts such as the *Mencius* describe the complex mutual influence of intention and *qi*.

---

[2] I am grateful to Karyn Lai for comments on this point.

This inquiry also raises many questions about what it means to be a human person. These include matters of the constitution of the self, the idea of locus, the nature of agency, and a view of normative and cognitive judgments that is significantly embodied. In this spirit, I conclude with three brief examples.

Inner and Outer Reconsidered

The complex interactions between clearly physical forms and frames, embodied persons, heart–minds, and spirits present a multilayered picture of human personhood that cannot be reduced to binaries of body and mind. They raise many questions whose answers are beyond the scope of the present study. How does the distinction between inner and outer (*neiwai*) frame notions of motivation, and the rightness or wrongness of actions and motivations? Which parts, and in which configurations, are the relationships between frames, embodied persons, heart–minds, and spirits constitutive of self? Are they all necessary? Can we say, without any one of them, that there is no self or no person? Are any or all of them defining aspects of humanity, distinguishing it from other species (or from nonterrestrials, or artificial intelligences)?

We can speculate that *all* these categories are necessary to, or constitutive of, self but to varying degrees. It seems clear that any human being requires a physical form, frame, and limbs, whether or not they correspond to human norms. One can lack substantial parts of the form and substance of a human body—arms and legs, for example—and still clearly be a person, but both the head and, at least most of the contents of the body cavity seem necessary for both physical and psychological survival. Similarly, plants and animals clearly have physical frames and forms and can exist without, or recover substantial parts of them, with details varying by species.

A more complex question is whether we can imagine a human being without a *shēn*. Can we say, for example, that a person who is brain dead or so psychopathic as to lack the "self" of an embodied person can truly be called a human being? Plants, nonhuman animals, and humans share (to varying degrees) the ability to survive without substantial parts of their form and frame. By contrast, only humans have embodied persons and the potential to become ritual persons, through the process of self-cultivation.[3] While

---

[3] The process of becoming a fully developed ritual person is thus dynamic and ongoing, and an important and distinctively Confucian understanding of personhood.

they may survive as biological beings without them, it is not clear that such survivors can truly be called human.

An interesting speculative perspective on this question comes from the East Asian affairs specialist Paul Myron Anthony Linebarger (1913–1966), who wrote science fiction under the pseudonym (closely guarded during his lifetime) of Cordwainer Smith. He imagined a future universe in which humans were modified extensively to be able to inhabit planets unfriendly to the human form and frame. As a result, you could "look like scrambled eggs," and legally be a "true human." By contrast, human-animal hybrids called "Underpeople" were legally confined to the human norm but classified as homunculi, and robots implanted with the essential personality of dead human high-level experts were legally classified as machines.[4] In other words, in the thought experiment of these stories, identity as a "true human" was explicitly independent of the aspects of the body determined by both form and frame, which, in turn, were constitutive in the identities of Underpeople and (conscious machines). In the early Chinese context, plants and animals have form and frame, but only humans have embodied persons (*shēn*).

Another important feature of accounts of body, mind, and spirit in early China is the porosity of these categories, both in interactions between body, mind, spirit, and related psychological faculties "within" a person and in interactions with "external" entities, including the external environment and the ritual boundaries between external spirits and internal spirit. In strong contrast to Cartesian substance dualism, body, mind, and spirit consist of the same fundamental stuff—*qi*, albeit from multiple sources and varying degrees of refinement and concentration. This is not to deny strongly dualist elements within Chinese thought but only the extreme claims of substance dualism.

This complex view of bodies and persons also challenges the conventional polarity of inner and outer (*neiwai*), which are disordered by the porosities between frame, form, embodied person, heart–mind, and spirit. On the physical level, the intake and transformation of *qi* provide a continuity between the "inner-outer" boundaries of the body. The mind-centered view makes a clear distinction between the "greater part" (the mind) that rules the body and the "lesser part" that is ruled, even if both are ontologically continuous and composed of the same substances. The spirit-centered view

---

[4] These themes are especially explored in the stories "The Ballad of Lost C'Mell," "The Dead Lady of Clown Town," and "A Planet Named Shayol," in C. Smith 1975.

presents more complex boundaries between external and internal *qi*, since essence and *qi* are refined to produce internal spirit, which in turn pervades the body and affects, or even has power over, the external world.

Several texts, discussed especially in Chapter 4, describe the refinement of essence and *qi* via the heart–mind and spirit in techniques that integrate physical, emotional, cognitive, and spiritual well-being. The locus of these activities seems to be the heart–mind, where essence is refined and spirit is ultimately housed. Is this "locus" or residence a *physical* location, or is it metaphorical? I would suggest that it is physical but in the context of a series of porous "containers." The form and frame of the body (*xingti*) contain the heart–mind, which "contains" internal spirit. But internal spirit also moves through the body, which in turn has a porous boundary with the external environment, including the larger spatial framework of the cosmos itself.

An important implication of porous boundaries between interior regions of the body, the body and its exterior, and between body, mind, and spirit is to raise questions about what is "interior" and what is "physical," entities that are ontologically distinct in substance dualism. This matters because the evidence of anthropology makes clear that these categories are not universal.[5] For example, Marilyn Strathern argues that, far from being regarded as unique entities, Melanesian persons are understood as both individuals and "dividuals." In this sense, singular persons are also understood as social microcosms, constructed as the plural and composite site of the relationships that produced them. The singular person, understood as a derivative of multiple identities, may be transformed into a dividual composed of distinct male and female elements. These elements are fundamental to relationships, social life, and the understanding of gender.[6]

Concepts of inner and outer are also challenged by the Amazonian anthropologist Philippe Descola. He argues that some perceived distinction between "interiority" and "physicality" is a human universal. Interiority is the attribution of mental processes—subjectivity and intentionality—which is described, at least metaphorically, as interior. Physicality refers to the world available to sense experience and the properties of beings related to behavior or form, again described metaphorically as exterior.[7]

---

[5] See, for example, Fowler 2004 and Scheper-Hughes and Lock 1987.
[6] Strathern 1988: 12–15, 275, 348–49n7. The term *dividual* was originally coined by McKim Marriott (1976: 109 and 111) to describe South Asian theories of the person as not "individual" in the sense of indivisible, bounded units, but rather as "dividual" or divisible. As a result: "What goes on *between* actors are the same connected processes of mixing and separation that go on *within* actors"
[7] Descola 1996 and 2013: 116–19. This view has occasioned substantial debate.

But the details of distinctions based on interiority and physicality are culturally specific, and culturally specific schemas of practice reflect different ontologies that give rise to different modes of structuring relations of "selves" and others. Descola identifies four basic ontologies based on the four combinations of shared and distinct attributions of interiority and physicality to different kinds of living beings. Animism (which he identifies with Amazonia) sees interiority as continuous across all living things; in an animist ontology, all living things have agency and intentionality. Humans, nonhumans, and spirit entities have different physical forms, but all have interiority. Totemism (identified with indigenous Australia) sees interiority and exteriority as continuous, with the result that human groups (tribes) are identifiable with nonhuman counterparts (totems). Naturalism (which Descola identifies with the modern West) sees exteriority as continuous and interiority as discontinuous. Naturalist ontologies restrict intentionality and agency to human "culture," and deny it to nonhuman "nature." Cultural humans, in contrast to mechanical and determinist nature, have agency. Analogism (which he identifies with much of Asia, the Andes, and medieval Europe) sees no continuity in interiority or exteriority. With no continuous ontology or cosmology, identity or order arise only from artificial analogies between radically dissimilar elements, for example, astrology, polytheism, and belief in metempsychosis.[8]

But what happens to the perception of interiority when the boundary between the clearly delimited physical "body" (*xing, ti, shēn*) and the not clearly delimited subject of "interiority" is porous, and both are composed of the same physical substance? Whether or not we agree with Descola's schema, it problematizes distinctions between "inner" and "outer," especially the view that associates mind and self with an "inner" space, linked to psychological interiority, and contrasted with a corporealized "outer" space defined by the physical body.

The mind-centered views presented in Chapter 3 broadly support this view, especially if spirit stays home and occupies its dwelling in the heart-mind in the center of the chest. The spirit-centered views of Chapter 4 and the medical texts surveyed in Chapter 6 complicate matters. Here, there seems to be no firm boundary between spirit and body. Spirit(s) circulate(s) in it, and arises from essence (*jing*) and *qi*, which also constitute the embodied person. Indeed, the practices that create or enhance spirit and spirit illumination

[8] Descola 2013: 121–25.

seem coterminous with practices that enhance physical health and longevity. Body and spirit seem to be composed of the same substances. A partial exception is the *Huainanzi* cosmology in which spirit is provided by Heaven and frame and bones by Earth. Yet even here, they come together at the time of birth, and a major part of the self-cultivation process is to keep them together as along as possible.

Descola's schema also raises questions about locus, and what is understood as interior, or as physical. For example, self-cultivation texts such as the *Neiye* describe the heart–mind as the "residence" of spirit, but is this a literal, physical location, or is it metaphorical? Genre differences matter. Medical texts such as the *Huangdi neijing* clearly identify the heart as a physical organ in the center of the chest. But philosophical texts also at least suggest that this is a literal, rather than a metaphorical location; in several cases, the mind-ruler analogy specifically draws on the central position of the ruler in the state and the heart–mind in the body. In such analogies, the brain (*nao* 腦) is never identified with the mind. (For instances of this term in the *Huangdi neijing*, see Appendix 3.)

In summary, inner-outer distinctions are problematic for the texts surveyed here because the various bodies and nonbody categories (heart-mind, spirit) are ontologically continuous and composed of the same substances.

Personal Identity and Persistence

Accounts of body, mind, and spirit also have implications for theories of the nature of personal identity in contemporary philosophy, especially with regard to whether there is such a thing as a stable self, and if so, what is the basis of its persistence. A full account of these theories is beyond the scope of the present discussion, but the kind of thought experiments used to argue these positions is striking. The arguments differ, but they consistently imagine that a body can be separated from the mind, spirit, soul, or some other kind of nonmaterial psychological persistence. A few examples illustrate this point, beginning with the arguments of John Locke (1632–1704).

Against claims that the mind, spirit, or immortal soul is the basis of personal identity, Locke argued that personal identity consists in psychological continuity through memory. For Locke a person is: "a thinking intelligent Being, that has reason and reflection, and can consider itself as itself, the same thinking thing, in different times and places; which it does only by that consciousness which is inseparable from thinking."[9] Thus, for Locke, consciousness constitutes the self and personal identity. In one of the many thought experiments he used to explore these questions, Locke imagines that the soul of a prince, with his consciousness and memories, is transposed into the body of a cobbler. Locke argues that the "person" of the prince persists in the body of a man who is recognized by others as the cobbler.[10] But the prince's soul, consciousness, and memories can only be separable from his body if they are ontologically distinct from it.

Locke's view remains influential, and many contemporary philosophers continue to use psychological continuity as the criterion for personal identity.[11] By contrast, David Hume (1711-1776) argued that enduring personal identity does *not* exist and that there is no self. Each of us is: "nothing but a bundle or collection of different perceptions, which succeed each other with an inconceivable rapidity, and are in a perpetual flux and movement ... nor is there any single power of the soul, which remains unalterably the same."[12] Hume concludes that, while perceptions seem to resemble or cause each other, no "self" links them together, and it is a mistake to talk about personal identity.[13]

Both Locke and Hume assume that mind and body are ontologically different. By contrast, it is almost impossible to imagine the authors of the *Mencius*, *Zhuangzi*, or *Xunzi* proposing this kind of dislocation. Would Locke have been so unwilling to take soul or spirit as the basis for personal identity if they were significantly corporeal, as they are in the *Yellow Emperor's Classic of Internal Medicine*?

Hume's views are also informed by an implicit rejection of the very notion of an embodied person. His objection to the idea of self-consciousness is that it is particular and embodied. As he puts it: "when I enter most intimately into what I call *myself*, I always stumble on some particular perception." He adds: "I never can catch *myself* at any time without a perception, and never can observe anything but the perception."[14] Why is this an objection? Hume's

---

[9] Locke 1999[1689]: 2.27.9: 318-19. He rejects the soul as the criterion for personal identity because that criterion would allow the same person to exist in different bodies at different times (2.27.6: 315).
[10] Locke 1999[1689]: 2.27.15: 324.
[11] For details see Olson 2021, J. Smith 2020, and Sorabji 2006.
[12] Hume 1978 [1739-40] 1.4.6: 252.
[13] Hume 1978 [1739-40] 1.4.6: 259. Thus, memory is the source for the perception of personal identity, but that perception is an illusion (1.4.6: 261-62). A number of analytic philosophers have followed Hume in denying the existence of a self. See Sorabji 2006: 18-20.
[14] Hume 1978 [1739-40]: 1.4.6: 252.

problem with self-consciousness is not that it does not occur but that it is corporeal.

Dualist thought experiments also populate claims for somatic continuity as the basis of personal identity. For example, in "The Self and the Future," Bernard Williams argues for a criterion of somatic continuity. He imagines a complex "body-change" in which two individuals exchange memories, and which future "self" each one is most concerned for.[15] Again, the creation of "Body A/memory B" and "Body B/memory A" would be unimaginable without substance dualism.[16]

Derek Parfit redefined the debate on personal identity in "Personal Identity" (1971) and *Reasons and Persons* (1984) with the view that personal identity may not be determinate and that it also is not what is important.[17] What matters is psychological continuity and connectedness. Parfit describes a person as an entity with a brain, a body, and the occurrence of a series of interrelated physical and mental events.[18] The person is constituted by these but is not identical to them: "personal identity over time just consists in physical and/or psychological continuity."[19] He thus rejects accounts of persons as separately existing entities who "own" their experiences, and he claims that psychological continuity and connectedness are "what matters." Psychological continuity is a chain of overlapping psychological connections, such as the memory of prior acts, experiences, or intentions, or psychological traits that persist over time. We care about our future states because our present states share psychological continuity and connectedness with them.[20] Parfit uses the science fiction thought experiment of a Teletransporter that destroys the body and re-creates it in the new location. If it malfunctions and fails to destroy the original body, "I" may exist in two locations. But which body has psychological connectedness and continuity that matters to my personal identity?[21] Parfit's arguments are too rich and too complex to do

---

[15] Williams 1970: 163–68.
[16] A very different approach to somatic continuity is the "animalist" view that personal identity is the identity of a living human animal, constituted by biological continuity. These views turn on the question of the status of humans as animals: the view that persons are human animals, and as a result, the persistence conditions of persons are biological rather than psychological. See Olson 1997, 2007. For discussion, see Shoemaker 2008: 315.
[17] Parfit 1984: especially 202–4 and 234–43.
[18] Parfit 1984: 204.
[19] Parfit 1995: 19. In his earlier "Reductionism," a person X's identity over time consists simply in facts that can be described impersonally, without presupposing the identity of X. Parfit claims that experiences in X's life were had by X, or even that X exists. See Parfit 1984: 204–17.
[20] Parfit 1984: 219–23.
[21] Parfit 1984: 199–200, with discussion in Shoemaker 1985: 443–44.

them justice here, but it is important to note that his version of psychological continuity and connectedness presumes the separability of the body from something else that provides continuity and connectedness, which he seems to identify with the brain.

In summary, it seems impossible to imagine the personal identity thought experiments of Locke, Williams, and Parfit applied to early Chinese conceptions of a person, either on the mind-centered or spirit-centered view. Even notwithstanding Parfit's focus on the brain (and its irrelevance to early Chinese views of personhood), the real problem lies in the attempt to detach the heart–mind or spirit from the body in early Chinese texts. For example, following Mencius, how does one pry the intentions apart from the *qi* Mencius says they command? How, following medical texts, does one separate the spirit from a body that physically dies if spirit dissipates?

In summary, a range of modern and contemporary Western accounts of personal identity are predicated on the unstated assumption of the separability of body and soul/brain. That separability simply doesn't work with ontologically continuous models, grounded in accounts of *qi* that make such claims for separability problematic in early China. The same point is also applicable to a long and nuanced history of Greek and Western views on the separability of the soul from the body.

Embodied Cognition

Embodied cognition is an emerging (and not unified) discipline that challenges Cartesian assumptions by underscoring how the body affects the mind. (It also offers important challenges to the models of cognitive science.) Cognition is embodied when it deeply depends on an agent's physical body insofar as somatic aspects (beyond the brain) play significant causal or physically constitutive roles in cognition.[22] The properties of an organism's body constrain the concepts it can acquire, and its understanding of its environment depends on the kind of body it has. This new discipline includes experimental results from neuropsychology, neuroscience, and developmental and social psychology. It includes a wide range of disciplinary and methodological perspectives, but most share the views that somatic experience,

---

[22] Shapiro 2011: 4. For a similar definition, see Wilson and Foglia 2011. For another account of embedded cognition in the context of Chinese philosophy, see Slingerland 2019: 262–67.

sensorimotor capacities, and the environment shape cognition in important ways; and cognition is not the sole prerogative of the mind. Examples include Lakoff and Johnson's arguments that metaphors reflect embodied experience, and the arguments of Varela, Thompson, and Rosch that the standard division of experience between given, external features of the world and internal symbolic representations should be dropped. They use the concept of enaction to emphasize that experience of the world arises from mutual interactions between an organism's physiology, its sensorimotor apparatus, and its environment.[23] In contrast to traditional disembodied views of the mind, these studies argue that embodied experience fundamentally shapes cognition; and perception, concepts, mental imagery, memory, reasoning, cognitive development, language, emotion, and consciousness are grounded in embodied experience. A full discussion of this issue is beyond the scope of the present discussion, but three examples provide illustrations.

Raymond Gibbs, a psychologist who specializes in embodiment, attributes a historical denial of the body's role in thought to the legacy of a dualist Western intellectual tradition. Since Descartes, the body has been understood as a solid object, somehow infused with a nonmaterial "self" and "mind," analogized to a range of mechanical objects (telephone switchboard, computer, etc.). Gibbs distinguishes three levels of personhood affected by embodiment: the level of neural events, the cognitive unconscious, and the level of phenomenological experience.[24]

A second, different account of somatic cognition comes from neuroscience and a growing literature on the concept of interoception: the representation of the internal states of an organism. Interoception includes the processes by which an organism senses, interprets, integrates, and regulates signals from within itself. As such, it contrasts with "exteroception," the primary sensory systems of sight, hearing, smell, taste, and touch. The term was originally coined in the nineteenth century, and it played an important role in the development of Pavlovian concepts of conditioning.[25] Butcher Ding's account of how he carved the ox flawlessly by seeing with his spirit rather

---

[23] See Lakoff and Johnson 1980 and 1999 (discussed in Chapter 1) and Varela, Thompson, and Rosch 2016. For other examples, see Gallagher 2005, Johnson 2017, and Menary 2007 and 2010. For useful overviews of this literature, see Shapiro 2014 and Shapiro and Spaulding 2021.
[24] Gibbs 2005: 3–10.
[25] W. Chen 2021: 3. The concept of interoception was first defined in the nineteenth century by Ivan Sechanov (quoted in Cameron 2001: 697. For further information see Bulgvii 1954), who referred to "dim feelings," "faint sensations," and an "obscure muscular sense" at the border of consciousness. Charles Sherrington (1906) originally used the term to refer to the physiological parameters that defined the normal internal state of an organism.

than his eyes, and moving with the patterns of what is inherently so is surely not a description of interoception, but from the anachronistic viewpoint of a modern description, it probably involves it.

A third perspective is the distinction between two very different body systems: the body image and the body schema. Shaun Gallagher describes the body image as a system of perceptions, attitudes, and beliefs about one's own body. By contrast, a body schema is a system of sensory-motor capacities that work without any awareness (or any need for conscious attention).[26] It operates at a level below personal awareness, interacts with the environment, and motivates action. An important difference is that the body image is available to consciousness; but the body schema is not. Nonetheless, conscious intentions also shape corporeal behavior controlled by the body schema. For example, the intention to drink a cup of tea causes the hand and arm to move appropriately to reach for the cup, with no need for awareness of the detailed muscle movements involved, which conform to the intention. While a body schema is not a form of consciousness, it can support (or undermine) intentional activity and cognition. When attention and awareness center on a willed action, the body acts with smoothness and coordination, with no involvement of the body image.[27]

Similarly, for Mencius, the will is the commander of the *qi*, but the *qi* in turn affects the will. It is striking that the mind-ruler metaphor which is so characteristic of the mind-centered approach described in Chapter 3 is articulated in terms of what contemporary theorists would call the body image: in this case, the heart–mind occupying the center of the body and governing its outlying regions. By contrast, the self-cultivation procedures described in Chapter 4 seem to act by the intentions operating on the body schema.

Karyn Lai has argued that the explanatory frameworks and perspectives of embodied cognition theory can help explain the views on knowledge and action and many important elements of mastery in the Zhuangzi skill stories from a very different viewpoint than the dominant epistemological frameworks in Western philosophy.[28] I raise the issue of embedded cognition here to make two very limited points. First, this description also fits the Chinese accounts of body, mind, and spirit presented here, especially the spirit-centered accounts. As a consequence, "self-consciousness" has a

---

[26] Gallagher 2005: 24.
[27] Gallagher 2005: 25.
[28] K. Lai 2019b.

somatic dimension in early China. Second, both the early Chinese accounts described here and a range of scientific perspectives in both cognitive science and embodied cognition theory, in quite different ways, all challenge dualist models of mind and body.

As these examples show, the corporealized mind–body–spirit boundary in early China has implications for self-awareness, as do the different perspectives of the mind-centered and spirit-centered views discussed herein. The term *self-awareness* or *self-consciousness* has traditionally referred to an "internal" awareness of a "mental" self, with little connection to somatic awareness. The texts studied here, across the early Chinese ideological spectrum, suggest a reconsideration of that view, leading to a much more corporeal understanding of self-awareness and a more complex understanding of the interrelations between body, mind, and spirit.

Glossary

Camp qi (*yingqi* 營氣) "Constructive" *qi*. By contrast, "guard *qi*" (*weiqi* 衛氣) refers to "protective" *qi*. Both are military terms and refer to two types of *qi* in the body that were believed to protect it and ward off intruders.

Chunqiu 春秋 (literally "Springs and Autumns"). An official chronicle of events in the state of Lu in the years 722–481 BCE. The events are arranged by year, month, and day on annalistic principles.

Earth Branches. See Sexagenary Cycle.

Fangshi 方士 (recipe masters). First mentioned. prominently during the reign of Han Wu Di 漢武帝 (r.141–87 BCE).

Fu viscera. See *Zang* viscera.

Ganzhi 干支. The sexagenary cycle of Ten Heaven Stems and Twelve Earth Branches. See Sexagenary Cycle.

Gong 躬 person[ality]. The ritual, performative person, or self that is associated with the deliberate and public display of virtuous conduct. It is exclusive to human beings.

Guard *qi*. See Camp *qi*.

Guishén 鬼神 Ghosts and spirits.

Heaven Stems. See Sexagenary Cycle.

Hexagram (*gua* 卦). A (bottom-to-top) vertical sequence of six yin or yang "lines."

Huangdi neijing 黃帝內經 (Inner Classic of the Yellow Lord). First major Chinese medical work (c. 100 BCE). It is divided into two sections: the *Suwen* 素問 (Basic Questions) and the *Lingshu* 靈樞 (Spiritual Pivot).

Hun 魂. Literally, "cloud soul." See Hunpo.

Hunpo 魂魄. Two types of soul. The *hun* or "cloud soul" was yang, noncorporeal, and was believed to leave the body at death. The *po* or "white soul" was yin, corporeal, and was believed to remain with or close to the corpse at death.

Jiaguwen 甲骨文. Oracle bone inscriptions. Inscriptions on turtle plastrons or bones used for divination, especially during the Shang dynasty.

Jing 精. Essence. One of the major components of the body in traditional Chinese medicine and self-cultivation practices, closely linked to *qi* and *shén*.

Jing 經. Bibliographic classification as "classic" (classification of textual genres).

Junzi 君子. "Gentleman." Term used by Confucius and his followers to describe the ideal human being or moral agent.

Li 禮. Ritual propriety. One of four virtues associated with the teachings of Confucius.

Neiwai 內外. The complementary realms of "inner" and "outer."

Oracle bone inscriptions. See *Jiaguwen*.

Po 魄. Literally, "white soul." See *Hunpo*.

Qi 氣 (also spelled *ch'i*). Matter, energy, breath, the vital energy that constitutes and organizes matter and makes growth possible; also, the force in living matter that influences other things.

Qu 軀. Physical frame; dysfunctional body of a petty person.

Ren 仁. Humane or benevolent. One of four virtues associated with the teachings of Confucius.

Ru 儒. A textual specialist, scholar, or literatus. The term is also used to describe specifically Confucian scholars.

Sexagenary Cycle. The traditional Chinese calendric system; a cyclic numeral system of the sixty possible combinations of Ten Heaven Stems and Twelve Earth Branches used in divination and astrology. It was also used to number days and years in China, Japan, Korea, and Vietnam.

Shēn 身. Embodied person. It refers to the lived body, the physical and social person, and the personality. Embodied persons are physically distinct and discrete, but they are socially permeable with other persons, especially parents and children. It is exclusive to human beings.

Shén 神. "Spirit" or "Spirits," sometimes translated as "numinous," "divine," or "spiritual. It originally referred to extrahuman (or formerly human) spirit powers, including ancestors, divine powers, and the spirit inhabitants of mountains, lakes, and forests. It later came to refer to humans with extraordinary "spirit-like" sagacity and power; as well as to the "spirit" quality within humans that could be cultivated to make a human being "spirit-like." In some medical contexts, spirit is a fundamental constituent of a human being and is necessary for survival.

Shénming 神明. Both the faculty of "spirit illumination" and two linked divine powers: *Shén* 神 [Spirit] and *Ming* 明 [Illumination].

Taiyi 太乙. "Great One." A star and the divinity (in anthromorphic form) associated with it.

Ti 體. Frame. The concrete physical frame of the body of humans or other animals, including limbs, major parts, and substantial physical form (as distinct from outline or visible shape).

Wuxing 五行. Five Agents, also called Five Phases. Its meaning changed over time from five processes ("Five Agents") to the five transformations of *qi* ("Five Phases") associated with correlative cosmology. In an astronomical context, it refers to the "five courses" of planetary motion. In other contexts, it refers to other groupings of five categories.

Xici 繫辭. An important commentary in the *Yijing* or Classic of Changes.

Xin 心. The heart–mind, heart, or mind.

Xing 形 Form. The visible form, shape, or structure of the body. It is solid and three-dimensional, with clear boundaries.

Yi 意. Thought, awareness. One of five psychological capacities associated with the five *zang* viscera.

Yi 義. Righteousness, propriety, or rightness. One of four virtues associated with the teachings of Confucius.

Yijing 易經. Classic of Change. In its present form, the *Yijing* consists of the Zhou Changes (*Zhouyi*) and seven commentaries.

Yin and yang 陰陽. Two complementary and fundamental forces whose constant interactions create change in the universe.

Zang 藏 viscera. The *Huangdi neijing* distinguishes two kinds of viscera. Five *zang* 臟 (modern form 藏) "depots" or "treasuries" (the heart, lungs, liver, spleen, and kidneys) are concerned with transformation and storage. Five *fu* 腑 (modern form 府) viscera; the gall bladder, stomach, large and small intestine, and urinary bladder) provide reception and passage.

Zhi 志. Will or intentions. One of five psychological capacities associated with the five *zang* viscera. *Zhi* is associated with the liver.

Zhi 知. Knowledge or consciousness.

Zhouyi 周易. "Zhou Changes." The core of the *Yijing*.

Zi 子. "Masters." Classification of textual genres.

APPENDIX 1

Time Lines

Chinese Time Lines and Dynasties

Shang 1700–c.1100 BCE
Zhou c.1100–256 BCE
   c.1100–771 Western Zhou
   770–256 Eastern Zhou
      770–475 Spring and Autumn
      551–479 Confucius
      475–222 Warring States
         c.430 Mo Di fl.
         372–289 Mencius
         4th century Zhuangzi
         310–237 Xunzi
         179–122 Liu An (*Huainanzi*)
Qin 221–209 BCE
Western Han 206 BCE–9 CE
   c.100 BCE comp. *Huangdi neijing*
Xin 9–23 CE
Eastern Han 25–220 CE
Three Kingdoms 220–265 CE
Six Dynasties 220–589 CE
   Jin 265–420
   Northern Dynasties 386–581
Sui 581–618
Tang 618–907
Five Dynasties (north) 907–960
Ten Kingdoms (south) 907–979
Liao 907–1279
Song 960–1279
   Northern Song 960–1127
   Southern Song 1127–1279
Jin 1115–1234
Yuan 1271–1368
Ming 1368–1644
Qing 1644–1911
Republic of China 1912–1949
People's Republic of China 1949–

Comparative Time Line

	Chinese	Greek
7th century BCE		750–700 writing of Homeric poems
6th century	551–479 Confucius	c.580–496 Pythagoras
5th century	c.430 Mo Di fl.	470–c.385 Philolaus of Croton
		437–347 Plato
		c.450–350 Hippocratic corpus
4th century	372–289 Mencius	c.384–322 Aristotle
	4th century Zhuangzi	341–270 Epicurus
3rd century	310–237 Xunzi	280–207 Chrysippus
2nd century	179–122 Liu An (Huainanzi)	
1st century BCE	c.100 comp. *Huangdi neijing*	99–55 Lucretius
1st century CE		45–120 Plutarch
		c.55–135 Epictetus
2nd century		129–200 Galen
		fl. 2nd century Hierocles

APPENDIX 2

Semantic Fields of Body, Mind, Soul, and Spirit

English	Chinese
Body elements	*jing* 精 vital essence
	qi 氣 breath/vital energy/force
	shén 神 spirit
Body [person]	*gong* 躬 person[ality]
	qu 軀 physical frame; dysfunctional body of a petty person
	shēn 身 physical person, personality
	ti 體 body, limbs, physical form
	xing 形 form or shape
	wu 吾 (I/my), *yu* 予, *wo* 我 (I/my/me)
	zi 自 (reflexive)
	ji 己 (person/self)
Mind	*xin* 心 mind, heart
	zhi 志 will or intentions
	zhi 知 awareness/knowledge/consciousness
	yi 意 thought/awareness
Spirit	*shén* 神 spirit
Soul	*guishén* 鬼神
	shénqi 神氣
	shénming 神明
	jingshén 精神
	shénling 神靈
	hun 魂 (lit. "cloud soul")
	po 魄 (lit. "white soul)
	hunpo 魂魄 soul compound

APPENDIX 3

The Brain in the *Huangdi Neijing*

The *Huangdi neijing* refers to the brain (*nao* 腦) forty-four times, in several contexts: (1) it associates the brain with bone marrow. (2) Less frequently, it associates the brain with tears and snot, including statements that the brain is yin and is linked to Earth. It is also linked to the eyes. (3) A few passages link the brain to heat diseases or to *qi* deficiencies. References to the brain also occur in (4) needling prohibitions and descriptions of the courses of various vessels, and (5) incidentally, in descriptions of other diseases. Finally, (6) two passages include both the brain and the heart.

This appendix uses the following additional abbreviations in citation:
U 2016 Unschuld 2016
UT 2011 Unschuld and Tessenow 2011

Bone Marrow

SW 10 Discourse on the Generation and Completion of the Five Depots (五藏生成論)

諸脈者皆屬於目，諸髓者皆屬於腦，諸、筋者皆屬於節，諸血者皆屬於心

All vessels are tied to the eyes. All marrow is tied to the brain. All sinews are tied to the joints. All blood is tied to the heart. (SW 10: 276–77; UT 2011: 1: 190)

SW 11 Further Discourse on the Five Depots (五藏別論)

Huangdi asks about contradictions in the views of the recipe masters (*fangshi* 方士):

或以腦髓為藏，或以腸胃為藏，或以為府，... 歧伯對曰：腦髓骨脈膽女子胞，此六者，地氣之所生也。皆藏於陰而象於地

Some consider the brain and the marrow to be depots; others consider the intestines and the stomach to be depots; still others consider them to be palaces. . . . Qi Bo responded: "The brain, the marrow, the bones, the vessels, the gallbladder, and the female uterus, these six are generated by earth *qi*. Their storing is associated with yin; their image is that of the earth." (SW 11: 294; UT 2011: 1: 203)

SW 47 Discourse on Strange Diseases (奇病論)

髓者以腦為主

The marrow is ruled by the brain. (SW 47: 960; UT 2011: 1: 695)

LS 9 End and Beginning (終始)

形體淫泆，乃消腦髓

When the form and frame are taxed by excessive lust, brain and bone marrow melt. (LS 9: 227–28; U 2016: 172)

LS 10 The Conduit Vessels (經脈)

人始生成精，精成而腦髓生

At the beginning of a person's life, essence [is the first to] form. Once essence has formed, brain and marrow are generated. (LS 10: 233; U 2016: 175–76)

LS 30 Differentiation of *Qi* (決氣)

In the context of a discussion of why there are distinct names for six kinds of *qi* in the body (essence, *qi*, *jin* liquids, *ye* liquids, blood, and vessels):

穀入氣滿，淖澤注于骨，骨屬屈伸，泄澤補益腦髓，皮膚潤澤是謂液。

When the grains enter and fill it [the body] with the *qi*, viscous liquid pours into the bones, enabling the bone connections to bend and stretch. [*Qi*] flows out to fill the brain with marrow and provide the skin with dampness. That is what is called *ye* liquid. (LS 30: 590; U 016: 352)

A later question asks how to know "whether the brain marrow is depleted or replete" (腦髓之虛實). The answer is:

液脫者，骨屬屈伸不利，色夭，腦髓消，脛痠，耳數鳴。

When *ye* liquids [are lost], the bone connections cannot bend and stretch freely, the complexion is one of early death, the brain marrow melts, the lower legs have a blockage-illness, and the ears are filled with frequent noises. (LS 30: 591; U 2016: 353)

LS 33 On the Seas (海論)

In a description of the "four seas" of the human body (of marrow, blood, *qi*, and water and grain):

腦為髓之海，其輸上在於其蓋，下在風府。

The brain is the sea of bone marrow. Its transport [openings] are in the upper region at the top of the skull and below the *fengfu* [opening]. (LS 33: 606; U 2016: 363)

髓海不足，則腦轉耳鳴，脛痠眩冒，目無所見，懈怠安臥。

When the sea of bone marrow has an insufficiency, the brain revolves and there are noises in the ears. The lower legs cramp, and vision is dimmed. The eyes see nothing. [Patients] are relaxed and sleep peacefully. (LS 33: 608; U 2016: 365)

LS 36 Separation of the Five Protuberance-Illness Jin and Ye Liquids (五癃津液別)

五穀之津液，和合而為膏者，內滲入于骨空，補益腦髓，而下流於陰股。

When the *jin* and *ye* liquids of the five types of grain come together, they generate a paste. Internally it seeps into the hollow spaces in the bones and supplements the brain with bone marrow, and descends to flow into the inner side of the thighs. (LS 36: 634; U 2016: 385)

LS 59 When the Guard *Qi* Lose their Regularity (衛氣失常)

According to a discussion about the physical appearance of disease, and the sections of the body:

筋部無陰無陽，無左無右，候病所在。骨之屬者，骨空之所以受益而益腦髓者也。

The sinews regions are not distinguished in yin and yang, there is no "left" and no "right". One examines where a disease may be. The joints of the bones are the places where the hollow space in the bones is filled and where the brain marrow is augmented. (LS 59: 812; U 2016: 541)

Tears, Snot, and the Eyes

SW 37 Discourse on Qi Recession (氣厥論)

膽移熱於腦，則辛頞鼻淵。鼻淵者，濁涕下不止也。傳為衄衊瞑目，故得之氣厥也。

When the gallbladder moves heat to the brain, then [this results in] xin'e and biyuan. Biyuan is turbid snot flowing down without end. Further transmission causes nosebleed and blurred vision. The fact is that one acquires these [states] from qi recession. (SW 37: 795–96; UT 2011: 1: 573)

SW 81 Discourse on Explaining the Subtleties of Essence (解精微論)

泣涕者腦也，腦者陰也，髓者骨之充也，故腦滲為涕。志者骨之主也，是以水流而涕從之者，其行類也。

Tears and snot are brain. The brain is yin. Marrow is what fills the bones. Hence, when the brain leaks, this generates snivel. The will is the ruler of the bones. Therefore, when water flows and snot follows it, this is because their passage is of one type. (SW 81: 1402–3; UT 2011: 2: 724–25)

LS 80 On Massive Confusion (大惑論)

In a discussion of causes of disorientation and confusion, Qi Bo explains that the essence of the sinews collects in the black parts of the eyes, and:

氣之精為白眼，肌肉之精為約束，裹擷筋骨血氣之精，而與脈并為系，上屬於腦後，出於項中。故邪中於項，因逢其身之虛。其入深，則隨眼系以入於腦，入于腦則腦轉，腦轉則引目系急，目系急則目眩以轉矣。

The essence of *qi* [collects in] the white of the eyes; the essence of the sinews and the flesh [collects in] the eyelids. They enclose the essence of sinews, bones, blood, and *qi*. They are tied to the vessels and form a connection that is linked to the brain and comes out in the nape of the neck. The fact is: When evil [*qi*] strikes the nape, it connects to the person's [regions of] depletion. When it enters deeply, it follows the eye connection and enters the brain. When it enters the brain, the brain rotates. When the brain rotates, it pulls the eye connection which becomes tense. When the eye connection is tense, the eyes are dizzy and [one feels as if] rotating. (LS 80: 1089–90; U 2016: 754–55)

Brain Linked to Heat Diseases and *Qi* Deficiencies

SW 35 Discourse on Malaria (瘧論)

溫瘧者，得之冬中於風寒，氣藏於骨髓之中，至春則陽氣大發，邪氣不能自出，因遇大暑，腦髓爍，肌肉消

Warmth malaria is acquired in winter through being struck by wind. Cold *qi* is stored in the bone and marrow. By spring, yang *qi* is effused massively, and evil *qi* cannot leave by itself. If subsequently [the patient] encounters massive summer heat, the brain and marrow melt; the muscles and flesh wane. (SW 35: 760; UT 2011: 1: 550)

LS 23 Heat Diseases (熱病)

熱病面青，腦痛，手足躁，取之筋間，以第四鍼於四逆。

When a heat disease is accompanied by a greenish facial complexion, as well as an aching brain and a rapid movement of hands and feet, the [disease] is to be removed from the sinews with the needle number 4. (LS 21: 509; U 2016: 297)

LS 28 Oral Inquiry (口問)

凡此十二邪者，皆奇邪之走空竅者也。故邪之所在皆為不足，故上氣不足，腦為之不滿，耳為之苦鳴，頭為之苦傾，目為之眩。

All these twelve evil [*qi*] are unusual evil [*qi*] that pass into the hollow spaces. Where such evil [*qi*] are present, this is always because of an insufficiency of [the proper *qi*] When the *qi* above are insufficient, it is because of this that the brain is not filled, that the ears suffer from hearing noises, that the head suffers from being bent to one side, and that the eyesight is dimmed. (LS 28: 572–73; U 2016: 336–37)

Needling Prohibitions and Locations

SW 52 Discourse on Prohibitions in Piercing (刺禁論)

刺頭中腦戶，入腦立死。

When needling, if one hits the head, one hits the Brain's Door [point], if [the needle] enters the brain, [the patient] dies immediately. (SW 52: 1028; UT 2011: 1: 745)

SW 60 Discourse on Bone Hollows (骨空論)

The Supervisor vessel (du mai 督脈) is described as:

少陰上股內後廉，貫脊屬腎。與太陽起於目內眥，上額交巔上，入絡腦

merging with the [foot] minor yin [conduit] and rise on the inner back edge of the upper thighs, penetrating the spine, connected with the kidneys, emerging together with the major yang [conduit] from the inner canthi of the eyes, rising to the forehead, intersecting [with the major yang conduit] on the peak of the skull, entering and enclosing the brain. (SW 60: 1168; UT 2011: 2: 79)

髓空，在腦後三分

There are marrow hollows. They are located three fen behind the brain. (SW 60: 1177; UT 2011: 2: 83)

LS 10 The Conduit Vessels (經脈)

膀胱足太陽之脈，起於目內眥，上額交巔；其支者，從巔至耳上角，其直者，從巔入絡腦

The four major yang vessels of the urinary bladder originate in the inner corner of the eyes, ascend at the forehead, and cross on the skull. Their branches extend from the top of the skull to the upper corner of the ears. Their straight courses extend from the top of the skull into [the head] and connect with the brain. (LS 10: 275–76; U 2016: 187)

LS 21 Cold and Heat Disease (寒熱病)

足太陽，有通項入于腦者，正屬目本，名曰眼系。...入腦乃別陰蹻、陽蹻

Where the foot major yang [conduit] passes through the nape and enters the brain, the main [course] is tied to the base of the eye. That is called "eye ribbon".... Where it enters the brain, it branches out into the yin walker and the yang walker [vessels]. (LS 21: 480–81; U 2016: 283)

LS 62 Transports (動輸)

胃氣上注于肺，其悍氣上沖頭者，循咽，上走空竅，循眼系，入絡腦，出顪，下客主人

Stomach *qi* ascends and flows into the lung. The more aggressive *qi* ascends and pours into the head. It follows the throat and ascends to enter the hollow spaces. It follows the eye connection, enters the brain, emerges at the cheeks, and descends to the *ke zhu ren* [opening]. (LS 62: 836; U 2016: 567)

Incidental Descriptions

SW 42 Discourse on Wind (風論)

風氣循風府而上，則為腦風。風入係頭，則為目風

When wind *qi* follows the wind palace and rises, then this causes brain wind. When the wind enters the connection with the head, then this causes eye wind. (SW 42: 877; UT 2011: 1: 629–30)

LS 24 Receding *Qi* Diseases (厥病)

真頭痛，頭痛甚，腦盡痛，手足寒至節，死，不治。

If genuine headache [manifests itself as] severe headache, with the entire brain aching and hands and feet being cold up to the joints, [the patient] will die. A cure is impossible. (LS 21: 526; U 2016: 306)

LS 52 Guard *Qi* (衛氣)

According to a discussion of *qi* paths (*qi jie* 氣街), and the path of head *qi*: "When the [evil] *qi* are in the head, they are to be stopped in the brain (氣在頭者，止之於腦). (LS 52: 774; U 2016: 506).

Passages that Feature Both Brain and Heart

SW 76 Discourse on Demonstrating a Natural Approach (示從容論)

五藏六府，膽胃大小腸脾胞膀胱，腦髓涕唾，哭泣悲哀，水所從行，此皆人之所生。

The five depots and the six palaces, the gallbladder, stomach, large and small intestines, spleen, uterus, and urinary bladder; the brain, marrow, snot and saliva, weeping, sadness, and grief, as well as the paths where water moves, all these together form the basis of human life. (SW 81: 1320; UT 2011: 2: 652)

LS 81 Obstruction and Impediment Illnesses (癰疽)

In a discussion of obstruction illnesses manifesting in the nape of the neck:

陽氣大發，消腦留項，名曰腦爍。...煩心者，死不可治。

If yang *qi* breaks out massively, the brain melts and collects in the nape. That is called "brain fire".... If [the patient] is vexed in his heart, he will die. No cure is possible. (LS 81: 1108; U 2016: 768)

References

Akahori, Akira 赤堀昭. (1978). "Bu-i Kandai ikan ni tsuite" 武威漢代醫簡について [Regarding the Han dynasty medical strips from Wuwei]. *Tōyō Gakuhō*, 50: 75–107.

Akahori, Akira 赤堀昭, and Yamada Keiji 山田慶兒. (1985). *Shinhatsugen Chūgoku kagakushi shiryō no kenkyū* 新發現中國科學史資料の研究 [Research on newly discovered Chinese scientific history materials]. Kyoto: Kyōto Daigaku Jinbun Kagaku Kenkyūjo.

Allan, Sarah. (1991). *The Shape of the Turtle: Art, Myth and Cosmos in Early China*. Albany: State University of New York Press.

Allan, Sarah. (1997). *The Way of Water and the Sprouts of Virtue*. Albany: State University of New York Press.

Allan, Sarah [Ai Lan 艾兰]. (2000). "Taiyi, shui, Guodian 'Laozi'" 太一, 水, 郭店老子 [Taiyi, water, and the Guodian Laozi]. In *Guodian Chujian guoji xueshu yantaohui lunwenji* 郭店楚簡國際學朮研討會論文集 [Proceedings of the International Symposium on the Chu Slips from Guodian], eds. Wuhan daxue Zhongguo wenhua yanjiuyuan. Wuhan: Hubei renmin chubanshe, 524–32.

Ames, Roger T. (1984). "The Meaning of the Body in Classical Chinese Philosophy." *International Philosophical Quarterly*, 24(1): 39–54. Rpt. in *Self as Body in Asian Theory and Practice*, ed. T. Kasulis, Roger T. Ames, and Wimal Dissanayake. Albany: State University of New York Press, 1994, 157–77.

Ames, Roger T. (1991). "Reflections on the Confucian Self: A Response to Fingarette." In *Rules, Rituals, and Responsibility: Essays Dedicated to Herbert Fingarette*, ed. Mary Bockover. La Salle, IL: Open Court, 103–14.

Ames, Roger T. (1993). "On Body as Ritual Practice." In *Self as Body in Asian Theory and Practice*, ed. T. Kasulis, Roger T. Ames, and Wimal Dissanayake. Albany: State University of New York Press, 149–56.

Ames, Roger T. (1994) "The Meaning of the Body in Classical Chinese Philosophy." *International Philosophical Quarterly* 24.1 (1984): 39–54, rpt. in *Self as Body in Asian Theory and Practice*, ed. T. Kasulis, R. T. Ames, and W. Dissanayake. Albany: State University of New York Press: 157–177.

Ames, Roger T. (1998). "The Problematic of Self in Western Thought." In *Thinking from the Han: Self, Truth, and Transcendence in Chinese and Western Culture*, ed. David Hall and Roger T. Ames. Albany: State University of New York Press, 3–21.

Ames, Roger T., Wimal Dissanayake, and Thomas Kasulis (eds.). (1994). *Self as Person in Asian Theory and Practice*. Albany: State University of New York Press.

Andreini, Attilio. (2006). "The Meaning of *Qing* 情 in Texts from Guodian Tomb No. 1." In *Love, Hatred, and Other Passions: Questions and Themes on Emotions in Chinese Civilization*, ed. Paolo Santangelo and Donatella Guida. Leiden: Brill, 149–65.

Arrault, Alain. (2010). "Méthodes hémérologiques et activités médicales dans les calendriers de Dunhuang du IXe au Xe siècle: esprit humain (renshen) et esprit du jour (riyou)." In *Médecine, religion et société dans la Chine médiévale. Etude de manuscrits chinois de Dunhuang et de Turfan*, ed. Catherine Despeux. Paris: Collège de France, Institut des Hautes études chinoises, 285–332.

Baoshan Chumu 包山楚墓. (1991). Ed. Hubeisheng Jingsha tielu kaogudui. Beijing: Wenwu chubanshe.

Barsalou, Lawrence. (2016). "Situated Conceptualization: Theory and Applications." In *Foundations of Embodied Cognition*, ed. Y. Coello and M. H. Fischer, vol. 1, *Perceptual and Emotional Embodiment*. East Sussex, UK: Psychology Press, 11–37.

Billeter, Jean-François. (2009). *Leçons sur Tchouang-tseu*. Paris: Alia.

Brashier, Ken E. (1996). "Han Thanatology and the Division of Souls." *Early China*, 21: 125–58.

Bremmer, J. N. (1983). *The Early Greek Concept of the Soul*. Princeton, NJ: Princeton University Press.

Brindley, Erica. (2009). "The Perspicuity of Ghosts and Spirits and the Problem of Intellectual Affiliations in Early China." *Journal of the American Oriental Society*, 129(2): 215–36.

Brindley, Erica. (2010). *Individualism in Early China: Human Agency and the Self in Thought and Politics*. Honolulu: University of Hawaii Press.

Bulygii, I. A. (1954). "Razvitie idei I. M. Sechenova i I. P. Pavlova o kortikal'noi reguliatsii interotseptivnykh bezuslovnykh refleksov" [Development of I. M. Sechenov's and I. P. Pavlov's theories on cortical regulation of interoceptive unconditioned reflexes]. *Zhurnal Vysshei Nervnoi Deiatelnosti Imeni I P Pavlova*, 4(6): 913–23.

Cai, Biming 蔡璧名. (1997). *Shenti yu ziran: Yi "Huangdi nei jing suwen" wei zhongxin lun gudai sixiang chuantong zhong de shenti guan* 身體與自然: 以《黃帝內經素問》為中心論古代思想傳統中的身體觀 [The Body and Nature: On views of the body in antiquity according to the Yellow Emperor's Internal Classic: Basic Questions]. Taipei: Guoli Taiwan Daxue chuban weiyuanhui.

Cameron, Oliver G. (2001). "Interoception: The Inside Story—A Model for Psychosomatic Processes." *Psychosomatic Medicine*, 63: 697–710.

Cao, Feng 曹峰. (2010). "Shangbo Chujian 'Fanwu liuxing' de wenben jiegou yu sixiang tezheng" 上博楚簡《凡物流形》的文本結構與思想特徵 [Text structure and intellectual content of the Shanghai Bamboo text "All things flow into form"], *Qinghua daxue xuebao* (Zhexue shehui kexue ban) 清華大學學報(哲學社會科學版 [Journal of Tsinghua University (Philosophy and Social Sciences Edition)], 25(1): 73–82.

Cao, Feng. (2019). "*Qinghua jian 'Xin shi wei zhong' de xinlun yu minglun*" 清華簡 '心是謂中' 的心論與命論 [The Theory of Mind and Fate of Tsinghua Bamboo Slips 'The Heart Is Called the Center']. *Zhongguo Zhexue Shi* 中國哲學史 [History of Chinese Philosophy], 3: 5–29.

Carr, Michael. (1983). "Sidelights of *Xin*: 'Heart, Mind' in the *Shijing*." Paper presented at the Proceedings of the Thirty-first International Congress of the Human Sciences in Asia and North Africa, Tokyo and Kyoto.

Chan, Alan K. L. (2002). "A Matter of Taste: Qi (Vital Energy) and the Tending of the Heart (Xin) in Mencius 2A2." In *Mencius: Contexts and Interpretations*, ed. Alan K. L. Chan. Honolulu: University of Hawaii Press, 42–71.

Chan, Shirley (Chen Hui 陳慧). (2009a). "Human Nature and Moral Cultivation in the Guodian 郭店 Text of the Xing zi ming chu 性自命出 (Nature Derives from Mandate)." *Dao*, 8: 361–82.

Chan, Shirley (Chen Hui 陳慧). (2009b). "The Ruler/Ruled Relationship in the 'Black Robes' Contained in the Newly Excavated Guodian Bamboo Texts." *Journal of Asian History,* 1(43): 19–30.

Chan, Shirley (Chen Hui 陳慧). (2011). "Cosmology, Society and Humanity: Tian in the Guodian texts (Part I)." *Journal of Chinese Philosophy,* 38: 64–77.

Chan, Shirley (Chen Hui 陳慧). (2012). "Cosmology, Society, and Humanity: *Tian* in the Guodian Texts (Part II)." *Journal of Chinese Philosophy,* 39(1): 106–20.

Chan, Shirley. (2015). "Oneness: Reading the 'All Things Are Flowing in Form' (Fan Wu Liu Xing) 凡物流形 (with a translation)." *International Communication of Chinese Culture,* 2(3): 285–299.

Chan, Shirley (ed.). (2019). *Dao Companion to the Excavated Guodian Bamboo Manuscripts,* Dao Companions to Chinese Philosophy 10. Dordrecht: Springer.

Chang, Kwang-chih. (1983). *Art Myth and Ritual: The Path to Authority in Early China.* Cambridge, MA: Harvard University Press.

Chang, Leo S., and Yu Feng. (1998). *The Four Political Treatises of the Yellow Emperor— Original Mawangdui Texts with Complete English Translation and an Introduction.* Honolulu: University of Hawaii Press.

Chen, Guying 陳鼓應. (2001). *Zhuangzi jinzhu jinyi* 莊子今注今譯 [Contemporary Notes and Translations of the Zhuangzi]. Hong Kong: Zhonghua shuju.

Chen, Guying 陳鼓應. (2006). *Guanzi sipian quanshi: Jixia Daojia daibiao zuo jiexi* 管子四篇詮釋: 稷下道家代表作解析 [Guanzi's Four Interpretations: An Analysis of the Jixia Daoist Masterpieces]. Beijing: Shangwu yinshguan.

Chen, Guying 陳鼓應. (2007). *Huangdi sijing jinzhu jinyi: Mawangdui Hanmu chutu boshu* 黃帝四經今注今譯: 馬王堆漢墓出土帛書 [Contemporary Annotation and Translation of the Four Classics of the Yellow Emperor: Silk Books Unearthed from the Han Tomb of Mawangdui]. Beijing: Shangwu yinshuguan chubanshe.

Chen, Ligui, and Hiu Chuk Winnie Sung. (2015). "The Doctrines and Transformation of the Huang-Lao Tradition." In *Dao Companion to Daoist Philosophy,* ed. Liu Xiaogan. New York: Springer, 241–64.

Chen, Mengjia 陈梦家. (1936). *Shangdai de shenhua yu wushu* 商代的神話與巫術 [Myths and Magic of the *Shang* Dynasty]. *Yanjing xuebao,* 20: 485–576.

Chen, Minzhen 陳民鎮. (2018). "Qinghua jian (8) du zha," Qinghua Daxue Chutu Wenxian Yanjiu yu Baohu Zhongxin Wangzhan, 2018 nian 11 yue 17 ri" 《清華簡(捌)讀札》(清華大學出土文獻研究與保護中心網站，2018 年11 月17 日 [Qinghua Bamboo slips vol. 8: Reading Notes, Qinghua University Unearthed Document Research and Protection Center website, November 17, 2018].

Chen, Wei 陳偉. (2002). *Guodian zhushu bieshi* 郭店竹書別釋 [Another Explanation of Guodian Bamboo Books]. Wuhan, China: Wuhan University Press.

Chen, Wei 陳偉. (2018). "'Xin shi wei zhong' 'xin jun' zhangchubu yandu" '心是謂中' '心君' 章初步研讀 [Preliminary Study of the chapter '*Xin jun*' of '*Xin shi wei zhong*'], *Jianbo wang* 簡帛網 [Bamboo and silk website] http://www.bsm.org.cn/?chujian/7980.html.

Chen, Wen G., Dana Schloesser, Angela M. Arensdorf, Janine M. Simmons, Changhai Cui, Rita Valentino, et al. (2021). "The Emerging Science of Interoception: Sensing, Integrating, Interpreting, and Regulating Signals within the Self." *Trends in Neurosciences,* 44(1): 3–16.

Chen, Yan 陳言. (Wu Ze 無擇 fl. 1174). (2007). *Sanyin ji yi bing yuan lun cui* 三因極一病源論粹 [The three causes epitomized and unified: the quintessence of doctrine on the origins of medical disorders]. Published as *Sanyin ji yi ping zheng fang lun* 三因極一病證方論. Beijing: Zhonguo Zhong yiyao chubanshe.

Cheng, Shude 程樹德. (1996). *Lunyu jishi* 論語集釋 [Collected edition of the Analects]. 4 vols. Beijing: Zhonghua shuju.

Ching, Julia. (1997). *Mysticism and Kingship in China: The Heart of Chinese Wisdom*. Cambridge, UK: Cambridge University Press.

Chiu, Wai Wai. (2016). "Zhuangzi's Idea of 'Spirit': Acting and 'Thinging Things' without Self-assertion." *Asian Philosophy*, 26(1): 38–51.

Chomsky, Noam. (1975). *Reflections on Language*. New York: Pantheon.

Chong, Kim-Chong. (2003) "Autonomy in the Analects." In *The Moral Circle and the Self*, eds. Kim-Chong Chong, Sor-Hoon Tan, and C. L., Ten. LaSalle, IL: Open Court, 269–82.

Chong, Kim-chong. (2006). "Metaphorical Use versus Metaphorical Essence: Examples from Chinese Philosophy." In *Davidson's Philosophy and Chinese Philosophy: Constructive Engagement*, ed. Mou Bo. Leiden: Brill, 229–46.

Chong, Kim-chong. (2007). "Zhuangzi and the Nature of Metaphor." *Philosophy East and West*, 56(3): 370–91.

Chong, Kim-Chong, Sor-Hoon Tan, and C. L. Ten (eds.). (2003). *The Moral Circle and the Self*. LaSalle, IL: Open Court.

Clark, Andy. (1997). *Being There: Putting Mind, Body, and World Together Again*. Cambridge, MA: MIT Press.

Clark, Andy. (2008). *Supersizing the Mind: Embodiment, Action, and Cognitive Extension*. New York: Oxford University Press.

Clarke, Michael. (1999). *Flesh and Spirit in the Songs of Homer. A Study of Words and Myths*. Oxford, UK: Clarendon Press.

Cong, Chunyu 叢春雨. (1994). *Dunhuang Zhong yiyao quanshu* 敦煌中醫藥全書 [Complete collection of Dunhuang Medical Texts]. Beijing: Zhongyi guji.

Cook, Constance. (2006). *Death in Ancient China: The Tale of One Man's Journey*. Leiden: Brill.

Cook, Constance, and Paul Goldin (eds.). (2020). *A Source Book for Ancient Chinese Bronze Inscriptions, Revised Edition*. Early China Special Monograph. Berkeley CA: Society for the Study of Early China.

Cook, Scott [Gu Shikao 顧史考]. (2009a). "Shangbo jian "Fanwu liuxing chutan" 上博簡〈凡物流形〉初探 [Initial Investigation of the Shanghai Museum Bamboo Strips All Things Flow into Form], *Guoli Taiwan daxue zhexue lunping* 國立臺灣大學哲學論評, 38: 1–32.

Cook, Scott [Gu Shikao]. (2009b). "Shangbo qi *Fanwu liuxing* xiaban pian shijie" 上博七《凡物流行》下半篇試解 [Provisional Explanation of the Second Half of the Shanghai Museum 7, All Things Flow into Form]. In *Chutu wenxian yu chuanshi dianji quanshi* 出土文獻與傳世典籍詮釋, ed. Fudan daxue chutu wenxian yu guwenzi yanjiu zhongxin 復旦大學出土文獻與古文字研究中心. Shanghai: Shanghai guji, 333–59.

Cook, Scott. (2012). *The Bamboo Texts of Guodian: A Study and Complete Translation*. 2 volumes. Ithaca, NY: Cornell University Press.

Coulson, Seana. (2001). *Semantic Leaps: Frame-shifting and Conceptual Blending in Meaning Construction.* Cambridge, UK: Cambridge University Press.

Csikszentmihalyi, Mark. (2005). *Material Virtue Ethics and the Body in Early China.* Leiden: Brill.

Cua, Antonio. (1985). *Ethical Argumentation: A Study in Hsün Tzu's Moral Epistemology.* Honolulu: University of Hawaii Press.

Damasio, Antonio R. (1994). *Descartes' Error: Emotion, Reason, and the Human Brain.* New York: Putnam.

Damasio, Antonio R. (2010). *Self Comes to Mind: Constructing the Conscious Brain.* New York: Pantheon.

Defoort, Carine. (1997). *The Pheasant Cap Master (He guan zi)—A Rhetorical Reading.* Albany: State University of New York Press.

Demiéville, Paul. (1947). "Le Miroir Spirituel." *Sinologica*, 1(2): 112–37.

Descola, Philippe. (1996). "Constructing Natures: Symbolic Ecology and Social Practice." In *Nature and Society: Anthropological Perspectives*, ed. P. Descola and G. Pálsson. London: Routledge, 82–102.

Descola, Philippe. (2013). *Beyond Nature and Culture*, trans. J. Lloyd. Chicago: University of Chicago Press.

Despeux, Catherine. (1987). *Prescriptions d'acuponcture valant mille onces d'or: traité d'acuponcture de Sun Simiao du VII siècle.* Paris: Guy Trédaniel.

Despeux, Catherine. (2007). "Âmes et animation du corps: La notion de shen dans la médecine chinoise antique." *Extrême-Orient Extrême-Occident*, 29: 71–94.

Despeux, Catherine. (2008). "*Neijing tu* and *Xiuzhen tu*." In *The Encyclopedia of Taoism*, ed. Fabrizio Predagio. London: Routledge, 767–71.

Despeux, Catherine (ed.). (2010). *Médecine, religion et société dans la Chine médiévale. Etude de manuscrits chinois de Dunhuang et de Turfan.* Paris: Collège de France, Institut des Hautes études chinoises.

Ding, Sixin 丁四新. (2000). *Guodian Chumu zhujian sixiang yanjiu* 郭店楚墓竹簡思想研究 [Research on the thought of the bamboo Strips from the Chu tomb at Guodian]. Beijing: Wenwu.

Ding, Sixin 丁四新. (2006). "Shangbo Chujian 'Guishen' pian zhu shi" 上博楚简《鬼神》篇注释 [Notes on the Shanghai Museum Chu bamboo strip texts "Ghosts and Gods"]. Jianbo wang 簡帛網 [Bamboo and silk website] http://www.bsm.org.cn/show_article.php?id=337.

Ding, Sixin 丁四新. (2011). "A Study on the Dating of the Mozi Dialogues and the Mohist View of Ghosts and Spirits." *Contemporary Chinese Thought*, 42(4): 39–87.

Ding, Yuanzhi 丁原植. (2000). Guodian Chujian Rujia yi ji si zhong shi xi 郭店楚簡儒家佚籍四種釋析 [Analyses of the Four Lost Confucian Texts from the Guodian Chu slips]. Taipei: Taiwan Guji chubanshe.

Du, Guoxiang. (1962). "Xunzi cong Song Yin Huang-Lao xuepai jieshoule shenme?" 荀子從宋尹黃老學派接受了什么？ [What did Xunzi accept from the Song-Yin Huang-Lao School?]. In *Du Guoxiang wenji* 杜國庠文集 [Collected Works of Du Guoxian]. Beijing: Renmin, 134–57.

Durrant, Stephen. (1977–78). "A Consideration of Differences Grammar of the Mo Tzu 'Essays' and 'Dialogues.'" *Monumenta Serica*, 33: 268–85.

Eliade, Mircea. (1958). *Patterns in Comparative Religion*. Trans. Rosemary Sheed. New York: Meridian.

Emerson, John. (1996). "Yang Chu's Discovery of the Body." *Philosophy East and West*, 46(4): 533–66.

Falkenhausen, Lothar von. (1993a). *Suspended Music: Chime-Bells in the Culture of Bronze Age China*. Berkeley: University of California Press.

Falkenhausen, Lothar von. (1993b). "Issues in Western Zhou Studies: A Review Article." *Early China*, 18: 139–226.

Falkenhausen, Lothar von. (2006). *Chinese Society in the Age of Confucius (1000–250 BC): The Archeological Evidence*. Los Angeles: Cotsen Institute of Archeology, UCLA.

Fanwu liuxing 凡物流形 [All things flow into form]. In *Shanghai Bowuguan cang zhanguo Chu zhu shu VII* 上海博物館藏戰國楚竹書（七）[The Warring States Chu Bamboo Texts Collected by the Shanghai Museum, vol. 7], ed. Ma Chengyuan. Shanghai: Shanghai guji chubanshe, 219–300.

Fauconnier, Gilles, and Mark Turner. (2002). *The Way We Think: Conceptual Blending and the Mind's Hidden Complexities*. New York: Basic Books.

Fingarette, Herbert. (1972). *Confucius: Secular as Sacred*. New York: Harper Torchbooks.

Fingarette, Herbert. (2008). "Discovering the Analects." In *Confucius Now: Contemporary Encounters with the Analects*, ed. D. Jones. Chicago: Open Court, 1–12.

Fodor, Jerry. (1975). *The Language of Thought*. Cambridge, MA: Harvard University Press.

Fowler, Chris. (2004). *The Archaeology of Personhood: An Anthropological Approach*. London: Routledge.

Fraser, Chris. (2011). "Emotion and Agency in Zhuāngzi." *Asian Philosophy*, 21(1): 97–121.

Fraser, Chris. (2016). *The Philosophy of the Mòzǐ: The First Consequentialists*. New York: Columbia University Press.

Frisina, W. G. (2000). "Value and the Self: A Pragmatic-Process-Confucian Response to Charles Taylor's *Sources of the Self*." *Journal of Chinese Philosophy*, 27(1): 117–25.

Gallagher, Shaun. (2005). *How the Body Shapes the Mind*. New York: Oxford University Press.

Gansusheng bowuguan 甘肃省博物馆. (1975). *Wuwei Handai yijian* 武威漢代醫簡 [The Han dynasty medical strips from Wuwei]. Beijing: Wenwu.

Gao, Dalun 高大倫. (1992). *Zhangjiashan Hanjian "Maishu" jiaoshi* 張家山漢簡《脈書》校釋. [Interpretation and Annotation of the Zhangjiashan Bamboo Strip "Pulse Book"]. Chengdu: Chengdu chubanshe.

Gao, Dalun 高大倫. (1995). *Zhangjiashan Hanjian yinshu yanjiu* 張家山漢簡引書研究 [Research on the Zhangjiashan Bamboo Strips "Pulling Book"]. Chengdu: Bashu shushe.

Gassmann, Robert H. (2011). "Coming to Terms with dé 德: The Deconstruction of 'Virtue' and an Exercise in Scientific Morality." In *How Should One Live? Comparing Ethics in Ancient China and Greco-Roman Antiquity*, ed. Richard King and Dennis Schilling. Berlin: De Gruyter, 92–125.

Gavrylenko, V. (2012). "The 'Body without Skin' in the Homeric Poems." In *Blood, Sweat and Tears—The Changing Concepts of Physiology from Antiquity into Early Modern Europe*, ed. M. Horstmanshoff, H. King, and C. Zittel. Leiden: Brill, 481–502.

Geaney, Jane. (2002). *On the Epistemology of the Senses in Early Chinese Thought.* Honolulu: University of Hawaii Press.

Gibbs, Raymond W. (2005). *Embodiment and Cognitive Science.* Cambridge: Cambridge University Press.

Goldin, Paul R. (1999). "Self-Cultivation and the Mind." In *Rituals of the Way: The Philosophy of Xunzi.* LaSalle, IL: Open Court, 1–37.

Goldin, Paul. (2003). "A Mind–Body Problem in the Zhuangzi?" In *Hiding the World in the World: Uneven Discourses on the Zhuangzi,* ed. S. Cook. Albany: State University of New York Press, 226–47.

Goldin, Paul R. (2005). "Xunzi in the Light of the Guodian Manuscripts." In *After Confucius: Studies in Early Chinese Philosophy.* Honolulu: University of Hawaii Press, 36–57.

Goldin, Paul. (2015). "The Consciousness of the Dead as a Philosophical Problem in Ancient China." In *The Good Life and Conceptions of Life in Early China and Græco-Roman Antiquity,* ed. R. A. H. King. Berlin: DeGruyter, 59–92.

Goldin, Paul R. (2018). "Xunzi." *The Stanford Encyclopedia of Philosophy.* Ed. Edward N. Zalta. https://plato.stanford.edu/archives/fall2018/entries/xunzi.

Graham, Angus C. (1967). "The Background of the Mencian Theory of Human Nature." *Tsing Hua Journal of Chinese Studies,* 6: 215–71.

Graham, Angus C. (1978). *Later Mohist Logic, Ethics and Science.* Hong Kong: Chinese University Press and London: School of Oriental and African Studies.

Graham, Angus C. (1981). *Chuang-Tzu: The Inner Chapters.* London: Unwin Paperbacks.

Graham, Angus C. (1985). *Divisions in Mohism Reflected in the Core Chapters of Mo-tzu.* Institute of East Asian Philosophies Occasional Paper and Monograph Series 1. Singapore: Institute of East Asian Philosophies.

Graham, Angus C. (1989a). "A Neglected Pre-Han Philosophical Text: Ho-kuan-tzu." *BSOAS,* 52(3): 497–532.

Graham, Angus C. (1989b). *Disputers of the Tao: Philosophical Argument in Ancient China.* LaSalle, IL: Open Court.

Guanzi 管子. (2001). In *A Concordance to the Guanzi* (管子逐字索引), ed. D. C. Lau, Ho Che Wah, and Chen Fong Ching. ICS Series. Hong Kong: Commercial Press.

Gundert, Beata. (2000). "Soma and Psyche in Hippocratic Medicine." In *Psyche and Soma: Physicians and Metaphysicians on the Mind–Body Problem from Antiquity to the Enlightenment,* eds. J. P. Wright and P. Potter. Oxford: Clarendon, 13–36.

Guo, Jue. (2011). "Concepts of Death and the Afterlife Reflected in Newly Discovered Tomb Objects and Texts from Han China." In *Mortality in Traditional Chinese Thought,* ed. Amy Olberding and P. J. Ivanhoe. Albany: State University of New York Press, 85–116.

Guo, Moruo 郭沫若. (1944). "Song Xing Yin Wen yizhu kao" 宋鈃尹文遺著考 [On Remnants of the Writings of Song Xing and Yin Wen]. In *Guo Moruo wenji* 郭沫著文集 [Collected Works of Guo Moruo]. Beijing: Renmin chubanshe, rpt. 1962, 224–66.

Guo, Yi 郭沂. (2001). *Guodian zhujian yu xian Qin xueshu sixiang* 郭店竹簡與先秦學朮思想 The [Guodian Bamboo Strips and Pre-Qin Academic Thought]. Shanghai: Shanghai jiaoyu chubanshe.

Guodian Chumu zhujian 郭店楚墓竹簡 [Bamboo Slips from the Chu Tombs at Guodian]. (1998). Beijing: Wenwu.

Hall, David, and Roger T. Ames. (1998). *Thinking from the Han: Self, Truth, and Transcendence in Chinese and Western Culture*. Albany: State University of New York Press.

Haloun, Gustav. (1951). "Legalist Fragments: Part I: *Kuan-tsï* 55 and Related Texts." *Asia Major* (ns) 2(1): 85–120.

Hansen, Chad. (1985). "Individualism in Chinese Thought." In *Individualism and Holism: Studies in Confucian and Taoist Values*, ed. Donald Munro. Ann Arbor: Center for Chinese Studies, University of Michigan, 35–55.

Hansen, Chad. (1995). "Qing (Emotions) 情 in Pre-Buddhist Chinese Thought." In *Emotions in Asian Thought: A Dialogue in Comparative Philosophy*, ed. J. Marks and Roger T. Ames. Albany: State University of New York Press, 181–212.

Harper, Donald J. (1998). *Early Chinese Medical Literature: The Mawangdui Medical Manuscripts*. London: Routledge.

Harper, Donald J. (1999). "Physicians and Diviners: The Relation of Divination to the Medicine of the *Huangdi neijing* (Inner Canon of the Yellow Thearch)." *Extrême-Orient, Extrême-Occident*, 21: 91–110.

Harper, Donald J. (2001). "Iatromancy, Diagnosis, and Prognosis in Early Chinese Medicine." In *Innovation in Chinese Medicine*, ed. Elisabeth Hsu. Cambridge, UK: Cambridge University Press, 99–120.

Harper, Donald J. (2003). "Physicians and Diviners" and "Iatromancie." In *Divination et Société dans la Chine Médiévale*, vol. 1, ed. Marc Kalinowski. Paris: Bibliothèque nationale de France, 471–512.

Harper, Donald J. (2005). "Dunhuang Iatromantic Manuscripts P. 2856R° and P. 2675V°." In *Medieval Chinese Medicine: The Dunhuang Manuscripts*, ed. Vivienne Lo and Christopher Cullen. London: RoutledgeCurzon, 134–64.

Harper, Donald J. (2010). "Précis de connaissance médicale. Le Shanghan lun 傷寒論 (Traité des atteintes par le Froid) et le Wuzang lun 五臟論 (Traité des cinq viscères)." In *Médecine, religion et société dans la Chine médiévale. Etude de manuscrits chinois de Dunhuang et de Turfan*, ed. Catherine Despeux. Paris: Collège de France, Institut des Hautes études chinoises, 65–106.

Harper, Donald J., and Marc Kalinowski (eds.). (2017). *Books of Fate and Popular Culture in Early China: The Daybook Manuscripts of the Warring States, Qin, and Han*. Leiden: Brill.

He, Jianjin. (2007). "The Body in the Politics and Society of Early China." PhD Dissertation,. University of Oregon.

He, Shuangquan 何雙全. (1986). "Wuwei Handai yijian shiwen buzheng." 武威漢代醫簡釋文補正. *Wenwu*, 4: 39.

He, Zhiguo, and Vivienne Lo. (1996). "The Channels: A Preliminary Examination of a Lacquered Figurine from the Western Han Period." *Early China*, 21: 81–123.

Hsia, Emil C.H. et al. (1986). *The Essentials of Medicine in Ancient China and Japan: Yasuyori Tamba's Ishinpō*. Leiden: Brill, 2 vols.

Hsu, Elisabeth. (2010). "Le diagnostic du pouls dans la China médiévale d'après les manuscrits de Dunhuang." In *Médecine, religion et société dans la Chine médiévale. Etude de manuscrits chinois de Dunhuang et de Turfan*, ed. Catherine Despeux. Paris: Collège de France, Institut des Hautes études chinoises, 107–84.

Hu, Fuchen 胡孚琛. (1993). "Daojia he Daojiao xing, qi, shen sanchong jiegou de renti guan" 道家和道教形, 氣, 神 三重 結構的人體觀 [Body, qi and spirit, the tripartite structure of the human body in Daoist philosophy and Daoist religion]. In *Zhongguo gudai sixiang shi zhong de qi lun yu shenti guan* 中國古代思想史中的氣論與身體觀 [Theories of Qi and the Body in the History of Early Chinese Thought], ed. Yang Rubin 楊儒賓. Taipei: Juliu tushu gongsi, 177–192.

Huainanzi 淮南子. (1992). In *A Concordance to the Huainanzi* (淮南子逐字索引), ed. D. C. Lau, Ho Che Wah, and Chen Fong Ching. ICS Series. Hong Kong: Commercial Press.

Huang, Dekuan 黃德寬 and Xu, Zaiguo 徐在國. (1999). "Guodian chujian wenzi xukao 郭店楚簡文字續考" [A Continued Examination of the Guodian Chu Slips] *Jianghan Kaogu* 江漢考古 2: 75–77.

Huang, Junjie 黃俊傑. (1993). "Mawangdui Hanmu boshu 'Wuxing pian' [xing yu nei] de yi han – Mengzi houxue shenxin guan zhong de yige que lian wenti" 馬王堆帛書《五行篇》「形於內」的意涵—孟子後學身心觀中的一個關鏈問題 [The Meaning of 'Formed in the Inner' in the Mawangdui Silk Manuscript 'Five KAnds of action'—A Linked Problem in the Post-Mencius Study of Body and Mind]." In *Zhongguo gudai sixiang shi zhong de qi lun yu shenti guan* 中國古代思想史中的氣論與身體觀 [Theories of Qi and the Body in the History of Early Chinese Thought], ed. Yang Rubin 楊儒賓. Taipei: Juliu tushu gongsi, 127–32.

Huangdi neijing lingshu 黃帝內經靈樞. (2003). [The Inner Classic of the Yellow Lord: Spiritual Pivot]. See Shibue Chūsai 澀江抽齋 [LS].

Huangdi neijing suwen 黃帝內經素問. (2004). [The Inner Classic of the Yellow Lord: Basic Questions]. See Yamada Gyōkō 山田業廣 [SW].

Huangdi neijing zhangju suoyin 黃帝內經章句索引. (1986). [Concordance to the Yellow Emperor's Classic of Internal Medicine]. Ed. Ren Yingqiu 任應 秋. Beijing: Renmin weisheng.

Hume, David. (1978). *A Treatise of Human Nature*. Ed. L. S. Selby-Bigge, 2nd ed. Oxford: Clarendon Press.

Hunter, Michael. (2021). *The Poetics of Early Chinese Thought: How the Shijing Shaped the Chinese Philosophical Tradition*. New York: Columbia University Press.

Hutton, Eric L. (2014). *Xunzi* 荀子 *The Complete Text*. Princeton, NJ: Princeton University Press.

Ikeda, Tomohisa 池田知久. (1993). "Mawangdui Hanmu boshu 'Wuxing pian' suojian zhi shen xin wenti" 馬王堆漢墓帛書《五行篇》所見之身心問題 [Findings and problems regarding the Mawangdui silk manuscript 'Five kinds of action']. In *Zhongguo gudai sixiang shi zhong de qi lun yu shenti guan* 中國古代思想史中的氣論與身體觀 [Theories of Qi and the Body in the History of Early Chinese Thought], ed. Yang Rubin 楊儒賓. Taipei: Juliu tushu gongsi, 127–32.

Im, Manyul. (1999). "Emotional Control and Virtue in the Mencius." *Philosophy East and West*, 49(1): 1–27.

Im, Manyul. (2002). "Action, Emotion, and Inference in Mencius." *Journal of Chinese Philosophy*, 29(2): 227–49.

Ishida, Hidemi. (1989). "Body and Mind: The Chinese Perspective." In *Taoist Meditation and Longevity Techniques*, ed. Livia Kohn. Ann Arbor: University of Michigan Press, 41–72.

Ishida, Hidemi. 石田秀実. (1993). "You shenti shengcheng guocheng de renshi lai kan Zhongguo gudai shenti guan de tezhi" 由身體生成過程的認識來看中國古代身體觀的特質 [Ancient Chinese views of the body considered through processes of the formation of the body]. In *Zhongguo gudai sixiang shi zhong de qi lun yu shenti guan* 中國古代思想史中的氣論與身體觀 [Theories of Qi and the Body in the History of Early Chinese Thought], ed. Yang Rubin 楊儒賓. Taipei: Juliu tushu gongsi, 177–92.

Ishinpō. See Tamba Yasuyori.

Ji, Xusheng 季旭昇. (2004). "'Xingqing lun' yishi:" '性情論' 譯釋 [Translation and Interpretation of "Discussion of Qing and Xing"]. In *Shanghai Bowuguan cang Zhanguo Chu Zhujian* 上海博物館藏戰國楚竹簡 (1) [Warring States Chu Bamboo Texts Collected by the Shanghai Museum, vol. 1], ed. Ma Chengyuan 馬承源. Taipei: Wanjuanlou Tushu Fufen, 152–221.

Jia, Jinhua 賈晉華. (2014). "Shénming shiyi" 神明釋義 [Explanation of *Shénming*]. *Shenzhen daxue xuebao* (Renwen shehui kexue xueban) 深圳大學學報（人文社會科學版）, 31(3): 5–15.

Jiang, Guanghui. (2000). "The Guodian Chu Slips and Early Confucianism." *Contemporary Chinese Thought*, 32(2): 6–38.

Jiangling Zhangjiashan Hanjian zhengli xiaoozu 江陵張家山汉简整理小组. (1990). "Zhangjiashan Han jian Yin shu shiwen" 張家山漢簡《引書》釋文 [Explanatory interpretation of the Han bamboo manuscript Yin shu from Zhangjiashan]. *Wenwu*, (10): 82–86.

Johnson, Mark (ed.). (1981). *Philosophical Perspectives on Metaphor*. Minneapolis: University of Minnesota Press.

Johnson, Mark. (1987). *The Body in the Mind: The Bodily Basis of Meaning, Imagination, and Reason*. Chicago: University of Chicago Press.

Johnson, Mark. (1993). *Moral Imagination: Implications of Cognitive Science for Ethics*. Chicago: University of Chicago Press.

Johnson, Mark. (2017). *Embodied Mind, Meaning, and Reason: How Our Bodies Give Rise to Understanding*. Chicago: University of Chicago Press.

Jullien, François. (2007). *The Propensity of Things: Toward a History of Efficacy in China*, trans. J. Lloyd. New York: Zone Books.

Kane, Virginia C. (1982–83). "Aspects of Western Chou Appointment Inscriptions: The Charge, the Gifts, and the Response." *Early China*, 8: 14–28.

Karlgren, Bernhard. (1950). *The Book of Odes*. Stockholm: Museum of Far Eastern Antiquities.

Kasulis, Thomas, Roger T. Ames, and Wimal Dissanayake (eds.). (1993). *Self as Body in Asian Theory and Practice*. Albany: State University of New York Press, 157–77.

Keegan, David J. (1988). "The 'Huang-ti Nei-Ching': The Structure of the Compilation; The Significance of the Structure." PhD dissertation. University of California, Berkeley.

Keightley, David N. (1978). "The Religious Commitment: Shang Theology and the Genesis of Chinese Political Culture." *History of Religions*, 17(3/4): 211–25.

Keightley, David N. (1998). "Shamanism, Death, and the Ancestors: Religious Mediation in Neolithic and Shang China (ca. 5000–1000 B.C.)." *Asiatische Studien /Etudes Asiatiques*, 52(3): 763–828.

Keightley, David N. (2014) "The Making of the Ancestors: Late Shang Religion and Its Legacy." In *These Bones Shall Rise Again: Selected Writings on Early China*. Albany: State University of New York Press, 155–206.

Kern, Martin. (2002). "Methodological Reflections on the Analysis of Textual Variants and the Modes of Manuscript Production in Early China." *Journal of East Asian Archaeology*, 4(1–4): 143–48.

Kern, Martin. (2005). "The Odes in Excavated Manuscripts." In *Text and Ritual in Eary China*, ed. Martin Kern. Seattle: University of Washington Press, 149–93.

Klein, Esther, and Colin Klein. (2012). "Did the Chinese Have a Change of Heart?" *Cognitive Science*, 36: 179–82.

Kline, T. C., III and P. J. Ivanhoe (eds.). (2000). *Virtue, Nature, and Moral Agency in the Xunzi*. Indianapolis, IN: Hackett.

Knoblock, John. (1988, 1990, 1994). *Xunzi: A Translation and Study of the Complete Works*. 3 vols. Stanford, CA: Stanford University Press.

Komjathy, Louis. (2008). "Mapping the Daoist Body, Part One: The Neijing Tu in History." *Journal of Daoist Studies*, 1: 67–92.

Komjathy, Louis. (2009). "Mapping the Daoist Body, Part Two: The Text of the Neijing Tu." *Journal of Daoist Studies*, 2: 64–108.

Kosoto, Hiroshi 小曾戶洋. (1981). *Tōyō igaku zempon sōsho* 東洋醫學善本叢書. 8 vols. Osaka: Tōyō igaku kenkyūkai.

Lai, Guolong. (2005). "Death and the Otherworldly Journey in Early China as Seen through Tomb Texts, Travel Paraphernalia, and Road Rituals." *Asia Major*, 18(1): 1–44.

Lai, Guolong. (2015). *Excavating the Afterlife: The Archaeology of Early Chinese Religion*. Seattle: University of Washington Press.

Lai, Karyn. (2019a). "Emotional Attachment and Its Limits: Mengzi, Gaozi and the Guodian Discussions," *Frontiers of Philosophy in China* (1): 132–51.

Lai, Karyn. (2019b). "The Cicada Catcher: Learning for Life." In *Skill and Mastery: Philosophical Stories from the Zhuangzi*, ed. Karyn Lai and Wai Wai Chiu. London: Rowman & Littlefield International, 143–62.

Lakoff, George, and Mark Johnson. (1980). *Metaphors We Live By*. Chicago: University of Chicago Press.

Lakoff, George, and Mark Johnson. (1999). *Philosophy in the Flesh: The Embodied Mind and Its Challenge to Western Thought*. New York: Basic Books.

Lakoff, George, and M. Turner. (1989). "Life, Death, and Time." In *More than Cool Reason: A Field Guide to Poetic Metaphor*. Chicago: University of Chicago Press, 1–56.

Lau, D. C. (1984). *Mencius. Bilingual edition*. Hong Kong: Chinese University Press, 1984.

Lau, D. C. (1992). *The Analects. Bilingual Edition*. Hong Kong: Chinese University Press.

Le Blanc, Charles. (1985). *Huai-nan tzu: Philosophical Synthesis in Early Han Thought*. Hong Kong: Hong Kong University Press.

Le Blanc, Charles. (2000). *Le Wen zi à la lumière de l'histoire et de l'archéologie*. Montréal: Les Presses de l'Université de Montréal.

Lee, Janghee. (2005). "The Notion of Xin." In *Xunzi and Early Chinese Naturalism*. Albany: State University of New York Press, 33–56.

Lei Jing Tu Yi 類經圖翼. [Illustrated supplement to the classic of categories]. Siku chuanshu edition.

Lewis, Mark E. (2006). *The Construction of Space in Early China*. Albany: State University of New York Press.

Li, Daoping 李道平. (1994). *Zhouyi jijie zuanshu* 周易集解纂疏 [Annotation and Compilation of Zhouyi]. Beijing: Zhonghua shuju.

Li, Ling 李零. (1993). *Zhongguo fangshu kao* 中國方術考 [A study of the occult arts of China]. Beijing: Zhonghua shuju.

Li, Ling 李零. (1999). "Du Guodian Chujian 'Taiyi sheng shui'" 讀郭店楚簡《太一生水》[Reading the Guodian Slips "The Great One Gave Birth to Water"]. *Daojia Wenhua Yanjiu* 道家文化研究 17: 316–31.

Li, Ling 李零. (2002). *Guodian Chujian jiaodu ji* 郭店楚簡校讀記 [Proofreading Notes on Guodian Chu Bamboo Slips]. Beijing: Peking University Press.

Li, Shenghua 李盛華, and Zhang Yanchang 張延昌. (2014). *Wuwei Handai yijian yanjiu jicheng* 武威漢代醫簡研究集成 [Collected research on the Han dynasty medical slips from Wuwei]. Hefei: Anhui kexue jishu.

Li, Tianhong 李天虹. (2003). "'Xingzi mingchu' yanjiu"《性自命出》研究 [Research on the Xingzi mingchu]. Wuhan: Hubei Jiaoyu chubanshe.

Li, Xueqin 李學勤 (ed.). (2018). *Qinghua daxue cang Zhanguo zhujian* (8) 清華大學藏戰國竹簡 (捌) [The Tsinghua University Warring States Bamboo Strips: volume 8]. Shanghai: Zhongxi shuju.

Liao, Mingchun 廖名春. (2001). *Xinchu Chujian shilun* 新出楚簡試論 [On the Newly Excavated Chu Bamboo Slips]. Shanghai: Yuwan, 133–70.

Liji 禮記 (Book of Rites). (1992). In *A Concordance to the Liji* (禮記逐字索引), ed. D. C. Lau, Ho Che Wah, and Chen Fong Ching. ICS Series. Hong Kong: Commercial Press.

Lin, Yun 林澐. (1992). "Du Baoshan Chujian zhaji qi ze" 讀包山楚簡札記七則 [Seven Reading Notes on Baoshan Chu Bamboo Slips]. *Jiang Han kaogu*, 4: 83–85.

Link, Perry. (2013). *An Anatomy of Chinese: Rhythm, Metaphor, Politics*. Cambridge, MA: Harvard University Press.

Littré, E. (1839–61). *Oeuvres completes d'Hippocrate*, 10 vols. Paris [Littré].

Liu, Guozhong. (2016). *Introduction to the Tsinghua Bamboo-Strip Manuscripts*. Leiden: Brill.

Liu, Xinlan 劉昕嵐. (2000). "Guodian Chujian 'Xingzi mingchu' pian longshi" 郭店楚簡《性自命出》篇箋釋 [Explanation of Xingzi mingchu in the Guodian Chu Slips]. In *Guodian Chu jian guoji xueshu yantaohui lunwen ji* 郭店楚簡 國際學朮研討會論文集 [Proceedings of the international symposium on the Chu slips from Guodian], eds. Wuhan daxue Zhongguo wenhua yanjiu yuanben. Wuhan: Hubei renmin chubanshe, 330–54.

Liu, Zhao 劉釗. (2000). "Du Guodian Chujian jici zhaji" 讀郭店楚簡字詞札記 [Notes on Words in the Guodian Chu Slips]. In *Guodian Chu jian guoji xueshu yantaohui lunwen ji* 郭店楚簡 國際學朮研討會論文集 [Proceedings of the international symposium on the Chu slips from Guodian], eds. Wuhan daxue Zhongguo wenhua yanjiu yuanben. Wuhan: Hubei renmin chubanshe, Wuhan daxue Zhongguo wenhua yanjiu yuanben, 75–93.

Liu, Zhao 劉釗. (2003). *Guodian Chujian jiaoshi* 郭店楚簡校釋 [An Interpretation with Corrections of the Guodian Chu Slips]. Fuzhou: Fujian Renmin Chubanshe.

Lloyd, G. E. R. (1983). "The Development of Zoological Taxonomy." In *Science, Folklore and Ideology: Studies in the Life Sciences in Ancient Greece*. Cambridge, UK: Cambridge University Press, 7–57.

Lloyd, G. E. R. (1996). *Aristotelian Explorations*. Cambridge, UK: Cambridge University Press.

Lo, Vivienne. (2001). "Yellow Emperor's Toad Canon: The Huangdi Hama Jing." *Asia Major, 14*(2): 61–100.

Lo, Vivienne. (2005). "Self-cultivation and the Popular Medical Traditions." In *Medieval Chinese Medicine: The Dunhuang Medical Manuscripts*, eds. Vivienne Lo and Christopher Cullen. New York: RoutledgeCurzon, 207–25.

Lo, Vivienne. (2014). *How to Do the Gibbon Walk: A Translation of the Pulling Book (ca. 186 BCE)*. Cambridge, UK: Needham Research Institute Working Papers.

Lo, Yuet-Keung. (1992). "Fatalism and Retribution in Late Han religious Daoism." In *Contacts between Cultures*, ed. B. H.-K. Luk, Vol. 4. Eastern Asia: History and Social Sciences. Lewiston, NY: Edwin Mellen Press, 317–21.

Lo, Yuet-Keung. (2003). "Finding the Self in the *Analects*: A Philological Approach." In *The Moral Circle and the Self*, eds. Kim-chong Chong, Sor-Hoon Tan, and C. L. Ten. LaSalle: Open Court, 249–68.

Lo, Yuet-Keung. (2008). "From a Dual Soul to a Unitary Soul: The Babel of Soul Terminologies in Early China." *Monumenta Serica*, 56: 23–53.

Locke, John. (1999/1689). *An Essay Concerning Human Understanding*. Ed P. Nidditch. Oxford, UK: Clarendon Press.

Loewe, Michael (ed.). (1993). *Early Chinese Texts: A Bibliographical Guide*. Berkeley: Institute of East Asian Studies.

Loy, Hui-chieh. (2011). "*Individualism in Early China: Human Agency and the Self in Thought and Politics*, By Erica Fox Brindley." *Journal of Chinese Religions*, 39: 101–5.

Lunheng 論衡 [Weighing Discourses]. (1990). In *Lunheng jiaoshi* 論衡校釋, by Wang Chong 王充 (27–97), ed. Liu Pansui 劉盼遂. Beijing: Zhonghua shuju.

Lunheng 論衡 [Weighing Discourses]. (1996). In *A Concordance to the Lunheng* (論衡逐字索引), ed. D. C. Lau, Ho Che Wah, and Chen Fong Ching. ICS Series. Hong Kong: Commercial Press.

Lunyu 論語 [Analects]. (1995). In *A Concordance to the Lunyu* (論語逐字索引), ed. D. C. Lau, Ho Che Wah, and Chen Fong Ching. ICS Series. Hong Kong: Commercial Press.

Lüshi chunqiu jiaoshi 呂氏春秋校釋 [Interpretation and Annotation of the Springs and Autumns of Master Lü]. (1984). Ed. Chen Qiyou 陳奇猷. (1917–2006). Shanghai: Xuelin.

Ma, Chengyuan 馬承源 (ed.). (2001). *Shanghai Bowuguan cang Zhanguo zhushu* 上海博物館藏戰國楚竹書, vol. 1 [The Warring States Chu Bamboo Texts Collected by the Shanghai Museum, vol. 1]. Shanghai: Shanghai Guji chubanshe.

Ma, Chengyuan 馬承源 (ed.). (2005). *Shanghai bowuguan cang Zhanguo Chu zhushu* 上海博物館藏戰國楚竹書, vol. 5 [[The Warring States Chu Bamboo Texts Collected by the Shanghai Museum, vol. 5]. Shanghai: Shanghai guji chubanshe.

Ma, Chengyuan (ed.). (2008). *Shanghai Bowuguan cang zhanguo Chu zhu shu VII* 上海博物館藏戰國楚竹書（七）[The Warring States Chu Bamboo Texts Collected by the Shanghai Museum, vol. 7]. Shanghai: Shanghai guji chubanshe.

Ma, Jixing 馬繼興. (1990). *Zhongyi wenxian xue* 中醫文獻學 [Study Chinese Medical Texts]. Shanghai: Shanghai kexue jishu.

Ma, Jixing 馬繼興. (1992). *Mawangdui gu yishu kaoshi* 馬王堆古醫書考釋 [Explanation of the Ancient Medical texts from Mawangdui]. Changsha: Hunan kexue jishu chubanshe.

Ma, Jixing 馬繼興 et al. (eds.). (1998). *Dunhuang yiyao wenxian jijiao* 敦煌醫藥文獻輯校 [The Dunhuang medical texts edited and collated]. Nanjing: Jiangsu guji.

Ma, Yuancai 馬元材 [Ma Feibai 馬非百]. (1990). "'Guanzi neiye' pian jizhu"《管子內業》篇集注 [Collected Notes on *Guanzi* Neiye]. *Guanzi xuekan*, 1: 6–13.

Machle, E. J. (1992). "The Mind and the *Shen-ming* in the *Xunzi*." *Journal of Chinese Philosophy*, 19: 361–86.

Mair, Victor. (1994). *Wandering on the Way: Early Taoist Tales and Parables of Chuang Tzu Zhuangzi*. New York: Bantam Books.

Major, John S. (2003). *Heaven and Earth in Early Han Thought: Chapters Three, Four, and Five of the Huainanzi*. Albany: State University of New York Press.

Major, John S., Sarah A. Queen, Andrew Seth Meyer, and Harold D. Roth (trans.). (2010). *The Huainanzi: A Guide to the Theory and Practice of Government in Early Han China*. New York: Columbia University Press.

Marriot, M. (1976). "Hindu Transactions: Diversity without Dualism." In *Transaction and Meaning: Directions in the Anthropology of Exchange and Symbolic Behaviour*, ed. B. Kapferer. Philadelphia: Institute for the Study of Human Issues, 109–37.

Maspéro, Henri. (1933). "Le mot ming." *Journal Asiatique*, 223: 249–96.

Mattos, Gilbert L. (1997). Eastern Zhou Bronze Inscriptions." In *New Sources of Early Chinese History: An Introduction to the Reading of Inscriptions and Manuscripts*, ed. Edward L. Shaughnessy. Berkeley: Society for the Study of Early China and the Institute of East Asian Studies, University of California Berkeley, 85–124.

Mawangdui Hanmu boshu 馬王堆漢墓帛書. (1980). [The Silk Manuscripts from the Han Tombs at Mawangdui]. Ed. Mawangdui Hanmu boshu zhengli xiaozu 馬王堆漢墓帛書整理小組. Volume 1/2. Beijing: Wenwu. [MWD1]

Mawangdui Hanmu boshu 馬王堆漢墓帛書 (1985). [The Silk Manuscripts from the Han Tombs at Mawangdui]. Ed. Mawangdui Hanmu boshu zhengli xiaozu 馬王堆漢墓帛書整理小組. Volume 4. Beijing: Wenwu. [MWD4]

Mawangdui Hanmu boshu zhengli xiaozu 馬王堆漢墓帛書整理小組. (1975a). "Mawangdui Hanmu chutu yishu shiwen (1)." 馬王堆漢墓出土醫書釋文(一) [Interpretation of the medical texts excavated from the Han tombs at (1)]. *Wenwu*, 6: 1–5.

Mawangdui Hanmu boshu zhengli xiaozu 馬王堆漢墓帛書整理小組. (1975b). "Mawangdui Hanmu chutu yishu shiwen (2)" 馬王堆漢墓出土醫書釋文(二) [Interpretation of the medical texts excavated from the Han tombs at (2)]. *Wenwu*, 6: 35–48.

Meader, Erik W. (1992). "Some Observations on the Composition of the 'Core Chapters' of the Mozi," *Early China* 17: 27–82.

Menary, Richard. (2007). *Cognitive Integration: Mind and Cognition Unbounded*. London: Palgrave Macmillan.

Menary, Richard (ed.). (2010). *The Extended Mind. Life and Mind*. Philosophical Issues in Biology and Psychology Series. Cambridge, MA: MIT Press.

Mengzi 孟子. (1995). In *A Concordance to the Mengzi (孟子逐字索引)*, edited by D.C. Lau, Ho Che Wah, and Chen Fong Ching. ICS series. Hong Kong: Commercial Press.

Messner, Angelika. (2006). "Emotions, Body, and Bodily Sensations within an Early Field of Expertise Knowledge in China." In *From Skin to Heart: Perceptions of Emotions and Bodily Sensations in Traditional Chinese Culture*, ed. Paolo Santangelo and Ulrike Middendorf. Wiesbaden: Harrassowitz Verlag, 41–63.

Middendorf, Ulrike. (2008). "Again on 'Qing'. With a Translation of the Guodian 'Xing zi ming chu.'" *Oriens Extremus*, 47: 97–159.

Morgan, Jeffrey. (2018). "Zhuang Zi and the Education of the Emotions." *Comparative Philosophy*, 9(1): 32–46.

Mozi 墨子. (2001). In *A Concordance to the Mozi (墨子逐字索引)*, edited by D.C. Lau, Ho Che Wah and Chen Fong Ching. ICS series. Hong Kong: Commercial Press.

Munro, David. (2005). "Two Kinds of Models and the Value of Autonomy." In *A Chinese Ethics for the New Century* (Ch'ien Mu Lecture in History and Culture). Hong Kong: Chinese University Press, 33–43.

Nivison, David S. (1979). "Mencius and Motivation." *Journal of the American Academy of Religion*, 47(3): 417–32.

Nivison, David S. (1996). *Ways of Confucianism: Investigations in Chinese Philosophy*. Ed. Bryan Van Norden. Chicago: Open Court.

Nylan, Michael. (1996). "Confucian Piety and Individualism in Han China." *Journal of the American Oriental Society*, 116(1): 1–27.

Nylan, Michael. (2001). *The Five "Confucian" Classics*. New Haven, CT: Yale University Press.

Olson, Eric T. (1997). *The Human Animal" Identity without Psychology*. New York: Oxford University Press.

Olson, Eric T. (2007). *What Are We? A Study in Personal Ontology*. New York: Oxford University Press.

Olson, Eric T. (2021). "Personal Identity," *The Stanford Encyclopedia of Philosophy* (Spring 2021 Edition), ed. Edward N. Zalta. https://plato.stanford.edu/archives/spr2021/entries/identity-personal.

Pang, Pu 龐樸. (2000). "'Taiyi sheng shui' shuo" 《太一生水》說 [Explanation of "The Great One Gave Birth to Water"], *Zhongguo zhexue* 中國哲學 [Chinese Philosophy], 21: 189–197.

Pang, Pu 龐樸. (2000-2001). "From Confucius to Mencius: The Confucian Theory of Mind and Nature in the Guodian Chu Slips." *Contemporary Chinese Thought*, 32(2): 39–54. Translation of "Kong Meng zhi jian—Guodian Chujian zhong de rujia xinxingshuo 孔孟之間—郭店楚簡中的儒家心性說." *Zhongguo zhexue* 中國哲學 [Chinese Philosophy] 20: 22–35.

Parfit, Derek. (1971). "Personal Identity." *Philosophical Review*, 80(1): 3–27.

Parfit, Derek. (1984). *Reasons and Persons*. New York: Oxford University Press.

Parfit, Derek. (1995). *The Unimportance of Identity*. New York: Oxford University Press.

Peng, Hao 彭浩. (1990). "Zhangjiashan Hanjian Yinshu chutan" 张家山汉简《引书》初探 [Preliminary study of the Han Bamboo manuscript "Yinshu" from Zhangjiashan]. *Wenwu*, 10: 87–91 (*Yinshu*).

Peng, Hua彭華. (2016). "Shenming yijie—Guodian Chujian Taiyi sheng shui yanjiu zhier" 神明臆解—郭店楚簡太一生水研究之二 [A second study of the interpretation of shenming in the Guodian Chu text Taiyi sheng shui]. *Zhongyuan wenhua yanjiu* 中原文化研究, 5: 96–101.

Perkins, Franklin. (2002). "Mencius, Emotion and Autonomy." *Journal of Chinese Philosophy*, 29(2): 207–26.

Perkins, Franklin. (2009). "Motivation and the Heart in the Xing zi ming chu." *Dao*, 8: 117–31.

Perkins, Franklin. (2015). "Fanwu liuxing 凡物流形 ("All Things Flow into Form") and the "One" in the Laozi." *Early China*, 38: 195–232.

Pham, Lee-Moi 范麗梅. (2013). "Jiejie jianjian, yong si kui ru—Guodian 'Xingzi mingchu' ji zhi de de shen xin qi shuxie" 節節蹇蹇、永思喟如-郭店〈性自命出〉亟治德的身心氣書寫 [Body, Mind, Qi and Self-Cultivation in the Guodian Xingzi mingchu]. *Qinghua xuebao* 清華學報, 4(1): 53–96.

Pines, Yuri. (2002). *Foundations of Confucian Thought: Intellectual Life in the Chinqiu Period, 722–453 BCE*. Honolulu: University of Hawai'i Press.

Pinker, Steven. (1994). *The Language Instinct*. New York: Morrow.

Poo, Mu-chou. (1990). "Ideas Concerning Death and Burial in pre-Han and Han China." *Asia Major*, 3(2): 25–62.

Poo, Mu-chou. (1998). *In Search of Personal Welfare: A View of Ancient Chinese Religion*. Albany: State University of New York Press.

Poo, Mu-chou. (2005). "Afterlife: Chinese Concepts." In *The Encyclopedia of Religion*, 2nd ed., vol. 1, ed. Lindsay Jones. New York: Macmillan, 169–72.

Puett, Michael J. (2002). *To Become a God: Cosmology, Sacrifice, and Self-Divinization in Early China*. Cambridge MA: Harvard University Press.

Puett, Michael J. (2004). "The Ethics of Responding Properly: The Notion of Qing in Early Chinese Thought." In *Love and Emotions in Traditional Chinese Literature*, ed. H. Eifring. Leiden: Brill, 37–68.

Puett, Michael J. (2010). "The Haunted World of Humanity: Ritual Theory from Early China." In *Rethinking the Human*, ed. J. Michelle Molina and Donald K. Swearer. Center for the Study of World Religions, Harvard Divinity School, distributed by Harvard University Press, 95–110.

Puett, Michael J. (2015a). "Constructions of Reality: Metaphysics in the Ritual Traditions of Classical China." In *Chinese Metaphysics and Its Problems*, ed. Chenyang Li and Franklin Perkins. Cambridge, UK: Cambridge University Press, 120–29.

Puett, Michael J. (2015b). "Ritual and Ritual Obligations: Perspectives on Normativity from Classical China." *Journal of Value Inquiry*, 49: 543–50.

Qianjin yaofang 千金要方 [Essential Recipes Worth a Thousand in Gold]. By Sun Simiao 孫思邈 (581–682). Siku quanshu edn.

Qianjin yifang 千金翼方 [Supplementary Prescriptions Worth a Thousand Gold]. By Sun Simiao 孫思邈 (581–682). Beijing: Renmin weisheng chubanshe, 1982.

Qinghua daxue cang Zhanguo zhujian (8) 清華大學藏戰國竹簡 (捌). (2018). See Li Xueqin.

Qiu, Xigui 裘錫圭. (1992). "Mawangdui yishu shidu suoyi" 馬王堆醫書釋讀瑣議 [Notes and annotations on the Mawangdui medical texts]. In *Guwenzi lunji* 古文字論集 [Collected essays on ancient writings]. Beijing: Zhonghua, 526–36.

Qiu, Xigui 裘錫圭. (1998). "Qiu an" 裘按 [Notes]. In *Guodian Chumu zhujian* 郭店楚墓竹簡 [Bamboo Slips from the Chu Tombs at Guodian]. Beijing: Wenwu, 182–184.

Quigley, Karen S., et al. (2021). "Functions of Interoception: From Energy Regulation to Experience of the Self." *Trends in Neurosciences,* 44(1): 29–38.

Raphals, Lisa. (2013). *Divination and Prediction in Early China and ancient Greece.* Cambridge, UK: Cambridge University Press.

Raphals, Lisa. (2014). "Uprightness, Indirection, Transparency." In *Dao Companion to the Analects*, ed. Amy Olberding. Dordrecht: Springer, 159–70.

Raphals, Lisa. (2015). "Body and Mind in Early China and Greece." *Journal of Cognitive Historiography,* 2(2): 132–82.

Raphals, Lisa. (2018). "Human and Animal in China and Greece." In *Ancient Greece and China Compared*, ed. G. Lloyd and J. J. Zhao. Cambridge, UK: Cambridge University Press, 131–59.

Raphals, Lisa. (2019). "Body and Mind in the Guodian Manuscripts." In *Dao Companion to the Excavated Guodian Bamboo Manuscripts*, ed. Shirley Chan. Dordrecht: Springer, 239–57.

Raphals, Lisa. (2020). "Body, Mind, and Spirit in Early Chinese Medicine." *T'oung-pao,* 106(5–6): 525–51.

Raphals, Lisa. (2021). "Virtue, Body, Mind and Spirit in the *Shijing*: New Perspectives on Pre-Warring States Conceptions of Personhood and Virtue," *Journal of Chinese Philosophy,* 48(1): 28–39.

Ren, Yingqiu 任應秋 (ed.). (1986). *Huangdi neijing zhangju suoyin* 黃帝內經章句索引 [Concordance to the Yellow Emperor's Classic of Internal Medicine]. Beijing: Renmin weisheng chubanshe.

Richert, R. A., and P. L. Harris. (2008). "Dualism Revisited: Body vs. Mind vs. Soul." *Journal of Cognition and Culture,* 8: 99–115.

Rickett, W. Allyn. (1985, 1998). *Guanzi: Political, Economic and Philosophical Essays from Early China* (2 vols.). Princeton, NJ: Princeton University Press.

Robinet, Isabelle [He Bilai 賀碧來]. (1999). "Lun 'Taiyi sheng shui' 論《太一生水》[On "The Great One gave birth to water]. *Daojia Wenhua Yanjiu,* 17: 332–39.

Robins, Dan (2014) "Xunzi," *Stanford Encyclopedia of Philosophy*, ed. E. N. Zalta et al., http://plato.stanford.edu/archives/spr2014/entries/xunzi.

Robinson, Howard. (2017). "Dualism." *The Stanford Encyclopedia of Philosophy* (Fall 2017 Edition), ed. Edward N. Zalta. https://plato.stanford.edu/archives/fall2017/entries/dualism.

Rosemont, Henry, Jr. (1991a). "Rights-Bearing Individuals and Role-Bearing Persons." In *Rules, Rituals, and Responsibility: Essays Dedicated to Herbert Fingarette*, ed. Mary I. Bockover. La Salle, IL: Open Court, 71–101.

Rosemont, Henry, Jr. (1991b). "Who Chooses?" In *Chinese Texts and Philosophical Contexts*, ed. Henry Rosemont Jr. La Salle, IL: Open Court, 227–63.

Rosemont, Henry, Jr. (2006). "Two Loci of Authority: Autonomous Individuals and Related Persons." In *Confucian Cultures of Authority*, ed. P. D. Hershock and Roger T. Ames, Albany: State University of New York Press, 1–20.

Roth, Harold. (1990). "The Early Taoist Concept of Shen: A Ghost in the Machine?" In *Sagehood and Systematizing Thought in the Late Warring States and Early Han*, ed. Kidder Smith. Brunswick ME: Bowdoin College, 11–32.

Roth, Harold. (1991). "Psychology and Self-Cultivation in Early Taoist Thought." *Harvard Journal of Asiatic Studies*, 51(1): 599–650.

Roth, Harold. (1999). *Original Tao: Inward Training (Nei-yeh) and the Foundations of Taoist Mysticism*. New York: Columbia University Press.

Sabattini, Elisa (2015). "The Physiology of 'xin' (Heart) in Chinese Political Argumentation: The Western Han Dynasty and the Pre-imperial Legacy." *Frontiers of Philosophy in China*, 10(1): 58–74.

Sahlins, Marshall, with Frederick B. Henry, Jr. (2022). *The New Science of the Enchanted Universe: An Anthropology of Most of Humanity*. Princeton: Princeton University Press.

Santangelo, Paulo. (2007). "Emotions and Perception of Inner Reality: Chinese and European." *Journal of Chinese Philosophy*, 34(2): 289–308.

Sarkissian, Hagop. (2012). "Individualism in Early China: Human Agency and the Self in Thought and Politics (review)." *Philosophy East and West*, 62(3): 408–10.

Schechtman, M. (1996). *The Constitution of Selves*. Ithaca, NY: Cornell University Press.

Scheid, Volker. (2002). *Chinese Medicine in Contemporary Society: Plurality and Synthesis*. Durham, NC: Duke University Press.

Scheper-Hughes, N., and Lock, M. M. (1987). "The Mindful Body: A Prolegomenon to Future Work in Medical Anthropology." *Medical Anthropology Quarterly*, 1: 6–41.

Seidel, Anna. (1982). "Tokens of Immortality in Han Graves," *Numen*, 29(1): 79–122.

Shapiro, Lawrence. (2011). *Embodied Cognition*. Oxford: Routledge.

Shapiro, Lawrence (ed.). (2014). *Routledge Handbook of Embodied Cognition*. Oxford, UK: Routledge.

Shapiro, Lawrence, and Shannon Spaulding. (2021). "Embodied Cognition." *The Stanford Encyclopedia of Philosophy*, ed. Edward N. Zalta. https://plato.stanford.edu/archives/fall2021/entries/embodied-cognition.

Shaughnessy, Edward L. (1991) *Sources of Western Zhou History: Inscribed Bronze Vessels*. Berkeley: University of California Press.

Shaughnessy, Edward L. (2015). "Unearthed Documents and the Question of the Oral versus Written Nature of the "Classic of Poetry." *Early China*, 75(2): 331–75.

Shen, Jianhua 沈建华. (2018). "Chu du Qinghua jian <Xin shi wei zhong>" 初读清华简〈心是谓中〉 [First Reading of Tsinghua Bamboo Slips "Xin shi wei zhong"] *Chutu wenxian* 出土文献 [Excavated Texts], 13: 136–41.

Sherrington, Charles S. (1906). *The Integrative Action of the Nervous System*. New Haven, CT: Yale University Press.

Shibue, Chūsai 澀江抽齋. (2003). *Lingshu jiangyi* 靈樞講義, ed. Cui Zhongping et al. Beijing: Xueyuan [LS].

Shoemaker, Sydney. (1985). "Reasons and Persons" [Review of Reasons and Persons]. *Mind*, 94(375): 443–53.

Shoemaker, Sydney. (2008). "Persons, Animals, and Identity." *Synthese*, 162(3): 313–24.

Shun, Kwong-loi. (1997). *Mencius and Early Chinese Thought*. Stanford, CA: Stanford University Press.

Shun, Kwong-loi. (2002). "Ren and Li in the Analects." In *Confucius and the Analects: New Essays*, ed. Bryan van Norden. Oxford: Oxford University Press, 53–72.

Shun, Kwong-loi and David B Wong (eds.). (2004). *Confucian Ethics: A Comparative Study of Self, Autonomy, and Community*. Cambridge, UK: Cambridge University Press.

Sivin, Nathan. (1987). *Traditional Medicine in Contemporary China. Science, Medicine, and Technology in East Asia 2*. Ann Arbor, MI: Center for Chinese Studies, University of Michigan, 273–74.

Sivin, Nathan. (1993). "Huang ti nei ching 黃帝內經." In *Early Chinese Texts: A Bibliographical Guide*, ed. Michael Loewe. Berkeley: University of California Press, 196–215.

Sivin, Nathan. (1995). "State, Cosmos, and Body in the Last Three Centuries B.C." *Harvard Journal of Asiatic Studies*, 55(1): 5–37.

Sivin, Nathan. (1998). "On the Dates of Yang Shang-shan and the Huang-ti nei ching t'ai su." *Chinese Science*, 15: 29–36.

Slingerland, Edward T. (2003a). *Confucius Analects with Selections from Traditional Commentaries*. Indianapolis, IN: Hackett.

Slingerland, Edward T. (2003b). *Effortless Action: Wu-wei as Conceptual Metaphor and Spiritual Ideal in Early China*. New York: Oxford University Press.

Slingerland, Edward T. (2004). "Conceptions of the Self in the Zhuangzi: Conceptual Metaphor Analysis and Comparative Thought," *Philosophy East and West*, 54(3): 322–42.

Slingerland, Edward T. (2008). "The Problem of Moral Spontaneity in the Guodian Corpus." *Dao*, 7(3): 237–56.

Slingerland, Edward T. (2011). "Metaphor and Meaning in Early China." *Dao*, 10: 1–30.

Slingerland, Edward T. (2013). "Body and Mind in Early China: An Integrated Humanities–Science Approach." *Journal of the American Academy of Religion*, 81(1): 6–55.

Slingerland, Edward T. (2014). "Cognitive Science and Religious Thought: The Case of Psychological Interiority in the Analects." In *Mental Culture: Classical Social Theory and the Cognitive Science of Religion*, ed. Dimitris Xygalatas and Lee McCorkle. London: Routledge, 197–212.

Slingerland, Edward T. (2016). "Interdisciplinary Methods in Chinese Philosophy: Comparative Philosophy and the Case Example of Mind-body Holism." In *The Bloomsbury Research Handbook of Chinese Philosophy Methodologies*, ed. S.-H. Tan. London: Bloomsbury, 323–51.

Slingerland, Edward T. (2019). *Mind and Body in Early China: Beyond Orientalism and the Myth of Holism*. Oxford: Oxford University Press.

Slingerland, Edward T., and M. Chudek. (2011). "The Prevalence of Mind–Body Dualism in Early China." *Cognitive Science*, 35(5): 997–1007.

Small, Sharon Y. (2018). "A Daoist Exploration of *Shenming*." *Journal of Daoist Studies*, 11: 1–20.

Smith, Cordwainer [Paul Myron Anthony Linebarger]. (1975). *The Best of Cordwainer Smith*, ed. J. J. Pierce. Garden City, NY: Nelson Doubleday.

Smith, Joel. (2020). "Self-Consciousness." *The Stanford Encyclopedia of Philosophy* (Summer), Edward N. Zalta (ed.). https://plato.stanford.edu/archives/sum2020/entries/self-consciousness.

Sommer, Deborah. (2008). "Boundaries of the "Ti" Body." *Asia Major*, 3rd Series, 21(1): 293–324.

Sommer, Deborah. (2010). "Concepts of the Body in the Zhuangzi." In *Experimental Essays on Zhuangzi*, ed. Victor Mair, 2nd ed. Dunedin, FL: Three Pines Press, 212–28.

Sommer, Deborah. (2012). "The Ji Self in Early Chinese Texts." In *Selfhood East and West: De-Constructions of Identity*, ed. Jason Dockstader Hans-Georg Moller and Gunter Wohlfahrt. Traugott Bautz: 17–45.

Sorabji, Richard. (2006). *Self: Ancient and Modern Insights about Individuality, Life, and Death*. Chicago: University of Chicago Press.

Sterckx, Roel (2007) "Searching for Spirit: Shen and Sacrifice in Warring States and Han Philosophy and Ritual," *Extrême-Orient Extrême-Occident*, 29: 23–54.

Strathern, Marilyn. (1988). *The Gender of the Gift: Problems with Women and Problems with Society in Melanesia*. Berkeley: University of California Press.

Szabó, Sándor P. (2003). "The Term Shenming—Its Meaning in the Ancient Chinese Thought and in a Recently Discovered Manuscript." *Acta Orientalia Academiae Scientiarum Hungaricae*, 56(2/4): 251–74.

Tamba, Yasuyori 丹波康頼. (1955). *Ishinpō* 醫心方 [Recipes at the Heart of Medicine]. Beijing: Renmin weisheng chubanshe.

Tang, Junyi 唐君毅. (2005). *Zhongguo zhexue yuanlun: Yuanxing pian* 中國哲學原論：原性篇 [On the original discourse on Chinese Philosophy—the original dao]. Beijing: Zhongguo shehui kexue chubanshe.

Tang, Yijie. (2003). "Emotion in Pre-Qin Ruist Moral Theory: An Explanation of "Dao Begins in Qing." Trans. Brian Bruya and Hai-ming Wen. *Philosophy East and West*, 53(2): 271–81.

Tessenow, Hermann, and Paul U. Unschuld. (2008). *A Dictionary of the Huang Di Nei Jing Su Wen*. Berkeley: University of California Press.

Thote, Alain. (2009). "Shang and Zhou Funeral Practices: Interpretation of Material Vestiges." In *Early Chinese Religion: Part One: Shang through Han (1250 BC–22 AD)*, ed. John Lagerwey and Marc Kalinowski. Leiden: Brill, 103–42.

Unschuld, Paul U. (1985). *Medicine in China: A History of Ideas*. Berkeley: University of California Press.

Unschuld, Paul U. (1986). *Nan Jing: The Classic of Difficult Issues*. Berkeley: University of California Press.

Unschuld, Paul U. (2003). *Huang Di nei jing su wen: Nature, Knowledge, Imagery in an Ancient Chinese Medical Text*. Berkeley: University of California Press.

Unschuld, Paul U. (2016) *Huang Di nei jing ling shu: The Ancient Classic on Needle Therapy. The complete Chinese text with an annotated English translation*. Berkeley: University of California Press.

Unschuld, Paul U., and Hermann Tessenow. (2011). *Huang Di nei jing su wen: An Annotated Translation of Huang Di's Inner Classic—Basic Questions*. 2 vols. Berkeley: University of California Press.

Van Els, Paul, (2015). "The Philosophy of the Proto-Wenzi." In *Dao Companion to Daoist Philosophy*, ed. Liu Xiaogan. Dordrecht: Springer, 325–40.

Vankeerberghen, Griet. (2001). *The Huainanzi and Liu An's Claim to Moral Authority*. Albany: State University of New York Press.

Van Norden, Bryan W. (2000). "Mengzi and Xunzi: Two Views of Human Agency." In *Virtue, Nature, and Moral Agency in the Xunzi*, ed. T. C. Kline and P. J. Ivanhoe. Indianapolis, IN: Hackett, 103–34.

Varela, Francisco, Evan Thompson, and Eleanor Rosch. (2016). *The Embodied Mind: Cognitive Science and Human Experience*. Cambridge, MA: MIT Press.

Virág, Curie. (2016). "The Intelligence of Emotions? Debates over the Structure of Moral Life in Early China." *L'Atelier du Centre de recherches historiques*, 16 [Online, posted May 17, 2016: http://acrh.revues.org/6721.

Virág, Curie. (2017). *The Emotions in Early Chinese Philosophy*. Oxford, UK: Oxford University Press.

Wang, Bo 王博. (2001). *Jianbo sixiang wenxian lunji* 簡帛思想: 文獻論集 [Collected papers on the thought of the silk and bamboo manuscripts], Vol. 5 of *Chutu sixiang wenwu yu wenxian yanjiu congshu* 出土思想文物與文獻研究叢書 [Collected books on research on the thought of excavated materials and manuscripts], ed. Ding Yuanzhi 丁原植. Taipei: Taiwan Guji chuban youxian gongsi, 219–23.

Wang, Bo 王博. (2004). "'Taiyi shengshui' yanjiu" 《太一生水》研究 [Research on "The Great One gives birth to water]. In *Zhongguo zhexue yu yixue—Zhu Bokun xiansheng bashi shouqing jinian wenji* 中國哲學與易學 — 朱伯崑先生八十壽慶紀念文集 [Chinese philosophy and the Yijing: Collected Works of Mr. Zhu Bokun's 80th Birthday Celebration], Beijing: Peking University Press, 265–81.

Wang, Jianwen 王健文. (1993). "Guojun yiti—Gudai Zhongguo guojia gainian de yige mianxiang" 國君一體—古代中國國家概念的一個面向 [The Monarch as One Body—A Face of the Concept of Ancient China]. In *Zhongguo gudai sixiang shi zhong de qi lun yu shenti guan* 中國古代思想史中的氣論與身體觀 [Theories of Qi and the Body in the History of Early Chinese Thought], ed. Yang Rubin 楊儒賓. Taipei: Juliu tushu gongsi, 227–60.

Wang, Shumin. (2005a). "A General Survey of Medical Works Contained in the Dunhuang Medical Manuscripts." In *Medieval Chinese Medicine: The Dunhuang Medical Manuscripts*, eds. Vivienne Lo and Christopher Cullen. New York: RoutledgeCurzon, 45–58.

Wang, Shumin. (2005b). "Appendix 2: Abstracts of the medical manuscripts from Dunhuang." In *Medieval Chinese Medicine: The Dunhuang Medical Manuscripts*, eds. Vivienne Lo and Christopher Cullen. New York: RoutledgeCurzon, 374–434.

Wang, Xianqian 王先謙 (1988). *Xunzi jijie* 荀子集解 [Annotated edition of the Xunzi]. Eds. Shen Xiaohuan 沈嘯寰 and Wang Xingxian 王星賢. 2 vols. Beijing: Zhonghua.

Wang, Zhongjiang. (2016). *Order in Early Chinese Excavated Texts: Natural, Supernatural, and Legal Approaches*, trans. Misha Tadd. London: Palgrave Macmillan. Originally published as Yuzhou, Zhixu, Xinyang 宇宙、秩序、信仰. Beijing: Renmin University Press, 2015.

Wenzi 文子. (1992). *A Concordance to the Wenzi* (文子逐字索引). Eds. D. C. Lau, Ho Che Wah, and Chen Fong Ching. ICS series. Hong Kong: Commercial Press.

Wenzi shuyi 文子疏義 [Elucidation of the Wenzi]. (2009). Ed. Wang Liqi 王利器. (1912–1998). Xinbian Zhuzi Jicheng edition. Beijing: Zhonghua shuju.

Wheatley, Paul. (1971). *Pivot of the Four Quarters: A Preliminary Enquiry into the Origins and Character of the Ancient Chinese City*. Chicago: Aldine.

Wierzbicka, Anna. (1989). "Soul and Mind: Linguistic Evidence for Ethnopsychology and Cultural History." *American Anthropologist*, 1: 41–58.

Williams, Bernard. (1970). "The Self and the Future." *Philosophical Review*, 7(2): 161–80.

Wilson, Robert A., and Lucia Foglia. (2011). "Embodied Cognition." *The Stanford Encyclopedia of Philosophy* (Fall 2011 Edition). Ed. Edward N. Zata. https://plato.stanford.edu/archives/fall2011/entries/embodied-cognition.

Wong, David B. (1991). "Is There a Distinction between Reason and Emotion in Mencius?" *Philosophy East and West*, 41(1): 31–44.

Wong, David B. (2002). "Reasons and Analogical Reasoning in Mengzi." In *Essays on the Moral Philosophy of Mengzi*, ed. Liu Xiusheng and Philip J. Ivanhoe. Indianapolis, IN: Hackett, 187–220.

Wong, Ming (trans.). (1987). *LING-SHU: Base de l'acupuncture traditionnelle chinoise*. Paris: Masson.

Wong, Wan-chi 黃蘊智. (2014). "A Genealogy of Self in Chinese Culture." *Monumenta Serica*, 62(1): 1–54.

Wu, Hong. (1992). "Art in a Ritual Context: Rethinking Mawangdui." *Early China*, 17:111–44.

Wu, Hong. (1994). "Beyond the 'Great Boundary': Funerary Narrative in the Cangshan Tomb." In *Boundaries in China: Critical Views*, ed. J. Hay. London: Reaktion Books, 81–104.

Wu, Kuang-ming. (1997). *On Chinese Body Thinking: A Cultural Hermeneutics*. Leiden: Brill.

Wuhan daxue Zhongguo wenhua yanjiu yuanben (eds.). (2000). *Guodian Chujian guoji xueshu yantaohui lunwenji* 郭店楚簡國際學術研討會論文集 [Proceedings of the International Symposium on the Chu Slips from Guodian]. Wuhan: Hubei renmin chubanshe.

Wushier bingfang 五十二病方 [Recipes for fifty-two ailments]. (1985). In *Mawangdui Hanmu boshu*, ed. Mawangdui Hanmu boshu zhengli xiaozu, vol. 4. Beijing: Wenwu, 23–82.

Wuwei Handai yijian 武威漢代醫簡 [The Han dynasty Medical slips from Wuwei]. (1975). Ed. Gansusheng bowuguan 甘肅省博物館. Beijing: Wenwu.

Xiong, Tieji 熊鐵劑. (2000). "Dui 'shenming' de lishi kaocha—jianlun 'Taiyi sheng shui' de Daojia xingzhi 對"神明"的歷史考察—兼論太一生水的道家性質 [A historical examination of "Shenming"—and on the Daoist nature of "The Great One gives birth to water"]. In *Guodian Chujian guoji xueshu yantaohui lunwenji* 郭店楚簡國際學術研討會論文集 [Proceedings of the International Symposium on the Chu Slips from Guodian], eds. Wuhan daxue Zhongguo wenhua yanjiuyuan. Wuhan: Hubei renmin chubanshe, 533–537.

"*Xin shi wei zhong*" 心是謂中 [The heart–mind is what is called the center]. (2018). In *Qinghua daxue cang Zhanguo zhujian (8)* 清華大學藏戰國竹簡 (捌) [The Tsinghua University Warring States Bamboo Strips: volume 8], ed. Li, Xueqin 李學勤. Shanghai: Zhongxi shuju, 87–90 and 148–52.

Xunzi 荀子 in *A Concordance to the Xunzi* (荀子逐字索引). (1996). Eds. D. C. Lau, Ho Che Wah, and Chen Fong Ching. ICS series. Hong Kong: Commercial Press.

Yamada, Gyōkō 山田業廣. (2004). *Suwen cizhu jishu* 素問次注集疏, ed. Cui Zhongping 崔仲平 et al. Beijing: Xueyuan [SW].

Yamada, Keiji. (1979). "The Formation of the Huang-ti Nei-ching." *Acta Asiatica*, 36: 67–89.

Yang, Rubin 楊儒賓 (ed.). (1993). *Zhongguo gudai sixiang shi zhong de qi lun yu shenti guan* 中國古代思想史中的氣論與身體觀 [Theories of Qi and the Body in the History of Early Chinese Thought]. Taipei: Juliu tushu gongsi 巨流圖書公司.

Yang, Rubin 楊儒賓. (1999). *Rujia shenti guan* 儒家身體觀 [Confucian views of the body]. Taipei: Zhongyang yanjiyuan Zhongguo wen zhe yanjiusuo chou bei chu 中央研究院中國文哲研究所籌備處.

Yang, Yong, and Miranda Brown. (2017). "The Wuwei Medical Manuscripts: A Brief Introduction and Translation." *Early China*, 40: 241–301.

Yates, Robin D. S. (1994). "Body, Space, Time and Bureaucracy: Boundary Creation and Control Mechanisms in Early China." In *Boundaries in China: Critical Views*, ed. J. Hay. London: Reaktion Books, 56–80.

Yates, Robin D. S. (1997). *Five Lost Classics: Tao, Huang-Lao and yin and yang in Han China*. New York: Ballantine.

Yijing. See *Zhouyi* 1995.

Yin Zhou Jinwen jicheng 殷周金文集成. (1984). [Collection of bronze inscriptions from the time of the Shang and Zhou dynasties]. Beijing: Zhonghua.

Yin Zhou Jinwen jicheng yinde 殷周金文集成引得. (2001, rpt. 2021). [Concordance to the Collection of bronze inscriptions from the time of the Shang and Zhou dynasties]. Ed. Zhang Yachu 亞初. Beijing: Zhonghua.

Yu, Jiyuan. (2001). "The Moral Self and the Perfect Self in Aristotle and Mencius." *Journal of Chinese Philosophy*, 28(3): 235–56.

Yu, Ning. (1998). *The Contemporary Theory of Metaphor: A Perspective from Chinese*. Amsterdam: John Benjamins.

Yu, Ning. (2007). "Heart and Cognition in Ancient Chinese Philosophy." *Journal of Cognition and Culture*, 7: 27–47.

Yu, Ning. (2009). *The Chinese HEART in a Cognitive Perspective: Culture, Body, and Language*. Berlin: Mouton de Gruyter.

Yü, Ying-shih 余英時. (1985). "Individualism and the Neo-Taoist Movement in Wei-Chin China." In *Individualism and Holism: Studies in Confucian and Taoist Values*, ed. Donald J. Munro. Ann Arbor, MI: Center for Chinese Studies, University of Michigan, 121–56.

Yü, Ying-Shih. (1987). "O Soul, Come Back! A Study in the Changing Conceptions of the Soul and Afterlife in Pre-Buddhist China." *Harvard Journal of Asiatic Studies*, 47(2): 363–395.

Yuan, Guohua [Yuen Kwok Wa] 袁國華. (2000). "Guodian Chumu zhujian 'Wuxing' [chuo du] zi kaoshi" 郭店楚墓竹簡《五行》「辶度」字考釋 [Textual research and explanation of the Characters "辶度" in "Five Kinds of Action" in the Chu bamboo strips from Guodian]. *Zhongguo wenzi* N.S., 26(12): 169–76.

Zhang, Jiebin 張介賓 (1563–1640, ed.) (1965). *Lei Jing Tu Yi* 類經圖翼 [Illustrated supplement to the classic of categories]. Beijing: Renmin weisheng chubanshe.

Zhang, Jing 張靜(2004). "*Guodian Chujian wenzi shiyi sanzi*" 郭店楚簡文字釋遺三則 [Three Notes on Guodian Chu Bamboo Slips], *Guwenzi yanjiu,* 25(10): 361–63.

Zhang, Yanchang 張延昌. (2006). *Wuwei Handai yijian zhujie* 武威漢代醫簡注解 [Annotations to the Han Dynasty Medical strips from Wuwei]. Beijing: Zhongyi.

Zhang, Zailin 張再林. (2008). *Zuo wei shenti zhexue de Zhongguo gudai zhexue* 作爲身體哲學的中國古代哲學 [Traditional Chinese Philosophy as the Philosophy of the Body]. Beijing: Zhongguo shehui kexue chubanshe.

Zhang, Zhicong 張志聰. (1610–1674?). (ed.) (1670/1959, rpt. 1980). *Huangdi neijing suwen jizhu* 黃帝內經素問集注 [The Inner Classic of the Yellow Lord: Basic Questions]. Shanghai: Shanghai kexue jishu chubanshe: Xinhua shudian Shanghai faxing suo fa xing.

Zhang, Zhicong 張志聰 (1610–1674?). (ed.). (1672/1959, rpt. 1980). *Huangdi neijing lingshu jizhu* 黃帝內經靈樞集注 [The Inner Classic of the Yellow Lord: Spiritual Pivot]. Shanghai: Shanghai kexue jishu chubanshe: Xinhua shudian Shanghai faxing suo fa xing.

Zhang, Zhongjing 張仲景. (150–219 CE). (1940). *Jin kui yao lue fang lun* 金櫃要略方論 [Essentials and discussions of prescriptions in the golden casket]. In *Xinbian jin kui yaolue fanglun* 新编金櫃要略方論 Changsha: Shangwu yinshuguan.

Zhangjiashan Hanmu zhujian (247-hao mu) 張家山漢墓竹簡([二四七號墓]. (2001). [Bamboo Slips from the Han Tombs at Zhangjiashan]. ed. Zhangjiashan 247 hao Hanmu zhujian zhengli xiaozu 張家山二四七號漢墓竹簡整理小組. Beijing: Wenwu.

Zhao, Jianwei 趙建偉. (1999). "Guodian zhujian 'Zhongxin zhi dao,' 'Xingzi mingchu' jiaoshi" 郭店竹簡《忠信之道》、《性自命出》校釋 [Interpretation with Corrections of the Guodian Bamboo Slip texts Zhongxin zhi Dao and Xingzi Mingchu]. *Zhongguo zhexueshi* 中國哲學史 [History of Chinese Philosophy], 26: 34–39.

Zhao, Shoucheng 趙守正. (1989). *Guanzi tongjie* 管子通解. 2 vols. Beijing: Beijing jingji xueyuan chubanshe [Beijing Institute for Studies in Economics Press].

Zhongguo zhongyi yanjiuyuan 中國中醫研究院 and Guangzhou zhongyi xueyuan 廣州中醫學院. (1995). *Zhongyi dacidian* 中醫大辭典 [Dictionary of Traditional Chinese Medicine]. Beijing: Renmin weisheng chubanshe.

Zhou, Yimou 周一謀 & Xiao Zuotao 蕭佐桃 (1988). *Mawangdui yishu kaozhu* 馬王堆醫書考注 [Textual research and annotations to the medical texts from Mawangdui]. Tianjin: Kexue jishu chubanshe.

Zhouyi 周易. (1995). In *A Concordance to the Zhouyi* (周易逐字索引), ed. D. C. Lau, Ho Che Wah, and Chen Fong Ching. ICS series. Hong Kong: Commercial Press.

Zhuangzi 莊子. (2000). In *A Concordance to the Zhuangzi* (莊子逐字索引), ed. D. C. Lau, Ho Che Wah, and Chen Fong Ching. ICS series. Hong Kong: Commercial Press.

Zhuangzi jishi 莊子集釋. (1961). [Collected explanations of the Zhuangzi], ed. Guo Qingfan 郭慶藩 (1844–96). Beijing: Zhonghua.

Ziporyn, Brook. (2020). *Zhuangzi: The Complete Writings*. Indianapolis, IN: Hackett.

[Chunqiu] Zuozhuan zhu 春秋左传注. (1981). Ed. Yang Bojun 楊伯峻. Beijing: Zhonghua shuju.

Index

For the benefit of digital users, indexed terms that span two pages (e.g., 52–53) may, on occasion, appear on only one of those pages.

acting without acting. See *wuwei* 無為
alignment, 79–80, 82, 90–91, 127, 129, 132, 154–157
All things flow into form. See *Fanwu liu xing*
Ames, Roger, 3–4, 13, 18, 33n12, 39n26, 50, 77n2
Analects, 4–5, 6n23, 24, 27, 30–31, 40n32, 57n4, 73, 76, 78–83, 119, 121, 208
animals, 9, 11, 16, 18, 26, 32–33, 39, 56–58, 64, 67, 75, 77–78, 138, 139, 159–63, 166, 173, 208, 211–212, 217n16
artifice. See *wei* 偽
Arts of the Mind. See *Guanzi*

Black Robes. See *Ziyi*
body, 1–20, 30–40, 43–46, 51, 55, 58–64, 67, 72–81, 86–94, 98–99, 101–114, 116–20, 122–124, 127–32, 135–136, 139–149, 151, 153–58, 161–163, 171–176, 178–179, 180–185, 190, 194, 196–97, 199, 201–21
  discovery of, 12, 27, 122–24
brain, 1n2, 56, 210–211, 215–18, 231–37
breath cultivation, 53, 143
bronze inscriptions, 58, 61–62, 71–72, 208

Carr, Michael, 65, 68n26, 70
cautery prohibitions, 44, 197–200
cognition, 1–2, 15, 17, 20, 53n64, 65, 83–84, 94, 96, 98, 100–104, 114, 119, 121–22, 165, 181, 184, 205, 208–210, 218–20
coloration, 60, 91, 93, 175
Confucius, 5–7, 9, 31, 37, 40–42, 57, 64, 80–82, 84–85, 92, 122–23, 142–43, 163
Csikszentmihalyi, Mark, 10–11, 67, 91n23, 159, 160, 176n31, 179n35

dao 道, 14, 32, 38, 42, 49, 80, 87–89, 99–100, 103, 106, 123, 125, 136, 139–41, 143–44, 149–53, 160–61, 163–65, 167, 168–69, 200, 205
de 德 (power, virtue), 10, 14, 59, 60, 69, 73, 74, 87, 90, 107, 125, 128, 176
Descola, Philippe, 213–14
Despeux, Catherine, 20–23, 25, 53n63, 181–183, 191
dispositions. See *Qing* 情
dividual, 124n9, 213
dualism, 1–3, 15–25, 159, 160, 180–185, 202, 207, 209–13, 217
Dunhuang, 182, 197, 199, 203n66

embodied cognition, 218–221
embodied persons. See *shēn* 身
embodiment, 1, 2, 3–4, 8, 16, 31, 32, 34, 81, 210, 219
Emerson, John, 12, 122n3, 123, 124
emotions, 4–8, 17, 24, 26–28, 31, 39, 41, 42, 65, 68, 76, 102–104, 137, 159–160, 170, 177, 189, 200, 201, 219
essence. See *jing* 精
eyes and ears, 89n22, 96, 129

Falkenhausen, Lothar von, 61n10
Five Kinds of Action. See *Wuxing*
form. See *xing* 形
four sprouts, 92, 95

Gallagher, Shaun, 1n3, 220
Gaozi, 31, 92–95, 97
ghosts, 7, 17, 53–54, 85, 114, 126, 131, 139, 156
Gibbs, Raymond, 219
Goldin, Paul, 17, 58n5, 98, 108, 110–12

264　INDEX

gong 躬 self, 30, 32, 37–39, 58, 60–63
Guanzi, 3, 8, 9, 14, 24, 27, 43, 47, 49, 52, 54, 76, 78, 80, 87–93, 97, 99, 104, 119–35, 143, 148, 157, 180, 194, 203, 206, 208, 209
    Arts of the Mind, 9, 14, 27, 54, 87, 88–90, 124, 125, 129, 132, 157, 203, 206
    Neiye 內業 (Inner Workings), 8, 9, 14, 27, 49, 52, 54, 80, 87, 88, 91, 109, 122, 124–134, 139, 143, 151–152, 155–58, 203, 209, 215
Guodian 郭店, 6–7, 10, 14, 27–28, 33–34, 36, 38, 41–43, 46, 49, 54, 67, 78, 91, 94, 97, 110–112, 119–120, 159–179, 208, 209

heart–mind. See *xin* 心
Heart–Mind Is What Is at the Center. See *Xin shi wei zhong*
holism, 1, 14, 18, 24, 28, 179, 184, 207, 209
Hu, Fuchen, 22, 181n6, 182
Human Nature Comes from the Mandate. See *Xingzi mingchu*
Huainanzi, 24, 27, 51, 52, 78, 115–19, 121–22, 124, 149–56, 194, 209, 215
Huangdi hama jing, 197, 198n54
Huangdi neijing, 4, 24, 27, 28, 39, 43, 44, 46, 49, 76, 77, 149, 151, 180–86, 189–91, 194, 195, 200–207, 210, 215
    Lingshu, 149, 184, 185–90, 192–97, 199, 201–207
    Suwen, 149, 185, 186, 189–95, 202, 205, 207
Huangdi zhenjiu jiayi jing, 186–89, 191, 203
Hume, David, 216
hun and *po* souls, 55–56, 148, 184, 186–88, 191–93, 195n48, 198, 202, 204–205

individualism, 11, 13, 14
Inner Workings. See *Guanzi*
intentions, 28, 41, 42, 50, 93, 100, 136, 142, 159–164, 166–68, 171, 173, 175, 177, 179, 198, 209, 217, 218, 220
    fixed, 52, 94, 166, 168, 179, 209
interiority, 21, 57, 69, 208, 213, 214
Ishinpō, 198

jing 精 (essence), 9, 11, 14, 20, 24, 27, 39, 40, 46, 49–55, 59, 77, 89–91, 93, 98, 100, 108, 117–118, 121, 125–34, 140–142, 146–149, 152–158, 165, 182, 186–189, 191–193, 195, 200, 203–207, 209, 210, 213, 214
    and *qi*, 9, 11, 14, 24, 27, 39, 40, 46, 49, 51, 53, 54, 59, 77, 89, 90, 91, 93, 100, 121, 125–127, 130, 131, 134, 140–142, 146, 147, 149, 157, 186–188, 191, 192, 203, 205, 206, 209, 214
    and *shén*, 50, 52, 53, 98, 108, 117, 118, 134, 146, 148, 152, 153, 158, 192, 193, 195, 205, 209

Lai, Karyn, 13n42, 18, 19, 33n13, 97n35, 137n25, 210n2, 220
Lakoff, George and Mark Johnson, 15, 219
Lee, Janghee, 103n40, 104n46
Lewis, Mark, 3, 27, 42, 76, 81n10, 122, 124, 194
Li 禮 (ritual), 5–9, 12, 19, 20, 30–31, 38–39, 41, 48–51, 56, 64, 72, 75, 78, 79, 81–83, 85, 95, 105, 121–23, 125, 132, 163, 171, 176, 208, 211–212
Li, Tianhong, 161n4, 172
lingshu. See *Huangdi neijing*
Liude (Six Virtues), 42, 160, 164
Locke, John, 215–216, 218
longevity, 140, 143–147, 157, 205, 206, 210, 215
Lunyu. See *Analects*

mantic practices, 125
Masters texts, 47
Mawangdui 馬王堆, 10, 11, 24, 27, 35, 43–44, 46, 48–49, 55, 67, 91n23, 111, 121, 124, 134n20, 143, 147, 148, 150, 160n3, 183, 194
Mencius, 6, 10–11, 14, 24, 27, 31, 41, 51, 67, 91–99, 106, 108, 119, 121–23, 208, 210, 216, 218, 220
metaphor, 3, 15–16, 24, 26–27, 37, 42–43, 67, 76–78, 82, 87–91, 93, 99, 100, 111–12, 115, 119–20, 125, 129, 147, 160, 178
    amalgam, 16, 18, 26, 77, 183, 208, 210
    conceptual, 15, 16
    container, 16, 26, 27, 30, 43, 67, 77, 93, 99, 125–26, 129–30, 132, 134, 175, 180–81, 195, 206, 210
    mirror, 66, 100, 138, 143

root, 3, 16, 26
ruler, 16, 27, 43, 67, 76, 78, 87, 99, 111–12, 115, 125, 129, 147, 207, 220
water, 36, 100–101, 109, 138, 143, 145, 147, 164, 204
mind-centered view, 24, 76, 78, 92, 178, 210, 212, 214, 218, 220–21
monism, 1, 206
moral psychology, 10, 41, 67, 93–97, 102, 119, 159
motivation, 97, 166, 168, 211
Mozi, 10–11, 32–33, 54, 67, 78, 83–86, 119, 208
music, 5–6, 41, 55, 81–82, 105, 137, 149, 160, 163, 169, 173–74, 179, 206, 209

Nanjing (*Classic of Difficult Issues*), 190–91, 203
needling, 186–88, 193, 196, 201, 206
Neiye 內業 (Inner Workings). See *Guanzi*
nurturing life (*Yang sheng*), 11, 139, 187

oracle bone inscriptions, 18, 40, 47

Parfit, Derek, 217–18
Perkins, Franklin, 4n15, 6n21, 36n19, 145n40, 166, 168, 172, 178n33
persistence, 215, 217
personal identity, 20–21, 37, 55, 61, 181, 215–18
Pham, Lee-moi, 173–76
physicality, 213–14
physiognomy, 11, 67–68
porosity, 41, 56, 168, 176, 212
power or charismatic virtue. See *de* 德
psychological interiority, 18, 57, 67, 208, 214
Puett, Michael, 7–10, 46, 50–51, 72–73, 77n3, 78, 82, 88n21, 98, 105n48, 125, 132, 134, 148, 150, 153, 155–56

qi 氣, 2, 4–7, 11, 22, 24, 31, 39–41, 44–46, 49–56, 61, 66–67, 74–75, 77, 79, 89–95, 98, 105, 117–18, 121, 125–27, 129–32, 136, 141, 144, 146–49, 151–55, 157–58, 160–61, 163, 166–67, 173, 175–77, 179, 181–82, 186–93, 195–97, 199–207, 209–10, 212–14, 218, 220
floodlike, 93–95

Qianjin yaofang, 198–99
qing 情 (dispositions), 4, 6, 7, 74, 102–104, 113, 137, 159–60, 166–67, 170–71, 173–77, 179
Qiu, Xigui, 147, 169–70

ren 仁 (humaneness), 6, 34, 39, 50, 59, 65, 82, 93, 95, 106, 108, 137, 163, 168, 176–77, 199
ritual. See *li* 禮

sacrifice, 9, 47, 48, 51, 72–73, 75, 77–78, 82, 85
sagehood, 48, 98, 106, 153, 180
sages (*sheng ren* 聖人), 10–11, 27, 50, 54, 67, 80, 94, 98, 107–10, 125–26, 129–30, 134, 138–39, 150–51, 155–56, 161, 197
Sahlins, Marshall, 9
self-cultivation, 1–2, 8–12, 14, 22, 28, 34, 37, 39, 46, 48, 51, 67–68, 73, 76, 78, 82, 91, 94, 98, 104, 109, 121–22, 125, 132, 140, 153, 156–58, 160, 162, 166, 173, 175, 179–80, 182, 201, 206, 209–11, 215, 220
self-divinization, 10, 46, 51, 72–73, 78, 98, 157
selfhood, 2, 11–13, 15
semantic fields, 24, 26–27, 30, 46, 68, 70, 183–85, 208
senses, 8, 12, 24, 27–28, 30, 42–43, 76–77, 79, 88–92, 96, 98–99, 101–102, 104, 111, 114, 116–19, 121, 125, 127–29, 132, 139, 157, 160, 176, 180, 206, 208, 219
shēn 身 (embodied person), 4–5, 9–11, 13–16, 20–26, 29–30, 34, 37–39, 49, 52, 56, 58–65, 67, 71–77, 79–83, 86, 90, 92–93, 96, 98, 102, 112, 114, 116–17, 120, 123–24, 126, 128–30, 133, 138, 140–42, 149, 152–53, 156–60, 162–64, 170, 172, 178, 180–86, 188–90, 192, 195, 197, 203, 205, 207–208, 210–18
shén 神 (spirit), 4, 8, 20, 22–24, 27–28, 46–48, 51, 53–55, 72–73, 75–79, 82, 97–98, 106–107, 115, 118–19, 121, 124–25, 130, 134, 138, 141–42, 147–49, 151, 165, 180–92, 195–207, 210
external, 47, 49, 54, 72, 79, 84, 97, 125–26, 132, 157, 165, 212
human (*renshén*), 157, 197

shén 神 (spirit) (*cont.*)
  internal, 49–50, 76–78, 105, 115, 120–21, 132, 157, 165, 209, 212–13
  mobile, 197
  multiple, 182–83, 191
  spirit persons (*shénren*), 138, 143, 156
shénming 神明 (spirit illumination), 42, 46, 53, 54, 89, 105, 109–10, 127–129, 143–144, 146, 148, 149, 153, 157, 164, 165, 183, 191, 193, 201, 205–207, 214
shēnti guan 身體觀, 2
Shijing, (Book of Odes) 27, 57–75
Shiwen 十問 (Ten Questions), 24, 27, 35, 55, 121, 124, 143–48, 153, 157, 206, 209
Six Virtues. See *Liu de*
skill, 139, 141–42, 157, 209, 220
Slingerland, Edward, 2n5, 9–10, 18–21, 57, 66, 79–80, 119, 136, 179, 181–82, 184, 218
Smith, Cordwainer, 212
soul, 1–2, 4, 15–16, 18–23, 25–27, 29–30, 46, 55, 75, 85, 124, 140, 181–83, 191, 215–16, 218
spirit. See *Shén* 神
spirit illumination. See *shénming* 神明
spirit–body dualism, 203
spirit–centered view, 24–25, 51, 212, 214, 218, 221
Sterckx, Roel, 47–48, 53, 85, 106, 161
Strathern, Marilyn, 124, 213
Sun Simiao, 198
Suwen. See *Huangdi neijing*

Ten Questions. See *Shiwen* 十問
ti 體 (form), 32–33, 38–39, 56
tripartite self, 2, 22–26, 181–83, 210

virtue, 5, 6, 10–11, 38, 41–42, 50, 57, 59–60, 62, 64, 67, 69–76, 78–79, 82, 90–92, 95, 106, 109, 120, 125, 141, 160, 162–63, 177, 179, 209

wei 偽: (artifice), 102–3, 137, 166, 170–71
Wuwei 武威 (Gansu), 43–45, 182, 197, 199–200
Wuwei 無為 (acting without acting), 9–10, 80, 88–89, 140–141

Wuxing 五行 (Five Kinds of Action), 10, 28, 41, 43, 67, 91, 111, 160, 176, 190

xin 心 (heart-mind), 4, 5, 16, 17, 23–30, 34, 40–46, 50, 52, 55–57, 62, 65–72, 75–84, 87–96, 98–106, 108–123, 125–144, 147–149, 151, 154, 157–163, 166–184, 186, 188–190, 192–197, 199–200, 202–203, 205, 207–215, 218, 220
  hegemony of, 88, 119, 208
  inner, 177
  like a mirror, 138
  mind within the mind, 96, 129, 137, 143
  settled, 125–127, 157
  unmoved, 93–94
xing 形 (form), 4, 14, 22–24, 30, 32, 34–37, 56, 58, 64, 74–75, 86, 109, 111, 123, 126, 131, 133, 140, 146–47, 160, 166–67, 173, 176, 179–80, 184–85, 203, 214
xing 性 (essential nature), 160, 166
Xingzi mingchu, 性自命出 (Human Nature Comes from the Mandate), 6, 28, 41, 159, 166
xue qi 血氣 (blood and qi), 131, 154–55, 161, 176, 192, 203–204
Xunzi, 4, 9–11, 17, 24, 27, 34, 40, 43, 47–50, 67, 76, 78, 97–112, 118–22, 178, 183, 194, 208, 216
  autonomy of the heart–mind, 104
  Rectifying Names, 101, 103

Yang, Rubin, 4, 22, 40
Yang Zhu, 3, 12, 27, 121–24, 157, 209
yin viscera. See *zang* viscera
Yinqueshan, 11, 67
Yinshu 引書 (Pulling Book), 45, 200

zang viscera, 137, 153–55, 186–90, 192–95, 201–202, 204–206, 210
Zhangjiashan 張家山, 43, 45, 54, 183, 194, 200, 206
Zhuangzi, 8–10, 14, 17, 22, 24, 32, 40, 47, 49–51, 67, 78, 94, 121–24, 135–36, 137–43, 150, 157, 209, 216, 220
Ziyi 緇衣 (Black Robes), 14, 38, 41–43, 111–12, 159–60, 162–63, 178–79, 209
Zuozhuan (Zuo Annals), 3, 5–6, 18, 53, 94